# Introduction to DITA

## Second Edition

A User Guide to the

Darwin Information Typing Architecture

Including DITA 1.2

# Introduction to DITA

## Second Edition

## A User Guide to the Darwin Information Typing Architecture Including DITA 1.2

JoAnn Hackos

Comtech Services, Inc.

Publisher: Comtech Services, Inc.
Editor: Comtech Services, Inc.
Text Design and Composition: Comtech Services, Inc.



Published by Comtech Services, Inc., Colorado



Printed in the United States of America

***Library of Congress Cataloging-in-Publication Data:***

Comtech Services, Inc.
Introduction to DITA-Second Edition: A User Guide to theDarwin Information Typing ArchitectureIncluding DITA 1.2
ISBN 978-0-9778634-3-3

**Colophon**
This book was authored using DITA markup and methodology. The book was composed using the DITA-OT and Antenna House.

# Contents

# Introduction

Welcome to *Introduction to DITA Second Edition: A Basic User Guide to the Darwin Information Typing Architecture, Including DITA 1.2*. This book provides you with a task-oriented approach to learning the Darwin Information Typing Architecture. You will find conceptual overviews, background information, tutorials, and the sample XML markup you need to get started using DITA.

**What's new in the Second Edition**
The Second Edition of *Introduction to DITA* adds discussions and exercises relating to the following features introduced in the DITA 1.2 specification:

- Bookmaps
- Glossary topics
- Content reuse mechanisms, including conref push and range and keyref
- Authoring environment modifications, including document-type shells, constraints, and controlled attribute values

While adding the new DITA 1.2 information, we also reviewed all content in the first edition in light of emerging best practices in the use of DITA. We modified examples and exercises that conflicted with current accepted standards and inserted recommendations to guide you in developing good habits from the start. Recognizing that many use this guide as a tutorial, we also enhanced the end of lesson review questions, taking advantage of DITA 1.2's learning and training assessment topic and its supported question types.

Finally, taking into account comments and suggestions from readers of the first edition, we clarified confusing concepts and expanded exercises to include more of the commonly used elements. All content was tested and verified with the DITA Open Toolkit.

**Who should read this book**
*Introduction to DITA* provides a basic introduction to the DITA model. You may be trying to decide if the DITA model is right for your organization, or you may already be using DITA to create deliverables. In either case, you will find a helpful resource to

answer your questions. The book is designed as both a basic learning tool and a reference manual. This user guide is for you if you hold any of these roles in your organization:

- information developer who needs to know how to create DITA topics. Part 2 guides you through basic concepts and lessons to create DITA core information types: concept, task, and reference.
- information architect who needs to know how to create DITA maps, reuse content, and specialize the DITA DTD. Part 3 and Part 4 guide you step-by-step through creating DITA maps and using the many content reuse features of DITA. Part 5 introduces DITA specialization concepts.
- production specialist who needs to know how to create output using DITA processing. Part 6 guides you through installing and running the DITA Open Toolkit and processing final deliverables.

**What you should know**

Before you start using DITA, you may find understanding topic-based authoring helpful. Topic-based authoring encourages a new approach to developing information deliverables. For more information about topic-based authoring and content management strategies, refer to JoAnn Hackos's and Dawn Stevens's *Standards for Online Communication* (Wiley, 1997) and JoAnn Hackos's *Content Management for Dynamic Web Delivery* (Wiley, 2002).

You may find the lessons and examples easier to understand if you have a basic knowledge of HTML, XML, or other tagging languages.

**How to use this book**

The conventions used in this book allow you to easily identify DITA terms used in the lessons.

- <elements> — all elements are surrounded by angled brackets < and >
- *@attributes* — all DITA attributes are in italics and prefaced with an @ sign
- attribute "values" — all DITA attribute values are in quotes
- **lesson actions** — all tags and content added in the lesson steps are in **bold** in the examples

**Organization of this book**

Each part in this book covers a significant aspect of the DITA model, including DITA Topics, DITA Maps, Content Reuse, and Processing. Each part consists of sections that explain the concepts and include one or more lessons. The lessons include step-by-step procedures and reference information about the corresponding DITA elements and attributes.

**Lesson scenarios**

All lessons in this book are based on a scenario of creating a small user guide for the fictitious Comstar phone system. The final version of this guide and the corresponding DITA code for each section is included in the appendix.

**DITA version and Open Toolkit version**

We have based the information in this book on the *OASIS Darwin Information Typing Architecture (DITA) Version 1.2 (OASIS Standard, 1 December 2010)*.

We also provide processing information based on the SourceForge DITA Open Toolkit package. New versions of the Open Toolkit continue to be released. You should continue to check for new versions as you work with DITA.

**Additional resources**

Many people have written about the Darwin Information Typing Architecture. Articles about the model and approaches to using the model are available on the web. If you search on DITA, you will find many resources.

Here are some useful resources to get you started:

- The official DITA OASIS standards committee web site http://www.oasis-open.org/committees/tc_home.php?wg_abbrev=dita
- *OASIS Darwin Information Typing Architecture (DITA) Version 1.2 (OASIS Standard, 1 December 2010)* at http://docs.oasis-open.org/dita/v1.2/os/spec/DITA1.2-spec.pdf
- A web site and wiki, provided by the OASIS Technical Committee, that allow you to contribute and gather more information about the DITA standard at http://dita.xml.org
- A collection of articles gathered by the OASIS technical committee. This resource is, at present, the most extensive collection of articles, presentations, and facts about DITA at http://xml.coverpages.org/dita.html
- The web site managed by IBM, the original DITA developer, with a rich collection of DITA information at http://www.ibm.com/developerworks/xml/library/x-dita1/
- The forum for DITA questions at http://tech.groups.yahoo.com/group/dita-users/ and http://tech.groups.yahoo.com/group/framemaker-dita/

A number of local DITA User Groups have been established. User groups continue to be formed to provide resources for people interested in learning more about the DITA model. You can find information about local DITA user groups at http://dita.xml.org.

Comtech Services, Inc. provides an extensive program of workshops and webinars to help you learn more about DITA. Find information about upcoming events at http://www.comtech-serv.com/workshops and http://www.comtech-serv.com/webinars. Also consider attending one of the conferences sponsored by the Center for Information-Development Management (CIDM). Content

Management Strategies/DITA North America occurs in the spring and DITA Europe occurs in early winter. See the announcement at http://www.infomanagementcenter.com.

# Acknowledgments

Many people contributed to the development and success of the second edition of *Introduction to DITA*. I would first like to acknowledge Jennifer Linton, Kylene Bruski, and Bill Hackos for their significant contributions to the first edition. For the second edition, I have greatly benefited from the contributions of Anne Bovard, Frank Miller, Dawn Stevens, and Hal Trent. Each has generously provided guidance, best practices, support, code samples, and time to produce this book. In particular, Dawn Stevens completed a thorough review of all first edition and new content and helped us make many corrections and improvements to the text and the samples. This project has truly been a team effort.

Throughout the development of our understanding of the OASIS DITA Specification, Don Day, Gershon Joseph, Robert Anderson, Eliot Kimber, Kristen Eberlein, Su-Laine Yao, and other OASIS DITA Technical Committee members provided many explanations and much support. The frequent question-and-answer sessions with members helped clarify the details about DITA and, especially, about the DITA 1.2 Specification.

Thanks to all my colleagues at Comtech for their support and help in reviewing and editing the book. Our book would not be what it is without all of your contributions.

# PART I

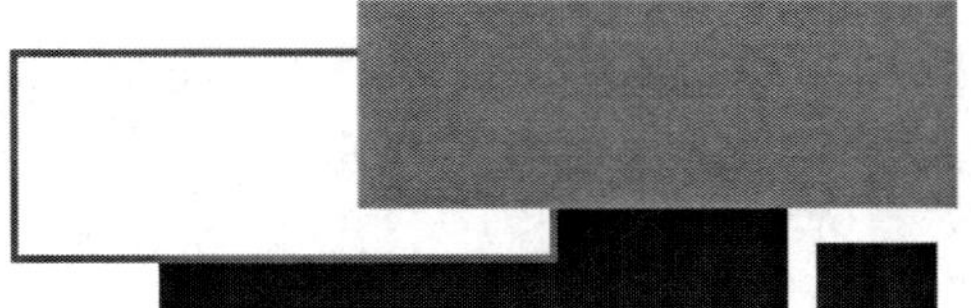

# The Darwin Information Typing Architecture

You've heard about XML as a potential tool for authoring technical content. You're thinking about developing individual topics of content and assembling them into PDFs, help systems, websites, and other deliverables rather than creating monolithic books. You've even heard about the Darwin Information Typing Architecture, a standard that makes topic-based information development easier and faster to implement. You've come to the right place—an introduction to using the DITA standard to produce your publications.

The Darwin Information Typing Architecture (DITA) is an OASIS Standard that defines an XML architecture for designing, authoring, publishing, and managing content. Content that you develop using the DITA (pronounced dit - uh) model can be easily published to print, PDF, the web, help systems, and other deliverables, depending upon the needs of your users.

The core set of DITA information types provides information architects and information developers with a solid starting point. These three information types, concept, task, and reference, represent the vast majority of content produced to support users of technical information. You will find that each core information type contains a standard set of content units, expressed as XML elements, that encompass the essential content that you need to develop useful and reusable content.

But developing individual topics that match the DITA information types is only the starting point. DITA provides many mechanisms that enable you to build print and online deliverables quickly and easily, accommodate unique information requirements, and make assembly faster and easier and search and retrieval more dynamic:

- DITA maps
- DITA relationship tables
- DITA specialization
- DITA metadata attributes and XML element names

DITA maps provide you with the means of assembling any number of topics into sequences like tables of contents for print and online deliverables. You add DITA topics one by one to a DITA map, using the map construction principles to organize your topics into first-, second-, or third-order headings. The hierarchies you now manage with heading levels are easily managed by the hierarchy of a DITA map.

DITA maps are only one way of handling relationships among topics. By creating DITA relationship tables in your DITA maps, you can easily add and manage related-topic links. The relationships help you build an information-centered web site or a help system that leads users from one topic to related information that supports successful task performance.

DITA doesn't stop there. If you find that your content does not easily conform to the structure already built into the standard set of information types, DITA provides a mechanism that lets you create special structures. By using DITA specialization techniques, you can start with standard information types and build new XML elements that best describe your content or you can remove or rename standard DITA elements that your information developers do not need. Specialization allows you, for example, to add a list of required tools to a hardware installation task and label the list precisely or to create a special reference information type to accommodate specifications, parameters, or other data your customers require.

Finally, DITA accommodates the requirement of most information developers to handle content variations within a single topic, rather than creating multiple copies of the content with slight variations. The task of maintaining multiple instances of the same or nearly the same content has always been a thorn in the side of most information developers. DITA helps you manage the pain by providing you with conditional processing capabilities to specify elements of content you want to include or exclude from a particular deliverable. For example, if you have instructions that differ in detail among product versions, you can accommodate those differences by labeling them with metadata attributes. The process is very similar to using conditional text in desktop publishing but it is more reliable and precise.

DITA also provides the mainstay of XML authoring by using XML element names to identify content units in a topic. By labeling your task content as steps rather than ordered lists, you can easily find and reuse specific steps rather than all ordered lists in your content. By labeling reference material as a syntax diagram rather than as a paragraph, you can easily develop a dictionary-like deliverable with all the command names and their syntax diagrams. Meaningful labels in DITA are used to replace the standard format labels that we have traditionally used in desktop publishing. A style name like paragraph becomes short description, context, information, or step result in DITA.

Once your content conforms to the standards for DITA topics and you have mapped your content into the various deliverables your customers require, you can use the DITA Open Toolkit or the tools available through your content management system to produce your output. During the production processing steps, you associate one or more style sheets with your format-free XML content, accommodating various print specifications, PDF, HTML, and any number of help systems and other deliverables. You can also transfer your XML topics, DITA maps, and relationship tables to your localization service provider. Because you are working in format-free XML, you or your service provider can transform your XML topics into the forms required by translation memory systems and other translators' tools. Using the same transforms, your localization service provider can return the translated versions of your topics back to your content repository.

By using all the mechanisms available to you in DITA, you can support the full range of tasks that make up your information-development life cycle.

**Reaping the benefits of DITA**

DITA is more than a set of XML-based tools or out-of-the-box Document Type Definitions (DTDs) or schemas that you can immediately use to begin authoring topics with sound XML structure. DITA provides you with an open-source, enabling technology that you can download at no cost. It also provides you with the energy, commitment, and investment of DITA developers worldwide who contribute to the OASIS DITA Technical Committee to improve the DITA specification and tools. With DITA, you receive

- a fully tested DTD or schema for XML-based authoring
- a community of developers investing in improvements to the DITA model
- an open source toolkit you can use to produce your own output in multiple media without having to invest in proprietary tools
- a thoroughly developed approach to information development originating with OASIS and now encompassing many other companies, large and small, that find value in a standards-based approach

DITA represents a standard for the design and development of technical content, the first such broadly based standard in the information-development community.

**What business advantages do you gain with DITA?**

DITA provides a number of advantages to organizations that are seriously committed to managing information. Both large organizations with content contributors dispersed globally and small organizations with a few individuals working together will benefit from a topic-based, standards-governed approach to content management. DITA adopters find that they can

- reuse information quickly and easily across multiple deliverables
- respond positively to requests for customized information delivery
- respond quickly to changing business and customer needs
- reduce the cost of maintaining and updating information
- enable continuous publishing to keep abreast of content changes
- share information across the global enterprise
- assemble content from multiple resources
- share information with business partners throughout the product support life cycle
- collaborate on content creation with marketing, sales, support, training, and information development
- reduce the cost of localization and the time to market for translated content
- increase the global reach of information, products, and services
- reduce the technical debt caused by inadequate, incorrect, and unusable legacy information

By using DITA to produce topics according to the rules of each information type, you create content that can easily be shared among a wide variety of deliverables. Because the topics are designed and developed to promote consistency of presentation and content, you can develop a repository of building blocks that can be assembled in multiple ways, including new ways that you have not invented yet. You can assemble the topics based on products, services, audiences, geographies, languages, customer job roles, industries—almost anything that presents you with a business advantage.

The promise organizations and information developers have made for years of providing customized information to meet the specific needs of individual customers is possible without prohibitive expense and time commitments. Many information developers are reluctant to promise support for customization because they cannot support the cost of transforming information for individual customers given their existing desktop publishing tools. With DITA's ability to facilitate new mappings of topics to tables of content and its ability to support conditional processing from master documents that contain a range of information, you are able to respond quickly to requests for customized content without creating a burden on authors and publishers.

As business and customer needs change, you can add new topics to your repository, modify existing topics, add variations to the topics, and publish restructured content. You can respond quickly to changing needs by implementing continuous publishing. Rather than waiting for a new product release to correct errors in content or revise topics so that they answer user questions more successfully, you can update individual topics immediately.

Because topics are authored once and used in multiple DITA maps, you reduce the cost of maintaining and revising topics. You can include task topics in assemblies delivered to different audience groups, add basic concepts for new users and advanced concepts for expert users, and link to detailed reference information that can be extracted directly from source material.

DITA facilitates sharing information across your enterprise because authoring is based on a common XML standard. Some authors will use XML-based authoring tools that provide a full range of functionality. Some authors will continue to use well-known word processing tools with the addition of XML capabilities. Some authors will complete XML-based forms with required information. Others will import XML content into high-end design tools to support creative information design. Some authors, especially software professionals, might even choose to author by inputting tags directly in basic text editors. All of these methods are supported by the DITA standard.

Not only can you share information with colleagues throughout your enterprise and from every part of the development life cycle and the product support chain, but you can also share information with business partners. If you and your suppliers agree to use the DITA standard, you have the means to exchange information resources without laborious and time-consuming restructuring. If you send information to customer organizations, you can provide those resources using the DITA standard. Even if you and your business partners have your own DITA specializations, the hierarchical design principles upon which DITA is built enable you to generalize those individual specializations back to the core information types.

Perhaps one of the most powerful advantages you gain using the DITA standard is to reduce the cost of localization and translation. Once topics are written, reviewed, and approved, they can be transformed to the sources required by translation memory systems. Only new or revised topics need to be sent for translation, eliminating the need to reapply translation memory to unchanged topics. By building localization and translation early into the information-development life cycle, you give the translators more time to research terminology and develop sound content in your target languages, and you begin to reduce the time needed at the end of the cycle waiting for translations to be completed.

Because DITA maps can be assembled for every language you need, you also eliminate the high costs of desktop publishing at the end of a project. By referencing the translated topics in your DITA maps, you can generate multiple-language output quickly.

Finally, DITA and topic-based authoring, by enabling content reuse, decreasing content assembly time and costs, facilitating localization and translation, and giving authors a standard for content creation, allow you to devote valuable time to minimalizing existing content, promoting usability, correcting errors, filling gaps, and making your content more valuable to your customers and your organization.

**How do you get started with DITA?**

One of the best ways to get started using the OASIS DITA standard is with a combination of workshops and the lessons in this book. However, a DITA implementation is actually part of a much larger organizational change. We recommend that you follow a DITA roadmap that encompasses the following activities:

- Build your business case by evaluating current costs of information development and localization, and demonstrate how DITA will help reduce those costs.
- Investigate minimalism to ensure that you move forward only with the content that customers find valuable.
- Create an information-architecture team to develop a targeted Information Model for your organization. Your Information Model provides the rules your team members must follow and specifies which parts of the complete DITA information architecture you intend to use.
- Evaluate your legacy content and decide what you need to move forward into DITA. Rarely will you want to convert everything, especially at the beginning. You are likely to discover that your current content needs reshaping to work in an information-typed, structured-authoring environment.
- Specify your publishing requirements so that you are ready to develop stylesheets to support PDF, XHTML, Help, and other output types. If you need help in developing your publishing pipeline, consider those who are expert in the DITA Open Toolkit and stylesheet development, including Comtech Services.
- Focus on a small but important pilot project. During the pilot project, refine your Information Model, develop your DITA authoring guide, concentrate on structured authoring, help everyone learn the DITA templates and tags, and develop your localization and publishing pipeline.
- Consider the need to purchase a component content management system, one that specifically recognizes DITA and enables you to manage the details of your XML content and publishing and localization requirements. Recognize that you do not need a content management system to work with DITA, but once you have thousands of topics, a content management system will quickly become essential.
- Measure your success with your pilot project and with subsequent organization-wide and enterprise-wide rollouts. Compare your results with the return on investment promised in your original business case.

# PART II

# DITA Topics

Topic-based authoring has been a mainstay of technical information development since we first began developing help systems. We learned quickly enough that we couldn't split our existing books into help topics by making every heading level a new topic. Information originally designed with a unique narrative flow no longer made sense nor assisted users in finding exactly the content they needed. We had to rethink the types of information that our help systems should include and create a new set of standards for their development. The result is topic-based authoring.

Authoring in topics provides information developers with a way to create distinct modules of information that can stand alone for users. Each topic answers one question: "How do I ...?" "What is ...?" "What went wrong?" Each topic has a title to name its purpose and contains enough content for someone to begin and complete a task, grasp a basic concept, or look up critical reference information. Each topic has a carefully defined set of the basic content units that are required and accommodates other optional content. As information developers learn to author in topics and follow sound authoring guidelines consistently, you gain the flexibility to publish information written by many different writers and subject-matter experts that looks and feels the same to the users.

Not only has topic-based authoring become the norm for well-designed help systems, information architects have learned that designing consistently structured topics facilitates readability and information access in traditional, more linear book structures. Readers are able to identify task-based topics in sections and chapters because the tasks look the same and contain the same essential content units. Readers learn that conceptual and background information is always located in the same position in the table of contents with respect to the tasks. Readers come to depend upon standard reference sections that contain similarly structured details for ease of lookup.

The core information types in DITA—task, concept, and reference—support the structures that underlie most well-designed technical information. Any organization that follows best practices in information architecture will find the core DITA structure to be a good fit. But the core DITA information types also challenge us to become even more disciplined in structuring information according to a set of carefully defined business rules. The benefit of such disciplined information structuring is the consistent presentation of information that helps you build reader confidence and simplify the reader's task of knowing how to navigate and use your information.

**Use topic-based authoring to build customer value**

Authoring in structured topics provides you with a sophisticated and powerful way to deliver information to your user community. You experience benefits that decrease your development costs and time to market, as well as provide increased value to your users:

- Structured topics contain only the information needed to understand one concept, perform one procedure, or look up one set of reference information.
- Structured, topic-based authoring promotes consistency in the presentation of similar information.
- Topics can be reviewed by subject-matter experts as soon as they are ready. They need to be reviewed only once, even if they appear in multiple deliverables, reducing the burden on reviewers.
- Topics can be translated before entire volumes are complete, reducing the time to market for global customers. Topics in multiple languages can be combined into language-specific deliverables without extra desktop publishing time and expense.
- Assembling topics into multiple deliverables can be automated, reducing production time and costs.
- Consistently structured topics are easier to reuse in multiple deliverables.
- Structured topics can be combined in new ways to meet changes in product solutions, work structures, geographies, industries, or other customer configurations.
- Topics are easier to update immediately instead of waiting for the next release of an entire library of documents.
- Consistently structured topics help users build a firm mental model of the types of information you are presenting.
- Consistently structured topics help users navigate more quickly to the information they need.

If one of your business goals is to use information topics in multiple deliverables, you need to build a repository of topics that are clearly defined according to a standard set of information types. DITA provides you with such a standard as a starting point. DITA gives you the capability to expand upon its core information types when you need to accommodate the special needs of your customers and your information.

**Conducting a content inventory**

If your information is like most in the technical information industry, you have a great diversity of structures, especially if topics are embedded in the threaded narrative sections and chapters of books. Your first job is to inventory your content to identify its range and diversity. In most cases, you will find lots of tasks, containing step-by-step instructions for reaching a specific goal. The dominance of the task in technical information is why DITA includes the task as one of the three core information types. Accompanying tasks, you are likely to find background, descriptive, and conceptual information that explains what something is and how it works. DITA labels such supporting information "concepts." You will also find tables, lists, diagrams, process flows, and other information that can be labeled as "reference," the information that no one wants to memorize but must be easy to look up.

Once you have completed your content inventory, you need to carefully analyze the three core information types provided with DITA. The standard structure for task, concept, and reference is presented in detail in the this section of this book. Experiment with accommodating your content to the standard structure. In more than 80 percent of the cases we've researched, the content easily fits into a standard DITA structure.

Where you might encounter difficulties is with the diversity of your own content rather than with the DITA information types. Some of the content in your inventory will not even meet your own guidelines. Often, that content was written by people long gone from your organization or was influenced by subject-matter experts who wanted it their way rather than following your authoring guidelines.

Our recommendation is to focus on the essential underlying structure of your content rather than the idiosyncrasies and accidents of individual writers over the years. If you find an odd structure in a task, for example, ask if that structure is the best way of conveying the information to the user or if the task can be rewritten to follow the structure of a standard DITA information type. Most of the time, you will find that the standard is a good solution.

One of the more common problems you will find with some of the content you examine is mixed structure. Tasks start out with long discussions of background information. Concepts include step-by-step procedures. Tables of reference material end up with concepts in the footnotes or tasks incorporated into table cells. Although mixed information types are possible in DITA, in most cases, we don't recommend them. Consider that by separating information carefully and rigorously into the neat information-type buckets provided, you will have information that you can present much more dynamically and flexibly to users. If users want to know the steps of a task, they won't have to skip over background that they don't want to think about yet. You can refer them to that conceptual and background information through a related-topic reference or a hypertext link rather than embed lengthy conceptual information in the task.

Notice the difference between the two task topics in the following table. The well-structured task follows the DITA model, clearly omitting descriptive information about menus and screens. The well-structured task also ensures that action steps begin with commands and that step results are not incorrectly labeled as steps, as well as separating steps from additional information.

| Well-structured, Minimalism DITA Task | Poorly Structured Task |
|---|---|
| Selecting a Language, Product, Unit, and Lesson (task title)<br>Use the Menu Screen, the first screen you see, to select the Language, Product, Unit, and Lesson you want to work on. (short description)<br>**1.** Click on any Language/Product that appears in the left frame of the Menu screen. (step-command)<br>You may need to scroll to see all the Languages on your CD. (step-information)<br>**2.** Click on a Unit tab on the right frame. (step-command)<br>All the Lessons available in that Unit appear. (step-result)<br>**3.** Click once on any Lesson to go to the Activities Selection Screen. (step-command)<br>The selected Lesson may take a few minutes to load. (step-information)<br>Every time you return to the Menu screen, the last Unit and Lesson you worked on is highlighted. (task-result) | Selecting a Language, Product, Unit, and Lesson (task title)<br>The Menu Screen (another title)<br>When you run the RS program, the first screen you will see is the Menu Screen. In this screen, you select a Language, Product, Unit, and Lesson. (menu description)<br>The Menu Screen has two frames:<br>■ A frame for selecting a Language and Product (left side).<br>■ A frame for selecting a Unit and Lesson (right side). (more menu description)<br>All the Languages on the CD will appear in the Language/Product frame on the left. If you are using the online version of RS, all available Languages should be visible here. You may need to scroll to see all the Languages on your CD. (more menu description)<br>**1.** Select any Language/Product in the Language frame by clicking on it. (step-command)<br>**2.** The Units will appear. (no step; a result?)<br>**3.** All the Lessons available to you in that Unit will appear, after you click on a Unit tab. (misstated step with result first)<br>**4.** Click once on any Lesson to continue to the Activities Selection Screen. There may be a delay as the program loads the selected Lesson. (step-command and step-information)<br>Every time you return to the Menu Screen, the last Unit and Lesson you worked on will be highlighted. (task-result) |

**Table 1: Comparison of DITA and non-DITA task structures**

By authoring in topics according to well-defined DITA information types rather than combining types randomly, you gain flexibility in distributing your information to people who need it most. You also make the relationships among sets of content more obvious. If you believe that users will profit from reading background information before performing a task, you can use related-topic links to ensure that they know about the relationship and why reviewing the concept or background is advantageous.

**Note:** Tabbed interfaces in help topics facilitate the movement back and forth among related topics. Once users find a concept, they can immediately link to one or more tasks simply by clicking on a task tab at the top of the screen. At any point in the online navigation, you can make clear the relationships among a concept, one or more tasks, and a set of reference material.

### Adding your own information types to the core DITA set

Although you will find that most technical information fits neatly into the core DITA information types (task, concept, and reference), you may discover that you have special information types that cannot be accommodated by the standard content units or that you want to label those content units with more descriptive XML tag names. At that point, you need to pursue specialization.

Consider an example in the semiconductor industry. Much detailed information about a chip design is contained in an information type called a register description. Although a register description falls into the class of reference information types, it has some specific and detailed content that should be presented consistently and labeled by its semantic content. By specializing the core reference information type, you can build a register description specialization that standardizes the register content with appropriate XML element names, assisting the writers and providing additional metadata to facilitate search. Many similar opportunities for specialization may present themselves in your content. But be careful to exhaust the possibilities of the core information types before pursuing the differences.

Create information-type specializations only when you are certain that they will benefit your writers and your content. The more different information types you present to writers and readers, the more opportunities there are for confusion. With too many choices of information types, an information developer is more likely to choose incorrectly. With too many subtle differences in the presentation of information, your users are more likely to become confused when they are unable to find the standard set of content that they have come to expect.

# SECTION A

# Understanding DITA Information Types

DITA 1.2 provides many information types to support topic-based authoring in any number of industries, organizations, and subject areas. While DITA 1.0 included only the core DITA technical-communication information types, DITA 1.2 added Learning and Training information types, glossary-related information types, and the machine industry task model.

Each DITA information type is based on a common structure, called the DITA topic. The DITA topic serves as a starting point for the information-type specializations that are an integral part of the DITA framework, and it can also be used as the base for further specializations.

The base structure of the DITA topic has the following required and optional components:

| | |
|---|---|
| **Topic Element** | Is the root element for the DITA topic with the *@id* and *@xml-lang* attributes (required) |
| **Title** | Describes the subject of the topic (required) |
| **Short Description or Abstract** | Provides a short description or an abstract that describes the topic (optional) |
| **Prolog** | Allows for various kinds of topic metadata, such as change history, audience, product, and so on (optional) |
| **Body** | Contains the topic content that is permitted by the information type (optional) |
| **Related links** | Contains cross references to supporting information (optional) |

**Table 2: Base structure of the core information types**

Starting with the DITA topic's base structure, the DITA 1.2 specification includes the following information types that are specialized from the base structure:

- concept
- general task
- reference
- learning base

Concept, general task, and reference are the primary information types for technical communication, while the learning base is the basis for specialized information types for the Learning and Training industry, including learning plan, learning overview, assessments, and others.

Each of these information types has a unique set of content units that define the internal structure of that information type. For example, each information type begins with header information followed by <body> information and <related-links>. The header information begins with a required @*id* and an optional <prolog> which contains metadata and index terms for the topic. In the concept, task, and reference information types, the header information also includes an optional <shortdesc> or <abstract>.

In each concept, task, or reference topic, the <body> is specialized as <conbody, <taskbody>, and <refbody> and defines the specific content units that you can use within it. The <taskbody> element, for example, contains steps and other content units needed to structure procedural information. The unique content units in the three technical-communication information types are illustrated in the following table.

Each of the core information types can be used as the basis for other specialized topics. For example, both the strict task model and the machine task model were created by modifying the general task, and the glossary entry model is a specialization of the concept information type. You can learn about the various ways to specialize information types in The DITA Information-Development Environment on page 305.

| **Concept** | **General Task** | **Reference** |
|---|---|---|
| Header Information<br>Unique @*id*<br>Title<br>Short Description<br>Prolog | Header Information<br>Unique @*id*<br>Title<br>Short Description<br>Prolog | Header Information<br>Unique @*id*<br>Title<br>Short Description<br>Prolog |
| conbody<br>Section<br>Paragraph<br>List<br>Table<br>Figure<br>Example | taskbody<br>Pre-requisites<br>Context<br>Section<br>Steps or steps-unordered or steps-informal<br>Various step elements<br>Result<br>Example<br>Post-requisite | refbody<br>Section<br>Properties table<br>Table<br>Syntax<br>Example |
| Related links | Related links | Related links |

**Table 3: Core Information Types**

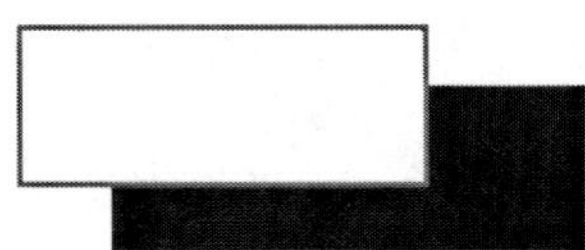

# LESSON 1

## Concept Information Type

Concepts provide information that users need to complete tasks successfully. They respond to the user's question, "What is this about?" In implementing a topic-based architecture, you want to begin by developing your tasks. But, for each task, you may need to develop conceptual, descriptive, or background information. Based on your list of tasks, consider if your user needs more knowledge of the product, service, or environment to complete the task.

Unfortunately, much of the conceptual information included in technical documentation is not related to task performance. Others in the organization often ask writers to include snippets of information with little or no relevance to the user's performance. In the DITA model, consider first what concepts are absolutely essential and then ensure that the concepts are stand-alone topics that you can reuse in more than one context.

You may find that identifying and writing a concept is difficult. You may also find it difficult to differentiate between concept information and reference information. Concepts should directly support task performance. If users understand a core concept or know how a product functions, they should be able to perform tasks and reach their goals more quickly, confidently, and with fewer errors. Some examples of concepts are product overviews, process maps, and introductions to groups of tasks.

Remember that the DITA concept information type is derived from the DITA topic structure as shown in Figure 1 on page 22. The root concept element is derived from the root topic element in the base structure, and the concept body is derived from the body element in the base structure. Concepts must include a title and a concept body. Short description, prolog, and related links are all optional.

A simple concept consists of a title and one or more paragraphs contained in the concept body. You can include additional structural content units in the concept body, such as paragraphs, sections, examples, and definition lists. For example, a concept body can contain one or more sections or examples with their own titles.

Following the lesson, you will find a list and detailed descriptions of the concept elements, including elements not discussed in this lesson. For a complete list of elements you can use to write a concept, see the *OASIS Darwin*

*Information Typing Architecture (DITA) Version 1.2 (OASIS Standard, 1 December 2010).*

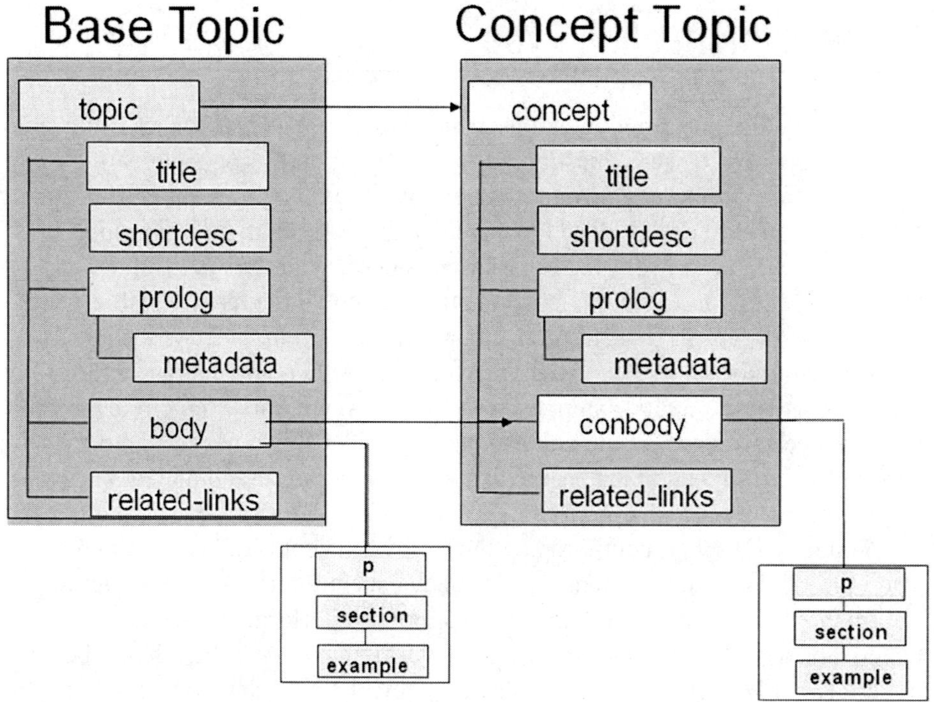


**Figure 1: Structure of the concept topic**

### Creating a concept topic

This lesson explains the basic DITA elements you use to create a concept topic. In this lesson, you learn to

- add elements used in each information type, such as <title>, <shortdesc>, <prolog>, and <related-links>
- add a unique *@id* attribute to your topic root element
- add elements specific to the concept information type, such as <concept>, <conbody>, <p>, <dl>, <dlentry>, <dt>, and <dd>

1. Start a new DITA concept topic.

   You can start a new DITA topic in an XML editor or in a text editor. In most XML editors, you can choose **file** > **new** > **DITA concept topic** . The XML tool usually includes a DTD declaration and XML declaration automatically. If you choose to use a text editor, start your concept topic by including the example markup shown below. The first line is the XML declaration and identifies the file as an XML document. The second line is the DTD declaration which uses a relative path to point to the DTD you want to validate your topic structure against. Finally, the start and end tags for the root element, concept, form the container element for all other elements and identify the topic as a concept.

```
<?xml version="1.0" encoding="utf-8"?>
<!DOCTYPE concept PUBLIC "-//OASIS//DTD DITA CONCEPT//EN"
    "concept.dtd">
<concept>
</concept>
```

2. Assign an *@id* attribute and value to the <concept> element.

   Each *@id* you add to your topic must be unique to that topic. You use the unique *@id* to reference the topic in a DITA map. You can use letters, numbers, and underscores in your *@id*.

   Most content management systems assign a unique *@id* to every topic you create automatically. If you are not using a content management system, consider using your topic title as the unique *@id*. Be careful to omit the spaces between words.

   For this concept, use the unique *@id*: "AboutConferenceCalls".

```
<?xml version="1.0" encoding="utf-8"?>
<!DOCTYPE concept PUBLIC "-//OASIS//DTD DITA CONCEPT//EN"
   "concept.dtd">
<concept id="AboutConferenceCalls">
</concept>
```

3. Assign an *@xml:lang* attribute and value to the <concept> element.

   The *@xml:lang* attribute specifies the language of the element content. Using markup to identify language is strongly recommended to make the document as portable as possible.

```
<?xml version="1.0" encoding="utf-8"?>
<!DOCTYPE concept PUBLIC "-//OASIS//DTD DITA CONCEPT//EN"
   "concept.dtd">
<concept id="AboutConferenceCalls" xml:lang="en-us">
</concept>
```

4. Insert <title> start and end tags between the <concept> start and end tags and include title text.

   The title is the first content unit you include in every topic. The title may be used as a heading when the topic is rendered. Adding the title at the beginning of every topic ensures that the end user can identify the topic. You can include the topic title in your table of contents and site maps, and you can use it as link text for navigation through your topic set. Be certain that your concept title clearly communicates the subject of your topic. Consider developing a naming convention for your task, concept, and reference topic titles to distinguish the topics for the user.

For this concept, use the title: "About conference calls".

```
<concept id="AboutConferenceCalls">
   <title>About conference calls</title>
</concept>
```

5. Add <shortdesc> start and end tags after your title and include a short description of your topic.

   The short description briefly introduces the content of your concept topic. Although the short description is not required, we recommend that you include it in every topic. You can use the short description to provide a brief statement to display in search engine results or as a mouse-over for a help topic. Depending on your stylesheet, the short description may or may not appear in your rendered output.

```
<concept id="AboutConferenceCalls" xml:lang="en-us">
   <title>About conference calls</title>
   <shortdesc>Use a conference call to speak with more
      than two people in two different locations at the
      same time.</shortdesc>
</concept>
```

6. Add <prolog> start and end tags after your short description.

   The <prolog> container holds the metadata for your concept topic. For more information about prolog metadata elements, see Prolog Metadata on page 101. You can also refer to the *OASIS Darwin Information Typing Architecture (DITA) Version 1.2 (OASIS Standard, 1 December 2010)* for a complete list of prolog elements.

```
<concept id="AboutConferenceCalls" xml:lang="en-us">
   <title>About conference calls</title>
   <shortdesc>Use a conference call to speak with more
      than two people in two different locations at the
      same time.</shortdesc>
   <prolog>
   </prolog>
</concept>
```

7. Add <author> start and end tags between the <prolog> start and end tags and include the author's name.

   The <author> element is one of the metadata attributes you can use in the <prolog> container. In the <author> element, enter the topic author's name; in our example code, we use "John Smith".

```
<concept id="AboutConferenceCalls" xml:lang="en-us">
   <title>About conference calls</title>
```

```
   <shortdesc>Use a conference call to speak with more
      than two people in two different locations at the
      same time.</shortdesc>
   <prolog>
      <author>John Smith</author>
   </prolog>
</concept>
```

8. Add <conbody> start and end tags after the prolog.

   The concept body contains most of the content in a concept topic. Place the information you write about a concept inside the <conbody> element container.

```
<concept id="AboutConferenceCalls" xml:lang="en-us">
   <title>About conference calls</title>
   <shortdesc>Use a conference call to speak with more
      than two people in two different locations at the
      same time.</shortdesc>
   <prolog>
      <author>John Smith</author>
   </prolog>
   <conbody>
   </conbody>
</concept>
```

9. Add <p> start and end tags between the <conbody> start and end tags.

   A concept can include any of the basic block elements, such as paragraph, bulleted list, numbered list, and table. Use block elements to structure your concept information in the concept body. For more information about block elements, see Block Elements on page 65.

```
<conbody>
   <p>Use one of the following types of conference calls
      to speak with multiple people.</p>
</conbody>
```

10. Add a definition list to your concept topic.

    A definition list provides a convenient structure for defining terms, describing components of a system or product, or including information that falls naturally into a two-column table. For this lesson, create a definition list describing the different types of conference calls, as shown in the example code below.

    a. Add <dl> start and end tags within your <conbody> element.

       The <dl> element is the container element for your definition list.

    b. Add <dlentry> start and end tags between the <dl> start and end tags.

       The <dlentry> element is a container for a single term and definition in the definition list. Use a separate <dlentry> for each new term and definition.

c. Add <dt> start and end tags between your <dlentry> start and end tags.

   Use <dt> (definition term) to identify the word or phrase to be defined. For each <dlentry> you must include at least one <dt>. If multiple terms share the same definition, you can add multiple <dt> elements to the <dlentry> element.

d. Add <dd> start and end tags after your <dt> end tag.

   Use the <dd> (definition description) to provide the definition for the corresponding term. For each <dlentry> you must include at least one <dd>. If a term has multiple definitions, you can add multiple <dd> elements to the <dlentry> element.

```
<conbody>
   <p>Use one of the following types of conference calls
      to speak with multiple people.</p>
   <dl>
      <dlentry>
         <dt>Three-way conference call</dt>
         <dd>Three-way conference calling connects two
             other people to a call.</dd>
      </dlentry>
      <dlentry>
         <dt>Multi-line conference call</dt>
         <dd>Multi-line conference calling connects you
             to more than two but fewer than eight other
             people on a call.</dd>
      </dlentry>
      <dlentry>
         <dt>Dial-in conference call</dt>
         <dd>Dial-in conference calling uses a single
             conference call number to connect multiple
             people.</dd>
      </dlentry>
   </dl>
</conbody>
```

11. Add a link to point the user to other related concept, task, or reference topics.

    You can use the <related-links> element to point your user to other topics, external files, or websites. However, we strongly recommend using a relationship table to add related links to your topics rather than the <related-links> element. Relationship tables free you from hardcoding links and are far easier to maintain. See Understanding Relationship Tables on page 179 for more information.

    a. Add <related-links> start and end tags between your <conbody> end tag and your <concept> end tag.

       The <related-links> element is a container for all links that relate to this topic.

    b. Add <link> start and end tags to your <related-links> container.

Include a link tag for each individual topic that you want to link to.

c. Add an *@href* attribute to the <link> element and set the *@scope* attribute to "local".

The *@href* attribute provides a link to the task topic with the file name you provide. For this example, use "SettingUpConfCall.dita". The *@scope* attribute indicates the position of the topic in relation to this topic. For this example, use "local" to indicate that the target topic is in the same directory as this one. For more information about the *@scope* attribute, refer to Scope Attribute on page 141.

d. Add a <linktext> element between the start and end tags of the <link> element to display text other than the topic title as the link.

The <linktext> element allows you to add a title or other text to the related link that appears at the end of the topic. If you link to a local DITA topic, as you have in this exercise, the title of the target topic appears automatically when you process the topic. However, if you link to a peer or external target, you need to supply link text. In this example, add different link text for the target topic, "Conference call set-up".

```
</conbody>
<related-links>
   <link href="SettingUpConfCall.dita" scope="local">
      <linktext>Conference call set-up</linktext>
   </link>
</related-links>
</concept>
```

12. Save your concept topic as AboutConferenceCalls.dita.

The following example shows the complete concept topic you created.

```
<?xml version="1.0" encoding="utf-8"?>
<!DOCTYPE concept PUBLIC "-//OASIS//DTD DITA Concept//EN"
   "concept.dtd">
<concept id="AboutConferenceCalls" xml:lang="en-us">
   <title>About conference calls</title>
   <shortdesc>Use a conference call to speak with more
      than two people in two different locations at the
      same time.</shortdesc>
   <prolog>
      <author>John Smith</author>
   </prolog>
   <conbody>
      <p>Use one of the following types of conference calls
         to speak with multiple people.</p>
      <dl>
         <dlentry>
            <dt>Three-way conference call</dt>
            <dd>Three-way conference calling connects
                two other people to a call.</dd>
         </dlentry>
```

```
        <dlentry>
        <dt>Multi-line conference call</dt>
           <dd>Multi-line conference calling connects
               you to more than two but fewer than eight
               other people on a call.</dd>
        </dlentry>
        <dlentry>
           <dt>Dial-in conference call</dt>
           <dd>Dial-in conference calling uses a single
               conference call number to connect multiple
               people.</dd>
        </dlentry>
     </dl>
  </conbody>
  <related-links>
     <link href="SettingUpConfCall.dita" scope="local">
        <linktext>Conference call set-up</linktext>
     </link>
  </related-links>
</concept>
```

The example below shows what a PDF rendering of the concept topic might look like. Output will vary depending on the stylesheet applied.

> **About conference calls**
>
> Use a conference call to speak with more than two people in two different locations at the same time.
>
> Use one of the following types of conference calls to speak with multiple people.
>
> **Three-way conference call**
> Three-way conference calling connects two other people to a call.
>
> **Multi-line conference call**
> Multi-line conference calling connects you to more than two but fewer than eight other people on a call.
>
> **Dial-in conference call**
> Dial-in conference calling uses a single conference call number to connect multiple people.

**Structure elements**

Structure elements are the base elements that you can use with every DITA information type. Use structure elements to create the base topic structure and organize the content. Structure elements are the topic container, title, short description, prolog, and body. The DITA DTD requires that you include a topic container, title, and body in every topic you develop. The other structure elements are optional. You use the elements described in this lesson in the core information types—concept, task, and reference. The structure elements are listed here in the order that you might use them.

**<task> <concept> <reference> root elements**

Use one of the core DITA information types as the top-level container (root element).

**<title> title**

Use the <title> element at the beginning of a topic to specify the heading for the entire topic. You can also use the <title> element to label sections or examples.

**<titlealts> title alternatives**

Use the <titlealts> element to specify alternative titles for your topic. The alternative titles may appear in web navigation, a table of contents, related links, or search results. The <titlealts> is a container for the <navtitle> and <searchtitle> elements. The <titlealts> element is optional. If you do not use the <titlealts> element, the text in the <title> element is used for navigation windows, table of contents, related links, and search results.

**<navtitle> navigation title**

Use the <navtitle> element to specify an alternative title for your topic. The navtitle is usually shorter than the full title in the <title> element. The <navtitle> element is used in navigation windows or other online tables of content. The <navtitle> element is located in the <titlealts> element and is optional.

**<searchtitle> search title**

Use the <searchtitle> element to specify a meaningful search title for your topic. The <searchtitle> element is used in search result summaries. It is located in the <titlealts> element and is optional.

**<shortdesc> short description**

Use the <shortdesc> element to provide the initial sentence or paragraph that summarizes the purpose or content of the topic. The <shortdesc> adds information to the topic title in search results and link previews. If you do not want to use the short description in your link previews or search results, you can turn off the short description with your stylesheet.

**<abstract> abstract**

Use the <abstract> element to provide a longer summary of the purpose or content of the topic than you might provide in the short description. You can label the first sentence or paragraph of your abstract as a <shortdesc> if you intend to use the short description in your online link previews and search results

**<prolog> prolog**

Use the <prolog> element as a container for the topic-level metadata. The metadata you can specify in the <prolog> element includes author, audience, copyright information, tracking dates, and permissions. For a complete list of <prolog> elements, see Prolog Metadata on page 101.

**<body> body**

Use the <body> element as the container for the main content of the <topic> element. The <body> element can contain block elements, phrase elements, and links. In the core task, concept, and reference information types, the <taskbody>, <conbody>, and <refbody> elements take the place of the base <body> element.

**<related-links> related links**

Use the <related-links> element to specify topics that the reader might want to consult after reading the topic. Although you can add related links to every topic with this element, we strongly recommend that you create your linking structure using a relationship table rather than embedding links in each topic. Changing a relationship table once in a DITA map is much easier than changing links embedded in individual topics. To create a relationship table, see Understanding Relationship Tables on page 179.

The following example illustrates how to use the structure elements described above.

```
<concept>
   <title>How PUB$ Estimator simplifies project
      planning</title>
      <titlealts>
         <navtitle>Simplified project
            planning</navtitle>
         <searchtitle>Simplified project planning with
            PUB$ Estimator</searchtitle>
      </titlealts>
   <abstract>
      <shortdesc>This section explains how PUB$ can simplify
         project planning.</shortdesc>
      <p>Included are the tasks accomplished with PUB$ and the
         worksheets that correspond to each task.</p>
   </abstract>
   <prolog>
      <author>John Smith</author>
   </prolog>
   <conbody>
   </conbody>
   <related-links>
      <link href="PlanningWorksheets.dita" scope="local"/>
   </related-links>
</concept>
```

## Concept elements

The elements you can use in a concept are primarily block elements. For definitions of block elements, see Block Elements on page 65. Concepts restrict the structure that authors can use but provide considerable flexibility.

For example, you can begin a concept with paragraphs of other block elements. To create a second level of heading within the concept, you must first add a

<section> or <example> element followed by a <title> and various block elements. Once you begin using a section or example, you can add additional sections or examples but you cannot add subsections or subexamples. DITA only allows one heading level below the title in a concept information type.

The following example illustrates how to use the elements in a concept topic.

```
<conbody>
   <p>The two-phase method of planning is so named
      because the planning and estimating process is
      comprised of two phases: the information planning
      phase and the content planning phase.  As you will
      see, the phases of project planning closely resemble
      the phases of product development.</p>
   <section>
      <title>The information planning phase</title>
      <p>During the information planning phase, the
         nature of the project is defined. The information
         plan can be likened to a product requirements
         document for a software development project.</p>
      <p>While studying the information needed by
         potential users and deciding on the best method to
         package the information, you can also create
         preliminary estimates based upon your initial
         research.</p>
   </section>
   <example>
      <image href="informationplanphase.jpg"></image>
   </example>
   <section>
      <title>The content planning phase</title>
      <p>After reviewing and gaining approval for your
         information plan, you reach the content planning
         phase. The content plan is analogous to the product
         specifications for a software or hardware
         project.</p>
      <p>During the content planning phase, you revise
         your preliminary estimates to reflect your detailed
         project specifications. At this point, you have
         enough information to develop a more reliable
         estimate of the time, staffing, and budget
         necessary.</p>
   </section>
   <example>
      <image href="contentplanphase.jpg"></image>
   </example>
</conbody>
```

## Concept review questions

You cannot insert a <p> element between sections and examples in a concept topic.

- True
- False

What question does a concept topic try to answer for the user?

Arrange the elements into the proper order for a concept topic.

1. <prolog/>
2. <conbody/>
3. <concept/>
4. <shortdesc/>
5. <related-links/>
6. <title/>

Where may a short description appear in your final output? Select all that apply.

a. In your table of contents
b. In search engine results
c. As a mouse-over for a help topic
d. In your printed text

What is the preferred method for referencing other topics from a DITA topic?

a. Using a <link> element in a <related-links> container
b. Using a relationship table
c. Using the <related-links> element in the <prolog> container
d. Using an unordered list of <xref> block elements within the <conbody> container

# LESSON 2

## Task Information Type

Tasks are the essential building blocks of technical content. They respond to the user's question, "How do I …?" When you implement a topic-based architecture, you should always begin by planning and authoring the tasks that the users must perform. To identify tasks for your information plan, consider performing a user and task analysis. Associate tasks with each user role you identify. Then, follow the basic instructions in this lesson to develop your task topics.

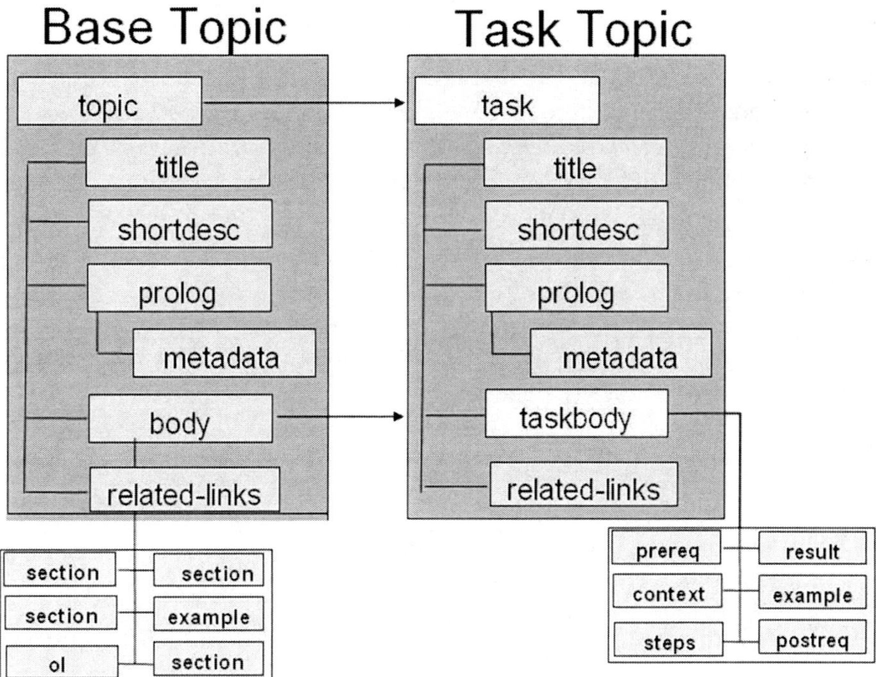


**Figure 2: Structure of the task topic**

The structure of the task information type is derived from the DITA topic structure as shown in Figure 2. The task body contains steps, substeps, and other content units required to structure the steps in a procedure.

The only required elements in a task are the title and the task body. A simple task includes a title and one or more steps in the task body. All other elements are optional. In the task body, you can include semantic elements, such as prerequisites, steps, examples, and results. The order and number of these semantic elements depends on whether you are following the original Strict Task Model or the General Task Model, released with DITA 1.2.

The General Task Model provides a less restrictive task model as an alternative to the Strict Task Model. It allows for variations in the way organizations create procedural information and can be used to develop a unique task specialization or to constrain the task model in a new way. The primary difference between the General and the Strict Task Model is the order of the elements before and after the steps. In addition, the General Task Model adds the <section> element to the elements preceding the steps. Table 4 shows the differences between the two task models. For more information about task elements, see Task elements on page 43. For a complete list of task elements, see the *OASIS Darwin Information Typing Architecture (DITA) Version 1.2 (OASIS Standard, 1 December 2010)*.

Although the Strict Task Model is valid for all versions of DITA, the General Task Model is not valid for DITA versions prior to 1.2. In addition, you cannot mix the task models in your content. We use the Strict Task Model in all lessons within this book.

| **Element** | **General Task Model** | **Strict Task Model** |
|---|---|---|
| title | required | required |
| prolog | optional | optional |
| prerequisite | optional, in any order, any number | optional, one only, must precede context |
| context | optional, in any order, any number | optional, one only, must follow prerequisite |
| section | optional, in any order, any number, may include a title | not supported |
| steps | optional, one only (excludes steps-unordered and steps-informal) | optional, one only (excludes steps-unordered) |

| Element | General Task Model | Strict Task Model |
|---|---|---|
| steps-unordered | optional, one only (excludes <steps and steps-informal) | optional, one only (excludes steps) |
| steps-informal | optional, one only (excludes steps and steps-unordered) | not supported |
| result | optional, one only, must precede example | optional, one only, must precede example |
| example | optional, any number, must precede post-req | optional, one only, must precede post-req |
| post-requisite | optional, any number | optional, one only |
| related links | optional | optional |

**Table 4: Comparison of the General and Strict Task Models**

### Creating a task topic

Many of the elements added to the beginning of your task topic are general topic structure elements. If you would like more information about the purpose of the <title>, *@id* attribute, <shortdesc>, and <prolog> elements and how to use them, see Concept Information Type on page 21.

This lesson explains the basic DITA elements you use to create a task topic using the Strict Task Model. In this lesson, you learn to

- add elements to the task information type, such as <task>, <taskbody>, <context>, <steps>, <step>, <cmd>, <info>, <note>, and <result>
- create a choice table using elements such as <choicetable>, <chhead>, <choptionshd>, <chdeschd>, <chrow>, <choption>, and <chdesc>

**1.** Start a new DITA task topic.

You can start a new DITA topic in an XML editor or in a text editor. In most XML editors, you can choose **file** > **new** > **DITA task topic**. The XML tool usually includes a DTD declaration and XML declaration automatically. If you choose to use a text editor, start your task topic by including the example markup shown below. The first line is the XML declaration and identifies the file as an XML document. The second line is the DTD declaration which uses a relative path to point to the DTD you want to validate your topic structure against. Finally, the start and end tags for the root element, task, form the container element for all other elements and identify the topic as a concept.

```
<?xml version="1.0" encoding="utf-8"?>
<!DOCTYPE task PUBLIC "-//OASIS//DTD DITA TASK//EN"
   "task.dtd">
<task>
</task>
```

2. Assign an *@id* attribute and value to the <task> element.

   Each *@id* you add to your topic must be unique to that topic. You use the unique *@id* to reference the topic in a DITA map. You can use letters, numbers, and underscores in your *@id*.

   Most content management systems assign a unique *@id* to every topic you create automatically. If you are not using a content management system, consider using your topic title as the unique *@id*. Be careful to omit the spaces between words.

   For this task, use the unique *@id*: TransferringACall.

```
<?xml version="1.0" encoding="utf-8"?>
<!DOCTYPE task PUBLIC "-//OASIS//DTD DITA TASK//EN"
   "task.dtd">
<task id="TransferringACall">
</task>
```

3. Assign an *@xml:lang* attribute and value to the <task> element.

   The *@xml:lang* attribute specifies the language of the element content. Using markup to identify language is strongly recommended to make the document as portable as possible.

```
<?xml version="1.0" encoding="utf-8"?>
<!DOCTYPE task PUBLIC "-//OASIS//DTD DITA TASK//EN"
   "task.dtd">
<task id="TransferringACall" xml:lang="en-us">
</task>
```

4. Insert <title> element start and end tags between the <task> start and end tags and include title text.

   The title element is the first content unit you include in every topic. The title may be used as a heading when the topic is rendered. Adding the title at the beginning of every topic ensures that the end user can identify the topic. You can include the topic title in your table of contents and site maps, and you can use it as link text for navigation through your topic set. Be certain that your task title clearly communicates the action the user must take. Consider developing a naming convention for your task, concept, and reference topic titles to distinguish the topics for the user.

For this task, use the title: "Transferring a call".

```
<task id="TransferringACall" xml:lang="en-us">
   <title>Transferring a call</title>
</task>
```

5. Add <shortdesc> element start and end tags after your title and include a short description of your topic.

   The short description briefly introduces the content of your task topic. Although the short description is not required, you should include it in every topic. The short description for a task provides your readers with an overview of what they will accomplish in the task. You can use the short description to provide a brief statement to display in search engine results or as a mouse-over for a help topic. Depending on your stylesheet, the short description may or may not appear in your rendered output.

```
<task id="TransferringACall" xml:lang="en-us">
   <title>Transferring a call</title>
   <shortdesc>When you transfer a call to another
      person in your office, you have two ways of handling
      the transfer.</shortdesc>
</task>
```

6. Add <prolog> element start and end tags after your short description.

   The <prolog> container holds the metadata for your concept topic. For more information about prolog metadata elements, see Prolog Metadata on page 101. You can also refer to the *OASIS Darwin Information Typing Architecture (DITA) Version 1.2 (OASIS Standard, 1 December 2010)* for a complete list of prolog elements.

```
<task id="TransferringACall" xml:lang="en-us">
   <title>Transferring a call</title>
   <shortdesc>When you transfer a call to another person
      in your office, you have two ways of handling the
      transfer.</shortdesc>
   <prolog>
  </prolog>
</task>
```

7. Add <author> start and end tags between the <prolog> start and end tags and include the author's name.

   The <author> element is one of the metadata attributes you can use in the <prolog> container. In the <author> element, enter the topic author's name; in our example code, we use "John Smith".

```
<task id="TransferringACall" xml:lang="en-us">
   <title>Transferring a call</title>
   ⋮
   <prolog>
      <author>John Smith</author>
   </prolog>
</task>
```

8. Add <taskbody> element start and end tags after the prolog.

   The task body contains most of the content in the task topic. Place the information you write about the task inside the <taskbody> element container.

```
<task id="TransferringACall" xml:lang="en-us">
   <title>Transferring a call</title>
   ⋮
   <prolog>
      <author>John Smith</author>
   </prolog>
   <taskbody>
   </taskbody>
</task>
```

9. Add <context> element start and end tags as the first element between your <taskbody> start and end tags, and provide text.

   The <context> element helps the user understand the purpose of the task and provides required background information. The context for a task should not include an entire concept topic. If the user needs more context, consider developing a concept topic.

```
<taskbody>
   <context>When you transfer the call without speaking to
      the person, it is an unannounced transfer. When you
      speak to the person receiving the transferred call,
      it is an announced transfer.</context>
</taskbody>
```

10. Add <steps> element start and end tags after the <context> container.

    The <steps> container surrounds all individual steps in a task so you can more easily reuse the group of steps in another task.

11. Add a <step> element start and end tag for each step in your procedure.

    Each <step> must begin with a command. Use the <cmd> element to write a single sentence stating the action for the step.

```
<taskbody>
   <context>When you transfer the call without speaking to
      the person, it is an unannounced transfer. When you
      speak to the person receiving the transferred call,
      it is an announced transfer.</context>
   <steps>
      <step>
         <cmd>Press the transfer button.</cmd>
```

```
      </step>
      <step>
         <cmd>Dial the number.</cmd>
      </step>
      <step>
         <cmd>Transfer the call.</cmd>
      </step>
   </steps>
</taskbody>
```

12. Add additional information for any step that requires it using an <info> element container after the <cmd> element end tag.

    In the <info> element container, you can add block elements such as paragraphs, lists, and notes. For example, you can include a <note> element in the <info> element container and further classify it as a note, tip, or caution using the *@type* attribute.

```
<steps>
   <step>
      <cmd>Press the transfer button.</cmd>
   </step>
   <step>
      <cmd>Dial the number.</cmd>
      <info>Dial the number manually, use your pre-defined
         speed dial keys, or go to your company directory.
      </info>
   </step>
   <step>
      <cmd>Transfer the call.</cmd>
      <info>
         <note type="tip">If you announce a call and the person
            refuses the transfer, do not hang up the phone.
            Press the transfer button again to retrieve the
            call on your phone.</note>
     </info>
   </step>
</steps>
```

13. Add a choice table in the <step> element container.

    A choice table allows you to present your user with different options to complete the step.

    a. Add <choicetable> element start and end tags.

       The <choicetable> element sets up a table with one row and two columns to display a choice option in one column and a description in the second column.

    b. Add <chhead> element start and end tags.

       The <chhead> element allows you to label the columns.

    c. Add <choptionhd> and <chdeschd> start and end tags and enter the headings for each column.

For this example, use "Type of Announcement" and "Steps to complete" as the column heads.

**d.** Add <chrow> containers for each row in the table.

For this example, add two rows.

**e.** Add <choption> and <chdesc> elements within each <chrow> container.

Add text for each element as shown in the example code. Note that the contents of each cell can include any number of block elements, such as paragraphs and lists.

```
<steps>
   ⋮
   <step>
      <cmd>Transfer the call.</cmd>
      <choicetable>
         <chhead>
            <choptionhd>Type of Announcement
            </choptionhd>
            <chdeschd>Steps to complete
            </chdeschd>
         </chhead>
         <chrow>
            <choption>Announce a call transfer
            </choption>
            <chdesc>
               <ol>
                  <li>Speak to the person.</li>
                  <li>Hang up the phone.</li>
               </ol>
            </chdesc>
         </chrow>
         <chrow>
            <choption>Transfer a call unannounced
            </choption>
            <chdesc>
               <ul>
                  <li>Hang up the phone.</li>
               </ul>
            </chdesc>
         </chrow>
      </choicetable>
      <info>
         <note type="tip">If you announce a call and the person
            refuses the transfer, do not hang up the phone.
            Press the transfer button again to retrieve the
            call on your phone.</note>
      </info>
   </step>
</steps>
```

**14.** Add task <result> start and end tags before your <taskbody> end tag.

Task topics do not require a result, but a result statement helps the users verify that they performed the task correctly. In the <result> element, provide the users with information about what they accomplished in the task. You can also add a task example and a post requirement. For more information about the <example> and the <postreq> elements, see Task elements on page 43.

```
<taskbody>
   ⋮
   </steps>
   <result>The call is transferred.</result>
</taskbody>
```

15. Add a link to point the user to other related concept, task, or reference topics.

    You can use the <related-links> element to point your user to other topics, external files, or websites. For example, you might use a related link to lead the reader to the next tasks in a sequence of tasks. However, we strongly recommend using a relationship table to add related links to your topics rather than the <related-links> element. Relationship tables free you from hardcoding links and are far easier to maintain. See Understanding Relationship Tables on page 179 for more information.

    **a.** Add <related-links> start and end tags between your <taskbody> end tag and your <task> end tag.

    The <related-links> element is a container for all links that relate to this topic.

    **b.** Add <link> start and end tags to your <related-links> container.

    Include a link tag for each individual topic that you want to link to.

    **c.** Add an *@href* attribute to the <link> element.

    The *@href* attribute provides a link to the task topic with the file name you provide. For this example, use "AboutTransfer.dita".

    **d.** Close your link tag with a "/" prior to the ">".

    When your element does not require other tags or text between its start and end tags, it is considered an "empty" element. Rather than using a close tag, you can close an empty element by inserting a "/" prior to the final ">".

```
<task>
   <taskbody>
   ⋮
   </taskbody>
   <related-links>
      <link href="AboutTransfer.dita"/>
   </related-links>
</task>
```

16. Save the task topic as TransferringACall.dita.

The following example shows the complete task topic you created.

```
<?xml version="1.0" encoding="utf-8"?>
<!DOCTYPE task PUBLIC "-//OASIS//DTD DITA Task//EN"
   "task.dtd">
<task id="TransferringACall" xml:lang="en-us">
   <title>Transferring a call</title>
   <shortdesc>When you transfer a call to another person
      in your office, you have two ways of handling the
      transfer.</shortdesc>
   <prolog>
      <author>John Smith</author>
   </prolog>
   <taskbody>
      <context>When you transfer the call without speaking to
         the person, it is an unannounced transfer. When you
         speak to the person receiving the transferred call,
         it is an announced transfer.</context>
      <steps>
         <step>
            <cmd>Press the transfer button.</cmd>
         </step>
         <step>
            <cmd>Dial the number. </cmd>
            <info>Dial the number manually, use your
               pre-defined speed dial keys, or go to your
               company directory. </info>
         </step>
         <step>
            <cmd>Transfer the call.</cmd>
            <choicetable>
               <chhead>
                  <choptionhd>Type of Announcement
                  </choptionhd>
                  <chdeschd>Steps to complete
                  </chdeschd>
               </chhead>
               <chrow>
                  <choption>Announce a call transfer
                  </choption>
                  <chdesc>
                     <ol>
                        <li>Speak to the person.
                        </li>
                        <li>Hang up the phone.</li>
                     </ol>
                  </chdesc>
               </chrow>
               <chrow>
                  <choption>Transfer a call
                     unannounced</choption>
                  <chdesc>
                     <ul>
                        <li>Hang up the phone.</li>
                     </ul>
                  </chdesc>
               </chrow>
            </choicetable>
            <info>
               <note type="tip">If you announce a call and the
                  person refuses the transfer, do not hang
```

```
                up the phone. Press the transfer button
                again to retrieve the call on your phone
                station.</note>
            </info>
        </step>
    </steps>
    <result>The call is transferred.</result>
  </taskbody>
  <related-links>
      <link href="AboutTransfer.dita"/>
  </related-links>
</task>
```

The following example shows what a PDF rendering of the task topic might look like. Output will vary depending on the stylesheet applied.

> **Transferring a call**
>
> When you transfer a call to another person in your office, you have two ways of handling the transfer.
>
> When you transfer the call without speaking to the person, it is an unannounced transfer. When you speak to the person receiving the transferred call, it is an announced transfer.
>
> 1. Press the transfer button.
> 2. Dial the number.
>    Dial the number manually, use your pre-defined speed dial keys, or go to your company directory.
> 3. Transfer the call.
>
> | Type of Announcement | Steps to complete |
> |---|---|
> | Announce a call transfer | 1. Speak to the person.<br>2. Hang up the phone. |
> | Transfer a call unannounced | Hang up the phone. |
>
> **Tip:** If you announce a call and the person refuses the transfer, do not hang up the phone. Press the transfer button again to retrieve the call on your phone station.
>
> The call is transferred.

### Task elements

You can use the elements described below in the task information type. The task elements are listed here in the order that you might use them when writing a task. The descriptions note the difference in the way the elements might be used between the General and the Strict Task Models when such a difference occurs.

### <prereq> prerequisite

Use the <prereq> element to specify anything that the user needs to know or do before starting the task. This information might include actions that must be completed first or a list of equipment that the user needs to complete the task.

If you are referring the user to another section, put the reference links needed for the prerequisite in the related-links section rather than into the prerequisite paragraph.

In the Strict Task Model, the <prereq> element must precede the <context> element. Only one <prereq> element is permitted. In the General Task Model, you may include more than one <prereq> element and the <prereq> elements may occur in any order before <steps>.

```
<taskbody>
   <prereq> Before you generate a new dependencies
      worksheet, research your organization's average hours
      per page for similar documents. You can base this
      average on past project histories, industry averages,
      or an educated guess.</prereq>
</taskbody>
```

### <context> context

Use the <context> element to identify the purpose or goal of the task, as well as to indicate to the users what they gain by completing the task. While the context information may contain some basic conceptual information, it should not replace or recreate a related concept topic.

In the Strict Task Model, the <context> element must follow the <prereq> element. Only one <context> element is permitted. In the General Task Model, you may include more than one <context> element and the <context> elements may occur in any order before <steps>.

```
<taskbody>
   <context>PUB$ sets up your dependencies worksheet with
      an average ranking of 3 for each dependency. After
      PUB$ returns control to you, you may want to change
      the rankings to reflect your specific
      circumstances.</context>
</taskbody>
```

### <section> section

Use the <section> element to create divisions in your task topic before beginning the steps. You can add a title to a section to label the information, providing a second heading level if necessary.

<section> is available only in the General Task Model.

```
<taskbody>
   <context>
      <p>PUB$ sets up your dependencies worksheet with
         an average ranking of 3 for each dependency. After
         PUB$ returns control to you, you may want to change
         the rankings to reflect your specific
```

```
         circumstances.</p>
   </context>
   <section>
      <title>Dependency ranking levels</title>
      <p>Dependency ranking levels must be defined by your
         organization to reflect your project metrics.</p>
   </section>
</taskbody>
```

**<steps> steps and <steps-unordered> steps unordered**

Use the <steps> element to create a numbered list of all the steps that the user must follow to complete the task. The <steps> element is the container for all of the individual <step> elements that your task contains. If your task only has one step or if the steps do not need to be performed in order, use a <steps-unordered> element instead.

**<step> step**

Use the <step> element to develop each step that the user must follow to complete the task. Each <step> element must be in the <steps> container element and must begin with a <cmd> element. Each <step> in a <steps> list is rendered as a numbered step while each <step> in a <steps-unordered> list is rendered as an unnumbered step. You can use one or more <step> elements within each <steps> or <steps-unordered> element.

**<cmd> command**

Use the <cmd> element to describe the action the user needs to take in a <step> element. The description should be written in the imperative (Press the button), and it should be no more than one sentence. The <cmd> element must be the first element in the <step> element.

**<info> information**

Use the <info> element to add information needed to complete a step beyond the instruction in the <cmd> element. The description should be brief and should contain minimal conceptual information.

**<note> note**

Use the <note> element to call attention to a particular point in the <info> element. Use the *@type* attribute value to specify the kind of note; for example, note, tip, caution, danger, and so on. In DITA 1.2, the values danger, warning, and notice are based on ANSI Z535 and ISO 3864 regulations.

**<stepxmp> step example**

Use the <stepxmp> element to show the user how to perform the step. The example may include a few words, a paragraph, a figure, a table, or other information to illustrate the task. Step examples often provide specific data-entry characters.

**<stepresult> step result**

Use the <stepresult> element to explain the expected outcome of a step, such as a dialog box opening or a progress indicator appearing. Step results assure users that they are on track.

**<substeps> sub-steps**

Use the <substeps> element to break a step down into a series of actions. This element is a container for the individual <substep> elements. If you need to use <substeps>, consider creating a new task instead so that the steps are not embedded in another task. Use <substeps> only when necessary.

**<substep> sub-step**

Use the <substep> element to develop each sub-step that a user must follow to complete the step. The <substep> element has the same structure as the <step> element, but it cannot contain another level of <substeps> or <choices> or <choicetable> elements.

**<steps-informal> steps informal**

Use the <steps-informal> element to describe procedural task information without placing each step in an individual container element. For example, <steps-informal> may contain a paragraph that describes more than one step in a single sentence, or it may contain sentences that mix steps together with information about the steps. <steps-informal> is available only in the General Task Model.

```
<taskbody>
   <steps>
      <step>
         <cmd>Rank each dependency.</cmd>
         <substeps>
            <substep><cmd>Select a cell in the dependency row you
               want to change.</cmd>
               <info>After setting up the dependencies
                  worksheet, PUB$ selects a cell in the first
                  dependency row. If you don't want to change this
                  dependency ranking, select a cell in another
                  dependency row.</info>
            </substep>
            <substep><cmd>While holding down the Control key,
               type the appropriate ranking (1 to 5).</cmd>
               <info>The cell that corresponds to your
                  entry is shaded.
                  <note type="caution"> The Control key
                     works only with the number keys at the
                     top of your keyboard. Use those numbers
                     to change dependency rankings. If you
                     use the keypad on the right side of
                     your keyboard, you delete information
                     in the selected cell.</note>
               </info>
            </substep>
            <substep><cmd>Repeat for each dependency.</cmd>
            </substep>
         </substeps>
         <stepresult>After you change the dependency
            ranking, PUB$ multiples your average hours per
```

```
            page by each multiple to calculate a new hours
            per page projection. PUB$ then selects a cell in
            the next dependency row and returns control to
            you.</stepresult>
      </step>
      <step><cmd>Multiply the modified hours per page from the
         dependency calculator by the number of pages to get a
         total project budget.</cmd>
      </step>
   </steps>
</taskbody>
```

**<choices> choices**

Use the <choices> element to create a list of options that the user can select to complete the task. The <choices> element is a container for individual <choice> elements.

**<choice> choice**

Use the <choice> element to list each option that the user can select. The <choice> element must be in a <choices> container. The <choice> items typically render as bullets.

```
<taskbody>
   <steps>
      <step><cmd>Start the PUB$ program.</cmd>
         <choices>
            <choice>Click Yes if you want to include
               the new skill in the factor formula.
            </choice>
            <choice>Click No if you don't want to include
               the new skill in the factor formula.
            </choice>
         </choices>
      </step>
   </steps>
</taskbody>
```

**<choicetable> choice table**

Use the <choicetable> element to create a table of options that the user can select to complete the task. The <choicetable> element is a container for the<chhead> and <chrow> elements.

**<chhead> choice head**

Use the <chhead> element to define headings in a choice table. The <chhead> element is used in the <choicetable> container. It contains the <choptionhd> and <chdeschd> elements. If you do not include a <chhead> element, no column headings will appear on the table.

**<choptionhd> choice option head**

Use the <choptionhd> element to define the heading for the first column of a choice table. The <choptionhd> element is used in the <chhead> container.

**<chdeschd> choice description head**

Use the <chdeschd> element to define the heading for the second column of a choice table. The <chdeschd> element is used in the <chhead> container.

**<chrow> choice row**

Use the <chrow> element to create a row in a choice table. The <chrow> element is used in the <choicetable> container. The <chrow> element contains the <choption> and <chdesc> elements.

**<choption> choice option**

Use the <choption> element to describe an option that the user can choose to accomplish the step. One <choption> element is used in each <chrow> element.

**<chdesc> choice description**

Use the <chdesc> element to provide a description for the option in the corresponding <choption> element. The description explains why the user would choose that option or the result of making that choice. One <chdesc> element is used in each <chrow> element.

```
<taskbody>
   <steps>
      <step><cmd>Enter the file names of any labor costs
         summary reports.</cmd>
         <choicetable>
            <chhead>
               <choptionhd>If</choptionhd>
               <chdeschd>Then</chdeschd>
            </chhead>
            <chrow>
               <choption>You have previously generated
                  labor costs summary reports</choption>
               <chdesc>The links must be updated and
                  maintained. Type the file names in the
                  spaces provided, indicate whether each
                  file is currently open, and click Enter.
                  If a file is closed, PUB$ opens it before
                  updating the information.</chdesc>
            </chrow>
            <chrow>
               <choption>You have not generated one or
                  both of these reports.</choption>
               <chdesc>Check the box that corresponds
                  to the missing report, and click Enter.
               </chdesc>
            </chrow>
         </choicetable>
      </step>
   </steps>
</taskbody>
```

**<result> result**

Use the <result> element to describe the expected outcome of the entire task. The <result> element could include a final description using figures, tables, or audiovisual cues that show the users that they have successfully completed the task. The <result> element is used after the <steps> container.

```
<taskbody>
   <steps>
   ⋮
   </steps>
   <result>The weekly hours tracking workshop has been
      saved by PUB$. Control of the worksheet has been
      restored to you. </result>
</taskbody>
```

**<example> example**

Use the <example> element in a task to show an example of completing the task. The <example> element could include code samples, figures, screen shots, and other samples that show the users how to complete the task. The <example> element follows the <result> container.

```
<taskbody>
   <steps>
   ⋮
   </steps>
   <example>Let's take a look at the weekly total costs
      tracking worksheet that Renee generated for the month
      of March (Figure 5.21)
      <fig>
         <title>Serendipity's weekly total costs tracking
            worksheet</title>
         <image href="WeeklyTotalCostsExample.jpg"/>
      </fig>
   </example>
</taskbody>
```

**<postreq> post requirement**

Use the <postreq> element to specify anything that the user needs to know or do after completing the task. This information might include actions that need to be completed before the user can see the expected results, such as rebooting the computer, or information that the user needs to read or cross-reference to verify the completion of the task. The <postreq> element follows the <example> element and is often supported by links to the next task or tasks in the related-links section.

```
<taskbody>
   <steps>
   ⋮
   </steps>
   <postreq>After you have entered your initial
      dependency rankings, you can change any of them by
      repeating steps 1 and 2. Notice how the hours per page
      projection is affected by each change.</postreq>
</taskbody>
```

**Task review questions**

This code sample conforms to DITA code standards: `<step>Type your name.</step>`

- True
- False

What question does a task topic try to answer for the user?

Arrange the elements into the proper order for a strict task topic.

1. <context/>
2. <taskbody/>
3. <result/>
4. <shortdesc/>
5. <prereq/>
6. <example/>
7. <steps/>

What is the difference between the General Task and Strict Task Models? (Select all that apply.)

a. The Strict Task Model allows sections, while the General Task Model does not.
b. Only Strict Task Model topics are supported in DITA versions prior to 1.2
c. The General Task Model allows more flexibility in the order and number of elements before and after the steps.
d. The General Task Model replaces <steps-unordered> with <steps-informal>.
e. The Strict Task Model requires <prereq>, <context>, <steps>, <result>, and <example> elements all be present and in that order.

Match the description to each element.

| | |
|---|---|
| <steps> | Creates a bulleted list of all the steps contained within. |
| <steps-unordered> | Describes a procedure without requiring a list of steps. |
| <steps-informal> | Breaks a step down into a series of actions |
| <substeps> | Describes a specific sub-step that the user must follow to complete a step.. |
| <step> | Creates a numbered list of all the steps contained within.. |
| <substep> | Describes a specific step the user must follow to complete a task |

What is the difference between <choices> and <choicetable>?

- **a.** <choices> is used to display options for <steps>, while <choicetable> is used in <substeps>.
- **b.** <choices> formats as a bulleted list, while <choicetable> creates a two-column table of options.
- **c.** <choices> can be used for any number of options, while <choicetable> is limited to two.

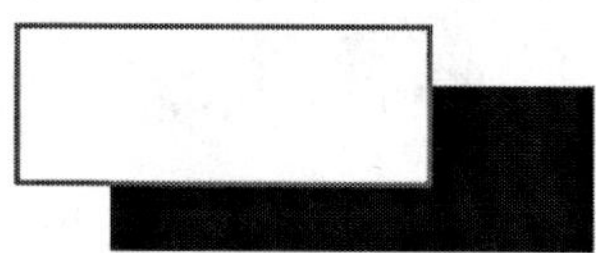

# LESSON 3

## Reference Information Type

Reference topics are essential for the successful performance of technical tasks. In fact, many competent and expert users depend more heavily on reference information than they do on step-by-step tasks. By building stand-alone reference topics, you have the flexibility of building unique deliverables that emphasize reference content, including command reference lists, parts and equipment lists, error codes, specifications, parameters, and glossary terms.

The structure of the reference information type is derived from the DITA topic. The reference body includes the properties content unit, which uses the same structure as a simple table in the DITA topic structure. Figure 3 provides a visual representation of the relationship between the DITA topic structure and the structure of the reference information type.

The only required elements in a reference topic are the title and the reference body. Because reference information is often presented in lists or tables, the reference information type provides elements that facilitate list and table development. A simple reference topic consists of a title and a list or a table contained in the reference body. You can structure your information further within the reference body using a properties table, ordered and unordered lists, simple tables, and complex tables. Following the lesson, you will find a list and more detailed descriptions of the reference elements, including elements not discussed in this lesson. For a complete list of elements you can use to write a reference topic, see the *OASIS Darwin Information Typing Architecture (DITA) Version 1.2 (OASIS Standard, 1 December 2010).*

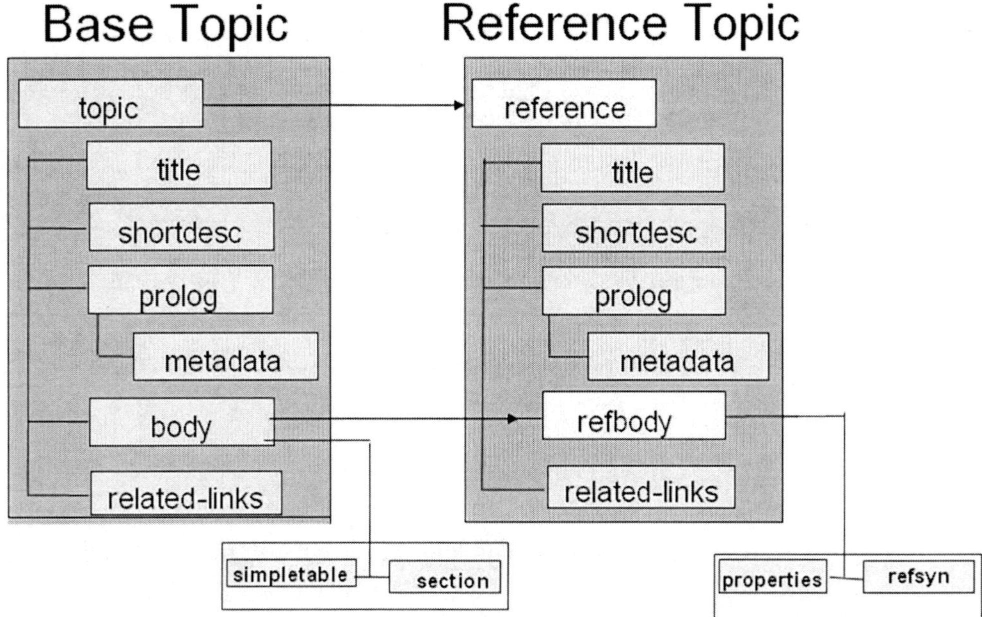


Figure 3: Structure of the reference topic

### Creating a reference topic

This lesson explains the basic DITA elements you use to create a reference topic.

Many of the elements added to the beginning of your reference topic are general topic structure elements that have been explained in detail in the concept and task creation lessons. Refer to those lessons if you need a refresher on these common elements, including <title>, <shortdesc>, and <prolog>, or on the *@id* attribute.

In this lesson you learn to

- add standard elements used in the reference information type such as <reference> and <refbody>
- create a properties table using elements such as <properties>, <prophead>, <proptypehd>, <propvaluehd>, <propdeschd>, <property>, <proptype>, <propvalue>, and <propdesc>

**1.** Start a new DITA reference topic.

You can start a new DITA topic in a text editor or in an XML editor. In most XML editors, you can choose **file** > **new** > **DITA reference topic**.

```
<?xml version="1.0" encoding="utf-8"?>
<!DOCTYPE reference PUBLIC "-//OASIS//DTD DITA
   REFERENCE//EN" "reference.dtd">
<reference>
</reference>
```

2. Assign an *@id* attribute and value to the <reference> element.

   For this lesson, use the unique *@id*: "QuickGuide".

```
<?xml version="1.0" encoding="utf-8"?>
<!DOCTYPE reference PUBLIC "-//OASIS//DTD DITA
   REFERENCE//EN" "reference.dtd">
<reference id="QuickGuide">
</reference>
```

3. Assign an *@xml:lang* attribute and value to the <reference> element.

```
<?xml version="1.0" encoding="utf-8"?>
<!DOCTYPE reference PUBLIC "-//OASIS//DTD DITA
   REFERENCE//EN" "reference.dtd">
<reference id="QuickGuide" xml:lang="en-us">
</reference>
```

4. Insert <title> element start and end tags between the <reference> start and end tags and include title text.

   Reference topic titles need to facilitate quick lookup. Be certain that your reference title clearly communicates the subject of your topic.

```
<reference id="QuickGuide" xml:lang="en-us">
   <title>Quick Guide to Basic Telephone Use</title>
</reference>
```

5. Add <shortdesc> element start and end tags after your title and include a short description of your topic.

   The short description for a reference topic provides your users with an overview of the lists, tables, and other reference information in the topic.

```
<reference id="QuickGuide" xml:lang="en-us">
   <title>Quick Guide to Basic Telephone Use</title>
   <shortdesc>The Quick Guide provides a brief
      description of the buttons on your phone.
   </shortdesc>
</reference>
```

6. Add <prolog> start and end tags after your short description and include metadata specific to your reference topic.

For your reference topic, include author metadata. See the *OASIS Darwin Information Typing Architecture (DITA) Version 1.2 (OASIS Standard, 1 December 2010)* for a complete list of prolog elements.

```
<reference id="QuickGuide" xml:lang="en-us">
   <title>Quick Guide to Basic Telephone Use</title>
   <shortdesc>The Quick Guide provides a brief
      description of each button on your phone.
   </shortdesc>
   <prolog>
      <author>John Smith</author>
   </prolog>
</reference>
```

7. Add <refbody> start and end tags after your <prolog> container.

   The <refbody> element contains most of the content in the reference topic. Place all reference information you write inside the <refbody> element container.

```
<reference id="QuickGuide" xml:lang="en-us">
   <title>Quick Guide to Basic Telephone Use</title>
   <shortdesc>The Quick Guide provides a brief
      description of the buttons on your phone.
   </shortdesc>
   <prolog>
      <author>John Smith</author>
   </prolog>
   <refbody>
   </refbody>
</reference>
```

8. Add a properties table for your reference information.

   A properties table informs users about terms, values, and descriptions. Properties tables are limited to three columns. If you need more columns, you must use simple or complex tables.

   a. Add <properties> element start and end tags between your <refbody> tags.

```
<refbody>
   <properties></properties>
</refbody>
```

   b. Define column heads for the table by embedding <proptypehd>, <propvaluehd>, and <propdeschd> elements in a <prophead> container within the <properties> start and end tags.

      The <proptypehd> element defines the column head for your property types, the <propvaluehd> element defines the column head for your property values, and the <propdeschd> element defines the column head for your property descriptions.

```
<refbody>
   <properties>
      <prophead>
         <proptypehd>Action</proptypehd>
         <propvaluehd>Indicator</propvaluehd>
         <propdeschd>Description</propdeschd>
      </prophead>
   </properties>
</refbody>
```

c. Add <property> element start and end tags for each row in your table.

d. Insert content into each row by embedding <proptype>, <propvalue>, and <propdesc> elements in your <property> container.

   The three element containers, property type, property value, and property description, allow you to create a three-column table. Use <proptype> to define the name of a particular parameter. Use <propvalue> to describe the values associated with the parameter. Use <propdesc> to include a detailed description of the parameter. If you decide you don't want to include data in one of the table cells defined by the <proptype>, <propvalue>, and <propdesc> elements, add the element tags without adding text.

**Note:** Content need not be limited to text. You might choose to embed a figure in one of the table cells. In this exercise, we include the icons associated with each telephone action in the Indicator column. To include figures, use the <image> element and include the name of the graphic file in the *@href* attribute as shown in the example.

```
<refbody>
   <properties>
      <prophead>
         <proptypehd>Action</proptypehd>
         <propvaluehd>Indicator</propvaluehd>
         <propdeschd>Description</propdeschd>
      </prophead>
      <property>
         <proptype>Talk</proptype>
         <propvalue>
            <image href="talk.jpg"/>
         </propvalue>
         <propdesc>Press the talk key to receive a dial
            tone.</propdesc>
      </property>
      <property>
         <proptype>Speaker phone</proptype>
         <propvalue>
            <image href="speakerphone.jpg"/>
         </propvalue>
         <propdesc>Press the speaker phone button to
            place a call on speaker phone.</propdesc>
```

```
            </property>
            <property>
               <proptype>Forward</proptype>
               <propvalue>
                  <image href="forward.jpg"/>
               </propvalue>
               <propdesc>Press the forward button to forward
                  all incoming calls to another phone number or
                  voice mail.</propdesc>
            </property>
            <property>
               <proptype>Transfer</proptype>
               <propvalue>
                  <image href="transfer.jpg"/>
               </propvalue>
               <propdesc>Press the transfer button to transfer
                  a call to another person.</propdesc>
            </property>
            <property>
               <proptype>Hold</proptype>
               <propvalue>
                  <image href="hold.jpg"/>
               </propvalue>
               <propdesc>Press the hold button to place a call
                  on hold.</propdesc>
            </property>
            <property>
               <proptype>Mute</proptype>
               <propvalue>
                  <image href="mute.jpg"/>
               </propvalue>
               <propdesc>Press the mute button to mute your
                  end of the call.</propdesc>
            </property>
         </properties>
      </refbody>
```

9. Add a link to point the user to other related concept, task, or reference topics.

    **Note:** In reference topics, you rarely use related links because reference topics relate to so many other task, concept, and reference topics. If you include links to all task, concept, and reference topics in your reference topic, it might overwhelm the user.

```
<reference id="QuickGuide" xml:lang="en-us">
   ⋮
   </refbody>
   <related-links>
      <link href="TransferringACall.dita"/>
   </related-links>
</reference>
```

10. Save the reference topic as QuickGuide.dita.

The following example illustrates the complete reference topic you created.

```
<?xml version="1.0" encoding="utf-8"?>
<!DOCTYPE reference PUBLIC "-//OASIS//DTD DITA
   Reference//EN" "reference.dtd">
```

```
<reference id="QuickGuide" xml:lang="en-us">
   <title>Quick Guide to Basic Telephone Use</title>
   <shortdesc>The Quick Guide provides a brief
      description of the buttons on your phone.
   </shortdesc>
   <prolog>
      <author>John Smith</author>
   </prolog>
   <refbody>
      <properties>
         <prophead>
            <proptypehd>Action</proptypehd>
            <propvaluehd>Indicator</propvaluehd>
            <propdeschd>Description</propdeschd>
         </prophead>
         <property>
            <proptype>Talk</proptype>
            <propvalue>
               <image href="talk.jpg"/>
            </propvalue>
            <propdesc>Press the talk key to receive a
               dial tone.</propdesc>
         </property>
         <property>
            <proptype>Speaker phone</proptype>
            <propvalue>
               <image href="speakerphone.jpg"/>
            </propvalue>
            <propdesc>Press the speaker phone button to
               place a call on speaker phone.</propdesc>
         </property>
         <property>
            <proptype>Forward</proptype>
            <propvalue>
               <image href="forward.jpg"/>
            </propvalue>
            <propdesc>Press the forward button to
               forward all incoming calls to another phone
               number or voice mail.</propdesc>
         </property>
         <property>
            <proptype>Transfer</proptype>
            <propvalue>
               <image href="transfer.jpg"/>
            </propvalue>
            <propdesc>Press the transfer button to
               transfer a call to another person.
            </propdesc>
         </property>
         <property>
            <proptype>Hold</proptype>
            <propvalue>
               <image href="hold.jpg"/>
            </propvalue>
            <propdesc>Press the hold button to place a
               call on hold.</propdesc>
         </property>
         <property>
            <proptype>Mute</proptype>
            <propvalue>
               <image href="mute.jpg"/>
```

```
            </propvalue>
            <propdesc>Press the mute button to mute
               your end of the call.
            </propdesc>
         </property>
      </properties>
   </refbody>
   <related-links>
      <link href="TransferringACall.dita"/>
   </related-links>
</reference>
```

The following example shows what a PDF rendering of the reference topic might look like. Output will vary depending on the stylesheet applied.

**Quick Guide to Basic Telephone Use**

The Quick Guide provides a brief description of the buttons on your phone.

| Action | Indicator | Description |
|---|---|---|
| Talk | TALK | Press the talk key to receive a dial tone. |
| Speaker phone | SPEAKERPHONE | Press the speaker phone button to place a call on speaker phone. |
| Forward | FORWARD | Press the forward button to forward all incoming calls to another phone number or voice mail. |
| Transfer | TRANSFER | Press the transfer button to transfer a call to another person. |
| Hold | HOLD | Press the hold button to place a call on hold. |
| Mute | MUTE | Press the mute button to mute your end of the call. |

### Reference elements

You can use the reference elements described below in the reference information type. The reference elements are listed here in the order that you might use them when authoring a properties table.

**<properties> properties**

Use the <properties> element to create a properties table to list all the details the user must know for the corresponding task topic. The <properties> element is the container for all the individual <property> elements your reference contains.

**<prophead> property head**

Use the <prophead> element to specify the property type, property value, and property description column heads for the properties table. The <prophead> element is the container for the <proptypehd>, <propvaluehd>, and <propdeschd> elements. Each of these elements can only occur once within the <properties> element.

**<proptypehd> property type head**

Use the <proptypehd> element to specify the type heading for the properties table. The <proptypehd> is the first element in the <prophead> element.

**<propvaluehd> property value head**

Use the <propvaluehd> element to specify the value heading for the properties table. The <propvaluehd> is the second element in the <prophead> element.

**<propdeschd> property description head**

Use the <propdeschd> element to specify the description head for the properties table. The <propdeschd> is the last element in the <prophead> element.

**<property> property**

Use the <property> element to create a row in a property table. The <property> element contains the <proptype>, <propvalue>, and <propdesc> elements. A properties table can contain any number of <property> elements.

**<proptype> property type**

Use the <proptype> element to define the property type for the row in the properties table. Each <property> element can include only one <proptype> element.

**<propvalue> property value**

Use the <propvalue> element to define the value of the specified property type. Each <property> element can include only one <propvalue> element.

**<propdesc> property description**

Use the <propdesc> element to describe the property type in one row of the properties table. Each <property> element can include only one <propdesc> element.

The following example illustrates how to use the <properties> elements.

```
<properties>
   <prophead>
      <proptypehd>Character Graphic</proptypehd>
      <propvaluehd>Code Point</propvaluehd>
      <propdeschd>Description</propdeschd>
   </prophead>
   <property>
```

```
      <proptype>A</proptype>
      <propvalue>41</propvalue>
      <propdesc>A Capital</propdesc>
   </property>
   <property>
      <proptype>a</proptype>
      <propvalue>61</propvalue>
      <propdesc>a Small</propdesc>
   </property>
      <property>
      <proptype>B</proptype>
      <propvalue>42</propvalue>
      <propdesc>B Capital</propdesc>
   </property>
   <property>
      <proptype>b</proptype>
      <propvalue>62</propvalue>
      <propdesc>b Small</propdesc>
   </property>
   <property>
      <proptype>C</proptype>
      <propvalue>43</propvalue>
      <propdesc>C Capital</propdesc>
   </property>
   <property>
      <proptype>c</proptype>
      <propvalue>63</propvalue>
      <propdesc>c Small</propdesc>
   </property>
</properties>
```

The following table illustrates a rendered properties table. The table format will vary depending on your stylesheet.

| **Character Graphic** | **Code Point** | **Description** |
|---|---|---|
| A | 41 | A Capital |
| a | 61 | a Small |
| B | 42 | B Capital |
| b | 62 | b Small |
| C | 43 | C Capital |
| c | 63 | c Small |

**Reference review questions**

Reference topics may consist of list and table elements only.

- True
- False

Which elements are required in a reference topic? (Select all that apply.)

a. <title>
b. <shortdesc>
c. <prolog>
d. <refbody>
e. <related-links>

What is wrong with this code?

```
<property>
   <prophead>
      <proptypehd>Character Graphic</proptypehd>
      <propvaluehd>Code Point</propvaluehd>
      <propdeschd>Description</propdeschd>
   </prophead>
   <properties>
      <proptype>A</proptype>
      <proptype>41</proptype>
      <proptype>A capital</proptype>
   </properties>
   <properties>
      <proptype>a</proptype>
      <proptype>61</proptype>
      <proptype>A small</proptype>
   </properties>
</property>
```

If you want to leave a cell blank within a properties table, omit the corresponding element tag.

- True
- False

How many columns can you have in a properties table?

**a.** 2

**b.** 3

**c.** Up to 5

**d.** Unlimited

# SECTION B

# Understanding DITA Elements

In the first three lessons, you learned to apply structure elements to a DITA concept, task, and reference topic. DITA has many more elements that you can use to create your DITA topics. In addition, the DITA elements may contain attributes that enhance their functionality. In this guide, we do not discuss all elements or all the attributes. For a complete list of the DITA elements and their attributes, see the *OASIS Darwin Information Typing Architecture (DITA) Version 1.2 (OASIS Standard, 1 December 2010)*.

DITA topic elements can be grouped into five categories:

**Structure elements**
: Provide the overall structure for each information type. These elements were introduced in the previous lessons.

**Block elements**
: Provide structure for basic content, such as paragraphs and lists, and also provide containers for other elements.

**Phrase elements**
: Used to label information semantically or provide formatting options. Phrase elements are categorized into Domain and Highlight elements. Domain elements describe text associated with a specific subject area, such as programming, software, or user interface elements. Highlight, or typographic, elements override the formatting associated with a semantic DITA tag, allowing you to specify formatting such as italic, bold, and underscore.

**Related-link elements**
: Enable you to link topics together.

**Metadata elements**
: Enable you to categorize your information to facilitate search and retrieval and conditional processing.

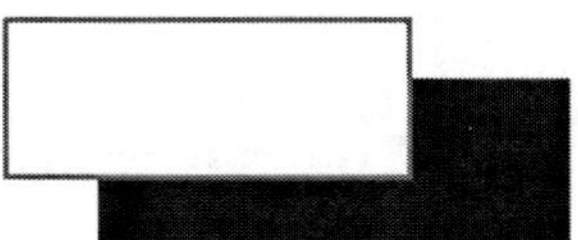

# LESSON 4

## Block Elements

Block elements are the standard content units used by authors to define the structure of blocks of text. Some block elements may look familiar because they share the same names as HTML elements. Block elements include paragraph, list, table, and example. Section is a block element that serves as a container element for other block elements. You can use most block elements in every information type. However, the rules in the Document Type Definition (DTD) for each information type restrict the use of some block elements. For example, you can use a section in a concept but not in a strict task.

**Adding block elements**

In this lesson, you learn to add basic block elements, such as <p>, <ul>, and <li>, to a DITA topic.

1. Start a new concept topic.

   Refer to the Concept Information Type on page 21 to create the basic structure.

   ```
   <?xml version="1.0" encoding="utf-8"?>
   <!DOCTYPE concept PUBLIC "-//OASIS//DTD DITA CONCEPT//EN"
      "concept.dtd">
   <concept id="AboutTelephoneFeatures" xml:lang="en-us">
      <title>About using the telephone's features</title>
      <shortdesc>Your Comstar telephone has many features
         that allow you to handle calls in a variety of
         powerful ways.</shortdesc>
      <conbody>
      </conbody>
   </concept>
   ```

2. Add <p> start and end tags between the <conbody> element start and end tags.

   You can include any of the basic block elements, such as paragraph, unordered list, numbered list, and tables in your topics. However, each information type allows or disallows block elements in different places. See the *OASIS Darwin Information Typing Architecture (DITA) Version 1.2 (OASIS Standard, 1 December 2010)* to determine where you can add block elements in your information types.

   For this lesson, enter two paragraphs as shown.

```
<conbody>
   <p>In this chapter, you will learn how to use the
      features of your phone. If you have any questions
      about these features, contact your system
      administrator.</p>
   <p>The features discussed in this chapter are</p>
</conbody>
```

3. Add <ul> start and end tags to your concept after the second paragraph container.

   An unordered list presents information to the user when the order of the item is not relevant, such as a list of tools needed to complete a task. The unordered list container uses <li> elements to separate each list item. Using a list item container allows you to reuse the set of items in other contexts.

   For this lesson, enter a six-item list as shown.

```
<conbody>
   <p>In this chapter, you will learn how to use the
      features of your phone. If you have any questions
      about these features, contact your system
      administrator.</p>
   <p>The features discussed in this chapter are</p>
   <ul>
      <li>automatic callback</li>
      <li>automatic preselect</li>
      <li>automatic speakerphone answer</li>
      <li>background music</li>
      <li>call forwarding</li>
      <li>call waiting</li>
   </ul>
</conbody>
```

4. Save the topic as AboutTelephoneFeatures.dita.

The following example illustrates the complete concept topic you created in this lesson.

```
<?xml version="1.0" encoding="utf-8"?>
<!DOCTYPE concept PUBLIC "-//OASIS//DTD DITA CONCEPT//EN"
   "concept.dtd">
<concept id="AboutTelephoneFeatures" xml:lang="en-us">
   <title>About using the telephone's features</title>
   <shortdesc>Your Comstar telephone has many features
      that allow you to handle calls in a variety of
      powerful ways.</shortdesc>
   <conbody>
      <p>In this chapter, you will learn how to use the
         features of your phone. If you have any questions
         about these features, contact your system
         administrator.</p>
      <p>The features discussed in this chapter are</p>
      <ul>
         <li>automatic callback</li>
         <li>automatic preselect</li>
         <li>automatic speakerphone answer</li>
         <li>background music</li>
```

```
        <li>call forwarding</li>
        <li>call waiting</li>
     </ul>
  </conbody>
</concept>
```

The following example shows what a PDF rendering of the topic might look like.

> **About using the telephone's features**
>
> Your Comstar telephone has many features that allow you to handle calls in a variety of powerful ways.
>
> In this chapter, you will learn how to use the features of your phone. If you have any questions about these features, contact your system administrator.
>
> The features discussed in this chapter are
>
> - automatic callback
> - automatic preselect
> - automatic speakerphone answer
> - background music
> - call forwarding
> - call waiting

**Block element definitions**

The following block elements are used in the DITA model.

**<p> paragraph**

Use the <p> element to group text. The <p> element is the most common element used in a topic. You can use the <p> element in the body of your topic, in a <section>, or in an <example>. The number of <p> elements used in a topic is unlimited.

**<section> section**

Use the <section> element to organize subtopics in the body of a larger topic. All information types except strict task allow the <section> element in the body element. You cannot include a section in an example, but you can follow an example with a section and vice versa. You can include a title in a section. One of the ways you can build hierarchy within your topic is to add a title to your section. However, you will need to design your stylesheet so that the section title will appear in your table of contents.

**<example> example**

Use the <example> element to illustrate the content of a topic. Illustrations used in the <example> element may include images, code, output, and discussions. You cannot include an example in a section; you can follow a section with an example and vice versa. You can include a title in an example. One of the ways you can build hierarchy within your topic is to add a title to your example.

**<fig> figure**

We recommend that you always use the <fig> element as a container to include a figure caption and an image in your content. Adding a figure caption to your figure is optional. To add a figure capture, embed a <title> element in the <fig> element.

**<image> image**

Use the <image> element to reference a graphic. The <image> element has one required attribute, *@href*. Use the *@href* attribute to point to the location of your graphic. Other <image> element attributes are optional and allow you to set values related to placement, alignment, size, and scale. We recommend that you use the *@height*, *@width*, and *@scale* attributes sparingly. You should maintain the graphic's dimensions in the original source if at all possible.

```
<conbody>
   <p>The two-phase method of planning is so named
      because the planning and estimating process comprises
      two phases: the information planning phase and the
      content planning phase. As you will see, the phases of
      project planning closely resemble the phases of
      product development.</p>
   <section>
      <title>The information planning phase</title>
      <p>During the information planning phase, the
         nature of the project is defined. The information
         plan can be likened to a product requirements
         document for a software development project.
         You conduct preparatory research to learn the
         nature of the product and its potential market.
         You learn who will use the product and what tasks
         they will accomplish with the product.</p>
   </section>
   <example>
      <fig><title>Product Information Plan</title>
      <image href="ProductInfoPlan.jpg"/></fig>
   </example>
</conbody>
```

**<sl> simple list**

Use the <sl> element as the container for all simple list items. The output of a simple list does not use bullets or numbers to introduce each list item. Therefore, the simple list should only be used for short lists that do not need additional formatting to distinguish each item. If your list is more complex, we recommend using the <ul> or <ol> elements.

**<sli> simple list item**

Use the <sli> element to separate each item in the list.

```
<conbody>
   <p>When creating a bulleted list, choose from the following
      bullets:</p>
   <sl>
      <sli>▪</sli>
      <sli>◊</sli>
      <sli>•</sli>
   </sl>
</conbody>
```

**<ul> unordered list**

Use the <ul> element to list items when the sequence of each item is not relevant. The items within the <ul> element are typically formatted with bullets, circles, or other symbols. To create sub-unordered lists, nest <ul> elements in other <ul> elements. However, nesting more than one level of <ul> elements makes the list more difficult for the reader to understand. The <ul> element is the container for all unordered list items.

**<ol> ordered list**

Use the <ol> element to list items when the sequence of each item is important. The items in an ordered list are typically numbered. To create sub-ordered lists, nest <ol> elements in other <ol> elements. However, nesting more than one level of <ol> elements can make the list more difficult for the reader to understand. The <ol> element is the container for all ordered list items.

**<li> list item**

Use the <li> element to separate each item in an unordered or ordered list. You can add more than one <li> element to each <ul> or <ol> element.

The following example illustrates how to use the <ul> and <ol> elements.

```
<conbody>
   <p>Before adding or deleting a row or column in your
      projected hours worksheet, gather the following
      information:</p>
   <ul>
      <li>File names of the linked projected labor and
         total costs worksheets</li>
      <li>File names of the linked monthly hours, labor,
         and total costs tracking worksheets</li>
   </ul>
   <p>To ensure your links update correctly, open your
      worksheets in the following order:</p>
   <ol>
      <li>Projected hours worksheet</li>
      <li>Projected labor worksheet</li>
      <li>Total costs worksheet</li>
      <li>Monthly hours worksheet</li>
      <li>Monthly labor worksheet</li>
      <li>Monthly total costs worksheet</li>
   </ol>
</conbody>
```

**<dl> definition list**
: Use the <dl> element to list terms and their corresponding definitions. The <dl> element is the container for all elements in a definition list.

**<dlhead> definition list head**
: Use the <dlhead> element as the container for term and description column headings. This element is optional and may be used only once in a definition list.

**<dthd> definition term head**
: Use the <dthd> element to specify a term column head for the definition list. One <dthd> element can be added to the <dlhead> element but is not required. The <dthd> element is the first element added to the definition list head.

**<ddhd> definition description head**
: Use the <ddhd> element to specify a definition column head for the definition list. One <ddhd> element can be added to the <dlhead> element but is not required.

**<dlentry> definition list entry**
: Use the <dlentry> element in the <dl> element as a container for each term and definition. Use a separate <dlentry> element each time you introduce a new term and definition. You can use multiple <dlentry> elements for each <dl>.

**<dt> definition term**
: Use the <dt> element to identify the word or phrase to be defined. If multiple terms share the same definition, you can add multiple <dt> elements to the <dlentry> element.

**<dd> definition description**
: Use the <dd> element to provide the definition for the corresponding term. If a term has multiple definitions, you can add multiple <dd> elements to the <dlentry> element.

```
<conbody>
   <dl>
      <dlhead>
         <dthd>term</dthd>
         <ddhd>definition</ddhd>
      </dlhead>
      <dlentry>
         <dt>dome</dt>
         <dd>A hemispherical vault or roof.</dd>
         </dlentry>
      <dlentry>
         <dt>doctor</dt>
         <dt>PhD</dt>
         <dd>A person trained and licensed to practice
            the healing arts, as medicine or surgery.
         </dd>
      </dlentry>
      <dlentry>
         <dt>staple</dt>
```

```
            <dd>A principal raw material or commodity
               grown or produced in a region.</dd>
            <dd>A thin piece of wire in the shape of a
               square bracket that is driven by a device
               through sheets of paper or similar material
               and flattened to serve as a fastening.
            </dd>
         </dlentry>
      </dl>
   </conbody>
```

**<table> table**

Use the <table> element to create a complex table. Complex tables provide you with control over the display properties and layout of the table. The <table> element is the container for all of the complex table elements. For a list of all table element attributes, see the *OASIS Darwin Information Typing Architecture (DITA) Version 1.2 (OASIS Standard, 1 December 2010).*

**<tgroup> table group**

Use the <tgroup> element to specify the display properties for the columns, rows, spanning, header, footer, and body of the complex table. The <tgroup> element with column specifications is required when using a complex table.

**<colspec> column specification**

Use the <colspec> element to specify column information using attributes such as column name (*@colname*), number (*@cols*), cell content alignment (*@align*), and column width (*@colwidth*).

**<thead> table head**

Use the <thead> element to define the heads for the table columns. The <thead> element is used in the <table> container. It contains multiple <row> and <entry> elements.

**<tbody> table body**

Use the <tbody> element to define the body of the table. The <tbody> element is the container for multiple <row> and <entry> elements.

**<row> row**

Use the <row> element to define a single row in the table. Each <row> element contains multiple <entry> elements, each indicating a different column.

**<entry> entry**

Use the <entry> element to define a single cell in the table. Use this element to define both the content for each cell and the column heads for the entire table. The number of <entry> elements defined in the <tbody> element must match the number of <entry> elements defined in the <thead> element unless you specify that a cell should span multiple rows or columns. To span a cell across multiple rows, use the *@morerows* attribute and enter the number of rows to span. To span a cell across multiple columns, use the *@namest* and *@nameend* attributes to indicate the name of the first and last columns in the span.

The following example illustrates how to create a complex table.

```
<conbody>
   <table>
      <tgroup cols="4">
         <colspec colname="COLSPC0" colwidth="76*"/>
         <colspec colname="COLSPC1" colwidth="76*"/>
         <colspec colname="COLSPC2" colwidth="25*"/>
         <colspec colname="COLSPC3" colwidth="25*"/>
         <thead>
            <row>
               <entry colname="COLSPC0" align="left">
                  Worksheet</entry>
               <entry colname="COLSPC1" align="left">
                  Orientation</entry>
               <entry colname="COLSPC2" valign="top">
                  US Letter</entry>
               <entry colname="COLSPC3" valign="top">
                  US Legal</entry>
            </row>
         </thead>
         <tbody>
            <row>
               <entry morerows="1">Dependencies worksheet</entry>
               <entry>Vertical</entry>
               <entry namest="COLSPC2" nameend="COLSPC3"
                  align="center">100%</entry>
            </row>
            <row>
               <entry>Horizontal</entry>
               <entry namest="COLSPC2" nameend="COLSPC3"
                  align="center">100%</entry>
            </row>
            <row>
               <entry morerows="1">Weekly tracking worksheets</entry>
               <entry>Vertical</entry>
               <entry namest="COLSPC2" nameend="COLSPC3"
                  align="center">No</entry>
            </row>
            <row>
               <entry>Horizontal</entry>
               <entry align="center">45%</entry>
               <entry align="center">60%</entry>
            </row>
         </tbody>
      </tgroup>
   </table>
</conbody>
```

The following example shows what the rendered table looks like.

<table>
<tr><th>Worksheet</th><th>Orientation</th><th>US Letter</th><th>US Legal</th></tr>
<tr><td rowspan="2">Dependencies worksheet</td><td>Vertical</td><td colspan="2">100%</td></tr>
<tr><td>Horizontal</td><td colspan="2">100%</td></tr>
<tr><td rowspan="2">Weekly tracking worksheets</td><td>Vertical</td><td colspan="2">No</td></tr>
<tr><td>Horizontal</td><td>45%</td><td>60%</td></tr>
</table>

**<simpletable> simple table**

Use the <simpletable> element to describe tabular information that has a simple layout. The simple table is less sophisticated than the complex table. You cannot control the format of the table. The <simpletable> element is the container for <sthead>, <strow>, and <stentry> elements.

**<sthead> simple table head**

Use the <sthead> element to define the heads for the table columns. The <sthead> element contains one or more <stentry> elements. It is optional and can be used only once within the <simpletable> element.

**<strow> simple table row**

Use the <strow> element to create a row in the simple table. The <strow> element is used in the <simpletable> container. It contains the <stentry> element.

**<stentry> simple table cell (entry)**

Use the <stentry> element to define a single cell in the table. Use this element to define both the content for each cell and the column heads for the entire table. The number of <stentry> elements within each <strow> element must match the number of <stentry> elements used within the <sthead> element.

The following example illustrates how to create a simple table.

```
<conbody>
   <simpletable>
      <sthead>
         <stentry>Worksheet</stentry>
         <stentry>Prerequisites</stentry>
      </sthead>
      <strow>
         <stentry>Monthly hours tracking worksheet</stentry>
         <stentry>Projected hours worksheet</stentry>
      </strow>
      <strow>
         <stentry>Monthly labor costs tracking worksheet</stentry>
         <stentry>Projected hours worksheet</stentry>
      </strow>
   </simpletable>
</conbody>
```

The following example shows what the rendered simple table looks like.

| **Worksheet** | **Prerequisites** |
|---|---|
| Monthly hours tracking worksheet | Projected hours worksheet |
| Monthly labor costs tracking worksheet | Projected hours worksheet |

**Block element review questions**

DITA allows you to nest multiple levels of unordered and ordered lists.

- True
- False

Which attributes are required for the <image> element? Select all that apply.

**a.** *@height*
**b.** *@width*
**c.** *@scale*
**d.** *@href*

Which of these elements can include a title? Select all that apply.

**a.** Section
**b.** Paragraph
**c.** Example
**d.** Figure
**e.** Definition list
**f.** Table

What is the difference between a table and a simple table?

**a.** A simple table is limited to no more than three columns.
**b.** You cannot define column headings for a simple table.
**c.** You cannot control the format of a simple table.
**d.** A simple table does not show borders between cells.

The <li> element is used to define list items for simple, ordered, and unordered list types.

- True
- False

How do you include more than one definition for a single term in a definition list?

- **a.** Create multiple <dlentry> elements, leaving the corresponding <dt> blank for each additional definition.
- **b.** Include multiple <dt> and <dd> pairs within a single <dlentry> element, leaving the extra <dt> elements blank.
- **c.** Create multiple <dlentry> elements, omitting the <dt> entry for each additional definition.
- **d.** Include multiple <dd> elements within a single <dlentry> element.

What element is the container for the display properties of a complex table?

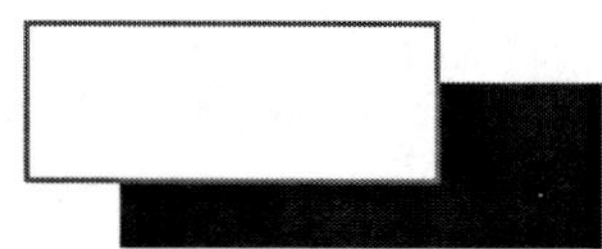

# LESSON 5

## Phrase Elements

Phrase elements describe the words or phrases that occur inside a structure or block element. Phrase elements include elements used inline in sentences to mark items, such as index terms, keywords, and cross references. Phrase elements also include domain and highlight elements. Domain elements occur inline to describe specific subject matter, such as a syntax diagram or an interface control. Highlight elements affect the output format of a word or phrase. Highlight elements include italic, bold, and underscore.

**Domain elements**
Domain elements describe text associated with a specific subject area. Use domain elements to add structure and semantic tags to your information. The information contained in your domain tags is used to optimize search and retrieval. The domains included in DITA are associated with programming information, software products, and user interfaces. Other domains may include elements for training material and Application Programming Interfaces (APIs). Depending on the subject matter you are writing about, you may want to add new domain-specific elements by specializing DITA. For more information about specialization, see Part V The DITA Information-Development Environment on page 305.

**Highlight elements**
Use highlight, or typographic, elements when your information cannot be formatted properly using the semantic DITA tags. In DITA, the highlight tags include italic, bold, teletype, superscript, subscript, and underscore.

DITA best practices discourage the use of most highlight elements. We recommend that you find or define an appropriate semantic tag that identifies text by its content rather than its formatting. For example, if you identify a word as a <uicontrol>, you can easily format it on output as bold, italic, or underscore. If you tag the same word as bold, your format cannot be easily changed on output. Remember that the word you emphasize in your source language may not be the same word that a translator must emphasize in a target language. Many languages do not include any of the common typographic elements found in English, so use highlight elements sparingly if your information is translated into other languages.

**Adding phrase elements**
This lesson explains the basic phrase elements to add to a DITA topic. In this lesson, you learn how to add phrase elements, such as <keyword>, <uicontrol>, and <xref>, that you can use in each information type.

1. Open the TransferringACall.dita task topic you created in Task Information Type on page 33.

```
<?xml version="1.0" encoding="utf-8"?>
<!DOCTYPE task PUBLIC "-//OASIS//DTD DITA Task//EN"
   "task.dtd">
<task id="TransferringACall" xml:lang="en-us">
   <title>Transferring a call</title>
   <shortdesc>When you transfer a call to another person
      in your office, you have two ways of handling the
      transfer.</shortdesc>
   <prolog>
      <author>John Smith</author>
   </prolog>
   <taskbody>
      <context>When you transfer the call without speaking to
         the person, it is an unannounced transfer. When you
         speak to the person receiving the transferred call,
         it is an announced transfer.</context>
      <steps>
         <step>
            <cmd>Press the transfer button.</cmd>
         </step>
         <step>
            <cmd>Dial the number.</cmd>
            <info>Dial the number manually, use your
               pre-defined speed dial keys, or go to your
               company directory. </info>
         </step>
         <step>
            <cmd>Transfer the call.</cmd>
            <choicetable>
               <chhead>
                  <choptionhd>Type of Announcement</choptionhd>
                  <chdeschd>Steps to complete</chdeschd>
               </chhead>
               <chrow>
                  <choption>Announce a call transfer</choption>
                  <chdesc>
                     <ol>
                        <li>Speak to the person.</li>
                        <li>Hang up the phone.</li>
                     </ol>
                  </chdesc>
               </chrow>
               <chrow>
                  <choption>Transfer a call
                     unannounced</choption>
                  <chdesc>
                     <ul>
                        <li>Hang up the phone.</li>
                     </ul>
                  </chdesc>
               </chrow>
            </choicetable>
            <info>
               <note type="tip">If you announce a call and the
                  person refuses the transfer, do not hang
                  up the phone. Press the transfer button
                  again to retrieve the call on your phone
```

```
                station.</note>
            </info>
        </step>
    </steps>
    <result>The call is transferred.</result>
  </taskbody>
  <related-links>
    <link href="AboutTransfer.dita"/>
  </related-links>
</task>
```

2. Add <keyword> start and end tags around the word "Transferring" in your <title> element.

   The <keyword> element highlights words or phrases in an abstract, title, subject heading, content notes, or general text to identify words you may want to use in a special context, such as a glossary or a search engine. In the example below, "Transferring" might be a term a user looks up in a glossary or types into a search engine. See the *OASIS Darwin Information Typing Architecture (DITA) Version 1.2 (OASIS Standard, 1 December 2010)* to learn where you can add keywords.

```
<task id="TransferringACall" xml:lang="en-us">
   <title><keyword>Transferring</keyword>
      a call</title>
   ⋮
</task>
```

3. Add <uicontrol> element start and end tags around the word "transfer" in the first step command.

   You can use the user interface control element to identify button names, entry fields, menu items, or other user interface controls. Using semantic elements, such as <uicontrol>, helps users find information more easily. You can create a unique format for a semantically tagged phrase element without using a typographic element like bold or italic.

```
<taskbody>
⋮
   <steps>
      <step>
         <cmd>Press the <uicontrol>transfer
            </uicontrol> button.</cmd>
      </step>
⋮
</taskbody>
```

4. Add <xref> start and end tags around the phrase "company directory" in the second step info container.

   The <xref> container identifies a term or phrase you want to cross reference to another piece of information. To use the <xref> element correctly, you must include a path location and target file to the content you want to cross reference.

To add a cross reference path location and target file, add an *@href* attribute in the <xref> element. In the example, the *@href* attribute points to another DITA task, AccessingCompanyDirectory.dita. The cross-reference element creates a hyperlink to the information you reference in the *@href* attribute. You can link to information in the same topic using the topic filename, topic *@id*, and element *@id* in your *@href* attribute value. Or you can link to an external topic or document by using the topic file name and *@id* in your *@href* attribute value. You can also use the *@type* attribute to specify the type of link. In this case, set the *@type* attribute to "task" to link to another DITA task. You can also link to figures, tables, concepts, references, and other types of information.

```
<taskbody>
⋮
   <steps>
      ⋮
      <step>
         <cmd>Dial the number.</cmd>
         <info>Dial the number manually, use your
            pre-defined speed dial keys or go to your
            <xref href="AccessingCompanyDirectory.dita"
            type="task">company directory</xref>.
         </info>
      </step>
⋮
</taskbody>
```

**5.** Save the document as TransferringACall.dita.

The following example illustrates the Transferring a call topic using phrase elements.

```
<?xml version="1.0" encoding="utf-8"?>
<!DOCTYPE task PUBLIC "-//OASIS//DTD DITA Task//EN"
   "task.dtd">
<task id="TransferringACall" xml:lang="en-us">
   <title><keyword>Transferring</keyword>
      a call</title>
   <shortdesc>When you transfer a call to another person
      in your office, you have two ways of handling the
      transfer.</shortdesc>
   <prolog>
      <author>John Smith</author>
   </prolog>
   <taskbody>
      <context>When you transfer the call without speaking to
         the person, it is an unannounced transfer. When you
         speak to the person receiving the transferred call,
         it is an announced transfer.</context>
      <steps>
         <step>
            <cmd>Press the <uicontrol>transfer
```

```
            </uicontrol> button.</cmd>
      </step>
      <step>
         <cmd>Dial the number. </cmd>
         <info>Dial the number manually, use your
            pre-defined speed dial keys or go to your
            <xref href="AccessingCompanyDirectory.dita"
            type="task">company directory</xref>.
         </info>
      </step>
      <step>
         <cmd>Transfer the call.</cmd>
         <choicetable>
            <chhead>
               <choptionhd>Type of Announcement</choptionhd>
               <chdeschd>Steps to complete</chdeschd>
            </chhead>
            <chrow>
               <choption>Announce a call transfer</choption>
               <chdesc>
                  <ol>
                     <li>Speak to the person.</li>
                     <li>Hang up the phone.</li>
                  </ol>
               </chdesc>
            </chrow>
            <chrow>
               <choption>Transfer a call
                  unannounced</choption>
               <chdesc>
                  <ul>
                     <li>Hang up the phone.</li>
                  </ul>
               </chdesc>
            </chrow>
         </choicetable>
         <info>
            <note type="tip">If you announce a call and the
               person refuses the transfer, do not hang
               up the phone. Press the transfer button
               again to retrieve the call on your phone
               station.</note>
         </info>
      </step>
   </steps>
   <result>The call is transferred.</result>
</taskbody>
<related-links>
   <link href="AboutTransfer.dita"/>
</related-links>
</task>
```

The following example shows what a PDF rendering of the task topic might look like.

### Transferring a call

When you transfer a call to another person in your office, you have two ways of handling the transfer.

When you transfer the call without speaking to the person, it is an unannounced transfer. When you speak to the person receiving the transferred call, it is an announced transfer.

1. Press the transfer button.
2. Dial the number.
   Dial the number manually, use your pre-defined speed dial keys, or go to your company directory.
3. Transfer the call.

| Type of Announcement | Steps to complete |
|---|---|
| Announce a call transfer | **1.** Speak to the person.<br>**2.** Hang up the phone. |
| Transfer a call unannounced | Hang up the phone. |

**Tip:** If you announce a call and the person refuses the transfer, do not hang up the phone. Press the transfer button again to retrieve the call on your phone station.

The call is transferred.

**Phrase elements definitions**

The following phrase elements are used in the DITA model.

**<keyword> keyword**
: Use the <keyword> element to highlight important words or phrases in your text. The <keyword> element does not usually affect the format of the text during processing. Use keyword only when a more specific element name, such as, apiname, is not available. The <keyword> element cannot contain additional markup (elements or attributes) except for trademark.

**<ph> phrase**
: Use the <ph> element to assign metadata to your information to locate it for future reuse, flagging, or filtering. The <ph> element usually does not change the format of the text during processing. However, you can use the element to apply specific formatting and processing to the marked up phrases with your stylesheet.

```
<conbody>
   <p>This section explains how
      <ph><keyword>PUB$</keyword> simplifies
         project planning</ph>.  Included are the tasks
         accomplished with <ph><keyword>PUB$
         </keyword></ph> and the worksheets that
         correspond to each task.</p>
</conbody>
```

### <term> term

Use the <term> element to identify words requiring an extended definition or explanation. The <term> element also links the identified word to matching glossary entries. The <term> element does not affect the format of the text during output.

```
<conbody>
   <p>The first three major type concepts defined in
      this chapter are <term>type family</term>,
      <term>typeface</term>, and <term>type
      font</term>.  Illustrations help you compare type
      styles and select those most suitable for your
      applications.</p>
</conbody>
```

### <xref> cross reference link

Use the <xref> element to create a link in the content of your document. The <xref> element is used inline in the text of your topic, preferably at the end of a sentence. It is not used at the end of the topic like the <related-links> element. The target for this link can be a specific element in the same topic, another topic, or an external source. To link to an external source, use the *@scope* attribute.

Use the *@href* attribute to point to the file you are referencing. If you are working in a file system, the typical format for the *@href* attribute value when referencing a dita file is systempathandfilename.dita#topicid/elementID, where #topicID is the unique identifier of the topic you are referencing and /elementID is the unique identifier of the specific element you are referencing within that topic. If you omit the #topic id/elementID, the *@href* points to the root element (i.e., <concept>, <task>, or <reference>) in the target file.

Use the *@type* attribute in the <xref> element to specify the type of target for your link. Possible values for the *@type* attribute are "fig", "table", "li", "section", "concept", "task", and "reference".

The <xref> element should be used sparingly, if at all, because a link in the middle of a sentence may distract the reader and increase the cost of maintaining and translating the topic. Instead of <xref>, consider using either a relationship table in your map or the <related-links> element at the end of each topic.

```
<taskbody>
   <steps>
      <step>
         <cmd>Type <codeph>ant all</codeph> and
            press Enter to begin testing.</cmd>
         <stepresult>The testing process completes in
            3-10 minutes, depending on the speed of your
            machine. When testing completes, the
            confirmation message "BUILD SUCCESSFUL"
            displays.
            <note type="note">To read more about the DITA
               Open Toolkit options and functions, see
               <xref href="C:\DITAOT\doc\DITA-readme.html"
               scope="external">DITA-readme</xref> on
               your local hard drive.
            </note>
         </stepresult>
      </step>
   </steps>
</taskbody>
```

### <indexterm> index term

Use the <indexterm> element to identify terms that you want to compile into an alphabetized index. The <keyword> and <indexterm> elements are similar for Web content, but the <indexterm> element provides for additional processing that compiles the terms into an alphabetical list for media that include an index. In addition, unlike <keyword> elements, <indexterm> elements do not appear in output text. To have a word or phrase appear in the text as well as in the index, you must repeat the term in an <indexterm> element, rather than enclosing the term within an <indexterm> element where it appears in the text. For more information about index terms, see Prolog Metadata on page 101.

```
<conbody>
   <indexterm>PUB$</indexterm>
   <p>This section explains how
      <ph><keyword>PUB$</keyword> simplifies
         project planning</ph>.  Included are the tasks
         accomplished with <ph><keyword>PUB$
         </keyword></ph> and the worksheets that
         correspond to each task.</p>
</conbody>
```

## Domain elements

The following domain elements are used in the DITA model. The element descriptions refer to specific content used in programming, software, and user interfaces.

**Programming elements**

Use the programming elements to define programming syntax or give examples of programming-specific information. Some descriptions for the common programming elements are included here. For the complete list of programming elements, see the *OASIS Darwin Information Typing Architecture (DITA) Version 1.2 (OASIS Standard, 1 December 2010).*

**<codeblock> code block**

Use the <codeblock> element to represent multiple lines of programming code. The information in the <codeblock> element is formatted as a monospaced font and preserves carriage returns and spaces in the element.

```
<conbody>
   <section>
      <codeblock>
         <?xml version="1.0"?>
         <recipe>
            <title>Scrambled eggs</title>
               <ingredient>Ingredient</ingredient>
               <ingredient_list>
                  <list_item>5 eggs</list_item>
                  <list_item>1/2 cup milk</list_item>
                  <list_item>1 tbsp butter</list_item>
               </ingredient_list>
               <instructions>Melt butter.......
               </instructions>
         </recipe>
      </codeblock>
   </section>
</conbody>
```

**<parml> parameter list**

Use the <parml> element to describe the terms and definitions associated with parameters in an application programming interface. The <parml> is similar to the <dl> element but is designed for documenting programming parameters.

**<plentry> parameter list entry**

Use the <plentry> element in the <parml> element as a container for each parameter term <pt> and definition <pd>. Use a separate <plentry> element to introduce each new parameter term and definition. You can include multiple <plentry> elements for each <parml>.

**<pt> parameter term**

Use <pt> to identify the parameter term to be defined. If multiple terms share the same definition, you can add multiple <pt> elements can be added to the <plentry> element.

**<pd> parameter description**

Use the <pd> element to provide the definition for the corresponding term. If a term has multiple definitions, you can add multiple <pd> elements to the <plentry> element.

```
<conbody>
   <section>
      <p>Listed below are the available properties for a
         checkbox object located in an HTML form.</p>
      <parml>
         <plentry>
            <pt>Checked</pt>
            <pd>Sets the checkbox value to true if the
               checkbox is checked and false if the checkbox
               is not checked.</pd>
         </plentry>
         <plentry>
            <pt>Name</pt>
            <pd>Sets the name attribute for the checkbox
               object on the form.</pd>
         </plentry>
         <plentry>
            <pt>Form</pt>
            <pd>Associates the checkbox object to the form
               in which the checkbox object is located.</pd>
         </plentry>
      </parml>
   </section>
</conbody>
```

### <apiname> API name

Use the <apiname> element to describe the name of an application programming interface (API), such as a Java class or method name.

```
<conbody>
   <section>
      <p>Use <apiname>JavaScript</apiname> to
         increase the functionality of your website.
      </p>
   </section>
</conbody>
```

## Software elements

Use the software elements to describe the operations of a software program. Some of the most common software elements are described in this section. For the complete list of software elements, see the *OASIS Darwin Information Typing Architecture (DITA) Version 1.2 (OASIS Standard, 1 December 2010).*

### <msgph> message phrase

Use the <msgph> element to list the contents of a message produced by an application or program. Other elements, such as the <varname> element, can be used in the <msgph> element to make the semantic markup of your information more specific.

```
<taskbody>
   <steps>
      <step>
         <cmd>Delete the dependency for the weekly
            tracking worksheet.</cmd>
         <info>If you receive the following error, see
```

```
            the appendix on error messages:
            <msgph>Can't remove the dependency for the worksheet
                as it is currently in use.</msgph></info>
      </step>
   </steps>
</taskbody>
```

### <cmdname> command name

Use the <cmdname> element to specify software commands. You can add the <cmdname> element to several of the topic elements, including <title>, <shortdesc>, <body>, <section>, <filepath>, and <msgph>.

```
<taskbody>
   <steps>
      <step>
         <cmd>Type <cmdname>cmd</cmdname> in the  Run window.</cmd>
      </step>
   </steps>
</taskbody>
```

### <varname> variable name

Use the <varname> element to define software application variables. The <varname> element is similar to the <var> element except that the <varname> element exists outside of a syntax diagram.

```
<conbody>
   <p>Create a Visual Basic program where you create the
      output "Hello World" by adding two variables:
      <varname>x</varname> and
      <varname>y</varname></p>
</conbody>
```

### <filepath> file path

Use the <filepath> element to define the name and location of a reference file. When adding a file path, be sure to include the directories preceding the file to document the full system hierarchy.

```
<conbody>
   <p>Open the PUB$ weekly timesheet example from
      <filepath>D:\Samples\WeeklyTimesheet.xls</filepath>.
   </p>
</conbody>
```

### <userinput> user input

Use the <userinput> element to specify information the user must enter. Software programs usually prompt users for this type of information.

```
<taskbody>
   <steps>
      <step>
         <cmd>Type <userinput>ant -f ant\PUB$_PDF.xml
            </userinput></cmd>
      </step>
   </steps>
</taskbody>
```

### <systemoutput> system output

Use the <systemoutput> element to represent the output or responses from a software program. The <systemoutput> is a very general element that can represent multiple output types.

```
<taskbody>
   <steps>
      <step>
         <cmd>Click Enter.</cmd>
         <stepresult>When the build file has completed
            the processing, you will receive the
            <systemoutput>Build Successful </systemoutput>
            message if the process was successful. If the build
            failed during processing, you will receive the
            <systemoutput>Build Failed</systemoutput>
            message.</stepresult>
      </step>
   </steps>
</taskbody>
```

## User interface elements

Use the user interface elements to describe the user interface of a web or software application. Some of the most common user interface elements are listed below. For the complete list of user interface elements, see the *OASIS Darwin Information Typing Architecture (DITA) Version 1.2 (OASIS Standard, 1 December 2010)*.

### <menucascade> menu cascade

Use the <menucascade> element to indicate a series of menu choices in an application. The <menucascade> element is a container for one or more <uicontrol> elements. A simple menu cascade may be formatted as **Start** > **Programs** > **Accessories** .

### <uicontrol> user interface control

Use the <uicontrol> element to specify button names, entry fields, menu items, or other user interface controls. You can use multiple <uicontrol> elements in a <menucascade> element to identify a sequence of menu choices in a nested menu.

```
<taskbody>
   <steps>
      <step>
         <cmd>Select
            <menucascade>
               <uicontrol>Track</uicontrol>
               <uicontrol>Return to PUB$ Menu</uicontrol>
            </menucascade>
         </cmd>
      </step>
   </steps>
</taskbody>
```

### Highlight elements

The following highlight elements are used in the DITA model.

**<b> bold**
: Use the <b> element to provide bold emphasis to information.

**<i> italic**
: Use the <i> element to provide italic emphasis to information.

**<sub> subscript**
: Use the <sub> element to subscript a symbol or text.

**<sup> superscript**
: Use the <sup> element to superscript a symbol or text.

**<tt> teletype**
: Use the <tt> element to output words in a monospace font.

The following example illustrates how to use the highlight elements.

```
<conbody>
   <p>In the DITA User Guide examples, each
      <b>change</b> is bolded.</p>
   <p>In the DITA User Guide examples, each
      <i>attribute</i> is italicized.</p>
   <p>... H<sub>2</sub>CO<sub>3</sub></p>
   <p>... x<sup>2</sup></p>
   <p><tt>In the DITA User Guide examples,
      each codeblock is created in a monospace
      font.</tt></p>
</conbody>
```

The following example illustrates what rendered highlight elements look like.

> **Highlight elements rendered**
>
> In the DITA User Guide examples, each **change** is bolded.
>
> In the DITA User Guide examples, each *@attribute* is italicized.
>
> ... $H_2CO_3$
>
> ... $x^2$
>
> `In the DITA User Guide examples, each codeblock is created in a monospace font.`

**Phrase element review questions**

What is the difference between phrase elements and block elements?

- **a.** Phrase elements do not affect the format of text during processing.
- **b.** Phrase elements are used outside of the <body> element tags, while domain elements are used inside <body> element tags.
- **c.** Phrase elements describe the words or phrases within a block element.
- **d.** Phrase elements only affect the format of text during processing.

When might you use typographic elements? Select all that apply.

- **a.** When your information cannot be formatted properly using semantic DITA tags.
- **b.** When you need to change your format frequently on output.
- **c.** When you will be translating information into languages that do not include common typographic elements found in English.
- **d.** Whenever you need to provide special emphasis on a word or phrase.

Match the element to its function.

| | |
|---|---|
| <keyword> | Identifies words that may have or require extended definitions or explanations. |
| <phrase> | Flags terms for inclusion in an alphabetical list of terms. |
| <term> | Marks information that you want to locate for future reuse, flagging, or filtering. |
| <indexterm> | Identifies words or phrases that you want to use in a special context. |

What is the purpose of domain elements?

- **a.** To affect the output format of a word or phrase.
- **b.** To describe text associated with a specific subject area, such as programming information, software products, and user interfaces.
- **c.** To define the structure of blocks of text.
- **d.** To refer the reader to other topics, external references, or web pages.

The <parml> element is similar to the <dl> element, except that you cannot define multiple term elements for the same definition element or vice versa.

- True
- False

Which element preserves carriage returns and spaces within the element?

**a.** <tt>

**b.** <systemoutput>

**c.** <msgph>

**d.** <codeblock>

The <menucascade> element is a container for one or more of what user interface element?

You can add the <cmdname> element to several topic elements, including <title>, <shortdesc>, <body>, <section>, <filepath>, and <msgph>.

- True
- False

# LESSON 6

## Related Links

You can add related links to a topic to refer the reader to other topics, external references, or web pages.

Related-link elements specify the tags that you use to add related links at the end of a topic. Because related links are output as hyperlinks, they are most appropriate for electronic delivery. If your output is to print or PDF, the links may not appear in the print or PDF unless you specify a format for the link in your stylesheet.

Although the related-links section at the end of each topic is useful, we recommend that you create links using a relationship table as described in Understanding Relationship Tables on page 179. If you create related links at the end of each topic, you cannot as easily reuse the topic because you must ensure that all the linked topics are included in your DITA map. If a topic is missing, you will get a broken link. If you create a relationship table, all the links are in one place, making them easier to maintain.

Your related links can point to any topic, including

- topics in your information set
- topics outside of your information set but available in a repository in your organization
- documents outside your organization

If you include a link to a non-DITA topic, you should also include both a link title and short description in the link metadata. These items ensure that your users understand something about the topic in the link. If you link to a DITA topic in your information set, your processing pipeline extracts both the title and short description to create the link text in the topic. If you choose not to display a short description, you can change this feature when you create your stylesheets.

**Adding related links**

In this lesson, you learn to add related-link elements, such as <related-links>, <link>, <linktext>, and <desc>, to create related links in any information type.

1. Open the TransferringACall.dita task topic you created in Task Information Type on page 33 and modified in Phrase Elements on page 76.

In the TransferringACall.dita task topic, you added a <related-links> container and a <link> element to point to another DITA topic.

```
<?xml version="1.0" encoding="utf-8"?>
<!DOCTYPE task PUBLIC "-//OASIS//DTD DITA Task//EN"
   "task.dtd">
<task id="TransferringACall" xml:lang="en-us">
   <title><keyword>Transferring</keyword>
      a call</title>
   <shortdesc>When you transfer a call to another person
      in your office, you have two ways of handling the
      transfer.</shortdesc>
   <prolog>
      <author>John Smith</author>
   </prolog>
   <taskbody>
      <context>When you transfer the call without speaking to
         the person, it is an unannounced transfer. When you
         speak to the person receiving the transferred call,
         it is an announced transfer.</context>
      <steps>
         <step>
            <cmd>Press the <uicontrol>transfer
               </uicontrol> button.</cmd>
         </step>
         <step>
            <cmd>Dial the number. </cmd>
            <info>Dial the number manually, use your
               pre-defined speed dial keys or go to your
               <xref href="AccessingCompanyDirectory.dita"
               type="task">company directory</xref>.
            </info>
         </step>
         <step>
            <cmd>Transfer the call.</cmd>
            <choicetable>
               <chhead>
                  <choptionhd>Type of Announcement</choptionhd>
                  <chdeschd>Steps to complete</chdeschd>
               </chhead>
               <chrow>
                  <choption>Announce a call transfer</choption>
                  <chdesc>
                     <ol>
                        <li>Speak to the person.</li>
                        <li>Hang up the phone.</li>
                     </ol>
                  </chdesc>
               </chrow>
               <chrow>
                  <choption>Transfer a call unannounced</choption>
                  <chdesc>
                     <ul>
                        <li>Hang up the phone.</li>
                     </ul>
                  </chdesc>
               </chrow>
            </choicetable>
            <info>
               <note type="tip">If you announce a call and the
```

```
                    person refuses the transfer, do not hang
                    up the phone. Press the transfer button
                    again to retrieve the call on your phone
                    station.</note>
              </info>
           </step>
        </steps>
        <result>The call is transferred.</result>
     </taskbody>
     <related-links>
        <link href="AboutTransfer.dita"/>
     </related-links>
  </task>
```

2. Add two additional <link> elements in the <related-links> container after the AboutTransfer.dita link.

   For every related link you want to add, you must use a separate <link> element.

```
<related-links>
   <link href="AboutTransfer.dita"/>
   <link/>
   <link/>
</related-links>
```

3. Within each link element, specify a value for the *@href* attribute.

   In your *@href* attribute, you must point to the target information you want to include using absolute or relative path and file names. The file path must be relative to the topic you are authoring.

```
<related-links>
   <link href="AboutTransfer.dita"/>
   <link href="../GeneralTopic/Glossary.dita"/>
   <link href="http://www.comtech-serv.com/Comstar"/>
</related-links>
```

4. Include a value for the *@format* attribute.

   The *@format* attribute identifies the format of the file you are linking to.

```
<related-links>
   <link href="AboutTransfer.dita" format="dita"/>
   <link href="../GeneralTopic/Glossary.dita"
      format="dita"/>
   <link href="http://www.comtech-serv.com/Comstar"
      format="html"/>
</related-links>
```

5. Add the *@scope* attribute to each <link> element.

   You can set the value to "local", "peer", or "external", depending on the location of the target topic. The *@scope* attribute tells the processor how to process a link. For more information about the *@scope* attribute, see Scope Attribute on page 141.

```
<related-links>
   <link href="AboutTransfer.dita" format="dita"
      scope="local"/>
   <link href="../GeneralTopic/Glossary.dita"
      format="dita" scope="peer"/>
   <link href="http://www.comtech-serv.com/Comstar"
      format="html" scope="external"/>
</related-links>
```

6. Add a <linktext> element for the http://www.comtech-serv.com/Comstar link.

   For topics that don't have a DITA title element, use a <linktext> element to specify text for your link. For example, because the http://www.comtech-serv.com/Comstar isn't a DITA topic, you need to add link text because your processor can't pull text from the web page. If you do not use link text, your processor uses the value you provided in the *@href* attribute (in this case, http://www.comtech-serv.com/Comstar).

   Not all related links need link text because your processor automatically uses the title of your target topic. For example, when you create your output, your AboutTransfer.dita link uses the title "About Transfer" as the link text in your related links section.

   **Note:** Because you are adding an element to the <link> element, it is no longer empty. You need to add a separate end tag and remove the "/" from the end of the start tag.

   For this example, use "Comstar Phones" as the link text for the http://www.comtech-serv.com/Comstar link.

```
<related-links>
   <link href="AboutTransfer.dita" format="dita"
      scope="local"/>
   <link href="../GeneralTopic/Glossary.dita"
      format="dita" scope="peer"/>
   <link href="http://www.comtech-serv.com/Comstar"
      format="html" scope="external">
      <linktext>Comstar Phones</linktext>
   </link>
</related-links>
```

7. Add <desc> start and end tags after your <linktext> element.

   The <desc> element provides the user with a brief description of the linked topic or resource. We recommend adding a description for external links to provide your user with additional information about the target topic. If you don't provide a description, the processor creates a hyperlink of the text or *@href* value for your user to navigate and doesn't include any description.

```
<related-links>
   <link href="AboutTransfer.dita" format="dita"
      scope="local"/>
   <link href="../GeneralTopic/Glossary.dita"
      format="dita" scope="peer"/>
   <link href="http://www.comtech-serv.com/Comstar"
      format="html" scope="external">
      <linktext>Comstar Phones</linktext>
      <desc>Order your Comstar phone today.</desc>
   </link>
</related-links>
```

**8.** Save your work in the TransferringACall.dita file.

### TransferringACall.dita example

The following example shows the complete related-links section in your task topic.

```
<task id="TransferringACall" xml:lang="en-us">
   ⋮
   <taskbody>
   ⋮
   </taskbody>
   <related-links>
      <link href="AboutTransfer.dita" format="html"
         scope="local"/>
      <link href="../GeneralTopic/Glossary.dita"
         format="html" scope="peer"/>
      <link href="http://www.comtech-serv.com/Comstar"
         format="html" scope="external">
         <linktext>Comstar Phones</linktext>
         <desc>Order your Comstar phone today.</desc>
      </link>
   </related-links>
</task>
```

The following figure shows how these related links are rendered.

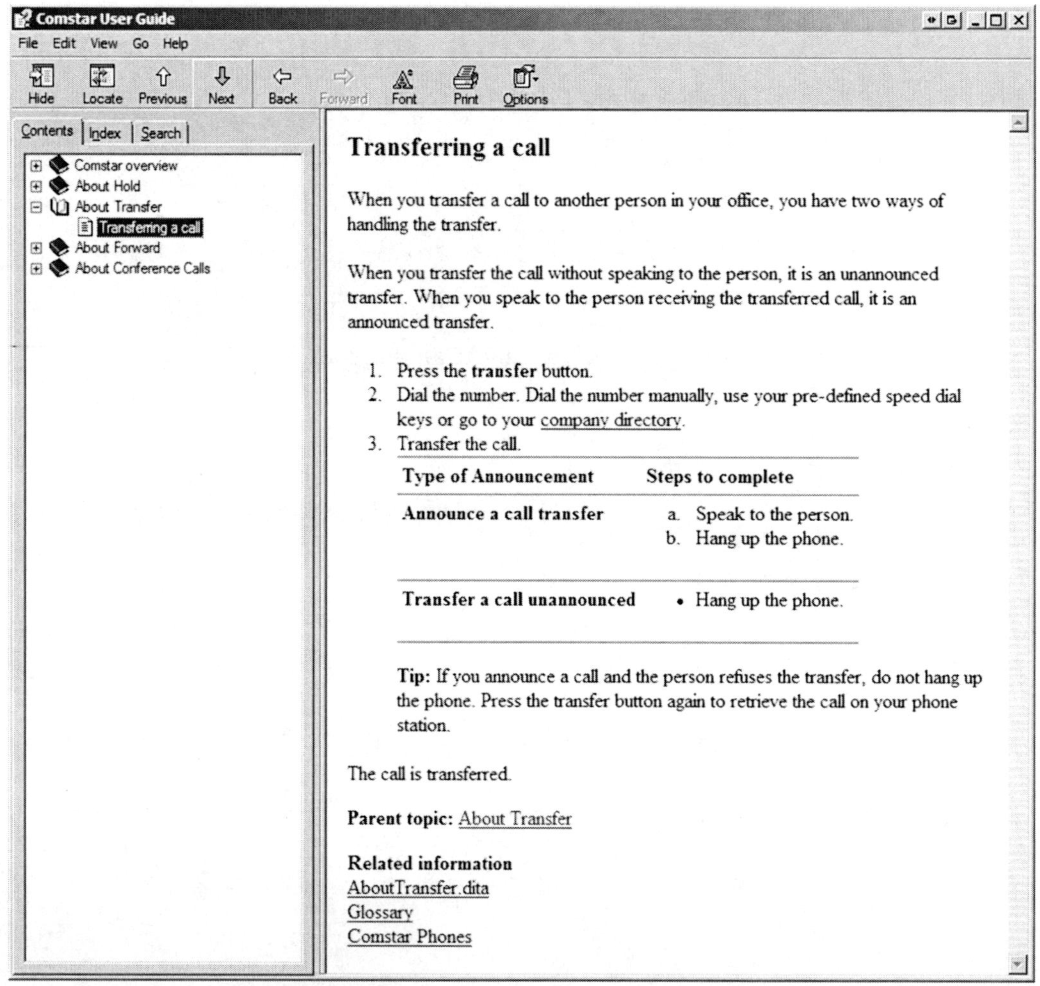

Comstar User Guide
File Edit View Go Help
Hide Locate Previous Next Back Forward Font Print Options
Contents Index Search
Comstar overview
About Hold
About Transfer
Transferring a call
About Forward
About Conference Calls
Transferring a call
When you transfer a call to another person in your office, you have two ways of handling the transfer.
When you transfer the call without speaking to the person, it is an unannounced transfer. When you speak to the person receiving the transferred call, it is an announced transfer.
1. Press the transfer button.
2. Dial the number. Dial the number manually, use your pre-defined speed dial keys or go to your company directory.
3. Transfer the call.
Type of Announcement
Steps to complete
Announce a call transfer
a. Speak to the person.
b. Hang up the phone.
Transfer a call unannounced
• Hang up the phone.
Tip: If you announce a call and the person refuses the transfer, do not hang up the phone. Press the transfer button again to retrieve the call on your phone station.
The call is transferred.
Parent topic: About Transfer
Related information
AboutTransfer.dita
Glossary
Comstar Phones


### Related-link elements

The following related-link elements are used in the DITA model.

**<desc> description**
: Use the <desc> element to provide a brief description of the linked topic or resource. Some processors display this information as hover text over the link.

**<link> link**
: Use the <link> element to define the relationships between topics. You can group similar links together using the <linklist> or <linkpool> elements.

**<linktext> link text**

Use the <linktext> element to specify the label or line of text for a link. Use the <linktext> element when the target reference cannot be reached or when the target is a non-DITA topic. During output, the <linktext> information will be output inline within the reference topic.

**<linklist> link list**

Use the <linklist> element to define a group of related links by giving the group a title. The *@collection-type* attribute defines the group of links and can be set to "unordered", "sequence", "choice", or "family". For more information on the *@collection-type* attribute, see Collection-type Attribute on page 161. The list of links will output in the same order you added them to your topic.

**<linkinfo> link information**

Use the <linkinfo> element to add a descriptive paragraph to a list of links.

```
<related-links>
   <linklist collection-type="sequence">
      <title>Hold</title>
      <link href="AboutHold.dita" type="concept"/>
      <link href="HoldingACall.dita" type="task">
         <linktext>Holding a call</linktext>
      </link>
      <linkinfo>Use these topics for background information
         about the process of holding a  call.</linkinfo>
   </linklist>
</related-links>
```

**<linkpool> link pool**

Use the <linkpool> element to group a set of related links that have a common characteristic, such as type, audience, source, etc. All links within a linkpool inherit any attribute associated with the <linkpool> element. Usually, the *@type* attribute defines the group of links attributes and can be set to "concept", "task", "reference", "other", and more. For more information on the *@type* attribute, see Type Attribute on page 149. Use the <linkpool> element in place of the <linklist> element. The order your links are listed in the <linkpool> element does not affect the output. Instead, the processor sorts through the links and determines the order for output.

```
<related-links>
   <linkpool type="concept">
      <link href="AboutHold.dita"/>
      <link href="AboutTransfer.dita"/>
      <link href="AboutForward.dita"/>
      <link href="AboutConfCalls.dita"/>
   </linkpool>
</related-links>
```

**Related links review questions**

What is the difference between the <xref> and <related-links> elements?

- **a.** <xref> elements cannot to external sources.
- **b.** <xref> identifies the type of files it is linking to using the *@type* attribute while <related-links> does the same thing with the *@format* attribute.
- **c.** Best practices recommend using <xref> elements rather than <related-links> elements.
- **d.** <xref> creates links inline in the text of your document while <related-links> appear at the end.

Because related links are output as hyperlinks, they cannot appear in a print or PDF file.

- True
- False

If you do not specify link text for a topic that does not have a DITA title, what will the processor use?

- **a.** The value provided in the *@id* attribute for the topic.
- **b.** The description text, if specified.
- **c.** The value provided in the href attribute.
- **d.** The link information text, if specified.

The *@format* attribute identifies the type of output you want to generate.

- True
- False

What attribute tells the processor how to process a link depending on the location of the target topic?

What is the different between <linklist> and <linkpool>? Select all that apply.

- **a.** <linklist> groups related topics under a common title. <linkpool> groups topics based on a common attribute.
- **b.** Links appear in the order specified in a <linklist>, while the processor controls the order in a <linkpool>.
- **c.** Links in <linkpool> elements can be of any @*type*. Links in <linklist> elements must have the same @*type*.
- **d.** Links in <linklist> elements can be of any @*type*. Links in <linkpool> elements must have the same @*type*.

# SECTION C

# Understanding Topic Metadata

Metadata means data or information about information. For example, the metadata you use to retrieve topics might include the names of the authors and contributors, dates of revisions, version numbers, or security rights. In DITA, you can add metadata to the prolog using elements, such as <author>, <revised>, <brand>, and <audience>.

In a DITA source document, you use descriptive element tags not only to control the content structure and reuse topics and elements, but you use additional markup to describe information in each topic. Because semantic element names are not always sufficient for search and retrieval, DITA provides general metadata markup for each topic. You use the metadata to find topics in your file system and your CMS. You can also build your search engine index using your topic metadata.

We strongly recommend that you plan your metadata at the beginning of your project. Once you add metadata to your topics, it is difficult to change. By planning your metadata, you ensure that your authors correctly apply metadata attributes and values as they create topics.

Be careful to limit the number of metadata attributes you ask authors to include. Too many attributes are harder to maintain and take time to add. Once you have defined your metadata, map the metadata categories to the metadata elements available in the DITA prolog. You will insert most of your topic metadata in the <prolog> element. You can also add metadata to any block of information by applying attributes to individual elements. If you find that the standard DITA metadata elements in the prolog do not meet your metadata needs, you may want to create a metadata specialization. See The DITA Information-Development Environment on page 305 for more information about specialization.

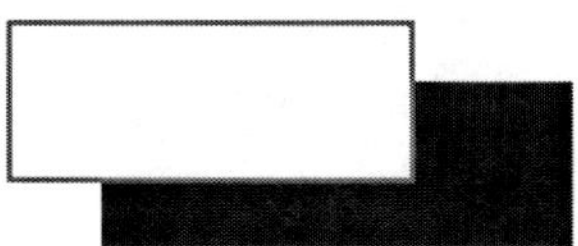

# LESSON 7

## Prolog Metadata

Use metadata elements in the <prolog> container to categorize, summarize, and label a topic. The base DITA prolog metadata elements specify the audience for which a topic is intended, the product with which the topic is associated, the hardware or software platform, the topic author, the copyright holder, and date-related information, such as copyright year, date created, and date revised. In addition, you can enter security filters for each topic you author. Prolog metadata elements are optional.

In addition to the general prolog metadata, you can add a <metadata> container with <keywords> elements and <indexterm> elements as prolog metadata. In HTML, the keywords metatag helps search engines retrieve a specific list of words to identify content in a full-text search. The search engine uses the keywords you provide to retrieve and rank your topic. You can transport the keywords you identify in your DITA topics to the HTML metatag using your stylesheet. Similarly, for PDF files, index-term entries are compiled into a comprehensive document index with page numbers. You can include index terms outside the prolog metadata as well. However, we recommend that you place terms that apply to the entire topic in the prolog metadata section.

**Adding prolog metadata**

This lesson explains how to add product information and keyword metadata to your topic <prolog> container. In this lesson, you learn to add prolog metadata elements such as <permissions>, <metadata>, and <keywords> that you can use in each information type.

1. Open the TransferringACall.dita task topic that you created in Task Information Type on page 33 and modified in Related Links on page 91.

   In the TransferringACall.dita task topic, you added a <prolog> container and an <author> element to identify topic author metadata.

   ```
   <?xml version="1.0" encoding="utf-8"?>
   <!DOCTYPE task PUBLIC "-//OASIS//DTD DITA Task//EN"
      "task.dtd">
   <task id="TransferringACall" xml:lang="en-us">
      <title><keyword>Transferring</keyword>
         a call</title>
      <shortdesc>When you transfer a call to another person
         in your office, you have two ways of handling the
         transfer.</shortdesc>
      <prolog>
         <author>John Smith</author>
   ```

```
</prolog>
<taskbody>
   <context>When you transfer the call without speaking to
      the person, it is an unannounced transfer. When you
      speak to the person receiving the transferred call,
      it is an announced transfer.</context>
   <steps>
      <step>
         <cmd>Press the <uicontrol>transfer
            </uicontrol> button.</cmd>
      </step>
      <step>
         <cmd>Dial the number. </cmd>
         <info>Dial the number manually, use your
            pre-defined speed dial keys or go to your
            <xref href="AccessingCompanyDirectory.dita"
            type="task">company directory</xref>.
         </info>
      </step>
      <step>
         <cmd>Transfer the call.</cmd>
         <choicetable>
            <chhead>
               <choptionhd>Type of Announcement</choptionhd>
               <chdeschd>Steps to complete</chdeschd>
            </chhead>
            <chrow>
               <choption>Announce a call transfer</choption>
               <chdesc>
                  <ol>
                     <li>Speak to the person.</li>
                     <li>Hang up the phone.</li>
                  </ol>
               </chdesc>
            </chrow>
            <chrow>
               <choption>Transfer a call unannounced</choption>
               <chdesc>
                  <ul>
                     <li>Hang up the phone.</li>
                  </ul>
               </chdesc>
            </chrow>
         </choicetable>
         <info>
            <note type="tip">If you announce a call and the
               person refuses the transfer, do not hang
               up the phone. Press the transfer button
               again to retrieve the call on your phone
               station.</note>
         </info>
      </step>
   </steps>
   <result>The call is transferred.</result>
</taskbody>
<related-links>
   <link href="AboutTransfer.dita" format="html"
      scope="local"/>
   <link href="../GeneralTopic/Glossary.dita"
      format="html" scope="peer"/>
   <link href="http://www.comtech-serv.com/Comstar"
```

```
            format="html" scope="external">
            <linktext>Comstar Phones</linktext>
            <desc>Order your Comstar phone today.</desc>
        </link>
    </related-links>
</task>
```

2. Add copyright information within the <prolog> element.
   a. Add <copyright> start and end tags after the author end tag within the prolog.
   b. Add a <copyryear> element with a *@year* attribute for the copyright date of the topic.
   c. Add <copyrholder> start and end tags and define who owns the copyright.

```
<prolog>
   <author>John Smith</author>
   <copyright>
      <copyryear year="2009"/>
      <copyrholder>Comtech Services, Inc.</copyrholder>
   </copyright>
</prolog>
```

3. Add a <permissions> element after the <copyright> element within the <prolog>, and use the *@view* attribute to define who can access the topic.

   The *@view* attribute provides a mechanism to add security roles to your topic. Choose from the values “all”, “classified”, “entitled”, or “internal”.

```
<prolog>
   <author>John Smith</author>
   <copyright>
      <copyryear year="2009"/>
      <copyrholder>Comtech Services, Inc.</copyrholder>
   </copyright>
   <permissions view="all"/>
</prolog>
```

4. Add <metadata> start and end tags in your <prolog> after the <permissions> tag.

```
<prolog>
   <author>John Smith</author>
   <copyright>
      <copyryear year="2009"/>
      <copyrholder>Comtech Services, Inc.</copyrholder>
   </copyright>
   <permissions view="all"/>
   <metadata>
   </metadata>
</prolog>
```

5. Add keywords to your <prolog>.

a. Add <keywords> start and end tags in your <metadata> container.

b. Add a <keyword> element within the <keywords> container for each term you want to include.

```
<prolog>
   <author>John Smith</author>
   <copyright>
      <copyryear year="2009"/>
      <copyrholder>Comtech Services, Inc.</copyrholder>
    </copyright>
    <permissions view="all"/>
    <metadata>
       <keywords>
          <keyword>phone</keyword>
          <keyword>transfer</keyword>
          <keyword>transferring a call</keyword>
       </keywords>
    </metadata>
</prolog>
```

6. Add index entries for the topic.

   Index terms that apply to the entire topic should be placed within the <keywords> element in the <prolog>. You can also place index terms directly in the body of a topic. However, we recommend placing index terms in the prolog or at the beginning of block-level elements for consistency and to minimize the impact on translation.

   a. Add <indexterm> start and end tags for each index term you want to include.

      For this example, add four index tags as shown.

```
<prolog>
   <author>John Smith</author>
   <copyright>
      <copyryear year="2009"/>
      <copyrholder>Comtech Services, Inc.</copyrholder>
   </copyright>
   <permissions view="all"/>
   <metadata>
      <keywords>
         <keyword>phone</keyword>
         <keyword>transfer</keyword>
         <keyword>transferring a call</keyword>
         <indexterm>transferring a call</indexterm>
         <indexterm>unannounced transfers</indexterm>
         <indexterm>announced transfers</indexterm>
         <indexterm>transfers</indexterm>
      </keywords>
   </metadata>
</prolog>
```

   b. Nest <indexterm> elements to create secondary and tertiary index entries.

For this example, nest two index terms within the transfers index term as shown.

```
<prolog>
   <author>John Smith</author>
   <copyright>
      <copyryear year="2009"/>
      <copyrholder>Comtech Services, Inc.</copyrholder>
   </copyright>
   <permissions view="all"/>
   <metadata>
      <keywords>
         <keyword>phone</keyword>
         <keyword>transfer</keyword>
         <keyword>transferring a call</keyword>
         <indexterm>transferring a call</indexterm>
         <indexterm>unannounced transfers</indexterm>
         <indexterm>announced transfers</indexterm>
         <indexterm>transfers
            <indexterm>unannounced</indexterm>
            <indexterm>announced</indexterm>
         </indexterm>
      </keywords>
   </metadata>
</prolog>
```

**c.** Add <index-see> and <index-see-also> tags as needed.

Use the <index-see> element to redirect readers to a term that they should see instead of the one they have looked up. Use the <index-see-also> element to redirect readers to a term that they should consult in addition to the term that they have looked up.

For this example, add a See Also reference to the unannounced transfers and announced transfers index tags as shown.

```
<prolog>
   <author>John Smith</author>
   <copyright>
      <copyryear year="2009"/>
      <copyrholder>Comtech Services, Inc.</copyrholder>
   </copyright>
   <permissions view="all"/>
   <metadata>
      <keywords>
         <keyword>phone</keyword>
         <keyword>transfer</keyword>
         <keyword>transferring a call</keyword>
         <indexterm>transferring a call</indexterm>
         <indexterm>unannounced transfers
            <index-see-also>transferring a call
            </index-see-also>
         </indexterm>
         <indexterm>announced transfers
            <index-see-also>transferring a call
            </index-see-also>
         </indexterm>
         <indexterm>transfers
```

```
                <indexterm>unannounced</indexterm>
                <indexterm>announced</indexterm>
            </indexterm>
        </keywords>
    </metadata>
</prolog>
```

7. Save your work in the TransferringACall.dita file.

### TransferringACall.dita

The following example shows how to use the <prolog> element in a task topic.

```
<?xml version="1.0" encoding="utf-8"?>
<!DOCTYPE task PUBLIC "-//OASIS//DTD DITA Task//EN"
   "task.dtd">
<task id="TransferringACall" xml:lang="en-us">
   <title><keyword>Transferring</keyword>
      a call</title>
   <shortdesc>When you transfer a call to another person
      in your office, you have two ways of handling the
      transfer.</shortdesc>
   <prolog>
      <author>John Smith</author>
      <copyright>
         <copyryear year="2009"/>
         <copyrholder>Comtech Services, Inc.</copyrholder>
      </copyright>
      <permissions view="all"/>
      <metadata>
         <keywords>
            <keyword>phone</keyword>
            <keyword>transfer</keyword>
            <keyword>transferring a call</keyword>
            <indexterm>transferring a call</indexterm>
            <indexterm>unannounced transfers
               <index-see-also>transferring a call
               </index-see-also>
            </indexterm>
            <indexterm>announced transfers
               <index-see-also>transferring a call
               </index-see-also>
            </indexterm>
            <indexterm>transfers
               <indexterm>unannounced</indexterm>
               <indexterm>announced</indexterm>
            </indexterm>
         </keywords>
      </metadata>
   </prolog>
   <taskbody>
      <context>When you transfer the call without speaking to
         the person, it is an unannounced transfer. When you
         speak to the person receiving the transferred call,
         it is an announced transfer.</context>
      <steps>
         <step>
            <cmd>Press the <uicontrol>transfer
               </uicontrol> button.</cmd>
```

```
         </step>
         <step>
            <cmd>Dial the number. </cmd>
            <info>Dial the number manually, use your
               pre-defined speed dial keys or go to your
               <xref href="AccessingCompanyDirectory.dita"
               type="task">company directory</xref>.
            </info>
         </step>
         <step>
            <cmd>Transfer the call.</cmd>
            <choicetable>
               <chhead>
                  <choptionhd>Type of Announcement</choptionhd>
                  <chdeschd>Steps to complete</chdeschd>
               </chhead>
               <chrow>
                  <choption>Announce a call transfer</choption>
                  <chdesc>
                     <ol>
                        <li>Speak to the person.</li>
                        <li>Hang up the phone.</li>
                     </ol>
                  </chdesc>
               </chrow>
               <chrow>
                  <choption>Transfer a call
                     unannounced</choption>
                  <chdesc>
                     <ul>
                        <li>Hang up the phone.</li>
                     </ul>
                  </chdesc>
               </chrow>
            </choicetable>
            <info>
               <note type="tip">If you announce a call and the
                  person refuses the transfer, do not hang
                  up the phone. Press the transfer button
                  again to retrieve the call on your phone
                  station.</note>
            </info>
         </step>
      </steps>
      <result>The call is transferred.</result>
   </taskbody>
   <related-links>
      <link href="AboutTransfer.dita" format="html"
         scope="local"/>
      <link href="../GeneralTopic/Glossary.dita"
         format="html" scope="peer"/>
      <link href="http://www.comtech-serv.com/Comstar"
         format="html" scope="external">
         <linktext>Comstar Phones</linktext>
         <desc>Order your Comstar phone today.</desc>
      </link>
   </related-links>
</task>
```

**Prolog metadata elements**

The following prolog metadata elements are listed in the order they might appear in the prolog. When using these elements, remember that some may be nested in others.

**<author> author**
: Use the <author> element to specify the name of the topic author. Use the optional *@type* attribute with the value of "creator" or "contributor" to indicate the primary author of the topic. You may add multiple <author> elements to the <author> metadata element.

**<copyright> copyright**
: Use the <copyright> element to specify the copyright information for a topic. The <copyright> element is the container for the <copyryear> and <copyrholder> elements.

**<copyryear> copyright year**
: Use the <copyryear> element to indicate the copyright year.

**<copyrholder> copyright holder**
: Use the <copyrholder> element to indicate the entity that holds the legal rights to the topic.

**<critdates> critical dates**
: Use the <critdates> element to track the important dates of your topic including the creation and multiple revision dates. The <critdates> element is the container for the <created> and <revised> elements.

**<created> created date**
: Use the <created> element to track the topic creation date. Use the *@date* attribute to document the creation date.

**<revised> revised date**
: Use the <revised> element to track the dates the topic was modified or changed. Use the *@modified* attribute to track the last date the topic was modified. Use the *@golive* attribute to track the date the product was released. Use the *@expiry* date to record when the information should be reviewed or retired.

**<metadata> metadata**
: Use the <metadata> element to add information regarding a particular audience, category, product, keyword, or other metadata. The <metadata> element allows you to include elements, such as <audience>, <keywords>, and <prodinfo>.

**<audience> audience**
: Use the <audience> metadata element to specify the intended audience, job, and experience level for a topic. Use the *@type* attribute in the <audience> element to specify the intended audience. Use the *@job* attribute to specify the high-level task they are trying to accomplish. Use the *@experiencelevel* attribute to specify the end users' expected experience level. You may add

more than one <audience> metadata element to the <prolog> element to indicate multiple audiences, jobs, or experience levels for the topic.

**<keywords> keywords**
: Use the <keywords> metadata element to specify index and keyword terms. These terms are used in search indexes and are added to the metadata for HTML output. The <keywords> element is a container for one or more <keyword> elements.

**<keyword> keyword**
: Use the <keyword> element to specify a single index or keyword term for your topic. Multiple <keyword> elements can be added to the <keywords> element.

**<prodinfo> product information**
: Use the <prodinfo> metadata element to provide information regarding the product or products described in your topic. The <prodinfo> metadata element is a container for the <prodname>, <vrmlist>, and <platform> metadata elements.

**<prodname> product name**
: Use the <prodname> metadata element to specify the name of the product described in the topic.

**<vrmlist> version, release, modification list**
: Use the <vrmlist> element to define information about the product. The <vrmlist> element is a container for the <vrm> element.

**<vrm> version, release, modification**
: Use the version, release, and modification attributes of the <vrm> element to define the version, release and modification of the product.

**<brand> brand**
: Use the <brand> element to indicate the manufacturer or brand associated with the product info.

**<platform> platform**
: Use the <platform> metadata element to describe the software or hardware associated with the product.

**<permissions> permissions**
: Use the <permissions> element to add security filters to your topics. The <permissions> element requires you to include a @*view* attribute. The possible values you can use for the @*view* attribute are "all", "classified", "entitled", or "internal".

```
<prolog>
   <author type="creator">JoAnn Hackos</author>
   <copyright>
      <copyryear year="2000"></copyryear>
      <copyrholder>Comtech Services, Inc.</copyrholder>
   </copyright>
   <critdates>
      <created date="1999-01-01"></created>
      <revised modified="2000-03-01"></revised>
   </critdates>
   <metadata>
```

```
      <audience type="administrator" job="planning"
         experiencelevel="novice"/>
      <keywords>
         <keyword>Costs</keyword>
         <keyword>Estimating</keyword>
         <keyword>Tracking</keyword>
         <keyword>Monitoring</keyword>
         <keyword>PUB$</keyword>
      </keywords>
      <prodinfo>
         <prodname>PUB$ Estimator</prodname>
         <vrmlist>
            <vrm version="1.1" release="2"
               modification="1"/>
         </vrmlist>
         <brand>Comtech Services</brand>
         <platform>Windows XP</platform>
      </prodinfo>
   </metadata>
</prolog>
```

**<indexterm> indexterm**

Use the <indexterm> element to contain a term that will appear in the index. You can nest <indexterm> elements within <indexterm> elements to create secondary and tertiary index terms. As a best practice, nesting should not exceed two levels. Place index terms that apply to the entire topic within the <prolog> element. You can also place index terms within the body of the topic at block-, sentence- and phrase-levels. We recommend placing index terms in the prolog or at the beginning of block-level elements for consistency and to minimize the impact on translation. Index terms in the prolog will generate page numbers based on the location of the topic title.

**<index-see> index see**

Use the <index-see> element to redirect readers to a term that they should see instead of the one they have looked up. The element <index-see> is contained within an <indexterm> element.

**<index-see-also> index see also**

Use the <index-see-also> element to redirect readers to a term that they should consult in addition to the term that they have looked up. The element <index-see-also> is contained within an <indexterm> element.

**<index-sort-as> index sort as**

Use the <index-sort-as> element to specify the sort order of an index term. The <index-sort-as> element is contained with an <indexterm> element. The <index-sort-as> element is helpful for sorting languages like Japanese where the order of terms may require per-word modification.

```
<prolog>
   ⋮
   <metadata>
      <audience type="administrator" job="planning"
         experiencelevel="novice"/>
      <keywords>
         ⋮
```

```
            <indexterm>Costs
               <indexterm>Estimating</indexterm>
               <indexterm>Tracking
                  <index-see-also>Monitoring</index-see-also>
               </indexterm>
            </indexterm>
            <indexterm>Expenses
               <index-see>Costs</index-see>
            </indexterm>
            <indexterm>PUB$</indexterm>
        </keywords>
         <prodinfo>
            ⋮
         </prodinfo>
      </metadata>
   </prolog>
```

**Metadata review questions**

What is the purpose of metadata?

- **a.** To categorize, summarize, and label a topic.
- **b.** To define the structure of the topic.
- **c.** To describe content associated with a specific subject area.
- **d.** To specify formatting associated with the tags within the topic.

Which of the following must be placed inside a metadata container within the prolog? Select all that apply.

- **a.** <audience>
- **b.** <permissions>
- **c.** <author>
- **d.** <indexterm>
- **e.** <copyright>
- **f.** <critdates>
- **g.** <keyword>
- **h.** <prodinfo>

What is wrong with this code: `<audience>administrator</audience>` ?

- **a.** A job and experience level must also be specified.
- **b.** The information provided must be placed into an attribute.
- **c.** The <audience> tag does not exist.
- **d.** The code is correct as is.

Insert most of your metadata by applying attributes to individual elements within your topic.

- True
- False

How do you create secondary and tertiary index terms?

**a.** Use the type attribute on the <indexterm> tag.
**b.** Nest <indexterm> tags.
**c.** Use the <index-sort-as> tag to specify the appropriate level.
**d.** Secondary and tertiary index terms are not supported in DITA.

Which two tags within the prolog specify critical dates for the topic?

Prolog metadata elements are optional.

- True
- False

# PART III

# DITA Maps

Using DITA maps to create collections of topics for print, web, help, or other deliverables helps you create a collaborative work environment and improve the quality of the information you deliver to your customers. You may want to establish a team of information developers to collaboratively develop the topics for a deliverable. You may want to deliver solution-oriented information to your users rather than sets of manuals specific to individual products. You may want to improve the time to market by synchronizing processes between information and product development. Using DITA maps to create collections of topics improves your ability to deliver information to specific audiences, assemble pre-translated topics for specific locales, and create deliverables for specific products and product solutions.

Mapping your topics into deliverables helps to

- improve writer collaboration
- create solution-oriented deliverables
- create customized deliverables
- synchronize information development with product-development schedules

**A collaborative work environment**

Information-development organizations often move to topic-oriented writing to avoid duplication of effort. They find that their colleagues write the same topics in slightly different ways for individual deliverables. Managers hope to reduce redundancy by developing a repository of unique topics that can be reused in multiple deliverables. DITA maps facilitate single sourcing and content reuse. By designing DITA maps for final deliverables early in the information-development life cycle, information developers avoid duplication of effort at the same time that they understand the context in which a topic will appear.

**Solution-oriented deliverables**

Users of technical information are often at a disadvantage when they try to use a variety of products, even when these products are developed by the same company. They find that each product has an independently developed set of manuals that might adequately describe how to use each product but fails to explain how the products work together.

Solutions documentation is designed to bridge product elements by documenting how they work together and how they can be used together efficiently and effectively.

Topic-based authoring facilitates the development of solution-oriented deliverables. When you use topics to create your information deliverables, you can create DITA maps that apply to a specific product or to a group of products. You can reference DITA maps for one deliverable into a master map to produce a solutions-oriented collection of your product information.

**Customized deliverables**

Users of technical information often would prefer to collect individual topics from larger documentation sets and create their own personal manuals. Experienced technicians administering and maintaining complex products may need only select reference information to support their tasks. Occasional users may profit from simple task-oriented information because they're unwilling to devote time to learning concepts and studying background.

By giving your users access to individual topics or enabling them to search for topics with a controlled vocabulary of metadata attributes and values, you can help them create personalized maps of the information they need. Using a DITA map, they build personalized deliverables by arranging selected topics into a recommended hierarchy. They might even add their own topics to the ones you provide. The map can then group concepts, tasks, and reference information about a particular subject matter into a single deliverable.

**Synchronized information and product development**

By moving from authoring books to authoring topics, information developers can more easily synchronize their schedules with the development of product features and functions. Beginning with user scenarios or use cases that describe how actual users will benefit from new and updated product features and functions, information developers first create a list of task topics. The task topics explain how users will accomplish their goals with the product.

After the task topics are outlined, the information developers begin to string the tasks together in DITA maps, using a hierarchy that best represents how the user might approach the activities. That hierarchy might be chronological, supporting a start-to-finish installation process, or it might reflect common and less common uses of the product. The DITA map prepares the hierarchy and renders it as a table of contents or the navigation in a help system or web site.

Concept and reference topics can then be developed and organized in the DITA map in relation to the task topics. With all the topics accounted for and the contexts developed in the maps, the information developers can author topics in whatever order is convenient and corresponds to the availability of source information from requirements, use cases, product specifications, and interviews with product developers, designers, and managers. If you are translating, you can send finished topics to translation while others are still in development, potentially reducing the translation turnaround time at the end of the project.

By synchronizing the information-development process with product development, you can create topics about more stable product features early, moving to less stable or completed features and functions when they are ready. If product management decides to remove a feature from a deliverable, you need only remove the topic from the DITA map, making last minute changes easier to accommodate. Adding, modifying, or deleting stand-alone topics in a map is more efficient than extracting topics embedded in chapters and sections of books.

# SECTION D

# Understanding DITA Map Basics

DITA maps are the backbone of DITA. Maps provide a mechanism for ordering topics and creating a topic hierarchy. For example, you can produce two different API reference manuals, one organizing functions and methods alphabetically and the other organizing them by family. By creating two different maps that reference the same source topics, you can create two deliverables to meet user needs. Because maps consist of lists of topic references, you can reorganize the content in a map simply by changing the order of the topic references. You can distinguish among your maps by applying map and topic metadata. Figure 4 illustrates two maps created from the same source topics.

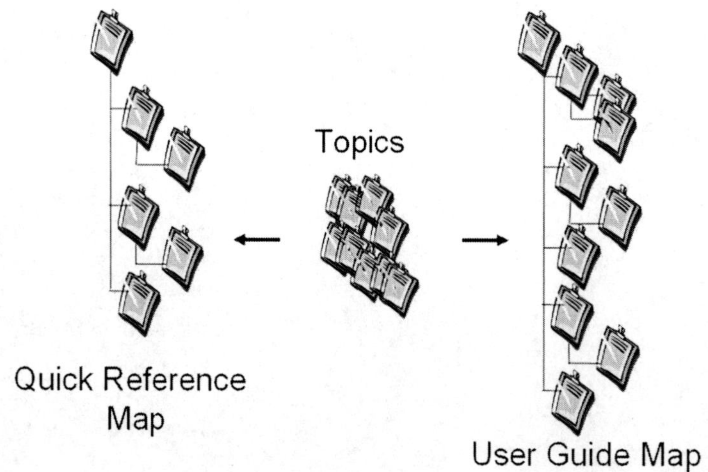


**Figure 4: Creating multiple maps from a single source**

When topics are authored in the chapters and sections of desktop publishing applications, restructuring them is difficult. In DITA, your deliverable isn't tied to the structure in which you author the topics. You can

- place topics in more than one position in a DITA map. For example, a task can occur in more than one place in a task flow
- create solutions-oriented maps that answer the question "how do these products work together?", task-oriented maps to answer the question "how do I accomplish my goals?", and feature-oriented maps to answer the question "what does this product do?"
- create maps to deliver information to specific audiences
- create hierarchies of topics depending on the way you format your output
- include topics in your navigation from different information sets, such as external web sites and other content your staff or another department may have created

The relationships among topics defined in a map can be used to create tables of contents (TOCs), site maps, and navigation. DITA maps provide functionality to customize how the output will be rendered using specific map metadata, such as the *@href*, *@format*, *@scope*, *@type*, *@linking*, and *@collection-type* attributes. Additionally, DITA map relationship tables provide linking among topics that do not have direct relationships in the hierarchy. You use the DITA map as the cornerstone for processing the output you need.

**Map location**

When you create a new map, it is best to place the map file in the same directory that contains the topics. DITA maps have a .ditamap extension so that they can be distinguished from other DITA source files. You might also consider creating smaller maps and storing them in subdirectories to help you manage topics better (for example, a folder for each major category of your deliverable, such as installation, troubleshooting, and operations). Then you can create a master map that references the smaller maps. Because you can nest the topic folders to any level, you should position the map in a higher level folder that contains all the topics. This folder organization ensures that processing runs without errors.

# LESSON 8

## DITA Map Structure

DITA maps use a small set of elements to help you create a topic collection and arrange topics into a useful hierarchy. The map elements enable you to reference topics, create groups of topics, create navigational headings, add map metadata, and more. Map elements dictate the structure of the topics in your final deliverables. Although the number of elements needed to create a map is significantly less than the number used to create topics, the map elements play a special role.

The <topicref> element builds the structure of the DITA map and is the most widely used map element. The topic reference points to a single topic and includes it in the deliverable. Topic reference elements create the hierarchical relationships needed to format the deliverable with more than one heading level. By embedding topic references in one another, you can create a hierarchy as many levels deep as you believe necessary.

Metadata in the map allows you to further customize deliverables. You can include the same metadata in your map that you include in your topic. Some metadata you might include in a DITA map are author, publisher, audience, category, copyright, critical dates, keywords, permissions, and product information.

When you include metadata in a topic, it is applied to a specific topic reference. However, when you include the metadata in a map, you can change the metadata based on the deliverable and manage the topic metadata in the map rather than in the topic. If you manage the metadata in the topic, it makes the topic less flexible. For example, if you want to include information about an audience, you might assign different audiences to a topic reference depending on the deliverable you are building. But, if you include one specific audience in your topic-level metadata, you may find it difficult to use that topic in more than one map.

This lesson contains four exercises that introduce you to the map elements and demonstrate how to use them to create a basic hierarchy:

- Starting a DITA map
- Adding topic references
- Adding topic metadata
- Creating a basic hierarchy

**Starting a DITA map**

This exercise explains the standard XML markup included in a DITA map. In this exercise, you learn to add the XML declaration, DTD declaration, the root <map> element and a <title> in your DITA map.

1. Start a new DITA map.

   You can start a new DITA map in a text editor or in an XML editor. In most XML editors, you can choose **file > new > DITA map** . As it does when you create any topic, your XML editor usually includes the DTD declaration, XML declaration, and <map> start and end tags automatically. If you choose to use a text editor, type the markup shown here.

   ```
   <?xml version="1.0" encoding="utf-8"?>
   <!DOCTYPE map PUBLIC "-//OASIS//DTD DITA Map//EN"
      "map.dtd">
   <map xml:lang="en-us">
   </map>
   ```

2. Add an *@id* attribute to your <map> element.

   The *@id* attribute must be unique. A unique *@id* allows you to easily identify the map you want to process. The *@id* can contain numbers, letters, and underscores, but it must start with a letter or a number.

   ```
   <map id="ComstarUserGuide" xml:lang="en-us">
   </map>
   ```

3. Add a <title> element and value to your map element.

   The processor uses the map's <title> element to create a title page for your print output or to add a window name to your online output.

   ```
   <map id="ComstarUserGuide" xml:lang="en-us">
      <title>Comstar User Guide</title>
   </map>
   ```

4. Save this file as ComstarUserGuide.ditamap.

**ComstarUserGuide.ditamap**

The following example illustrates the elements that must be included in every DITA map.

```
<?xml version="1.0" encoding="utf-8"?>
<!DOCTYPE map PUBLIC "-//OASIS//DTD DITA Map//EN"
   "map.dtd">
<map id="ComstarUserGuide" xml:lang="en-us">
   <title>Comstar User Guide</title>
</map>
```

**Adding topic references**

This exercise explains how to add topic references to your DITA map. You learn to

- add the <topicref> element
- apply an *@href* attribute and value to your topic references
- add the *@navtitle* attribute

1. Open the DITA map you started creating in the previous exercise in this lesson.
2. Insert an empty <topicref> element between the <map> start and end tags, after the <title> element.

   Create empty <topicref> elements if you are not going to nest topic references as child topics between start and end <topicref> tags. Using empty topic references helps you create a more maintainable map. If you use multiple open and close tags, you are more likely to create an error nesting your topic references. You can find out more about nesting topic references in Creating a basic hierarchy on page 126.

   ```
   <map id="ComstarUserGuide" xml:lang="en-us">
      <title>Comstar User Guide</title>
      <topicref/>
   </map>
   ```

3. Assign the *@href* attribute of the <topicref> element to the value "ComstarOverview.dita".

   The *@href* attribute is the most important attribute in a DITA map, pointing to the location of the DITA topic file you want to reference. The *@href* attribute value accepts absolute or relative path names to the location of your topic. Your topics may be named with a .dita or a .xml extension. We recommend using the .dita extension everywhere. Remember to include this file extension when referencing your file.

   For this example, assume the DITA topic is located in the same folder as the DITA map.

   ```
   <map id="ComstarUserGuide" xml:lang="en-us">
      <title>Comstar User Guide</title>
      <topicref href="ComstarOverview.dita"/>
   </map>
   ```

4. After the ComstarOverview.dita topicref, add two more empty <topicref> element containers and assign their *@href* attributes to Quickguide.dita and AboutHold.dita respectively.

Your map now points to three topics and puts them in the order in which you want them to appear in the table of contents. At this point, all the topic references are at the same level in the hierarchy.

```
<map id="ComstarUserGuide" xml:lang="en-us">
<title>Comstar User Guide</title>
   <topicref href="ComstarOverview.dita"/>
   <topicref href="QuickGuide.dita"/>
   <topicref href="AboutHold.dita"/>
</map>
```

5. Add a *@navtitle* attribute to your AboutHold.dita topic reference container.

   A *@navtitle* provides a way for authors to keep track of their topic titles. If you are using an XML editor, the program may automatically insert a *@navtitle* attribute based on the topic's title. Because, by default, the *@navtitle* attribute is ignored in processing, for the remainder of the exercises in this book, we will not include *@navtitle* attributes within <topicref> elements.

   In this example, the AboutHold.dita topic title is "About Hold." Bu using the *@navtitle* attribute, you shorten the navigation title to "Hold".

```
<map id="ComstarUserGuide" xml:lang="en-us">
<title>Comstar User Guide</title>
   <topicref href="ComstarOverview.dita"/>
   <topicref href="QuickGuide.dita" />
   <topicref href="AboutHold.dita" navtitle="Hold"/>
</map>
```

6. Save your work in the ComstarUserGuide.ditamap file.

### ComstarUserGuide.ditamap

At this point, your ComstarUserGuide.ditamap looks like the example below.

```
<?xml version="1.0" encoding="utf-8"?>
<!DOCTYPE map PUBLIC "-//OASIS//DTD DITA Map//EN"
   "map.dtd">
<map id="ComstarUserGuide" xml:lang="en-us">
<title>Comstar User Guide</title>
   <topicref href="ComstarOverview.dita"/>
   <topicref href="QuickGuide.dita"/>
   <topicref href="AboutHold.dita" navtitle="Hold"/>
</map>
```

## Adding topic metadata

This exercise explains how to apply topic metadata to each topic reference in your DITA map. Topic metadata assigned to a <topicref> in a map helps you define metadata for groups of topics in a particular map. Many of the metadata elements (but not all) cascade to child topic references. It is useful to define topic metadata in the map rather than within a topic since the metadata may differ from map to map.

Because you can also define metadata in the topics, you may not find it necessary to define metadata in the map. By default, the metadata assigned to topic references in the map override or supplement the topic metadata. To override the default behavior, you can assign a topicref's *@lockmeta* attribute with the value, "no".

In this exercise, you learn to

- add the <topicmeta> element needed to apply topic metadata in a map
- add three pieces of metadata to a map and topics including <copyright>, <navtitle>, and <audience>

1. Open your DITA map from the Adding Topic References exercise.
2. Insert <topicmeta> start and end tags after the map's title end tag.

   The topic metadata container inserted at this level in the hierarchy allows you to define metadata that applies to all topics in the map.

```
<map id="Comstaruserguide" xml:lang="en-us">
   <title>Comstar User Guide</title>
   <topicmeta></topicmeta>
   <topicref href="ComstarOverview.dita" />
   <topicref href="QuickGuide.dita" />
   <topicref href="AboutHold.dita"></topicref>
</map>
```

3. Add <copyright> element start and end tags after the <topicmeta> start tag.

   The <copyright> element requires <copyryear> and <copyrholder> elements.

```
<map id="Comstaruserguide" xml:lang="en-us">
   <title>Comstar User Guide</title>
   <topicmeta>
      <copyright>
      </copyright>
   </topicmeta>
   <topicref href="ComstarOverview.dita" />
   <topicref href="QuickGuide.dita" />
   <topicref href="AboutHold.dita"></topicref>
</map>
```

4. Insert <copyryear> and <copyrholder> elements within the <copyright> element.

   The copyright information will cascade to all topics in the Comstar User Guide ditamap.

a. To define the copyright year, add a *@year* attribute to the <copyryear> element.

b. To define the copyright holder, add the appropriate text between the <copyrholder>start and end tags.

```
<map id="Comstaruserguide" xml:lang="en-us">
   <title>Comstar User Guide</title>
   <topicmeta>
      <copyright>
         <copyryear year="2011" />
         <copyrholder>Comstar Phones</copyrholder>
      </copyright>
   </topicmeta>
   <topicref href="ComstarOverview.dita"/>
   <topicref href="QuickGuide.dita"/>
   <topicref href="AboutHold.dita" navtitle="Hold"/>
</map>
```

5. Change the QuickGuide.dita topic reference to a container element rather than an empty element.

   If you remove the end slash and insert a <topicref> end tag, you create a container element.

```
<map id="Comstaruserguide" xml:lang="en-us">
   ⋮
   <topicref href="ComstarOverview.dita"/>
   <topicref href="QuickGuide.dita"></topicref>
   <topicref href="AboutHold.dita" navtitle="Hold"/>
</map>
```

6. Insert <topicmeta> start and end tags between the QuickGuide.dita <topicref> start and end tags.

   The topic metadata container at this level allows you to define metadata about a topic that you reference in your map. The <topicmeta> element contains elements similar to those you include in the <prolog> topic metadata, such as author, copyright, keywords, and product information.

```
<map id="Comstaruserguide" xml:lang="en-us">
   <title>Comstar User Guide</title>
   <topicmeta>
      <copyright>
         <copyryear year="2011" />
         <copyrholder>Comstar Phones</copyrholder>
      </copyright>
   </topicmeta>
   <topicref href="ComstarOverview.dita" />
   <topicref href="QuickGuide.dita">
      <topicmeta></topicmeta>
   </topicref>
   <topicref href="AboutHold.dita"></topicref>
</map>
```

7. Add <navtitle> start and end element tags between the <topicmeta> start and end tags.

   Use the <navtitle> element when you want to use an alternative title for navigation in the table of contents or navigation pane instead of the title you originally defined in your topic. You may want to use the <navtitle> element if your topic has a long title and you want a shorter title in a navigation pane.

```
<map id="Comstaruserguide" xml:lang="en-us">
   <title>Comstar User Guide</title>
   <topicmeta>
      <copyright>
         <copyryear year="2011" />
         <copyrholder>Comstar Phones</copyrholder>
      </copyright>
   </topicmeta>
   <topicref href="ComstarOverview.dita" />
   <topicref href="QuickGuide.dita">
      <topicmeta>
         <navtitle>Get Started Now</navtitle>
      </topicmeta>
   </topicref>
   <topicref href="AboutHold.dita"></topicref>
</map>
```

8. Add a *@locktitle* attribute to the <topicref> element.

   By default, the processor uses the title from your topic for reference in the table of contents and navigation pane, but you can override this processing functionality when you define a <navtitle> and set the <topicref> *@locktitle* attribute value to "yes".

```
<map id="Comstaruserguide" xml:lang="en-us">
   <title>Comstar User Guide</title>
   <topicmeta>
      <copyright>
         <copyryear year="2011" />
         <copyrholder>Comstar Phones</copyrholder>
      </copyright>
   </topicmeta>
   <topicref href="ComstarOverview.dita" />
   <topicref href="QuickGuide.dita" locktitle="yes" />
      <topicmeta>
         <navtitle>Get Started Now</navtitle>
      </topicmeta>
   <topicref href="AboutHold.dita"></topicref>
</map>
```

9. Add <topicmeta> element start and end tags to the About Hold <topicref>.

```
<map id="Comstaruserguide" xml:lang="en-us">
   <title>Comstar User Guide</title>
   <topicmeta>
      <copyright>
         <copyryear year="2011" />
         <copyrholder>Comstar Phones</copyrholder>
      </copyright>
```

```
    </topicmeta>
    <topicref href="ComstarOverview.dita" />
    <topicref href="QuickGuide.dita" locktitle="yes" />
       <topicmeta>
          <navtitle>Get Started Now</navtitle>
       </topicmeta>
    <topicref href="AboutHold.dita">
       <topicmeta></topicmeta>
    </topicref>
</map>
```

**10.** Add two empty <audience> element tag after the <topicmeta> element start tag and define user and administrator audiences.

You must add a value to the *@audience* attribute in the <audience> element. You can add as many <audience> elements as needed, assigning a topic reference to multiple audiences, such as an end user or administrator. However, you can also add multiple values in a single audience *@metadata* attribute using space delimiters (i.e., audience="beginner intermediate").

```
<map id="Comstaruserguide" xml:lang="en-us">
   <title>Comstar User Guide</title>
   <topicmeta>
      <copyright>
         <copyryear year="2011" />
         <copyrholder>Comstar Phones</copyrholder>
      </copyright>
   </topicmeta>
   <topicref href="ComstarOverview.dita" />
   <topicref href="QuickGuide.dita" locktitle="yes" />
      <topicmeta>
         <navtitle>Get Started Now</navtitle>
      </topicmeta>
   <topicref href="AboutHold.dita">
      <topicmeta>
         <audience audience="user" />
         <audience audience="administrator" />
      </topicmeta>
   </topicref>
</map>
```

**11.** Save your work in the ComstarUserGuide.ditamap file.

### Comstaruserguide.ditamap

Your Comstar User Guide ditamap should look like this one.

```
<map id="Comstaruserguide" xml:lang="en-us">
   <title>Comstar User Guide</title>
   <topicmeta>
      <copyright>
         <copyryear year="2011" />
         <copyrholder>Comstar Phones</copyrholder>
      </copyright>
   </topicmeta>
```

```
    <topicref href="ComstarOverview.dita" />
    <topicref href="QuickGuide.dita" locktitle="yes" />
       <topicmeta>
          <navtitle>Get Started Now</navtitle>
       </topicmeta>
    <topicref href="AboutHold.dita">
       <topicmeta>
          <audience audience="user" />
          <audience audience="administrator" />
       </topicmeta>
    </topicref>
 </map>
```

### Creating a basic hierarchy

Up to this point, you have created a flat, one-level structure for your map. By nesting topic references, you create multiple heading levels in your deliverable. Nesting <topicref> elements sets up the sequence and hierarchy of topics in tables of contents and creates a navigation tree or site index for online output. In addition to nesting <topicref> elements, you can also nest maps in maps. Maps can be referenced with either a <topicref> or <mapref> element.

In this exercise, you learn to nest <topicref> and <mapref> elements to create hierarchical relationships among your topics.

1. Open your DITA map from the previous exercise.

   So far, you have three topic references in a flat, one-level structure.

2. Insert <topicref> start and end tags before the AboutHold.dita <topicref> end tags and assign its href attribute to "HoldingACall.dita".

   Inserting the HoldingACall.dita topic reference between the AboutHold.dita <topicref> start and end tags makes the AboutHold.dita topic the parent of HoldingACall.dita. When you output the map, the AboutHold.dita topic becomes a first-level heading and the HoldingACall.dita becomes a second-level heading. Notice in the example that the two </topicref> element end tags are next to each other. Two topic reference end tags next to each other close both the child topic reference container and its parent topic reference container. When you add the next topic in the map, the topic reference starts at the first level of hierarchy again.

```
<map id="ComstarUserGuide" xml:lang="en-us">
   <title>Comstar User Guide</title>
   <topicmeta>
      <copyright>
         <copyryear year="2011" />
         <copyrholder>Comstar Phones</copyrholder>
      </copyright>
   </topicmeta>
   <topicref href="ComstarOverview.dita"/>
   <topicref href="QuickGuide.dita" locktitle="yes">
      <topicmeta>
```

```
         <navtitle>Get Started Now</navtitle>
      </topicmeta>
   </topicref>
   <topicref href="AboutHold.dita" navtitle="Hold">
      <topicmeta>
         <audience type="user"/>
         <audience type="administrator"/>
      </topicmeta>
      <topicref href="HoldingACall.dita">
      </topicref>
   </topicref>
</map>
```

3. Insert additional topic references as shown to create more parent and child relationships.

   Remember to close child topic reference element containers with end tags before closing the parent topic reference elements. Nesting the topic references creates your hierarchy. You can continue to insert topic references at any level. However, it is better not to use more than three levels of topic references or the hierarchy may confuse the reader.

```
<map id="ComstarUserGuide" xml:lang="en-us">
   ⋮
   <topicref href="AboutHold.dita" navtitle="Hold">
      <topicmeta>
         <audience type="user"/>
         <audience type="administrator"/>
      </topicmeta>
      <topicref href="HoldingACall.dita">
      </topicref>
   </topicref>
   <topicref href="AboutTransfer.dita">
      <topicref href="TransferringACall.dita"/>
   </topicref>
   <topicref href="AboutForward.dita">
      <topicref href="ForwardingACall.dita"/>
   </topicref>
   <topicref href="AboutConferenceCalls.dita">
      <topicref href="PlacingACall.dita"/>
      <topicref href="LeavingAConferenceCallTemporarily.dita"/>
      <topicref href="ReenteringAConferenceCall.dita"/>
      <topicref
         href="ConsultingPrivatelyOnTheConferenceCall.dita/>
      <topicref href="ReenteringACallWithAllPeople.dita"/>
   </topicref>
   ⋮
</map>
```

4. Insert a map reference to add an entire submap to your high-level map.

   You might use a nested map to include content that stands alone in another publication. Collecting topics into small sub-maps can also help you group content for reuse. In the example, the Accessories section of the Phone Guide is organized into its own map. Note that the Accessories ditamap is not in the same folder as the rest of the topic references.

```
<map id="ComstarUserGuide" xml:lang="en-us">
   ⋮
   <topicref href="AboutConferenceCalls.dita">
      <topicref href="PlacingACall.dita"/>
      <topicref href="LeavingAConferenceCallTemporarily.dita"/>
      <topicref href="ReenteringAConferenceCall.dita"/>
      <topicref
         href="ConsultingPrivatelyOnTheConferenceCall.dita/>
      <topicref href="ReenteringACallWithAllPeople.dita"/>
   </topicref>
   <mapref href="../Components/Accessories.ditamap"/>
   ⋮
</map>
```

5. Save your work in the ComstarUserGuide.ditamap file.

#### ComstarUserGuide.ditamap

The following example shows the full map you have created in the ComstarUserGuide.ditamap file. The conference call section shows how to create multiple child topics.

```
<map id="ComstarUserGuide" xml:lang="en-us">
   <title>Comstar User Guide</title>
   <topicmeta>
      <copyright>
         <copyryear year="2011"/>
         <copyrholder>Comstar Phones</copyrholder>
      </copyright>
   </topicmeta>
   <topicref href="ComstarOverview.dita"/>
   <topicref href="QuickGuide.dita" locktitle="yes">
      <topicmeta>
         <navtitle>Get Started Now</navtitle>
      </topicmeta>
   </topicref>
   <topicref href="AboutHold.dita" navtitle="Hold">
      <topicmeta>
         <audience type="user"/>
         <audience type="administrator"/>
      </topicmeta>
      <topicref href="HoldingACall.dita">
      </topicref>
   </topicref>
   <topicref href="AboutTransfer.dita">
      <topicref href="TransferringACall.dita"/>
   </topicref>
   <topicref href="AboutForward.dita">
      <topicref href="ForwardingACall.dita"/>
   </topicref>
   <topicref href="AboutConferenceCalls.dita">
      <topicref href="PlacingACall.dita"/>
      <topicref href="LeavingAConferenceCallTemporarily.dita"/>
      <topicref href="ReenteringAConferenceCall.dita"/>
```

```
      <topicref
         href="ConsultingPrivatelyOnTheConferenceCall.dita"/>
      <topicref href="ReenteringACallWithAllPeople.dita"/>
   </topicref>
   <mapref href="../Components/Accessories.ditamap"/>
</map>
```

## Map elements

You can only use map elements in a DITA map. You cannot use the elements in topics or other DITA files. The map elements that you regularly use when creating a map are listed here. For more information on map elements, see the *OASIS Darwin Information Typing Architecture (DITA) Version 1.2 (OASIS Standard, 1 December 2010).*

### <topicref> topic reference

Use the <topicref> element to create a pointer to a single DITA topic. Use multiple <topicref> elements to point to multiple topics to build your deliverable. Nesting the <topicref> elements in one another creates a hierarchical structure for your readers. You can also use this hierarchy to represent your table of contents, site map, and online navigation. The topic reference *@href* attribute is the most important part of the <topicref> element. It points to the path and file name for the DITA topic or external information you reference.

```
<map>
   <topicref href="PUB$Overview.dita"/>
   <topicref href="PlanningAProject.dita"/>
   <topicref href="UsingTheDependenciesCalculator.dita"/>
   <topicref href="EstimatingProjectHours.dita"/>
   <topicref href="TrackingAProject.dita"/>
   <topicref href="EnteringWeeklyHours.dita"/>
   <topicref href="GeneratingProjectStatusReports.dita"/>
</map>
```

### <topichead> topic heading

Use the <topichead> element to add a title to your DITA map that is not used in any topic titles. For example, use the <topichead> element if you want to provide a title, such as "Section 3: Project Management," for a section or part that contains multiple topic references. Use the *@navtitle* attribute to enter the title text. Keep in mind you will need to translate the content in the *@navtitle* attribute if you produce deliverables for different languages. You may need to create a transform to put attribute values into translatable element containers.

```
<map>
   <topicref href="PUB$Overview.dita"/>
   <topichead navtitle="ProjectPlanning" locktitle="yes">
      <topicref href="PlanningAProject.dita"/>
      <topicref href="UsingTheDependenciesCalculator.dita"/>
```

```
      <topicref href="EstimatingProjectHours.dita"/>
   </topichead>
   <topichead navtitle="ProjectTracking" locktitle="yes">
      <topicref href="TrackingAProject.dita"/>
      <topicref href="EnteringWeeklyHours.dita"/>
      <topicref href="GeneratingProjectStatusReports.dita"/>
   </topichead>
</map>
```

### <topicgroup> topic group

Use the <topicgroup> element to create collections of topic references that are not already related by the hierarchy in the map. You can apply inheritable attributes to <topicgroup> elements. For example, you can specify that a large group of topics should be output only for an internal audience. Or, you can remove all the parent/child links among a set of topics for a particular deliverable. If you apply an attribute to a group of topic references between <topicgroup> start and end tags, all of the topic references also gain this attribute value. You learn about inheritable attributes in Understanding DITA Map Attributes on page 134.

This example illustrates the use of topic groups in a DITA map. The first group indicates that the included topics are appropriate for the marketing and project manager audiences, while the second group is appropriate for project managers and writers.

```
<map>
   <topicref href="PUB$Overview.dita"/>
   <topichead navtitle="ProjectPlanning" locktitle="yes">
      <topicgroup audience="marketing pm">
         <topicref href="PlanningAProject.dita"/>
         <topicref href="UsingTheDependenciesCalculator.dita"/>
         <topicref href="EstimatingProjectHours.dita"/>
      </topicgroup>
   </topichead>
   <topichead navtitle="ProjectTracking" locktitle="yes">
      <topicgroup audience="pm writers">
         <topicref href="TrackingAProject.dita"/>
         <topicref href="EnteringWeeklyHours.dita"/>
         <topicref href="GeneratingProjectStatusReports.dita"/>
     </topicgroup>
  </topichead>
</map>
```

### <topicmeta> topic metadata

Use the <topicmeta> element to apply topic metadata at the map level. The <topicmeta> element allows you to include alternative text for links, short descriptions that you want to use specifically for an output, author information, keywords, and more. If you apply topic metadata at the map level, it overrides any metadata that authors set in the topics.

This example illustrates the use of metadata in a DITA map. You can use the keywords to add to your search metadata.

```
<map>
   <topicref href="PUB$Overview.dita">
      <topicmeta>
         <navtitle>About PUB$ Estimator</navtitle>
         <keywords>
            <keyword>overview</keyword>
            <keyword>PUB$Estimator</keyword>
         </keywords>
      </topicmeta>
   ⋮
</map>
```

### <mapref> map reference

Use the <mapref> element to create a pointer to a DITA map. The map reference *@href* attribute is the most important part of the <mapref> element. It points to the path and file name for the DITA map you reference. If the child map referenced with the <mapref> element has a relationship table, that table will be added to the parent map.

```
<map>
   <topicref href="PUB$Overview.dita"/>
   <topichead navtitle="ProjectPlanning" locktitle="yes">
      <topicref href="PlanningAProject.dita"/>
      <topicref href="UsingTheDependenciesCalculator.dita"/>
      <topicref href="EstimatingProjectHours.dita"/>
   </topichead>
   <topichead navtitle="ProjectTracking" locktitle="yes">
      <topicref href="TrackingAProject.dita"/>
      <topicref href="EnteringWeeklyHours.dita"/>
      <topicref href="GeneratingProjectStatusReports.dita"/>
   </topichead>
   <mapref href="ProjectWrapUps.ditamap"/>
</map>
```

### Map review questions

What file extension is used for map files?

- **a.** *.map
- **b.** *.dita
- **c.** *.ditamap
- **d.** *.mapref

A topic can be used multiple times in the same map.

- True
- False

How do you establish topic hierarchy in a DITA map? Select all that apply.

- **a.** Use <mapref> elements to reference entire submaps.
- **b.** Nest <topicref> elements within other <topicref> elements.
- **c.** Nest <topicref> elements within <topicgroup> elements.
- **d.** Use <section> elements within the map file.

What's wrong with this code?

```
<map>
   <topicref href="QuickGuide.dita" locktitle="yes"/>
      <topicmeta>
      <audience type="user administrator"/>
      <keywords>
         <keyword>quick reference</keyword>
      </keywords>
   <topicref href="Overview.dita">
      <topicref href="Definitions.dita"/>
      <topicref href="Prerequisites.dita"/>
   </topicref>
</map>
```

- **a.** There needs to be two audience tags to define the two audiences.
- **b.** The QuickGuide.dita topic reference element is not closed properly.
- **c.** You cannot use a *@locktitle* attribute without a corresponding *@navtitle* attribute.
- **d.** The Overview.dita topic reference element is not closed properly.

What element would you use to embed a submap into your map?

When might you define topic metadata within a map rather than within a topic? Select all that apply.

- **a.** When metadata may differ from map to map
- **b.** When the same metadata will apply to multiple topics
- **c.** When you want to override the metadata within a topic
- **d.** When you are defining metadata keywords reserved for map use only

Match each element or attribute to its purpose.

| <navtitle> | Overrides default processing so that your alternative title is always used in the table of contents or navigation pane. |
|---|---|
| *@navtitle* | Provides an alternative title for navigation in the table of contents or navigation pane. |
| *@locktitle* | Assists authors in keeping track of their topic titles. |
| <title> | Used to create a title page for your print output of add a window name of your online output. |

Both <copyryear> and <copyrholder> are required when you include <copyright> in a map's metadata.

- True
- False

# SECTION E

# Understanding DITA Map Attributes

Even though maps provide the structure for your deliverables, map attributes add production functionality to the maps. The most important attribute in a DITA map is the required *@href* attribute. You've already been using this attribute both in topics (in <related-links> and <xref> elements) and in maps (in <topicref> and <mapref> elements) to define the file path and file name of the topic you are referencing. Other DITA map attributes facilitate dynamically linking topics and setting processing options and formatting rules.

This section introduces identification and processing attributes that you might assign to a topic or map reference within a DITA map:

- Use the *@format* attribute to indicate the file type you are referencing in your map. You may want to reference files other than DITA topics or maps in your map, such as PDFs, text files, XML files, or web pages.
- Use the *@scope* attribute to indicate the location of your source topics relative to the DITA map. By setting this attribute, you indicate whether a topic reference is a part of the immediate information set or if it points to an external topic.
- Use the *@type* attribute to specify the information type of each topic reference. This attribute allows you to specify whether a topic reference is a concept, task, reference, or topic.
- Use processing attributes to indicate whether a topic reference and its child topic references should be included in a particular output, such as a table of contents or print deliverable.

Although these attributes are not required and the default values apply in most situations, consider using them as a matter of habit in your coding for consistency. Having these attributes on each reference helps ensure that you remember to apply the appropriate values in situations where the defaults do not apply.

**Attribute inheritance**
Because maps create a hierarchical structure, they establish parent/child relationships among topics. If you add an attribute to a parent topic reference, all child topics have the same attribute and value, a relationship referred to as

inheritance. You can override the inheritance by applying a different value to the child topic reference. However, in general, you should avoid using processing attributes on child topics because they make your content less likely to be reused.

For example, if you assign a topic reference the *@toc* attribute value "no", the table of contents will not include that topic reference and all of its child references. However, if you set one of the child topic references to the *@toc* attribute value "yes", the table of contents will include that child topic. You can use inheritance to create different print and HTML output using the same DITA maps. You can exclude topics from the PDF output by setting the *@print* attribute value to "no".

The inheritable attributes you can use in a DITA map include *@linking*, *@print*, *@toc*, *@audience*, *@product*, *@platform*, *@importance*, *@otherprops*, *@rev*, *@type*, *@locktitle*, *@scope*, and *@format*.

# LESSON 9

## Format Attribute

Use the *@format* attribute to indicate the file type you are referencing in your map. You may want to reference other files than DITA topics or maps in your map, such as PDFs, text files, XML files, or web pages. Because a map allows you to reference different kinds of content, you need to indicate the format of what you are referencing by using the *@format* attribute. The default value for a topic reference's *@format* attribute is "dita", and for a map reference, it is "ditamap". Other possible formats include "html", "pdf", "txt", "zip", or any other resource you may reference in your deliverable.

If you assign the *@format* attribute the value “dita”, it instructs your processor to use DITA processing rules. If the topic reference points to a different file type, then the DITA processing engine will not try to process the file referenced. Setting *@format* to "pdf", for example, causes the PDF simply to be copied into the output directory with a link to it. Your processor will not attempt to process the PDF using DITA processing rules. Any non-DITA topic reference will open in a separate window or application

In this lesson, you learn to apply the *@format* attribute to your topic and map references. You should use this attribute for each topic reference to provide consistency in your output.

**Adding the format attribute**
In this lesson, you learn to

- add the *@format* attribute to <topicref> and <mapref> elements
- apply *@format* attribute values, such as "dita" and "html"

1. Open the DITA map you created at the end of DITA Map Structure on page 118.

```
<map id="ComstarUserGuide" xml:lang="en-us">
   <title>Comstar User Guide</title>
   <topicmeta>
      <copyright>
         <copyryear year="2011"/>
         <copyrholder>Comstar Phones</copyrholder>
      </copyright>
   </topicmeta>
   <topicref href="ComstarOverview.dita"/>
   <topicref href="QuickGuide.dita" locktitle="yes">
      <topicmeta>
```

```
         <navtitle>Get Started Now</navtitle>
      </topicmeta>
   </topicref>
   <topicref href="AboutHold.dita" navtitle="Hold">
      <topicmeta>
         <audience type="user"/>
         <audience type="administrator"/>
      </topicmeta>
      <topicref href="HoldingACall.dita">
      </topicref>
   </topicref>
   <topicref href="AboutTransfer.dita">
      <topicref href="TransferringACall.dita"/>
   </topicref>
   <topicref href="AboutForward.dita">
      <topicref href="ForwardingACall.dita"/>
   </topicref>
   <topicref href="AboutConferenceCalls.dita">
      <topicref href="PlacingACall.dita"/>
      <topicref href="LeavingAConferenceCallTemporarily.dita"/>
      <topicref href="ReenteringAConferenceCall.dita"/>
      <topicref
         href="ConsultingPrivatelyOnTheConferenceCall.dita"/>
      <topicref href="ReenteringACallWithAllPeople.dita"/>
   </topicref>
   <mapref href="../Components/Accessories.ditamap"/>
</map>
```

2. Add the *@format* attribute to your topic references, and set the value to "dita".

   Because all your topic references so far are DITA topics, it is unnecessary to explicitly assign the topic reference the format attribute. However, for consistency, include the *@format* attribute for each topic reference whether it is DITA or not.

```
<map id="ComstarUserGuide" xml:lang="en-us">
   ⋮
   <topicref href="ComstarOverview.dita" format="dita"/>
   <topicref href="QuickGuide.dita" locktitle="yes" format="dita">
      ⋮
   </topicref>
   <topicref href="AboutHold.dita" navtitle="Hold" format="dita">
      ⋮
      <topicref href="HoldingACall.dita" format="dita">
      </topicref>
   </topicref>
   <topicref href="AboutTransfer.dita" format="dita">
      <topicref href="TransferringACall.dita" format="dita"/>
   </topicref>
   <topicref href="AboutForward.dita" format="dita">
      <topicref href="ForwardingACall.dita" format="dita"/>
   </topicref>
   <topicref href="AboutConferenceCalls.dita" format="dita">
      <topicref href="PlacingACall.dita" format="dita"/>
      <topicref href="LeavingAConferenceCallTemporarily.dita"
         format="dita"/>
      <topicref href="ReenteringAConferenceCall.dita"
         format="dita"/>
```

```
        <topicref
           href="ConsultingPrivatelyOnTheConferenceCall.dita"
           format="dita"/>
        <topicref href="ReenteringACallWithAllPeople.dita"
           format="dita"/>
     </topicref>
     <mapref href="../Components/Accessories.ditamap"/>
  </map>
```

3. Add the *@format* attribute to your <mapref> element and set the value to "ditamap".

```
<map id="ComstarUserGuide" xml:lang="en-us">
   ⋮
   <mapref href="../Components/Accessories.ditamap"
      format="ditamap"/>
</map>
```

4. After the last topic reference in the map add a topic reference to http://www.comtech-serv.com/Comstar/ and assign the *@format* attribute a value of "html".

   Because the topic reference is an HTML web page, processing the topic through the DITA processing pipeline would cause errors. Indicating that the topic reference *@format* is "html" prevents processing errors because the processor doesn't try to process the target file as a DITA topic.

```
<map id="ComstarUserGuide" xml:lang="en-us">
   ⋮
   <topicref href="http://www.comtech-serv.com/Comstar/"
      format="html"/>
   <mapref href="../Components/Accessories.ditamap"
      format="ditamap"/>
</map>
```

5. After the web page topic reference in the map add a topic reference to ../../ComstarPricing.pdf and assign the *@format* attribute to a value to "pdf".

   The expected behavior of *@format*="pdf" is that a PDF opens in a new window. There are limitations and variability among rendering engines in the implementation of this feature.

```
<map id="ComstarUserGuide" xml:lang="en-us">
   ⋮
   <topicref href="http://www.comtech-serv.com/Comstar/"
      format="html"/>
   <topicref href="../../ComstarPricing.pdf" format="pdf"/>
   <mapref href="../Components/Accessories.ditamap"
      format="ditamap"/>
</map>
```

6. Save your work in the ComstarUserGuide.ditamap file.

### ComstarUserGuide.ditamap

The following example shows what your ComstarUserGuide.ditamap file should look like with the *@format* attribute defined for each <topicref> and <mapref> element. Most of the format values are "dita", but the example also indicates other topic references where you must use the *@format* attribute.

```
<map id="ComstarUserGuide" xml:lang="en-us">
   <title>Comstar User Guide</title>
   <topicmeta>
      <copyright>
         <copyryear year="2011"/>
         <copyrholder>Comstar Phones</copyrholder>
      </copyright>
   </topicmeta>
   <topicref href="ComstarOverview.dita" format="dita"/>
   <topicref href="QuickGuide.dita" locktitle="yes" format="dita">
      <topicmeta>
         <navtitle>Get Started Now</navtitle>
      </topicmeta>
   </topicref>
   <topicref href="AboutHold.dita" navtitle="Hold" format="dita">
      <topicmeta>
         <audience type="user"/>
         <audience type="administrator"/>
      </topicmeta>
      <topicref href="HoldingACall.dita" format="dita">
      </topicref>
   </topicref>
   <topicref href="AboutTransfer.dita" format="dita">
      <topicref href="TransferringACall.dita" format="dita"/>
   </topicref>
   <topicref href="AboutForward.dita" format="dita">
      <topicref href="ForwardingACall.dita" format="dita"/>
   </topicref>
   <topicref href="AboutConferenceCalls.dita" format="dita">
      <topicref href="PlacingACall.dita" format="dita"/>
      <topicref href="LeavingAConferenceCallTemporarily.dita"
         format="dita"/>
      <topicref href="ReenteringAConferenceCall.dita"
         format="dita"/>
      <topicref
         href="ConsultingPrivatelyOnTheConferenceCall.dita"
         format="dita"/>
      <topicref href="ReenteringACallWithAllPeople.dita"
         format="dita"/>
   </topicref>
   <topicref href="http://www.comtech-serv.com/Comstar/"
      format="html"/>
   <topicref href="../../ComstarPricing.pdf" format="pdf"/>
   <mapref href="../Components/Accessories.ditamap"
      format="ditamap" />
</map>
```

**Format attribute review questions**

What is the purpose of the *@format* attribute?

**a.** To declare the stylesheet to use when formatting the topic.
**b.** To prevent the processor from sending a non-DITA topic through DITA processing.
**c.** To help authors keep track of the file types used in their maps.
**d.** To group similar topic types in related link lists.

What is the default value for the format attribute of a topic reference?

The format attribute values are limited to "dita", "ditamap", "pdf", and "html".

- True
- False

# LESSON 10

## Scope Attribute

Use the *@scope* attribute to indicate the location of your source topics relative to the DITA map. By setting this attribute, you indicate whether a topic reference is a part of the immediate information set or if it points to an external topic.

In most cases, you want to set up your authoring environment so that maps point to topics in the same directory and subdirectories as the map. You should assign topic references the value of "local" to point to a file in the same directory or subdirectories. Any topics you process using this attribute value will output a file into your output directory. For any topic references you include in your map that you don't want the processor to copy to the output directory, set the *@scope* attribute to "peer". The third *@scope* attribute value option is "external". Use the external value to point to topics or resources outside the immediate information set. The processor will not copy the external topic reference files to the output directory.

Figure 5 illustrates a basic folder structure and topic files representing each of the values you might use in the *@scope* attribute.

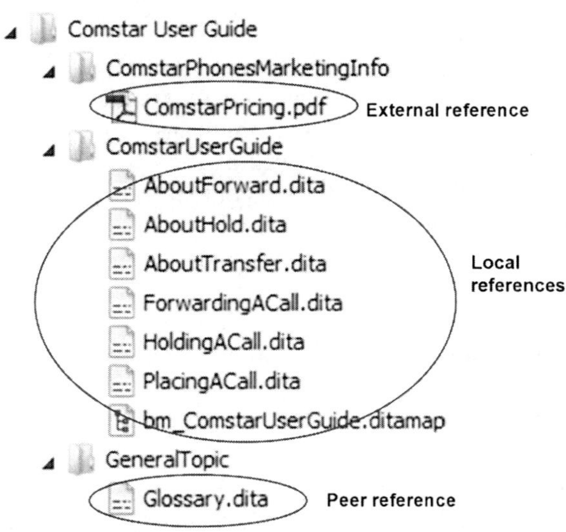


**Figure 5: Folder structure of local, peer, and external references**

**Local**

Local topic references point to topics that are part of the immediate information set, meaning the topic is in the same directory or subdirectory as the DITA map. When you set the *@scope* attribute to "local", the processor builds an output file and copies the file into your output directory as part of the final deliverable. Most topic references in your DITA maps will use the local *@scope* attribute. Therefore, the default value for the *@scope* attribute is "local".

**Peer**

To reference topics that are in a larger information set but should not be individually copied to the output directory, set the *@scope* attribute value to "peer". You might use "peer" if you have a folder for boilerplate information, such as a company glossary or legal pages. The *@href* value for a peer reference should be a relative path to another DITA topic depending on the map location. For a relative path in a file system, the *@href* value should look like ../common/topic.dita. The ../ common/ part of the path to the file tells the processor to back out of the directory where the map is located and go into the common folder to reference the topic.

Use the "peer" value when referencing a topic from a larger information set that you want to include in the navigation and linking as if it were part of your immediate information set. Keep in mind that when you assign a topic reference the "peer" value, your processor will generate an output topic but it will not copy it to the output directory. Setting the *@scope* attribute value to "peer" ensures you don't create duplicate copies of the output file each time you produce your deliverable. This practice helps to keep your file system or repository uncluttered with commonly used topics and boilerplate information.

**External**

For any topics you reference that are outside your information set, set the topic reference *@scope* attribute value to "external". In your map, any external topic reference should be an absolute URL or URI. An absolute path means you should include the full path and file name in the *@href* value. By setting the *@scope* to "external", the topic you are referencing will open in its own content frame or application and not appear to be part of your information set.

You should not include topic references as children of an external topic reference in the map hierarchy. Normally, the processor includes links from parent topic references to child topic references in the hierarchy using the title and short description. The links cannot be added to an external topic during processing.

**Adding the scope attribute**

In this lesson, you learn to

- add the *@scope* attribute to <topicref> elements
- identify when to use the *@scope* attribute values "local", "peer", and "external"
- add short descriptions in the metadata in the map topics

1. Open your DITA map from Format Attribute on page 136.

```
<map id="ComstarUserGuide" xml:lang="en-us">
   <title>Comstar User Guide</title>
   <topicmeta>
      <copyright>
         <copyryear year="2011"/>
         <copyrholder>Comstar Phones</copyrholder>
      </copyright>
   </topicmeta>
   <topicref href="ComstarOverview.dita" format="dita"/>
   <topicref href="QuickGuide.dita" locktitle="yes" format="dita">
      <topicmeta>
         <navtitle>Get Started Now</navtitle>
      </topicmeta>
   </topicref>
   <topicref href="AboutHold.dita" navtitle="Hold" format="dita">
      <topicmeta>
         <audience type="user"/>
         <audience type="administrator"/>
      </topicmeta>
      <topicref href="HoldingACall.dita" format="dita">
      </topicref>
   </topicref>
   <topicref href="AboutTransfer.dita" format="dita">
      <topicref href="TransferringACall.dita" format="dita"/>
   </topicref>
   <topicref href="AboutForward.dita" format="dita">
      <topicref href="ForwardingACall.dita" format="dita"/>
   </topicref>
   <topicref href="AboutConferenceCalls.dita" format="dita">
      <topicref href="PlacingACall.dita" format="dita"/>
      <topicref href="LeavingAConferenceCallTemporarily.dita"
         format="dita"/>
      <topicref href="ReenteringAConferenceCall.dita"
         format="dita"/>
      <topicref
         href="ConsultingPrivatelyOnTheConferenceCall.dita"
         format="dita"/>
      <topicref href="ReenteringACallWithAllPeople.dita"
         format="dita"/>
   </topicref>
   <topicref href="http://www.comtech-serv.com/Comstar/"
      format="html"/>
   <topicref href="../../ComstarPricing.pdf" format="pdf"/>
   <mapref href="../Components/Accessories.ditamap"
      format="ditamap" />
</map>
```

2. Assign a *@scope* attribute of "local" to all the topic references in the map that point to DITA files.

   The DITA files in this map are all part of the current set of content and are located in the same directory as the map itself.

```
<map id="ComstarUserGuide" xml:lang="en-us">
   ⋮
   <topicref href="ComstarOverview.dita" format="dita"
      scope="local"/>
   <topicref href="QuickGuide.dita" locktitle="yes" format="dita"
```

```
      scope="local">
      ⋮
   </topicref>
   <topicref href="AboutHold.dita" navtitle="Hold" format="dita"
      scope="local">
      ⋮
      <topicref href="HoldingACall.dita" format="dita"
         scope="local">
      </topicref>
   </topicref>
   <topicref href="AboutTransfer.dita" format="dita"
      scope="local">
      <topicref href="TransferringACall.dita" format="dita"
         scope="local"/>
   </topicref>
   <topicref href="AboutForward.dita" format="dita"
      scope="local">
      <topicref href="ForwardingACall.dita" format="dita"
         scope="local"/>
   </topicref>
   <topicref href="AboutConferenceCalls.dita" format="dita"
      scope="local">
      <topicref href="PlacingACall.dita" format="dita"
         scope="local"/>
      <topicref href="LeavingAConferenceCallTemporarily.dita"
          format="dita" scope="local"/>
      <topicref href="ReenteringAConferenceCall.dita"
         format="dita" scope="local"/>
      <topicref
         href="ConsultingPrivatelyOnTheConferenceCall.dita"
            format="dita" scope="local"/>
      <topicref href="ReenteringACallWithAllPeople.dita"
         format="dita" scope="local"/>
   </topicref>
   ⋮
</map>
```

3. Assign a *@scope* attribute of "peer" to the <mapref> element.

   Accessories.ditamap is part of a larger information set, common to many different product lines, and is stored outside the directory structure of the local files. Set its scope attribute to "peer" so you don't create duplicate copies of the output of this submap every time you produce your deliverable.

```
<map id="ComstarUserGuide">
   ⋮
   <mapref href="../Components/Accessories.ditamap"
      format="ditamap" scope="peer"/>
</map>
```

4. Assign a *@scope* attribute of "external" to your web page and PDF file.

   Both the web page and PDF file are outside of the main content for this map. With a scope attribute of "external", each will open in its own window.

```
<map id="ComstarUserGuide" xml:lang="en-us">
   ⋮
   <topicref href="http://www.comtech-serv.com/Comstar/"
      format="html" scope="external"/>
```

```
   <topicref href="../../ComstarPricing.pdf" format="pdf"
      scope="external"/>
   ⋮
</map>
```

5. Add metadata for the external references in your map.

   Since external topic references are not DITA or XML files, they are unlikely to have a title and short description. Use <topicmeta> to define these elements to assist your users in searching for information and determining if the information in the references is relevant to their needs.

   a. Add <topicmeta> start and end tags for each external topic reference.

      Remember that each <topicref> must be changed from an empty element to a container element as part of this step.

```
<map id="ComstarUserGuide" xml:lang="en-us">
   ⋮
   <topicref href="http://www.comtech-serv.com/Comstar/"
      format="html" scope="external">
      <topicmeta>
      </topicmeta>
   </topicref>
   <topicref href="../../ComstarPricing.pdf" format="pdf"
      scope="external">
      <topicmeta>
      </topicmeta>
   </topicref>
   ⋮
</map>
```

   b. Define a <navtitle> for the web site and set the locktitle attribute value on the <topicref> to "yes".

      If you don't provide the <navtitle> element and *@locktitle* attribute, some processors may use the entire value of the *@href* as the title in the table of contents or navigation.

```
<map id="ComstarUserGuide" xml:lang="en-us">
   ⋮
   <topicref href="http://www.comtech-serv.com/Comstar/"
      format="html" scope="external" locktitle="yes">
      <topicmeta>
         <navtitle>Comtech Services: Comstar Phone
            Information</navtitle>
      </topicmeta>
   </topicref>
   <topicref href="../../ComstarPricing.pdf" format="pdf"
      scope="external">
     <topicmeta>
      </topicmeta>
   </topicref>
   ⋮
</map>
```

   c. Define short descriptions for both the web site and the PDF.

The <shortdesc> element applied in the <topicmeta> element pertains to the referenced topic. Often used for external references, the <shortdesc> element provides an opportunity to add a short description to DITA and non-DITA resources. The content of the <shortdesc> element may be used as hover text in navigation or search-return text, or it may override the <shortdesc> defined in the topic. Including the <shortdesc> metadata element for external references allows your users to search and retrieve external references more easily.

```
<map id="ComstarUserGuide" xml:lang="en-us">
   ⋮
   <topicref href="http://www.comtech-serv.com/Comstar/"
      format="html" scope="external" locktitle="yes">
      <topicmeta>
         <navtitle>Comtech Services: Comstar Phone
            Information</navtitle>
         <shortdesc>Online ordering for your choice of any
            Comstar phones.</shortdesc>
      </topicmeta>
   </topicref>
   <topicref href="../../ComstarPricing.pdf" format="pdf"
      scope="external">
      <topicmeta>
         <shortdesc>Comstar phones provide a variety of
         different plans you can purchase to use with your
         phone.</shortdesc>
      </topicmeta>
   </topicref>
   ⋮
</map>
```

**6.** Save your work in the ComstarUserGuide.ditamap file.

### ComstarUserGuide.ditamap

The following example shows the complete ComstarUserGuide.ditamap using various *@scope* attributes and values and additional information to enhance the *@scope* attribute.

```
<map id="ComstarUserGuide" xml:lang="en-us">
   <title>Comstar User Guide</title>
   <topicmeta>
      <copyright>
         <copyryear year="2011"/>
         <copyrholder>Comstar Phones</copyrholder>
      </copyright>
   </topicmeta>
   <topicref href="ComstarOverview.dita" format="dita"
      scope="local"/>
   <topicref href="QuickGuide.dita" locktitle="yes" format="dita"
      scope="local">
      <topicmeta>
         <navtitle>Get Started Now</navtitle>
```

```
      </topicmeta>
   </topicref>
   <topicref href="AboutHold.dita" navtitle="Hold" format="dita"
      scope="local">
      <topicmeta>
         <audience type="user"/>
         <audience type="administrator"/>
      </topicmeta>
      <topicref href="HoldingACall.dita" format="dita"
         scope="local">
      </topicref>
   </topicref>
   <topicref href="AboutTransfer.dita" format="dita"
      scope="local">
      <topicref href="TransferringACall.dita" format="dita"
         scope="local"/>
   </topicref>
   <topicref href="AboutForward.dita" format="dita"
      scope="local">
      <topicref href="ForwardingACall.dita" format="dita"
         scope="local"/>
   </topicref>
   <topicref href="AboutConferenceCalls.dita" format="dita"
      scope="local">
      <topicref href="PlacingACall.dita" format="dita"
         scope="local"/>
      <topicref href="LeavingAConferenceCallTemporarily.dita"
         format="dita" scope="local"/>
      <topicref href="ReenteringAConferenceCall.dita"
         format="dita" scope="local"/>
      <topicref
         href="ConsultingPrivatelyOnTheConferenceCall.dita"
         format="dita" scope="local"/>
      <topicref href="ReenteringACallWithAllPeople.dita"
         format="dita" scope="local"/>
   </topicref>
   <topicref href="http://www.comtech-serv.com/Comstar/"
      format="html" scope="external" locktitle="yes">
      <topicmeta>
         <navtitle>Comtech Services: Comstar Phone
            Information</navtitle>
         <shortdesc>Online ordering for your choice of any
            Comstar phones.</shortdesc>
      </topicmeta>
   </topicref>
   <topicref href="../../ComstarPricing.pdf" format="pdf"
      scope="external">
   <topicmeta>
         <shortdesc>Comstar phones provide a variety of
         different plans you can purchase to use with your
         phone.</shortdesc>
   </topicmeta>
   </topicref>
   <mapref href="../Components/Accessories.ditamap"
      format="ditamap" scope="peer"/>
</map>
```

**Scope attribute review questions**

Match the scope attribute to the situation in which you would use it.

| | |
|---|---|
| Local | The topic will open it its own content frame or application, separate from your information set. |
| Peer | The topic reference is in the same directory or subdirectory as the DITA map. |
| External | The topic reference is from a larger information set that you want to include in the navigation and linking as if it were part of your immediate information set. |

Which of the following is true?

- **a.** You should not include topic references as children of an external topic reference because links between the parent and children cannot be added to an external topic during processing.
- **b.** When including topic references as children of an external topic reference, make sure you define <navtitle> and <shortdesc> elements for the external topic reference.
- **c.** The <shortdesc> element is used only for external topic references and ignored for local or peer references.
- **d.** If a <navtitle> element is not provided for an external topic reference, the topic cannot appear in the table of contents or navigation.

What is the default value for the @*scope* attribute of a topic reference?

Setting the @*scope* attribute to "external" helps keep your file system or repository uncluttered with frequently used topics and boilerplate information.

- True
- False

# LESSON 11

## Type Attribute

Use the *@type* attribute to specify the information type of each topic reference. This attribute allows you to specify whether a topic reference is a concept, task, reference, or topic. In the case of non-DITA resources, the *@type* attribute is not validated and can be left blank. Consider using the type attribute when your file naming convention does not include an easy way to identify topic type from the file name. It provides a quick, easy way for authors to see the topic type without having to open each file.

**Adding the type attribute**

In this lesson, you learn to

- add the *@type* attribute to each <topicref> element
- assign values to the *@type* attribute, such as "concept", "reference", "task", or "topic"

1. Open your DITA map from Scope Attribute on page 141.

```
<map id="ComstarUserGuide" xml:lang="en-us">
   <title>Comstar User Guide</title>
   <topicmeta>
      <copyright>
         <copyryear year="2011"/>
         <copyrholder>Comstar Phones</copyrholder>
      </copyright>
   </topicmeta>
   <topicref href="ComstarOverview.dita" format="dita"
      scope="local"/>
   <topicref href="QuickGuide.dita" locktitle="yes" format="dita"
      scope="local">
      <topicmeta>
         <navtitle>Get Started Now</navtitle>
      </topicmeta>
   </topicref>
   <topicref href="AboutHold.dita" navtitle="Hold" format="dita"
      scope="local">
      <topicmeta>
         <audience type="user"/>
         <audience type="administrator"/>
      </topicmeta>
      <topicref href="HoldingACall.dita" format="dita"
         scope="local">
      </topicref>
   </topicref>
   <topicref href="AboutTransfer.dita" format="dita"
      scope="local">
      <topicref href="TransferringACall.dita" format="dita"
```

```
            scope="local"/>
      </topicref>
      <topicref href="AboutForward.dita" format="dita"
         scope="local">
         <topicref href="ForwardingACall.dita" format="dita"
            scope="local"/>
      </topicref>
      <topicref href="AboutConferenceCalls.dita" format="dita"
         scope="local">
         <topicref href="PlacingACall.dita" format="dita"
            scope="local"/>
         <topicref href="LeavingAConferenceCallTemporarily.dita"
            format="dita" scope="local"/>
         <topicref href="ReenteringAConferenceCall.dita"
            format="dita" scope="local"/>
         <topicref
            href="ConsultingPrivatelyOnTheConferenceCall.dita"
            format="dita" scope="local"/>
         <topicref href="ReenteringACallWithAllPeople.dita"
            format="dita" scope="local"/>
      </topicref>
      <topicref href="http://www.comtech-serv.com/Comstar/"
         format="html" scope="external" locktitle="yes">
         <topicmeta>
            <navtitle>Comtech Services: Comstar Phone
            Information</navtitle>
            <shortdesc>Online ordering for your choice of any
               Comstar phones.</shortdesc>
         </topicmeta>
      </topicref>
      <topicref href="../../ComstarPricing.pdf" format="pdf"
         scope="external">
         <topicmeta>
            <shortdesc>Comstar phones provide a variety of
            different plans you can purchase to use with your
            phone.</shortdesc>
         </topicmeta>
      </topicref>
      <mapref href="../Components/Accessories.ditamap"
         format="ditamap" scope="peer"/>
   </map>
```

2. Assign the *@type* attribute to each topic reference as shown in the example.

   Assigning the topic references a *@type* provides an easy way to determine the kind of information the topic contains when you cannot tell from the title of the topic alone.
3. Save your work in the ComstarUserGuide.ditamap file.

### ComstarUserGuide.ditamap

The example shows the map with the *@type* attribute assigned to all DITA topic references. Non-DITA references, such as the URL and PDF, do not need a topic type.

```
<map id="ComstarUserGuide" xml:lang="en-us">
   <title>Comstar User Guide</title>
   <topicmeta>
```

```
    <copyright>
       <copyryear year="2011"/>
       <copyrholder>Comstar Phones</copyrholder>
    </copyright>
 </topicmeta>
 <topicref href="ComstarOverview.dita" format="dita"
    scope="local"/>
 <topicref href="QuickGuide.dita" locktitle="yes" format="dita"
    scope="local" type="reference">
    <topicmeta>
       <navtitle>Get Started Now</navtitle>
    </topicmeta>
 </topicref>
 <topicref href="AboutHold.dita" navtitle="Hold" format="dita"
    scope="local" type="concept">
    <topicmeta>
       <audience type="user"/>
       <audience type="administrator"/>
    </topicmeta>
    <topicref href="HoldingACall.dita" format="dita"
       scope="local" type="task">
    </topicref>
 </topicref>
 <topicref href="AboutTransfer.dita" format="dita"
    scope="local" type="concept">
    <topicref href="TransferringACall.dita" format="dita"
       scope="local" type="task"/>
 </topicref>
 <topicref href="AboutForward.dita" format="dita"
    scope="local" type="concept">
    <topicref href="ForwardingACall.dita" format="dita"
       scope="local" type="task"/>
 </topicref>
 <topicref href="AboutConferenceCalls.dita" format="dita"
    scope="local" type="concept">
    <topicref href="PlacingACall.dita" format="dita"
       scope="local" type="task"/>
    <topicref href="LeavingAConferenceCallTemporarily.dita"
       format="dita"  scope="local" type="task"/>
    <topicref href="ReenteringAConferenceCall.dita"
       format="dita" scope="local" type="task"/>
    <topicref
       href="ConsultingPrivatelyOnTheConferenceCall.dita"
       format="dita" scope="local" type="task"/>
    <topicref href="ReenteringACallWithAllPeople.dita"
       format="dita"  scope="local" type="task"/>
 </topicref>
 <topicref href="http://www.comtech-serv.com/Comstar/"
    format="html" scope="external" locktitle="yes">
    <topicmeta>
       <navtitle>Comtech Services: Comstar Phone
          Information</navtitle>
       <shortdesc>Online ordering for your choice of any
          Comstar phones.
       </shortdesc>
    </topicmeta>
 </topicref>
 <topicref href="../../ComstarPricing.pdf" format="pdf"
    scope="external">
    <topicmeta>
       <shortdesc>Comstar phones provide a variety of
```

```
        different plans you can purchase to use with your
        phone.</shortdesc>
      </topicmeta>
   </topicref>
   <mapref href="../Components/Accessories.ditamap"
      format="ditamap" scope="peer"/>
</map>
```

**Type attribute review questions**

What is the purpose of the *@type* attribute in a <topicref> element?

- **a.** To prevent the processor from sending a non-DITA topic type through DITA processing.
- **b.** To indicate the type of output processing that should be used.
- **c.** To identify the information type of the topic.
- **d.** To create relationships among topics that are closely associated.

For non-DITA resources, you must declare the type attribute as "other" to indicate that it is not an information type associated with DITA.

- True
- False

# LESSON 12

## Processing Attributes

In the DITA map, each topic reference can include two processing attributes, *@toc* and *@print*. The purpose of each of these attributes is to omit a topic reference and its child topic references from a particular output, such as a table of contents or a print deliverable. Use these attributes to process your deliverable for a particular output condition. Using the *@toc* attribute customizes your table of contents or navigation for a specific audience or medium. Using the *@print* attribute adds or removes topics from PDF output.

Both *@toc* and *@print* have "yes" and "no" as the possible values. For each attribute, the default value is "yes". Use these attributes if you want to create both an online and a print version of your deliverables. If you set the print attribute to "no" on any topic reference, you indicate that the topic should not be included in the PDF version of the deliverable. The print attribute also has the value "printonly". Use this value to mark topics that appear only in a PDF.

In your DITA map hierarchy, you can use processing attributes on parent topic references to control the *@print* and *@toc* of the child topics. If you want to include one of the child topics in your table of contents or print output, you can use these same attributes to override the value it inherits from its parent topic. However, you should avoid using processing attributes on child topics because they make your content less likely to be reused.

This simple DITA map example illustrates the inheritance feature of the processing attributes and shows how to override the inherited values in child topics.

```
<topicref href="A.dita">
   <topicref href="B.dita" toc="no">
      <topicref href="C.dita">
         <topicref href="D.dita" toc="yes">
            <topicref href="E.dita" />
         </topicref>
      </topicref>
   </topicref>
</topicref>
```

When you create the output, the resulting table of contents will include the following topic references.

```
A.dita
   D.dita
      E.dita
```

B.dita is omitted because the *@toc* attribute is set to "no". C.dita inherits the "no" value from B.dita. D.dita then overrides the inherited value from B.dita and sets the *@toc* attribute back to "yes". E.dita inherits the value from D.dita.

**Adding processing attributes**
In this lesson, you learn to

- add the *@print* attribute
- add the *@toc* attribute

1. Open your DITA map from Type Attribute on page 149.

```
<map id="ComstarUserGuide" xml:lang="en-us">
   <title>Comstar User Guide</title>
   <topicmeta>
      <copyright>
         <copyryear year="2011"/>
         <copyrholder>Comstar Phones</copyrholder>
      </copyright>
   </topicmeta>
   <topicref href="ComstarOverview.dita" format="dita"
      scope="local"/>
   <topicref href="QuickGuide.dita" locktitle="yes" format="dita"
      scope="local" type="reference">
      <topicmeta>
         <navtitle>Get Started Now</navtitle>
      </topicmeta>
   </topicref>
   <topicref href="AboutHold.dita" navtitle="Hold" format="dita"
      scope="local" type="concept">
      <topicmeta>
         <audience type="user"/>
         <audience type="administrator"/>
      </topicmeta>
      <topicref href="HoldingACall.dita" format="dita"
         scope="local "type="task">
      </topicref>
   </topicref>
   <topicref href="AboutTransfer.dita" format="dita"
      scope="local" type="concept">
      <topicref href="TransferringACall.dita" format="dita"
         scope="local" type="task"/>
   </topicref>
   <topicref href="AboutForward.dita" format="dita"
      scope="local" type="concept">
      <topicref href="ForwardingACall.dita" format="dita"
         scope="local" type="task"/>
   </topicref>
   <topicref href="AboutConferenceCalls.dita" format="dita"
      scope="local" type="concept">
      <topicref href="PlacingACall.dita" format="dita"
```

```
            scope="local" type="task"/>
         <topicref href="LeavingAConferenceCallTemporarily.dita"
            format="dita" scope="local" type="task"/>
         <topicref href="ReenteringAConferenceCall.dita"
            format="dita" scope="local" type="task"/>
         <topicref
            href="ConsultingPrivatelyOnTheConferenceCall.dita"
            format="dita" scope="local" type="task"/>
         <topicref href="ReenteringACallWithAllPeople.dita"
            format="dita" scope="local" type="task"/>
      </topicref>
      <topicref href="http://www.comtech-serv.com/Comstar/"
         format="html" scope="external" locktitle="yes">
         <topicmeta>
            <navtitle>Comtech Services: Comstar Phone
               Information</navtitle>
            <shortdesc>Online ordering for your choice of any
               Comstar phones.</shortdesc>
         </topicmeta>
      </topicref>
      <topicref href="../../ComstarPricing.pdf" format="pdf"
         scope="external">
         <topicmeta>
            <shortdesc>Comstar phones provide a variety of
               different plans you can purchase to use with your
               phone.</shortdesc>
          </topicmeta>
      </topicref>
      <mapref href="../Components/Accessories.ditamap"
         format="ditamap" scope="peer"/>
   </map>
```

2. Add the *@print* attribute to your http://www.comtech-serv.com/Comstar/ topic reference and assign a value of "no".

   Because this topic reference is an external web site, you do not want to include the web page in your PDF or print output. By setting the *@print* attribute value to "no", you exclude the topic from your PDF.

```
<map id="ComstarUserGuide" xml:lang="en-us">
   ⋮
   <topicref href="http://www.comtech-serv.com/Comstar/"
      format="html" scope="external" locktitle="yes" print="no">
      <topicmeta>
         <navtitle>Comtech Services: Comstar Phone
            Information</navtitle>
         <shortdesc>Online ordering for your choice of any
            Comstar phones.</shortdesc>
      </topicmeta>
   </topicref>
   ⋮
</map>
```

3. Add the *@toc* attribute for the Accessories.ditamap map reference and set the value to "no".

   You may want to link to your reference topics only from inside the content of other topics. When you set the *@toc* attribute to "no" on the

Accessories.ditamap map reference, you remove the hyperlink or topic reference from the hierarchical navigation and table of contents on output.

```
<map id="ComstarUserGuide">
   ⋮
   <mapref href="../Components/Accessories.ditamap"
      format="ditamap" scope="peer" toc="no"/>
</map>
```

4. Save your work in the ComstarUserGuide.ditamap file.

### ComstarUserGuide.ditamap

This example shows what the full ComstarUserGuide.ditamap looks like with the processing attributes.

```
<map id="ComstarUserGuide" xml:lang="en-us">
   <title>Comstar User Guide</title>
   <topicmeta>
      <copyright>
         <copyryear year="2011"/>
         <copyrholder>Comstar Phones</copyrholder>
      </copyright>
   </topicmeta>
   <topicref href="ComstarOverview.dita" format="dita"
      scope="local"/>
   <topicref href="QuickGuide.dita" locktitle="yes" format="dita"
      scope="local" type="reference">
      <topicmeta>
         <navtitle>Get Started Now</navtitle>
      </topicmeta>
   </topicref>
   <topicref href="AboutHold.dita" navtitle="Hold" format="dita"
       scope="local" type="concept">
      <topicmeta>
         <audience type="user"/>
         <audience type="administrator"/>
      </topicmeta>
      <topicref href="HoldingACall.dita" format="dita"
         scope="local" type="task">
      </topicref>
   </topicref>
   <topicref href="AboutTransfer.dita" format="dita"
      scope="local" type="concept">
      <topicref href="TransferringACall.dita" format="dita"
         scope="local" type="task"/>
   </topicref>
   <topicref href="AboutForward.dita" format="dita"
      scope="local" type="concept">
      <topicref href="ForwardingACall.dita" format="dita"
         scope="local" type="task"/>
   </topicref>
   <topicref href="AboutConferenceCalls.dita" format="dita"
      scope="local" type="concept">
      <topicref href="PlacingACall.dita" format="dita"
         scope="local" type="task"/>
      <topicref href="LeavingAConferenceCallTemporarily.dita"
```

```
         format="dita" scope="local" type="task"/>
      <topicref href="ReenteringAConferenceCall.dita"
         format="dita" scope="local" type="task"/>
      <topicref
         href="ConsultingPrivatelyOnTheConferenceCall.dita"
         format="dita" scope="local" type="task"/>
      <topicref href="ReenteringACallWithAllPeople.dita"
         format="dita" scope="local" type="task"/>
   </topicref>
   <topicref href="http://www.comtech-serv.com/Comstar/"
      format="html" scope="external" locktitle="yes" print="no">
      <topicmeta>
         <navtitle>Comtech Services: Comstar Phone
            Information</navtitle>
         <shortdesc>Online ordering for your choice of any
            Comstar phones.</shortdesc>
      </topicmeta>
   </topicref>
   <topicref href="../../ComstarPricing.pdf" format="pdf"
      scope="external">
      <topicmeta>
         <shortdesc>Comstar phones provide a variety of
            different plans you can purchase to use with your
            phone.</shortdesc>
       </topicmeta>
   </topicref>
   <mapref href="../Components/Accessories.ditamap"
      format="ditamap" scope="peer" toc="no"/>
</map>
```

**Processing attributes review questions**

What are the two processing attributes?

Which of the following indicates that the topic reference will be included in the printed output? Select all that apply.

- **a.** <topicref href="topic.dita">
- **b.** <topicref href="topic.dita" print="yes">
- **c.** <topicref href="topic.dita" print="no">
- **d.** <topicref href="topic.dita" print="printonly">

Based on this code, the topic F.dita will be included in the print output.

```
<topicref href="A.dita">
   <topicref href="B.dita" toc="no">
      <topicref href="C.dita" print="no">
         <topicref href="D.dita" print="printonly">
            <topicref href="E.dita" toc="yes"/>
            <topicref href="F.dita"/>
         </topicref>
      </topicref>
   </topicref>
</topicref>
```

- True
- False

# SECTION F

# Understanding Map Linking

By creating parent and child relationships among the topic references in the hierarchy, you can easily create links between topics. When you nest one topic reference inside another, the nested topic reference is considered a child. When you process the output, you can automatically insert the titles and short descriptions of the child topics into the parent topic and hyperlink them for ease of navigation. The child topics, in turn, may include links back to the parent. You can control the direction of these links using the *@linking* attribute.

Figure 6 shows a parent topic with links automatically inserted for each child topic.

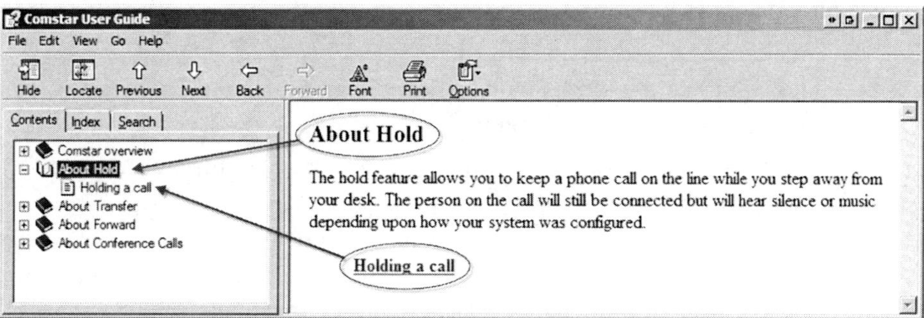


**Figure 6: Parent topic linking**

Figure 7 on page 160 shows that each child topic automatically includes a link back to the parent topic during processing.

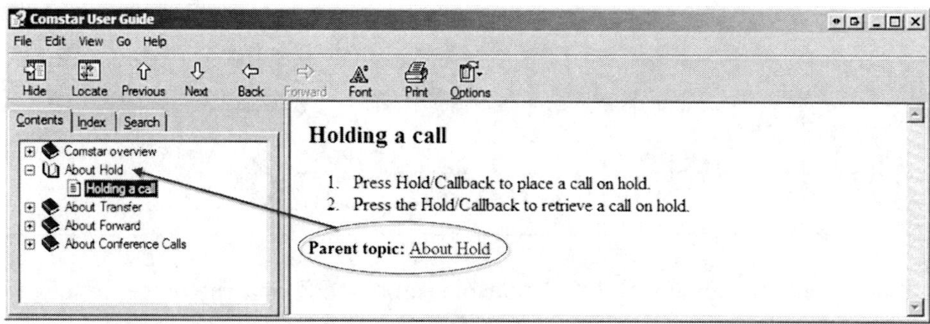


**Figure 7: Child topic linking**

You can further control linking with the *@collection-type* attribute to display topic references in a family or sequence. Family linking is normally formatted to place links to related topics at the end of the topic content. Sequential linking puts the links in a numbered list, suggesting an order in which the user might read the topics.

There are several advantages to maintaining links in your map rather than in the topics. You can

- quickly add, remove, and change topic reference links. Editing groups, hierarchies, and tables is more efficient and effective than managing the individual links in each topic.
- ensure accuracy and usability in one place, making it easier to identify patterns and holes in your information set.
- create customized information sets for specific audiences or product documentation. If you reuse information in a different context, you simply apply a different map without changing the topic content.
- continuously update topic content and easily recreate a map using additional or changed topics. You can incorporate links to topics throughout your information set without editing or hard coding the related-links content of each topic.

# LESSON 13

## Collection-type Attribute

Use the *@collection-type* attribute to create relationships among topics that are closely associated. The purpose of the *@collection-type* attribute is to group topics automatically, creating links in each topic for easier navigation and referencing. The two *@collection-type* attribute values you will most likely use are "family" and "sequence". The other possible values you use more rarely are "unordered" and "choice". You can use any of the collection-type values to override a previously set collection-type. You will most likely use the unordered and choice values to override the family and sequence values.

A basic DITA map creates relationships by nesting topic references to create a hierarchy. These relationships are known as parent and child relationships. However, in some cases, you want to create a relationship between topics that are not related through the parent and child pair. Sibling topics are often written about similar subject matter, but the sibling topics generally do not have links to one another. The purpose of a *@collection-type* attribute is to provide siblings with linking capabilities.

**Collection-type family**

Use the "family" value *@collection-type* attribute if you have a set of closely related concepts, tasks, or references that you want to link together. These topics may all be siblings in a particular part of a map. If these sibling topic references are all at the second level of the hierarchy and have the same parent topic, you can assign a *@collection-type* attribute to the parent topic that will link each of the sibling topics to one another.

For example, the following topic contains a *@collection-type* attribute set to family on the primary topic reference that includes all other topic references. As a result, all of the topic references under this parent are considered siblings.

```
<topicref href="AboutConferenceCalls.dita" format="dita"
   scope="local" type="concept" collection-type="family">
   <topicref href="PlacingACall.dita" format="dita"
      scope="local" type="task" />
   <topicref href="LeavingAConferenceCallTemporarily.dita"
       format="dita" scope="local" type="task"/>
   <topicref href="ReenteringAConferenceCall.dita"
      format="dita" scope="local" type="task"/>
   <topicref
      href="ConsultingPrivatelyOnTheConferenceCall.dita"
      format="dita" scope="local" type="task"/>
```

```
   <topicref href="ReenteringACallWithAllPeople.dita"
      format="dita" scope="local" type="task"/>
</topicref>
```

Figure 8 illustrates links to the selected topic's siblings in the collection. If "Reentering a conference call" had concept and reference siblings, headings for each would appear with the links below.

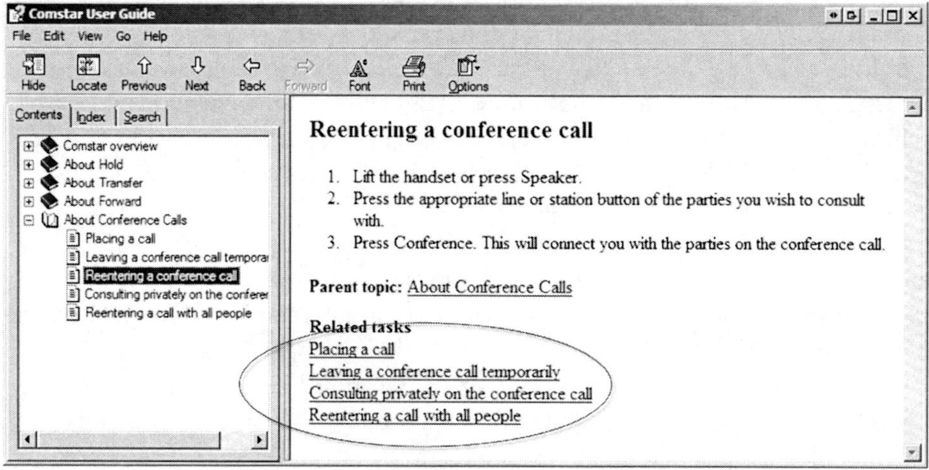


**Figure 8: Collection-type family result**

## Collection-type sequence

Use the "sequence" value on the *@collection-type* attribute to order your topics. You might use a "sequence" collection-type to present a series of tasks that the user should read in a particular order or a series of concepts that the user should read in a particular order. The greatest benefit of the "sequence" attribute value is that when you create the deliverable, the processor will generate the sequence in the order you include the topic references in the map. You don't have to number anything. Using the "sequence" collection type also creates links in each topic to the next and previous topics in the sequence. It allows you to indicate pre-requisite and post-requisite relationships automatically.

In the following map, all of the topics under the Conference call section are in a "sequence" collection-type.

```
<topicref href="AboutConferenceCalls.dita" format="dita"
   scope="local" type="concept" collection-type="sequence">
   <topicref href="PlacingACall.dita" format="dita"
      scope="local" type="task" />
   <topicref href="LeavingAConferenceCallTemporarily.dita"
       format="dita" scope="local" type="task"/>
   <topicref href="ReenteringAConferenceCall.dita"
       format="dita" scope="local" type="task"/>
```

```
  <topicref
    href="ConsultingPrivatelyOnTheConferenceCall.dita"
    format="dita" scope="local" type="task"/>
  <topicref href="ReenteringACallWithAllPeople.dita"
    format="dita" scope="local" type="task"/>
</topicref>
```

As a result, the processor generates normal links in the parent topic, AboutConferenceCalls.dita, except that the links are placed in the same order as the topic references in the map. In each of the sibling topics, the links at the end of the topic indicate the pre-requisite and post-requisite topics, as illustrated in Figure 9 and Figure 10.

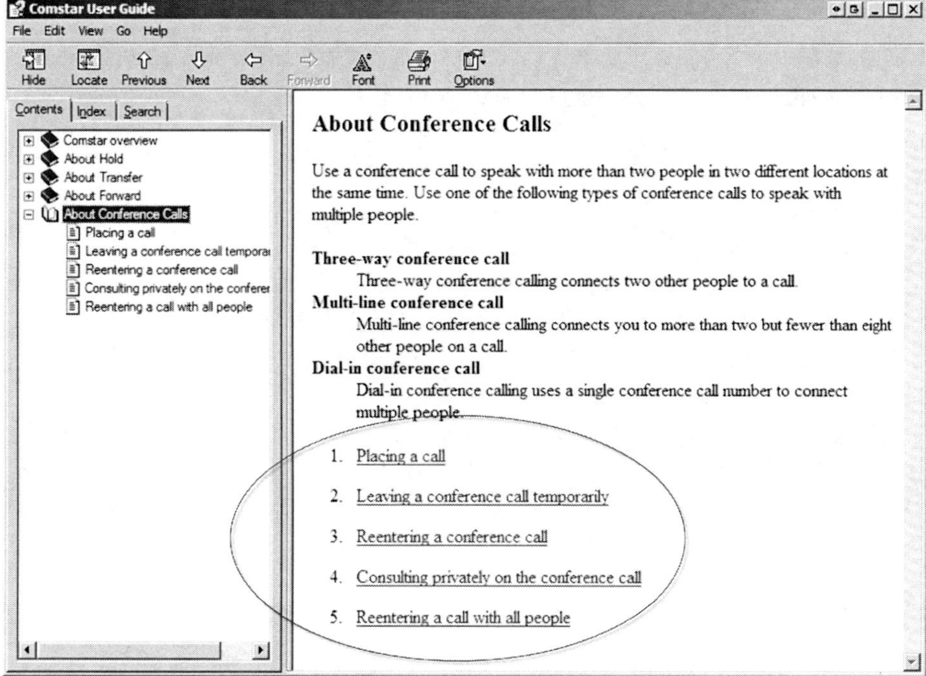


**Figure 9: Collection-type "sequence" result for the parent topic**

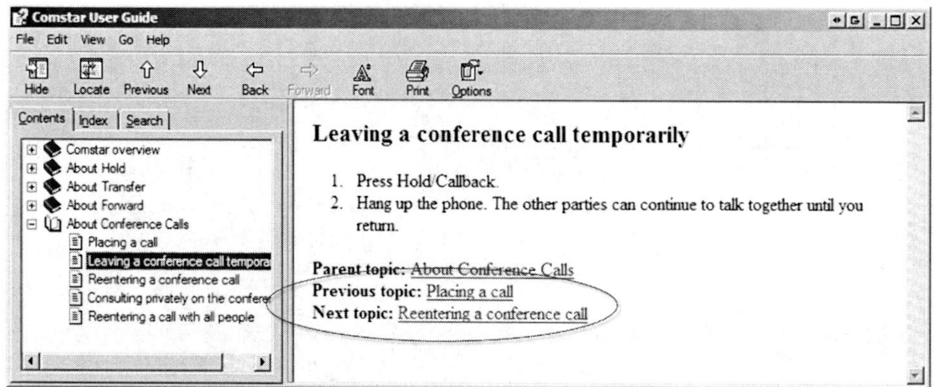


**Figure 10: Collection-type sequence result for the child topic**

### Adding the collection-type attribute

This lesson explains the *@collection-type* attribute and values you can use in your DITA map. In this lesson, you learn to

- add the *@collection-type* attribute to <topicref> elements
- add *@collection-type* values, such as "family" and "sequence"

1. Open the ComstarUserGuide.ditamap file from the Adding processing attributes on page 154 topic.

```
<map id="ComstarUserGuide" xml:lang="en-us">
   <title>Comstar User Guide</title>
   <topicmeta>
      <copyright>
         <copyryear year="2011"/>
         <copyrholder>Comstar Phones</copyrholder>
      </copyright>
   </topicmeta>
   <topicref href="ComstarOverview.dita" format="dita"
      scope="local"/>
   <topicref href="QuickGuide.dita" locktitle="yes" format="dita"
      scope="local" type="reference">
      <topicmeta>
         <navtitle>Get Started Now</navtitle>
      </topicmeta>
   </topicref>
   <topicref href="AboutHold.dita" navtitle="Hold" format="dita"
      scope="local" type="concept">
      <topicmeta>
         <audience type="user"/>
         <audience type="administrator"/>
      </topicmeta>
      <topicref href="HoldingACall.dita" format="dita"
         scope="local" type="task">
      </topicref>
   </topicref>
   <topicref href="AboutTransfer.dita" format="dita"
```

```
        scope="local" type="concept">
        <topicref href="TransferringACall.dita" format="dita"
           scope="local" type="task"/>
     </topicref>
     <topicref href="AboutForward.dita" format="dita"
        scope="local" type="concept">
        <topicref href="ForwardingACall.dita" format="dita"
           scope="local" type="task"/>
     </topicref>
     <topicref href="AboutConferenceCalls.dita" format="dita"
        scope="local" type="concept">
        <topicref href="PlacingACall.dita" format="dita"
           scope="local" type="task"/>
        <topicref href="LeavingAConferenceCallTemporarily.dita"
           format="dita" scope="local" type="task"/>
        <topicref href="ReenteringAConferenceCall.dita"
           format="dita" scope="local" type="task"/>
        <topicref
           href="ConsultingPrivatelyOnTheConferenceCall.dita"
           format="dita" scope="local" type="task"/>
        <topicref href="ReenteringACallWithAllPeople.dita"
           format="dita" scope="local" type="task"/>
     </topicref>
     <topicref href="http://www.comtech-serv.com/Comstar/"
        format="html" scope="external" locktitle="yes" print="no">
        <topicmeta>
           <navtitle>Comtech Services: Comstar Phone
              Information</navtitle>
           <shortdesc>Online ordering for your choice of any
              Comstar phones.</shortdesc>
        </topicmeta>
     </topicref>
     <topicref href="../../ComstarPricing.pdf" format="pdf"
        scope="external">
        <topicmeta>
           <shortdesc>Comstar phones provide a variety of
           different plans you can purchase to use with your
           phone.</shortdesc>
         </topicmeta>
     </topicref>
     <mapref href="../Components/Accessories.ditamap"
        format="ditamap" scope="peer" toc="no"/>
  </map>
```

**2.** Change QuickGuide.dita, AboutHold.dita, AboutForward.dita, AboutTransfer.dita, and AboutConferenceCalls.dita to child topics for ComstarOverview.dita.

To make these child topics, change the topicref for ComstarOverview.dita to a container and move its end tag to immediately after the end tag for AboutConferenceCalls.dita.

```
<map id="ComstarUserGuide" xml:lang="en-us">
  ⋮
  <topicref href="ComstarOverview.dita" format="dita"
     scope="local">
     <topicref href="QuickGuide.dita" locktitle="yes"
        format="dita" scope="local" type="reference">
        ⋮
     </topicref>
     <topicref href="AboutHold.dita" navtitle="Hold"
        format="dita" scope="local" type="concept">
        ⋮
        </topicref>
     </topicref>
     <topicref href="AboutTransfer.dita" format="dita"
        scope="local" type="concept">
        ⋮
     </topicref>
     <topicref href="AboutForward.dita" format="dita"
        scope="local" type="concept">
        ⋮
     </topicref>
     <topicref href="AboutConferenceCalls.dita" format="dita"
        scope="local" type="concept">
        ⋮
     </topicref>
  </topicref>
  ⋮
</map>
```

3. Add a *@collection-type* attribute to the ComstarOverview.dita topic reference, and assign the value "family".

   By default, the child topics of ComstarOverview.dita are unrelated except through their common parent. By adding the *@collection-type* attribute with the value "family" on the parent topic reference, you create linking relationships among its child topics; these relationships are referred to as sibling relationships. The sibling topic references in the example below are the five topic references you added in step 2.

```
<map id="ComstarUserGuide" xml:lang="en-us">
  ⋮
  <topicref href="ComstarOverview.dita" format="dita"
     scope="local" collection-type="family">
     <topicref href="QuickGuide.dita" locktitle="yes"
        format="dita" scope="local" type="reference">
        ⋮
     </topicref>
     <topicref href="AboutHold.dita" navtitle="Hold"
        format="dita" scope="local" type="concept">
        ⋮
     </topicref>
     </topicref>
     <topicref href="AboutTransfer.dita" format="dita"
        scope="local" type="concept">
        ⋮
     </topicref>
     <topicref href="AboutForward.dita" format="dita"
```

```
         scope="local" type="concept">
         ⋮
      </topicref>
      <topicref href="AboutConferenceCalls.dita" format="dita"
         scope="local" type="concept">
         ⋮
      </topicref>
   </topicref>
   ⋮
</map>
```

For the next part of the lesson, consider that you want the end user of the phone to do the tasks for conference calls in the order you included them in the map.

4. Add a *@collection-type* attribute assigned to "sequence" to the AboutConferenceCalls.dita topic reference.

```
<map id="ComstarUserGuide" xml:lang="en-us">
   ⋮
   <topicref href="AboutConferenceCalls.dita" format="dita"
      scope="local" type="concept" collection-type="sequence">
      <topicref href="PlacingACall.dita" format="dita"
         scope="local" type="task"/>
      <topicref href="LeavingAConferenceCallTemporarily.dita"
         format="dita" scope="local" type="task"/>
      <topicref href="ReenteringAConferenceCall.dita"
         format="dita" scope="local" type="task"/>
      <topicref
         href="ConsultingPrivatelyOnTheConferenceCall.dita"
         format="dita" scope="local" type="task"/>
      <topicref href="ReenteringACallWithAllPeople.dita"
         format="dita" scope="local" type="task"/>
   </topicref>
   ⋮
</map>
```

5. Save your work in the ComstarUserGuide.ditamap file.

### ComstarUserGuide.ditamap

The example shows the ComstarUserGuide.ditamap file with a topic reference hierarchy three levels deep. It has two collection types, "sequence" and "family". Setting the *@collection-type* attribute to "family" on the first topic reference results in each of the second-level topics linking to one another. The third-level topics, HoldingACall.dita, TransferringACall.dita, and ForwardingACall.dita inherit the family attribute; if they had sibling topics, they would link to those topics. The *@collection-type* on the About Conference Calls topic overrides the inherited value of "family" and creates a sequential relationship for the sibling topics in the conference call section.

**Note:** If you want to create a collection-type for a group of topics that do not have a common parent, you can add a topic group container element

<topicgroup> and assign the *@collection-type* attribute without disrupting the desired hierarchy. See the *OASIS Darwin Information Typing Architecture (DITA) Version 1.2 (OASIS Standard, 1 December 2010)* for further information about the <topicgroup> element.

```
<map id="ComstarUserGuide" xml:lang="en-us">
   <title>Comstar User Guide</title>
   <topicmeta>
      <copyright>
         <copyryear year="2011"/>
         <copyrholder>Comstar Phones</copyrholder>
      </copyright>
   </topicmeta>
   <topicref href="ComstarOverview.dita" format="dita"
      scope="local" collection-type="family">
      <topicref href="QuickGuide.dita" locktitle="yes"
         format="dita" scope="local" type="reference">
         <topicmeta>
            <navtitle>Get Started Now</navtitle>
         </topicmeta>
      </topicref>
      <topicref href="AboutHold.dita" navtitle="Hold"
         format="dita" scope="local" type="concept">
         <topicmeta>
            <audience type="user"/>
            <audience type="administrator"/>
         </topicmeta>
         <topicref href="HoldingACall.dita" format="dita"
            scope="local" type="task">
         </topicref>
      </topicref>
      <topicref href="AboutTransfer.dita" format="dita"
         scope="local" type="concept">
         <topicref href="TransferringACall.dita" format="dita"
            scope="local" type="task"/>
      </topicref>
      <topicref href="AboutForward.dita" format="dita"
         scope="local" type="concept">
         <topicref href="ForwardingACall.dita" format="dita"
            scope="local" type="task"/>
      </topicref>
      <topicref href="AboutConferenceCalls.dita" format="dita"
         scope="local" type="concept" collection-type="sequence">
         <topicref href="PlacingACall.dita" format="dita"
            scope="local" type="task"/>
         <topicref href="LeavingAConferenceCallTemporarily.dita"
            format="dita" scope="local" type="task"/>
         <topicref href="ReenteringAConferenceCall.dita"
            format="dita" scope="local" type="task"/>
         <topicref
            href="ConsultingPrivatelyOnTheConferenceCall.dita"
            format="dita"  scope="local" type="task"/>
         <topicref href="ReenteringACallWithAllPeople.dita"
            format="dita" scope="local" type="task"/>
      </topicref>
   </topicref>
   <topicref href="http://www.comtech-serv.com/Comstar/"
      format="html" scope="external" locktitle="yes" print="no">
      <topicmeta>
```

```
            <navtitle>Comtech Services: Comstar Phone
               Information</navtitle>
            <shortdesc>Online ordering for your choice of any
               Comstar phones.</shortdesc>
         </topicmeta>
      </topicref>
      <topicref href="../../ComstarPricing.pdf" format="pdf"
         scope="external">
         <topicmeta>
            <shortdesc>Comstar phones provide a variety of
            different plans you can purchase to use with your
            phone.</shortdesc>
         </topicmeta>
      </topicref>
      <mapref href="../Components/Accessories.ditamap"
         format="ditamap" scope="peer" toc="no"/>
   </map>
```

**Collection-type review questions**

What is the difference between family and sequence collection types? Select all that apply.

- **a.** The family collection type establishes relationships between topics that do not share the same parent.
- **b.** The sequence collection type establishes relationships between all first-level topics in the map, all second-level topics in the map, and so on.
- **c.** The family collection type establishes equal relationships between all child topics of the same parent.
- **d.** The sequence collection type establishes a relationship between child topics of the same parent based on the order in which they appear in the map.

Collection-type attributes establish relationships between parent and child topics.

- True
- False

Besides family and sequence, what other values can be assigned to the *@collection-type* attribute?

Why might you maintain links in maps rather than using the <related-links> element within a topic? Select all that apply.

- **a.** It is more efficient to add, remove, and change topic reference links in a map than in multiple, individual topics.
- **b.** You can create customized linking patterns for specific audiences or product documentation without changing topics.
- **c.** The <related-links> element does not provide a way to establish sequential relationships.
- **d.** Related topics are not grouped together within the map.

If you assign a "sequence" attribute value, the processor automatically creates links in each topic the next and previous topics of the sequence.

- True
- False

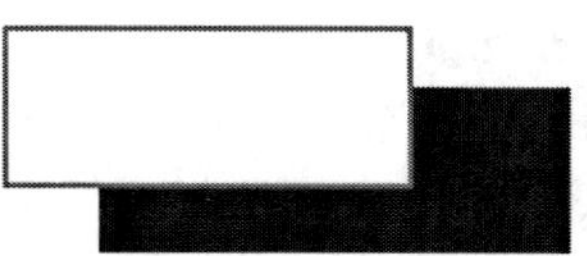

# LESSON 14

## Linking Attribute

Use the *@linking* attribute to control the direction of the links between your topic references. In some situations, you will want to apply dynamic *@linking* during your processing, but you don't necessarily want all the topics to link to each other.

For example, if you create a glossary, each topic reference should point to the glossary, but you will not want the glossary to point back to every other topic. You will want to control the direction of the links. Applying a *@linking* attribute to your topic references provides unidirectional *@linking*.

The *@linking* attribute has four possible values. The two most commonly used values are "targetonly" and "sourceonly". The other two values are "normal" and "none".

**Targetonly**

When a topic reference has a *@linking* attribute of "targetonly", other topics can link to the referenced topic; however, it cannot link to other topics. For example, add the "targetonly" *@linking* attribute when a topic relates to many other topics in the map. When a topic links to many related topics, the processor generates links to all the related topics. Too many links in a topic could overwhelm the reader.

Consider a case in which you have a common reference topic, such as a specification table that supports multiple tasks. The reference specification table should not include links back to all the tasks it supports. If you apply the *@linking* attribute to the specification table topic and set the value to "targetonly", the processor will create hyperlinks from the tasks to the reference topic, but the reference topic will not include hyperlinks back to the task topics.

**Sourceonly**

"Sourceonly" *@linking* is the opposite of "targetonly" *@linking*. When a topic reference has a *@linking* attribute of "sourceonly", the referenced topic can link to other topics, but other topics cannot link to it.

For example, you might have several reference topics that you want to set to targetonly so that they do not link to a task topic. It is easier to assign the task topic "sourceonly" and omit the *@linking* attribute from the reference topics. This way, you don't have to maintain all of the "targetonly" *@linking* attributes on the reference topics in the map.

**Normal**
The default for the *@linking* attribute is "normal". Normal means that a topic can be linked to or from any other topic. If you apply a "targetonly" or "sourceonly" *@linking* attribute to a topic reference, all child topics in the map inherit this value. In some situations, you might need to override a "sourceonly" or "targetonly" link by assigning the "normal" *@linking* attribute.

**None**
When you set the *@linking* attribute to "none" for a topic reference, the topic can neither be linked from nor linked to any other topic. You might set the *@linking* attribute to "none" for several reasons:

- You don't want the topic to affect your *@linking* for print output.
- You want to craft the links yourself in the DITA source files.
- You have a topic that you want to include in the table of contents or introductory boilerplate information, but you don't want it to link to other topics.

Setting the *@linking* attribute to "none" doesn't mean that you won't be able to access the topic from the table of contents, site map, or navigation; it just means that the topic will not have links in it to other topics and other topics will not link to it. For example, you may have a Preface in your map that you do not want other topics to link to, nor do you want to link the Preface to any other topics. Set the *@linking* attribute to "none".

**Adding the linking attribute**
This lesson explains the *@linking* attribute and the values you can use in your DITA map. In this lesson, you learn to

- add the *@linking* attribute to <topicref> elements
- add the values "sourceonly", "targetonly", and "normal" to your *@linking* attribute

1. Open the DITA map you created in Collection-type Attribute on page 161.

```
<map id="ComstarUserGuide" xml:lang="en-us">
   <title>Comstar User Guide</title>
   <topicmeta>
      <copyright>
         <copyryear year="2011"/>
         <copyrholder>Comstar Phones</copyrholder>
      </copyright>
   </topicmeta>
   <topicref href="ComstarOverview.dita" format="dita"
      scope="local" collection-type="family">
      <topicref href="QuickGuide.dita" locktitle="yes"
         format="dita" scope="local" type="reference">
         <topicmeta>
            <navtitle>Get Started Now</navtitle>
         </topicmeta>
      </topicref>
```

```
        <topicref href="AboutHold.dita" navtitle="Hold"
           format="dita" scope="local" type="concept">
           <topicmeta>
              <audience type="user"/>
              <audience type="administrator"/>
           </topicmeta>
           <topicref href="HoldingACall.dita" format="dita"
              scope="local" type="task">
           </topicref>
        </topicref>
        <topicref href="AboutTransfer.dita" format="dita"
           scope="local" type="concept">
           <topicref href="TransferringACall.dita" format="dita"
              scope="local" type="task"/>
        </topicref>
        <topicref href="AboutForward.dita" format="dita"
           scope="local" type="concept">
           <topicref href="ForwardingACall.dita" format="dita"
              scope="local" type="task"/>
        </topicref>
        <topicref href="AboutConferenceCalls.dita" format="dita"
           scope="local" type="concept" collection-type="sequence">
           <topicref href="PlacingACall.dita" format="dita"
              scope="local" type="task"/>
           <topicref href="LeavingAConferenceCallTemporarily.dita"
              format="dita" scope="local" type="task"/>
           <topicref href="ReenteringAConferenceCall.dita"
              format="dita" scope="local" type="task"/>
           <topicref
              href="ConsultingPrivatelyOnTheConferenceCall.dita"
              format="dita" scope="local" type="task"/>
           <topicref href="ReenteringACallWithAllPeople.dita"
              format="dita" scope="local" type="task"/>
        </topicref>
     </topicref>
     <topicref href="http://www.comtech-serv.com/Comstar/"
        format="html" scope="external" locktitle="yes" print="no">
        <topicmeta>
           <navtitle>Comtech Services: Comstar Phone
              Information</navtitle>
           <shortdesc>Online ordering for your choice of any
              Comstar phones.</shortdesc>
        </topicmeta>
     </topicref>
     <topicref href="../../ComstarPricing.pdf" format="pdf"
        scope="external">
        <topicmeta>
           <shortdesc>Comstar phones provide a variety of
           different plans you can purchase to use with your
           phone.</shortdesc>
        </topicmeta>
     </topicref>
     <mapref href="../Components/Accessories.ditamap"
        format="ditamap" scope="peer" toc="no"/>
  </map>
```

2. Add a *@linking* attribute to the QuickGuide.dita topic reference and set the value to "targetonly".

Setting the QuickGuide.dita topic reference to "targetonly" means the topic will not link to any other topics.

```
<map id="ComstarUserGuide" xml:lang="en-us">
   ⋮
   <topicref href="QuickGuide.dita" locktitle="yes"
      format="dita" scope="local" type="reference"
      linking="targetonly">
   ⋮
</map>
```

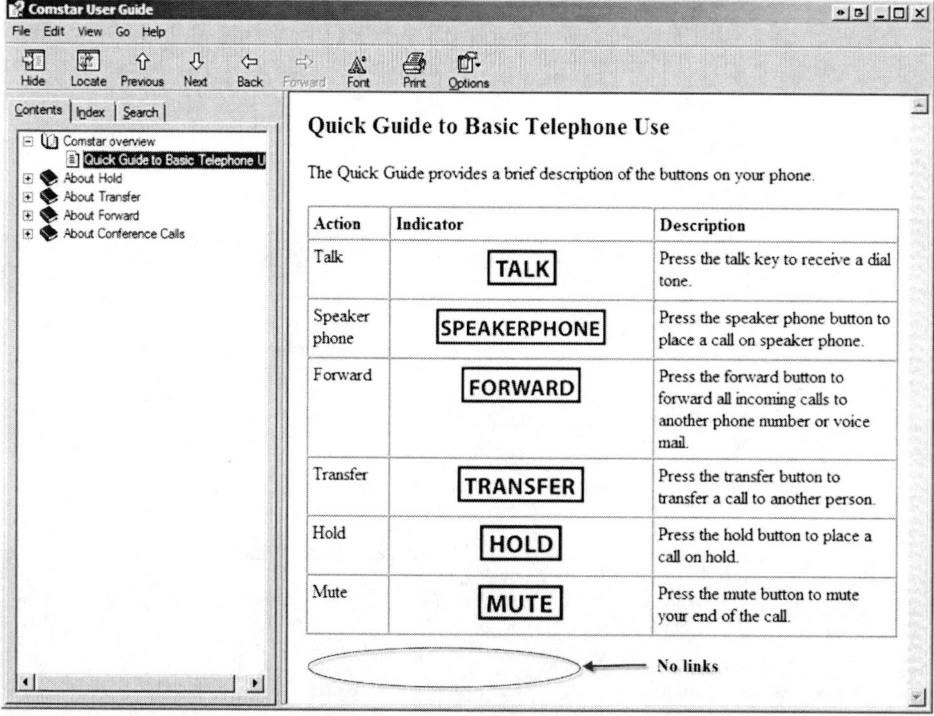


3. Add a *@linking* attribute to the AboutHold.dita topic reference and set the value to "sourceonly".

   Setting the AboutHold.dita topic reference to "sourceonly" means the topic output contains links to other topics, but other topics cannot link to it.

```
<map id="ComstarUserGuide" xml:lang="en-us">
   ⋮
   <topicref href="AboutHold.dita" navtitle="Hold"
      format="dita" scope="local" type="concept"
      linking="sourceonly">
   ⋮
</map>
```

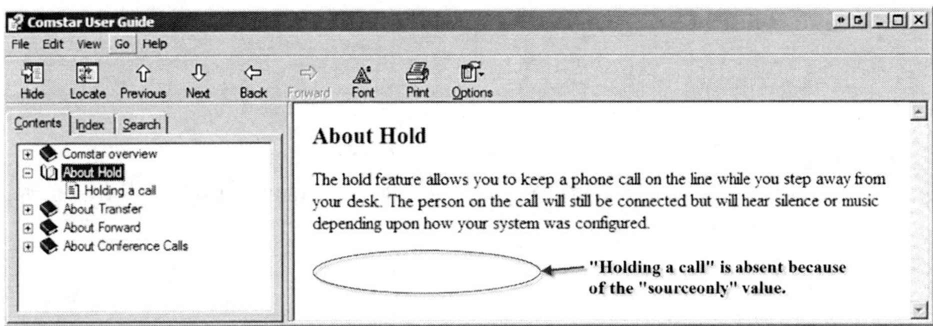


4. Set the *@linking* attribute for the HoldingACall.dita topic reference to "normal".

   Setting the topic reference to "normal" linking disables the inherited "sourceonly" linking from the AboutHold.dita topic reference.

```
<map id="ComstarUserGuide" xml:lang="en-us">
   ⋮
   <topicref href="AboutHold.dita" navtitle="Hold"
      format="dita" scope="local" type="concept"
      linking="sourceonly">
      <topicmeta>
         <audience type="user"/>
         <audience type="administrator"/>
      </topicmeta>
      <topicref href="HoldingACall.dita" format="dita"
        scope="local" type="task" linking="normal">
      </topicref>
   </topicref>
    ⋮
</map>
```

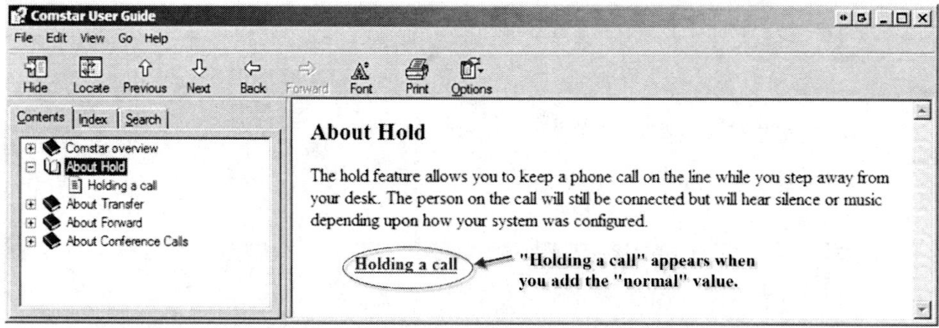


5. Repeat the previous two steps for the AboutTransfer.dita/ TransferringACall.dita and AboutForward.dita/ForwardingACall.dita topic references.

```
<map id="ComstarUserGuide" xml:lang="en-us">
   ⋮
   <topicref href="AboutTransfer.dita" format="dita"
      scope="local" type="concept" linking="sourceonly">
      <topicref href="TransferringACall.dita" format="dita"
         scope="local" type="task" linking="normal"/>
   </topicref>
   <topicref href="AboutForward.dita" format="dita"
      scope="local" type="concept" linking="sourceonly">
      <topicref href="ForwardingACall.dita" format="dita"
         scope="local" type="task" linking="normal"/>
   </topicref>
   ⋮
</map>
```

6. Save your work in the ComstarUserGuide.ditamap file.

The example shows the complete code used to produce the Comstar User Guide map in this lesson.

```
<map id="ComstarUserGuide" xml:lang="en-us">
   <title>Comstar User Guide</title>
   <topicmeta>
      <copyright>
         <copyryear year="2011"/>
         <copyrholder>Comstar Phones</copyrholder>
      </copyright>
   </topicmeta>
   <topicref href="ComstarOverview.dita" format="dita"
      scope="local" collection-type="family">
      <topicref href="QuickGuide.dita" locktitle="yes"
         format="dita" scope="local" type="reference"
         linking="targetonly">
         <topicmeta>
            <navtitle>Get Started Now</navtitle>
         </topicmeta>
      </topicref>
      <topicref href="AboutHold.dita" navtitle="Hold"
```

```
      format="dita" scope="local" type="concept"
      linking="sourceonly">
      <topicmeta>
         <audience type="user"/>
         <audience type="administrator"/>
      </topicmeta>
      <topicref href="HoldingACall.dita" format="dita"
         scope="local" type="task" linking="normal">
      </topicref>
   </topicref>
   <topicref href="AboutTransfer.dita" format="dita"
     scope="local" type="concept" linking="sourceonly">
      <topicref href="TransferringACall.dita" format="dita"
         scope="local" type="task" linking="normal"/>
   </topicref>
   <topicref href="AboutForward.dita" format="dita"
      scope="local" type="concept" linking="sourceonly">
      <topicref href="ForwardingACall.dita" format="dita"
         scope="local" type="task" linking="normal"/>
   </topicref>
   <topicref href="AboutConferenceCalls.dita" format="dita"
      scope="local" type="concept" collection-type="sequence">
      <topicref href="PlacingACall.dita" format="dita"
         scope="local" type="task"/>
      <topicref href="LeavingAConferenceCallTemporarily.dita"
         format="dita" scope="local" type="task"/>
      <topicref href="ReenteringAConferenceCall.dita"
         format="dita" scope="local" type="task"/>
      <topicref
         href="ConsultingPrivatelyOnTheConferenceCall.dita"
         format="dita" scope="local" type="task"/>
      <topicref href="ReenteringACallWithAllPeople.dita"
         format="dita" scope="local" type="task"/>
   </topicref>
</topicref>
<topicref href="http://www.comtech-serv.com/Comstar/"
   format="html" scope="external" locktitle="yes" print="no">
   <topicmeta>
      <navtitle>Comtech Services: Comstar Phone
         Information</navtitle>
      <shortdesc>Online ordering for your choice of any
         Comstar phones.</shortdesc>
   </topicmeta>
</topicref>
<topicref href="../../ComstarPricing.pdf" format="pdf"
   scope="external">
   <topicmeta>
      <shortdesc>Comstar phones provide a variety of
      different plans you can purchase to use with your
      phone.</shortdesc>
   </topicmeta>
</topicref>
<mapref href="../Components/Accessories.ditamap"
   format="ditamap" scope="peer" toc="no"/>
</map>
```

**Linking attribute review questions**

The linking attribute applies only to the topic reference to which it is assigned. Child topics do not inherit its value.

- True
- False

What should be the value of the linking attribute if you do not want any other topics to link to it?

What happens if you set the *@linking* attribute to "none"?

**a.** The topic will have no links to or from it, and you will not be able to access it from the table of contents, site map, or navigation.
**b.** The topic will have no links to other topics.
**c.** Any links defined in the topic's <related-links> element will be ignored.
**d.** The topic will have no links to or from other topics.

Suppose you want all tasks in your document to link to a command reference topic that defines the parameters available for each command. What *@linking* attribute should you assign to the reference topic to prevent it from pointing back to every task topic?

By default, links are bi-directional.

- True
- False

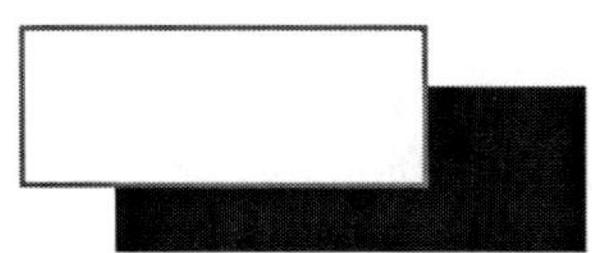

# LESSON 15

## Understanding Relationship Tables

DITA relationship tables, a feature exclusive to the DITA model, help you create dynamic and complete information sets. Users are often frustrated when they find task information that has no supporting concept information or tasks that refer to reference data that is in another book or set of information that they don't have. Using a relationship table to plan your topics helps you find information gaps that need to be filled. For example, you may find a task that is accurate and complete, but your users lack the background information they need to complete the task. You may also discover topics that don't seem to fit with the rest of the topics. For example, you may have concept topics that were added by product developers but add little to the user's understanding. If you choose to pursue a minimalist agenda, you will remove unnecessary topics from your information set.

DITA relationship tables also free you from the burden of creating and maintaining links in your topics or in your maps. Relationship tables enable you to create a well-defined, systematic linking structure for your topics and modify that structure in response to user needs. For example, you could use a relationship table to define an entire web site or help system by defining all the links to connect your topics without ever having to hardcode them. Hyperlinks hardcoded from topic to topic are usually hard to maintain and often break whenever you move or delete a target topic. If you maximize the features provided by relationship tables, you can create links for your topics without having to verify every hyperlink to make sure it works correctly for each release of your information.

**Relationship table construction**

Relationship tables are created using a table of rows and columns to define links. Each column in the table typically groups together the same information type. Each row in the table represents a unique relationship, which is generally rendered as a link, and each cell lists participants in the relationship. Each topic or map reference in a cell links to the topic and map references in the other cells in the same row. Using a set of topic references to build a table, you can easily link from concepts to tasks and back again, link reference information to multiple tasks, and link task information to supporting information needed to complete the task.

To build a simple relationship table, consider linking three topics: simpleconcept.dita, simpletask.dita, and simplereference.dita. The relationship table will look like the one in Figure 11. Each arrow represents a link that is created between the topics. Upon rendering, each link created in the table is placed at the end of each topic.

| type="concept" | type="task" | type="reference" |
| --- | --- | --- |
| simpleconcept.dita | simpletask.dita | simplereference.dita |

**Figure 11: Simple relationship table**

In practice, relationship tables are more complex than this simple example. When creating a more complex relationship table, consider the following guidelines:

- Each row in the table represents a separate set of relationships and links.
- No relationships exist between the rows in a table.
- Topic references are not needed in every cell in a row.
- Each cell can contain multiple topic references.
- Topic references can be repeated in multiple rows.

These guidelines are illustrated in the complex relationship table in Figure 12. Note that no arrows cross between rows or within cells, indicating there are no relationships between rows in the tables. Note also that some of the cells are blank, while others contain multiple references. Finally, note that simplereference1 and simplereference2 each appear in two different rows.

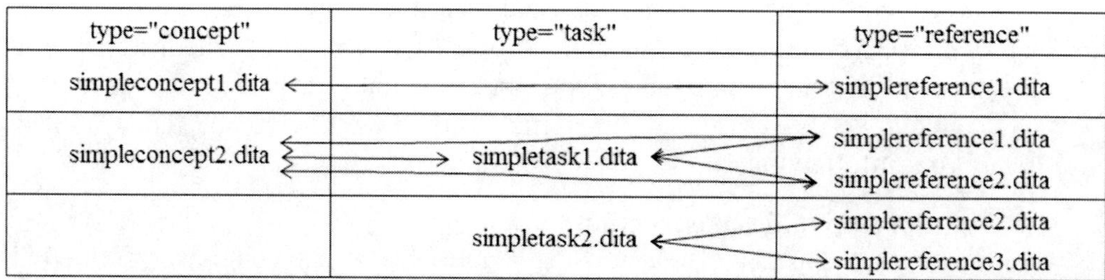

| type="concept" | type="task" | type="reference" |
| --- | --- | --- |
| simpleconcept1.dita | | simplereference1.dita |
| simpleconcept2.dita | simpletask1.dita | simplereference1.dita<br>simplereference2.dita |
| | simpletask2.dita | simplereference2.dita<br>simplereference3.dita |

**Figure 12: Complex relationship table**

### *@collection-type* and *@linking* attributes in relationship tables

You can use both the *@collection-type* and *@linking* attributes discussed in the previous lessons within a relationship table. For example, in a relationship table, topic references in a cell are not typically linked together. However, there are instances when they should be linked. Applying the *@collection-type* attribute in a <topicgroup> element allows you to link topic references inside a cell. For example, in Figure 13, simplereference1.dita and simplereference2.dita are related using collection-type="family". The *@collection-type* attribute affects the relationships only among topics in a cell; it does not affect relationships across cells. For more information about the collection-type attribute, see Collection-type Attribute on page 161.

Figure 13 also demonstrates the use of the *@linking* attribute to create one-way links in a relationship table. In the figure, the simpletask1.dita *@linking* attribute value is set to "sourceonly". Therefore, the link to simplereference1.dita and simplereference2.dita appears only in the simpletask1.dita. The simplereference1.dita and simplereference2.dita do not contain links back to the simpletask1.dita. For more information about the linking attribute, see Linking Attribute on page 171.

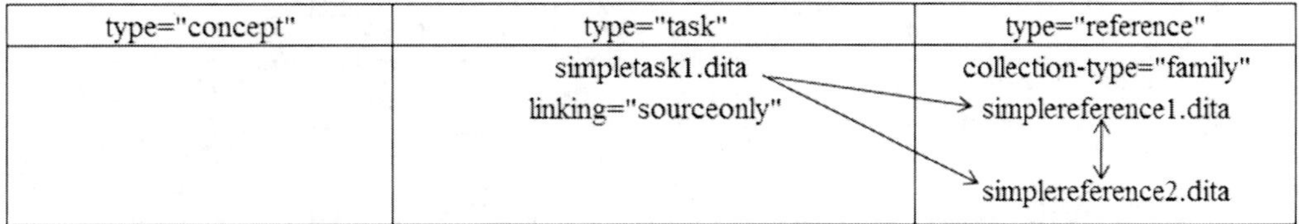


**Figure 13: Collection-type linking in relationship table**

### Creating a relationship table

This lesson explains how to build a relationship table in your DITA map. In this lesson, you learn to

- add the required elements needed to build a relationship table, such as <reltable>, <relrow>, and <relcell>
- add optional elements to enhance your relationship table, such as <relheader>, <relcolspec>, and the relcolspec *@type* attribute
- add topic references to your relationship table using the <topicref> element
- control linking capabilities in your relationship table using the *@linking* attribute

In this lesson, you will use a relationship table to duplicate the links you established in previous lessons using parent/child relationships, the collection-type attribute, and the linking attribute. In addition, you will link all topics to the Accessories.ditamap. Figure 14 on page 182 shows the relationships you will be creating. It's a good idea to draw a similar representation before you begin coding a relationship table.

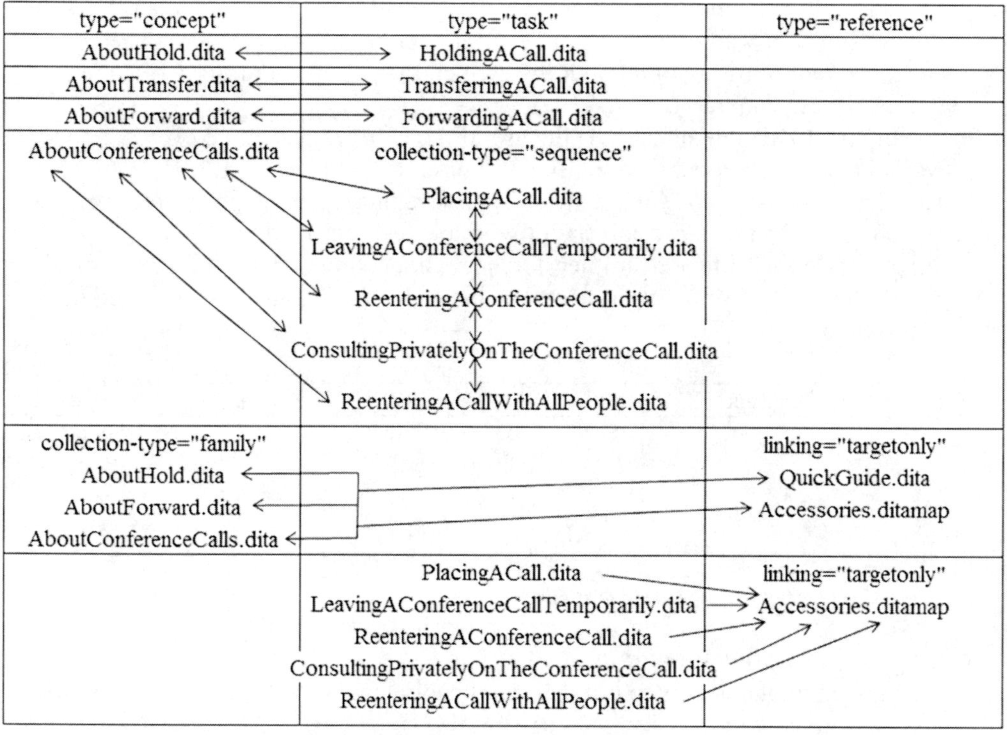

type="concept"
type="task"
type="reference"
AboutHold.dita
HoldingACall.dita
AboutTransfer.dita
TransferringACall.dita
AboutForward.dita
ForwardingACall.dita
AboutConferenceCalls.dita
collection-type="sequence"
PlacingACall.dita
LeavingAConferenceCallTemporarily.dita
ReenteringAConferenceCall.dita
ConsultingPrivatelyOnTheConferenceCall.dita
ReenteringACallWithAllPeople.dita
collection-type="family"
AboutHold.dita
AboutForward.dita
AboutConferenceCalls.dita
linking="targetonly"
QuickGuide.dita
Accessories.ditamap
PlacingACall.dita
LeavingAConferenceCallTemporarily.dita
ReenteringAConferenceCall.dita
ConsultingPrivatelyOnTheConferenceCall.dita
ReenteringACallWithAllPeople.dita
linking="targetonly"
Accessories.ditamap


**Figure 14: Comstar User Guide relationship table**

1. Create a new ditamap to hold the relationship table.

   Although you could create the relationship table in the same ditamap that you've been working in, it would duplicate the other coding you've done. Creating this second map allows you to review the code to better understand how different options achieve the same results.

```
<?xml version="1.0" encoding'"utf-8"?>
<!DOCTYPE map PUBLIC "-//OASIS//DTD DITA Map//EN"
   "map.dtd">
<map id="ComstarUserGuide" xml:lang="en-us">
   <title>Comstar User Guide</title>
   <topicref href="ComstarOverview.dita"/>
   <topicref href="QuickGuide.dita"/>
   <topicref href="AboutHold.dita">
      <topicref href="HoldingACall.dita"/>
   </topicref>
   <topicref href="AboutTransfer.dita">
      <topicref href="TransferringACall.dita"/>
   </topicref>
   <topicref href="AboutForward.dita">
      <topicref href="ForwardingACall.dita"/>
```

```
      </topicref>
      <topicref href="AboutConferenceCalls.dita">
         <topicref href="PlacingACall.dita"/>
         <topicref href="LeavingAConferenceCallTemporarily.dita"/>
         <topicref href="ReenteringAConferenceCall.dita"/>
         <topicref
            href="ConsultingPrivatelyOnTheConferenceCall.dita"/>
         <topicref href="ReenteringACallWithAllPeople.dita"/>
      </topicref>
      <mapref href="../Components/Accessories.ditamap"/>
   </map>
```

2. Add <reltable> start and end tags before the <map> end tag.

   The <reltable> element is the container for the entire relationship table.

```
<map id="ComstarUserGuide" xml:lang="en-us">
   ⋮
   <reltable>
   </reltable>
</map>
```

3. Add <relheader> start and end tags between the <reltable> start and end tags.

   The <relheader> element is the container for the column heads in the relationship table.

```
<map id="ComstarUserGuide" xml:lang="en-us">
   ⋮
   <reltable>
      <relheader>
      </relheader>
   </reltable>
</map>
```

4. Add empty <relcolspec> elements between the <relheader> start and end tags.

   In a relationship table, the <relcolspec> element defines one column heading. To create the example relationship table, add three <relcolspec> elements.

```
<map id="ComstarUserGuide" xml:lang="en-us">
   ⋮
   <reltable>
      <relheader>
         <relcolspec/>
         <relcolspec/>
         <relcolspec/>
      </relheader>
   </reltable>
</map>
```

5. Add the *@type* attribute to each <relcolspec> element, and set the attribute values.

   When you add attributes and values to the <relcolspec> element, you create default values for the entire column. For example, child <topicref> elements in a column with a <relcolspec> *@type* attribute set to "concept" and with no defined *@type* attribute themselves inherit the default value of the column. In this case, the default value is "concept." For this lesson, set the *@type* attributes to "concept", "task", and "reference", respectively.

```
<reltable>
   <relheader>
      <relcolspec type="concept"/>
      <relcolspec type="task"/>
      <relcolspec type="reference"/>
   </relheader>
</reltable>
```

6. Add <relrow> start and end tags after the <relheader> end tag.

   Each relationship row <relrow> start and end tag creates a new row in the relationship table. Each row defines a new set of linking relationships among the topic references in that row. The relationship table you are creating has six rows.

```
<reltable>
   <relheader>
      <relcolspec type="concept"/>
      <relcolspec type="task"/>
      <relcolspec type="reference"/>
   </relheader>
   <relrow></relrow>
   <relrow></relrow>
   <relrow></relrow>
   <relrow></relrow>
   <relrow></relrow>
   <relrow></relrow>
</reltable>
```

7. Add <relcell> start and end tags between each set of <relrow> start and end tags.

   The number of <relcell> elements in each <relrow> element must match the number of <relcolspec> elements used in the <relhead>. For this table, add three sets of <relcell> tags for each <relrow>.

```
<reltable>
   <relheader>
      <relcolspec type="concept"/>
      <relcolspec type="task"/>
      <relcolspec type="reference"/>
   </relheader>
   <relrow>
      <relcell></relcell>
      <relcell></relcell>
      <relcell></relcell>
   </relrow>
   <relrow>
      <relcell></relcell>
      <relcell></relcell>
```

```
      <relcell></relcell>
   </relrow>
   <relrow>
      <relcell></relcell>
      <relcell></relcell>
      <relcell></relcell>
   </relrow>
   <relrow>
      <relcell></relcell>
      <relcell></relcell>
      <relcell></relcell>
   </relrow>
   <relrow>
      <relcell></relcell>
      <relcell></relcell>
      <relcell></relcell>
   </relrow>
   <relrow>
      <relcell></relcell>
      <relcell></relcell>
      <relcell></relcell>
   </relrow>
</reltable>
```

**8.** Using your relationship table sketch as a guide, add empty <topicref> and <mapref> element tags to the appropriate cells, using the *@href* attribute to point to the topic locations.

You can add multiple topic references to each cell. When a <mapref> element is included in a relationship table, links are established with all individual topics contained in that map. For example, if the map contains three topics, each of the topics in the relationship table that refer to the map will link to each of the three topics in the map, and vice versa.

```
<reltable>
   <relheader>
      <relcolspec type="concept"/>
      <relcolspec type="task"/>
      <relcolspec type="reference"/>
   </relheader>
   <relrow>
      <relcell>
         <topicref href="AboutHold.dita"/>
      </relcell>
      <relcell>
         <topicref href="HoldingACall.dita"/>
      </relcell>
      <relcell></relcell>
   </relrow>
   <relrow>
      <relcell>
         <topicref href="AboutTransfer.dita"/>
      </relcell>
      <relcell>
         <topicref href="TransferringACall.dita"/>
      </relcell>
      <relcell></relcell>
   </relrow>
```

```
   <relrow>
      <relcell>
        <topicref href="AboutForward.dita"/>
      </relcell>
      <relcell>
         <topicref href="ForwardingACall.dita"/>
      </relcell>
      <relcell></relcell>
   </relrow>
   <relrow>
      <relcell>
         <topicref href="AboutConferenceCalls.dita"/>
      </relcell>
      <relcell>
         <topicref href="PlacingACall.dita"/>
         <topicref
            href="LeavingAConferenceCallTemporarily.dita"/>
         <topicref href="ReenteringAConferenceCall.dita"/>
         <topicref
            href="ConsultingPrivatelyOnTheConferenceCall.dita"/>
         <topicref href="ReenteringACallWithAllPeople.dita"/>
      </relcell>
      <relcell></relcell>
   </relrow>
   <relrow>
      <relcell>
         <topicref href="AboutHold.dita"/>
         <topicref href="AboutTransfer.dita"/>
         <topicref href="AboutForward.dita"/>
         <topicref href="AboutConferenceCalls.dita"/>
      </relcell>
      <relcell></relcell>
      <relcell>
         <topicref href="QuickGuide.dita"/>
         <topicref href="../Components/Accessories.ditamap"/>
      </relcell>
   </relrow>
   <relrow>
      <relcell></relcell>
      <relcell>
         <topicref href="HoldingACall.dita"/>
        <topicref href="TransferringACall.dita"/>
         <topicref href="ForwardingACall.dita"/>
         <topicref href="PlacingACall.dita"/>
         <topicref
            href="LeavingAConferenceCallTemporarily.dita"/>
         <topicref href="ReenteringAConferenceCall.dita"/>
         <topicref
            href="ConsultingPrivatelyOnTheConferenceCall.dita"/>
         <topicref href="ReenteringACallWithAllPeople.dita"/>
      </relcell>
      <relcell>
         <topicref href="../Components/Accessories.ditamap"/>
      </relcell>
   </relrow>
</reltable>
```

9. As required, add <topicgroup> start and end tags around related topic references within a cell.

Most processing engines do not generate links among the topics located in the same relationship cell. Instead, processing generates links among all topics located in the other cells in the same row. The <topicgroup> element groups topics located in the same cell to create relationships among topics of the same information type.

```
<reltable>
   ⋮
   <relrow>
      <relcell>
         <topicref href="AboutConferenceCalls.dita"/>
      </relcell>
      <relcell>
         <topicgroup>
            <topicref href="PlacingACall.dita"/>
            <topicref
               href="LeavingAConferenceCallTemporarily.dita"/>
            <topicref href="ReenteringAConferenceCall.dita"/>
            <topicref
               href="ConsultingPrivatelyOnTheConferenceCall.dita"/>
            <topicref href="ReenteringACallWithAllPeople.dita"/>
         </topicgroup>
      </relcell>
      <relcell></relcell>
   </relrow>
   <relrow>
      <relcell>
         <topicgroup>
            <topicref href="AboutHold.dita"/>
            <topicref href="AboutTransfer.dita"/>
            <topicref href="AboutForward.dita"/>
            <topicref href="AboutConferenceCalls.dita"/>
         </topicgroup>
      </relcell>
      <relcell></relcell>
      <relcell>
         <topicref href="QuickGuide.dita"/>
         <topicref href="../Components/Accessories.ditamap"/>
      </relcell>
   </relrow>
   ⋮
</reltable>
```

**10.** Add a *@collection-type* attribute to each <topicgroup> element as required.

Adding the *@collection-type* attribute to the <topicgroup> element container allows you to create links among topics in the same relationship cell. See Collection-type Attribute on page 161 for more information about the *@collection-type* attribute. For this example, group the topics related to conference call tasks in a sequence and the concept topics about basic telephone functions in a family.

```
<reltable>
   ⋮
   <relrow>
      <relcell>
         <topicref href="AboutConferenceCalls.dita"/>
      </relcell>
      <relcell>
         <topicgroup collection-type="sequence">
            <topicref href="PlacingACall.dita"/>
            <topicref
               href="LeavingAConferenceCallTemporarily.dita"/>
            <topicref href="ReenteringAConferenceCall.dita"/>
            <topicref
               href="ConsultingPrivatelyOnTheConferenceCall.dita"/>
            <topicref href="ReenteringACallWithAllPeople.dita"/>
         </topicgroup>
      </relcell>
      <relcell></relcell>
   </relrow>
   <relrow>
      <relcell>
         <topicgroup collection-type="family">
            <topicref href="AboutHold.dita"/>
            <topicref href="AboutTransfer.dita"/>
            <topicref href="AboutForward.dita"/>
            <topicref href="AboutConferenceCalls.dita"/>
         </topicgroup>
      </relcell>
      <relcell></relcell>
      <relcell>
         <topicref href="QuickGuide.dita"/>
         <topicref href="../Components/Accessories.ditamap"/>
      </relcell>
   </relrow>
   ⋮
</reltable>
```

11. Set any unidirectional links required using the *@linking* attribute on the appropriate <topicref> or <mapref> element.

    In this example, set the linking attribute to "targetonly" on the QuickGuide.dita topic reference and Accessories.ditamap map references.

```
<reltable>
   ⋮
   <relrow>
      <relcell>
         <topicgroup collection-type="family">
            <topicref href="AboutHold.dita"/>
            <topicref href="AboutTransfer.dita"/>
            <topicref href="AboutForward.dita"/>
            <topicref href="AboutConferenceCalls.dita"/>
      </relcell>
      <relcell></relcell>
      <relcell>
         <topicref href="QuickGuide.dita" linking="targetonly"/>
         <topicref href="../Components/Accessories.ditamap"
            linking="targetonly"/>
      </relcell>
```

```
      </relrow>
      <relrow>
         <relcell></relcell>
         <relcell>
            <topicref href="HoldingACall.dita"/>
            <topicref href="TransferringACall.dita"/>
            <topicref href="ForwardingACall.dita"/>
            <topicref href="PlacingACall.dita"/>
            <topicref
               href="LeavingAConferenceCallTemporarily.dita"/>
            <topicref href="ReenteringAConferenceCall.dita"/>
            <topicref
               href="ConsultingPrivatelyOnTheConferenceCall.dita"/>
            <topicref href="ReenteringACallWithAllPeople.dita"/>
         </relcell>
         <relcell>
            <topicref href="../Components/Accessories.ditamap"
               linking="targetonly"/>
         </relcell>
      </relrow>
   </reltable>
```

**12.** Save the file as ComstarUGRelTable.ditamap.

The following example shows the full ComstarUGRelTable.ditamap file. Compare this file to the ComstarUserGuide.ditamap file in terms of establishing relationships and links within the overall document. Each accomplishes the same thing; however, you may find the relationship table easier to set up and maintain.

```
<?xml version="1.0" encoding'"utf-8"?>
<!DOCTYPE map PUBLIC "-//OASIS//DTD DITA Map//EN"
   "map.dtd">
<map id="ComstarUserGuide" xml:lang="en-us">
   <title>Comstar User Guide</title>
   <topicref href="ComstarOverview.dita"/>
   <topicref href="QuickGuide.dita"/>
   <topicref href="AboutHold.dita">
      <topicref href="HoldingACall.dita"/>
   </topicref>
   <topicref href="AboutTransfer.dita">
      <topicref href="TransferringACall.dita"/>
   </topicref>
   <topicref href="AboutForward.dita">
      <topicref href="ForwardingACall.dita"/>
   </topicref>
   <topicref href="AboutConferenceCalls.dita">
      <topicref href="PlacingACall.dita"/>
      <topicref
         href="LeavingAConferenceCallTemporarily.dita"/>
      <topicref href="ReenteringAConferenceCall.dita"/>
      <topicref
         href="ConsultingPrivatelyOnTheConferenceCall.dita"/>
      <topicref href="ReenteringACallWithAllPeople.dita"/>
   </topicref>
   <mapref href="../Components/Accessories.ditamap"/>
   <reltable>
      <relheader>
         <relcolspec type="concept"/>
```

```
      <relcolspec type="task"/>
      <relcolspec type="reference"/>
   </relheader>
   <relrow>
      <relcell>
         <topicref href="AboutHold.dita"/>
      </relcell>
      <relcell>
         <topicref href="HoldingACall.dita"/>
      </relcell>
      <relcell></relcell>
   </relrow>
   <relrow>
      <relcell>
         <topicref href="AboutTransfer.dita"/>
      </relcell>
      <relcell>
         <topicref href="TransferringACall.dita"/>
      </relcell>
      <relcell></relcell>
   </relrow>
   <relrow>
      <relcell>
         <topicref href="AboutForward.dita"/>
      </relcell>
      <relcell>
         <topicref href="ForwardingACall.dita"/>
      </relcell>
      <relcell></relcell>
   </relrow>
   <relrow>
      <relcell>
         <topicref href="AboutConferenceCalls.dita"/>
      </relcell>
      <relcell>
         <topicgroup collection-type="sequence">
            <topicref href="PlacingACall.dita"/>
            <topicref
               href="LeavingAConferenceCallTemporarily.dita"/>
            <topicref href="ReenteringAConferenceCall.dita"/>
            <topicref
               href="ConsultingPrivatelyOnTheConferenceCall.dita"/>
            <topicref href="ReenteringACallWithAllPeople.dita"/>
         </topicgroup>
      </relcell>
      <relcell></relcell>
   </relrow>
   <relrow>
      <relcell>
         <topicgroup collection-type="family">
            <topicref href="AboutHold.dita"/>
            <topicref href="AboutTransfer.dita"/>
            <topicref href="AboutForward.dita"/>
            <topicref href="AboutConferenceCalls.dita"/>
         </topicgroup>
      </relcell>
      <relcell></relcell>
      <relcell>
         <topicref href="QuickGuide.dita" linking="targetonly"/>
         <topicref href="../Components/Accessories.ditamap"
            linking="targetonly"/>
```

```
            </relcell>
         </relrow>
         <relrow>
            <relcell></relcell>
            <relcell>
               <topicref href="HoldingACall.dita"/>
               <topicref href="TransferringACall.dita"/>
               <topicref href="ForwardingACall.dita"/>
               <topicref href="PlacingACall.dita"/>
               <topicref
                  href="LeavingAConferenceCallTemporarily.dita"/>
               <topicref href="ReenteringAConferenceCall.dita"/>
               <topicref
                  href="ConsultingPrivatelyOnTheConferenceCall.dita"/>
               <topicref href="ReenteringACallWithAllPeople.dita"/>
            </relcell>
            <relcell>
               <topicref href="../Components/Accessories.ditamap"
                  linking="targetonly"/>
            </relcell>
         </relrow>
      </reltable>
   </map>
```

**Relationship table elements**

Relationship table elements are found only in maps. The relationship table elements are listed here in the order that you use them when creating a relationship table in a map.

**<reltable> relationship table**

Use the <reltable> element to create the framework for the relationship table. Add all elements in the relationship table between the beginning and ending tags of the <reltable> element.

**<relheader> relationship head**

Use the <relheader> element as the container to define the column categories. The relationship header element is the first element in the relationship table and can only occur once.

**<relcolspec> relationship column specification**

Use the <relcolspec> element to define each column in the relationship table. Although you can build a one-column relationship table, you should add at least two <relcolspec> elements to form meaningful relationships among your topics. We recommend creating a relationship table with three columns to correspond to the three topic types: concept, task, and reference.

You can add attribute values to each <relcolspec> element to provide default values for each column. For example, the <relcolspec> element may serve as a container for a title or references to topics and maps.

**<relrow> relationship table row**

Use the <relrow> element to define the relationships among the topics in each relationship row. Each <relrow> element defines a new set of relationships. More than one <relrow> element can be added to each relationship table.

**<relcell> relationship table cell**

Use the <relcell> element to define the topic references. These topic references will be linked during processing.

The number of <relcell> elements must match the number of <relcolspec> elements. If you do not want to include a topic reference in one of the cells in a row, you must still add <relcell> start and end tags for the empty cell. Simply do not include topic references in the <relcell> in that case.

**Relationship table review questions**

What is the purpose of a relationship table?

- **a.** To define the hierarchy of the topic and map references within a map.
- **b.** To eliminate the need for the *@collection-type* attribute by grouping similar topics and maps into single cells within the table.
- **c.** To establish the navigation order for the topics in an online presentation format.
- **d.** To define the links that interconnect your topics.

Put these elements in the order they would occur within a relationship table.

1. <relcolspec>
2. <relcell>
3. <reltable>
4. <relheader>
5. <relrow>

What happens when a <mapref> element is placed into a relationship table?

- **a.** Every topic in the related row is linked to every topic within the <mapref> and vice versa in accordance with any *@linking* attributes defined.
- **b.** Every topic in the related row is linked to every topic within the <mapref>, but the <mapref> topics are not linked back to the other topics.
- **c.** You receive a compilation error. You cannot place a <mapref> into a relationship table.
- **d.** Every topic in the related row is linked to every topic within the <mapref> and vice versa regardless of any *@linking* attributes defined.

Every cell in a relationship table must contain a topic or map reference.

- True
- False

What element do you use to create relationships between topic references within the same cell?

An individual cell within a relationship table can contain multiple topic types.

- True
- False

Why might you need multiple rows in a relationship table?

a. One row defines bi-directional links, one row defines target-only links, and one row defines source-only links.
b. Each row defines a unique set of relationships; no relationships exist between the rows in a table.
c. Each <topicref> or <mapref> must have its own row.
d. Each call can contain only one topic or map reference, so multiple rows are required to define all the relationships.

Each topic within a map can only be used once within a relationship table.

- True
- False

What is the purpose of the <relcolspec> element?

a. To define each column in the relationship table and the default attribute values for references in that column.
b. To define the type of topics that must be included in that column.
c. To define the topic references that will be linked during processing.
d. To contain the <relheader> elements that define the column headers and attributes.

Select the true statements based on the given code.

```
<reltable>
   <relheader>
      <relcolspec type="concept"/>
      <relcolspec type="task"/>
      <relcolspec type="reference"/>
   </relheader>
   <relrow>
      <relcell>
         <topicref href="A.dita"/>
         <topicref href="B.dita"/>
         <topicref href="C.dita"/>
      </relcell>
      <relcell>
         <topicgroup collection-type="family>
            <topicref href="D.dita"/>
            <topicref href="E.dita"/>
            <topicref href="F.dita"/>
         </topicgroup>
      </relcell>
      <relcell>
         <topicref href="G.dita" linking="targetonly"/>
      </relcell>
   </relrow>
</reltable>
```

**a.** A.dita will be linked to B.dita.

**b.** All topics will link to G.dita, but G.dita will not link to any other topics.

**c.** G.dita will link to all other topics, but none of them will link back to G.dita.

**d.** E.dita will link to D.dita and F.dita.

**e.** B.dita will link to D.dita, E.dita, F.dita, and G.dita.

**f.** The link from D.dita to E.dita will be shown as "Next Topic".

# SECTION G

# Understanding Glossaries

DITA provides two different topic types for creating glossaries depending on your needs and approach:

- A <glossentry> topic contains a single term and provides a definition and related information about that term. Using this approach, every term in your glossary is a separate DITA topic. When you compile your glossary terms into a glossary list, you reference each topic in a DITA map. Some tools may provide a way to compile a glossary automatically by scanning the words in the text and producing a glossary that includes only those words.
- A <glossgroup> topic allows a title and multiple glossary entries in a single topic. You might choose to include all words in a single file or create multiple <glossgroup> topics that group related terms under a single title. For example, you might create glossary groupings by letter of the alphabet, product line, domain, or some other categorization.

There are advantages and disadvantages to each approach. Limiting a single file to an individual term and definition in a <glossentry> topic has obvious implications for reusability. With a repository of glossary term files, you can select only the appropriate words for each publication you produce or choose to output different glossary elements in different publications. If you intend to reference glossary terms through the keyref mechanism (see Referencing glossary terms on page 296), you need to use this approach. In addition, this approach also better supports translation. For example, translators will not need to re-alphabetize the file as they translate. However, creating a compiled glossary will likely require a transform to alphabetize your entries and stylesheet modifications to include letter-of-the-alphabet headings and to prevent each term from starting on a new page.

Conversely, a <glossgroup> topic might enable easier final production, but limits your ability for reuse and potentially puts more burden on the translation process. In addition, you cannot reference a specific term in a <glossgroup> topic using keyrefs. Nevertheless, in situations where you use a standard glossary in all your publications, this choice might be the better option.

Select the approach that works best for your individual needs. In this lesson, all glossary exercises use individual <glossentry> topics.

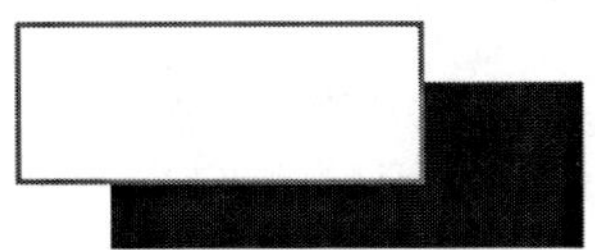

# LESSON 16

## Glossary Applications

A basic glossary topic contains a term and its definition. If a term has more than one definition, you must create a separate glossary topic for each definition. At publication, you should be able to assemble multiple definitions into one glossary item.

The DITA glossary topic was developed to serve as a rudimentary terminology database. You can use it to define terminology with information that could easily be transferred to a terminology database program. In addition to the term definition, you can include detailed information about each glossary term in the glossary body, including part of speech, acronyms and abbreviations, synonyms, and usage rules. You can indicate that a term is preferred or prohibited or define how and where a term should be used. Specifying the part of speech helps to facilitate the correct translation of a term.

In technical documentation, perhaps one of the more frequently used elements within the glossary body is the acronym. As part of the term's glossary body, use the element <glossSurfaceForm> to specify how the term and its acronym are used together and use the <glossAcronym> element to specify the acronym. For example, the term, "Darwin Information Typing Architecture", has a <glossSurfaceForm>, "Darwin Information Typing Architecture (DITA)", and a <glossAcronym>, "DITA". This construct allows you to reference terms in the text and let the processor determine the first time the term appears within the document being published. For the first instance of a term, you can specify that the full text in <glossSurfaceForm> be used. For subsequent occurrences, you can specify that only the acronym be used. For more information on referencing glossary terms, see the <abbreviated-form> element in the *OASIS Darwin Information Typing Architecture (DITA) Version 1.2 (OASIS Standard, 1 December 2010).*

The elements used to specify acronyms and abbreviations are designed to accommodate translations. Acronyms and abbreviations present special problems for translation because many languages may provide neither acronyms nor abbreviations for certain terms. In others, the order of term and acronym in the surface form may be reversed. The elements in the glossary topic allow you to translate terms correctly and supply acronyms or abbreviations if they exist.

## Creating a glossary

This exercise explains how to create a glossary using the <glossentry> topic type. You learn to

- create a <glossentry> topic
- add your glossary file to a map file and relationship table

1. Start a <glossentry> topic.

   If you are not using an editor that does so automatically, make sure to include the XML and DTD declarations and the root element, <glossentry>.

   ```
   <?xml version="1.0" encoding="UTF-8"?>
   <!DOCTYPE glossentry PUBLIC "-//OASIS//DTD DITA Glossary//EN"
      "http://docs.oasis-open.org/dita/v1.1/OS/dtd/glossary.dtd">
   <glossentry xml:lang="en-us">
   </glossentry>
   ```

2. Add an *@id* attribute and value to your <glossentry> element.

   The *@id* attribute is not required, but will enable you to reference the term within your topics more easily. In many cases, the ID will likely match the term; however, as shown here, you may want to shorten the term in the ID for easier referencing. Also keep in mind that if you provide more than one definition for a term, each must be in its own <glossentry>, and you will not be able to use the term as the ID for every definition of the term. As with all *@id* attributes, the ID must be unique. It can contain numbers, letters, and underscores, but it must start with a letter or a number. In this case, use "confcall".

   ```
   <?xml version="1.0" encoding="utf-8"?>
   <!DOCTYPE glossentry PUBLIC "-//OASIS//DTD DITA Glossary//EN"
      "http://docs.oasis-open.org/dita/v1.1/OS/dtd/glossary.dtd">
   <glossentry "xml:lang="en-us" id="confcall">
   </glossentry>
   ```

3. After the <glossentry> start tag, add a <glossterm> element and the content "conference call."

   ```
   <glossentry "xml:lang="en-us" id="confcall">
      <glossterm>conference call</glossterm>
   </glossentry>
   ```

4. After the <glossterm> end tag, add a <glossdef> element and a definition for the conference call term.

```
<glossentry "xml:lang="en-us" id="confcall">
   <glossterm>conference call</glossterm>
   <glossdef>a telephone call in which a caller may speak with
      several people in different locations at the same time
   </glossdef>
</glossentry>
```

5. Save your file as "g_confcall.dita".

   Using the "g_" at the beginning of your file name is a convenient way to indicate that the file is a glossary term.

6. Open the ComstarUGRelTable.ditamap file that you created in Creating a relationship table on page 181.

```
<?xml version="1.0" encoding'"utf-8"?>
<!DOCTYPE map PUBLIC "-//OASIS//DTD DITA Map//EN"
   "map.dtd">
<map id="ComstarUserGuide" xml:lang="en-us">
   <title>Comstar User Guide</title>
   <topicref href="ComstarOverview.dita"/>
   <topicref href="QuickGuide.dita"/>
   <topicref href="AboutHold.dita">
      <topicref href="HoldingACall.dita"/>
   </topicref>
   <topicref href="AboutTransfer.dita">
      <topicref href="TransferringACall.dita"/>
   </topicref>
   <topicref href="AboutForward.dita">
      <topicref href="ForwardingACall.dita"/>
   </topicref>
   <topicref href="AboutConferenceCalls.dita">
      <topicref href="PlacingACall.dita"/>
      <topicref href="LeavingAConferenceCallTemporarily.dita"/>
      <topicref href="ReenteringAConferenceCall.dita"/>
      <topicref href="ConsultingPrivatelyOnTheConferenceCall.dita"/>
      <topicref href="ReenteringACallWithAllPeople.dita"/>
   </topicref>
   <mapref href="../Components/Accessories.ditamap"/>
   <reltable>
      <relheader>
         <relcolspec type="concept"/>
         <relcolspec type="task"/>
         <relcolspec type="reference"/>
      </relheader>
      <relrow>
         <relcell>
            <topicref href="AboutHold.dita"/>
         </relcell>
         <relcell>
            <topicref href="HoldingACall.dita"/>
         </relcell>
         <relcell></relcell>
      </relrow>
      <relrow>
         <relcell>
            <topicref href="AboutTransfer.dita"/>
         </relcell>
         <relcell>
            <topicref href="TransferringACall.dita"/>
```

```
      </relcell>
      <relcell></relcell>
   </relrow>
   <relrow>
      <relcell>
         <topicref href="AboutForward.dita"/>
      </relcell>
      <relcell>
         <topicref href="ForwardingACall.dita"/>
      </relcell>
      <relcell></relcell>
   </relrow>
   <relrow>
      <relcell>
         <topicref href="AboutConferenceCalls.dita"/>
      </relcell>
      <relcell>
        <topicgroup collection-type="sequence">
          <topicref href="PlacingACall.dita"/>
          <topicref
            href="LeavingAConferenceCallTemporarily.dita"/>
          <topicref href="ReenteringAConferenceCall.dita"/>
          <topicref
            href="ConsultingPrivatelyOnTheConferenceCall.dita"/>
          <topicref href="ReenteringACallWithAllPeople.dita"/>
        </topicgroup>
      </relcell>
      <relcell></relcell>
   </relrow>
   <relrow>
      <relcell>
         <topicgroup collection-type="family">
            <topicref href="AboutHold.dita"/>
            <topicref href="AboutTransfer.dita"/>
            <topicref href="AboutForward.dita"/>
            <topicref href="AboutConferenceCalls.dita"/>
         </topicgroup>
      </relcell>
      <relcell></relcell>
      <relcell>
         <topicref href="QuickGuide.dita" linking="targetonly"/>
         <topicref href="../Components/Accessories.ditamap"
            linking="targetonly"/>
      </relcell>
   </relrow>
   <relrow>
      <relcell></relcell>
      <relcell>
         <topicref href="HoldingACall.dita"/>
         <topicref href="TransferringACall.dita"/>
         <topicref href="ForwardingACall.dita"/>
         <topicref href="PlacingACall.dita"/>
         <topicref
            href="LeavingAConferenceCallTemporarily.dita"/>
         <topicref href="ReenteringAConferenceCall.dita"/>
         <topicref
            href="ConsultingPrivatelyOnTheConferenceCall.dita"/>
         <topicref href="ReenteringACallWithAllPeople.dita"/>
      </relcell>
      <relcell>
         <topicref href="../Components/Accessories.ditamap"
```

```
                linking="targetonly"/>
          </relcell>
       </relrow>
    </reltable>
</map>
```

7. After the <mapref> element, add another <topicref> element and point its *@href* attribute to the g_confcall.dita topic.

```
<map id="ComstarUserGuide" xml:lang="en-us">
   ⋮
   <mapref href="../Components/Accessories.ditamap"/>
   <topicref href="g_confcall.dita"/>
   ⋮
</map>
```

8. In the relationship table, add the glossary topic as a "targetonly" relationship in the same rows that reference the Accessories.ditamap.

   The glossary topic is "targetonly" because you want the other topics in the relationship table row link to the glossary but you do not want the glossary topic to link back to the content. In the example, you include glossary in the same relationship table rows and cells that hold the other "targetonly" topics.

```
<map id="ComstarUserGuide" xml:lang="en-us">
   ⋮
   <mapref href="../Components/Accessories.ditamap"/>
   <topicref href="g_confcall.dita"/>
   <reltable>
   ⋮
      <relrow>
         <relcell>
            <topicgroup collection-type="family">
               <topicref href="AboutHold.dita"/>
               <topicref href="AboutTransfer.dita"/>
               <topicref href="AboutForward.dita"/>
               <topicref href="AboutConferenceCalls.dita"/>
            </topicgroup>
         </relcell>
         <relcell></relcell>
         <relcell>
            <topicgroup linking="targetonly">
               <topicref href="QuickGuide.dita"/>
               <topicref href="../Components/Accessories.ditamap"/>
               <topicref href="g_confcall.dita"/>
            </topicgroup>
         </relcell>
      </relrow>
      <relrow>
         <relcell></relcell>
         <relcell>
            <topicref href="HoldingACall.dita"/>
            <topicref href="TransferringACall.dita"/>
            <topicref href="ForwardingACall.dita"/>
            <topicref href="PlacingACall.dita"/>
            <topicref
               href="LeavingAConferenceCallTemporarily.dita"/>
            <topicref href="ReenteringAConferenceCall.dita"/>
```

```
            <topicref
               href="ConsultingPrivatelyOnTheConferenceCall.dita"/>
            <topicref href="ReenteringACallWithAllPeople.dita"/>
         </relcell>
         <relcell>
            <topicref href="../Components/Accessories.ditamap"
               linking="targetonly"/>
            <topicref href="g_confcall.dita"
               linking="targetonly"/>
         </relcell>
      </relrow>
   </reltable>
</map>
```

9. Save your work in the ComstarUGRelTable.ditamap file.

**Adding information to a glossary entry**

This exercise explains how to include information about a glossary term in addition to its basic definition. You learn to

- specify the part of speech for the term
- add acronym information

1. Open the glossary you created in the last exercise.

```
<?xml version="1.0" encoding="utf-8"?>
<!DOCTYPE glossentry PUBLIC "-//OASIS//DTD DITA Glossary//EN"
   "http://docs.oasis-open.org/dita/v1.1/OS/dtd/glossary.dtd">
<glossentry "xml:lang="en-us" id="fcc">
   <glossterm>Federal Communications Commission</glossterm>
   <glossdef>a government agency that regulates and oversees
      communications by radio, television, wire, satellite,
      and cable</glossdef>
</glossentry>
```

2. Add <glossBody> start and end tags after the <glossdef> end tag for the "Federal Communications Commission" term.

```
<glossentry "xml:lang="en-us" id="fcc">
   <glossterm>Federal Communications Commission</glossterm>
   <glossdef>a government agency that regulates and oversees
      communications by radio, television, wire, satellite,
      and cable</glossdef>
   <glossBody>
   </glossBody>
</glossentry>
```

3. Add an empty <glossPartOfSpeech> element between the <glossBody> start and end tags and assign a *@value* of "properNoun".

   If a part of speech is not defined, the default is "noun".

```
<glossentry "xml:lang="en-us" id="fcc">
   <glossterm>Federal Communications Commission</glossterm>
   <glossdef>a government agency that regulates and oversees
      communications by radio, television, wire, satellite,
      and cable</glossdef>
```

```
   <glossBody>
      <glossPartOfSpeech value="properNoun"/>
   </glossBody>
</glossentry>
```

4. Add <glossSurfaceForm> start and end tags for the "Federal Communications Commission", entering the term and its acronym as you would expect to see it in its first occurrence in a document.

   The <glossSurfaceForm> allows you to specify exactly how the term and its acronym should appear. In translation, some languages either do not have an acronym for a term or place the acronym before rather than after the term. By explicitly defining the <glossSurfaceForm>, you provide a mechanism for the translator to provide the correct translation.

```
<glossentry "xml:lang="en-us" id="fcc">
   <glossterm>Federal Communications Commission</glossterm>
   <glossdef>a government agency that regulates and oversees
      communications by radio, television, wire, satellite,
      and cable</glossdef>
   <glossBody>
      <glossPartOfSpeech value="properNoun"/>
      <glossSurfaceForm>Federal Communications Commission (FCC)
      </glossSurfaceForm>
   </glossBody>
</glossentry>
```

5. After the <glossSurfaceForm> end tag, add <glossAlt> start and end tags.

   The <glossAlt> element is a container element for all variants of the term. In addition to acronyms, you might include abbreviations and synonyms within this container.

```
<glossentry "xml:lang="en-us" id="fcc">
   <glossterm>Federal Communications Commission</glossterm>
   <glossdef>a government agency that regulates and oversees
      communications by radio, television, wire, satellite,
      and cable</glossdef>
   <glossBody>
      <glossPartOfSpeech value="properNoun"/>
      <glossSurfaceForm>Federal Communications Commission (FCC)
      </glossSurfaceForm>
      <glossAlt>
      </glossAlt>
   </glossBody>
</glossentry>
```

6. Within the <glossAlt> start and end tags, add a <glossAcronym> element and the content "FCC."

   By explicitly adding the <glossAcronym>, you provide a mechanism for the translator to add an acronym if appropriate. You should also inform your translator that this element can be left blank if the term has no acronym in the target language.

```
<glossentry "xml:lang="en-us" id="fcc">
   <glossterm>Federal Communications Commission</glossterm>
   <glossdef>a government agency that regulates and oversees
      communications by radio, television, wire, satellite,
      and cable</glossdef>
   <glossBody>
      <glossPartOfSpeech value="properNoun"/>
      <glossSurfaceForm>Federal Communications Commission (FCC)
      </glossSurfaceForm>
      <glossAlt>
         <glossAcronym>FCC</glossAcronym>
      </glossAlt>
   </glossBody>
</glossentry>
```

**7.** Save your work as g_fcc.dita.

### Glossary elements

The following glossary elements are used in the DITA model. The elements are listed here in the order that you might use them when creating a glossary.

**<glossgroup> glossary group**
: Use the <glossgroup> element to group a series of <glossentry> elements into a single topic. You can use include all your glossary terms in a <glossgroup> for publication in your map. However, you must alphabetize them manually, and the translator will have to re-alphabetize them after translation.

**<glossentry> glossary entry**
: Use the <glossentry> element as a container for one term and one definition. If a term has multiple definitions, use separate <glossentry> elements for each definition.

**<glossterm> glossary term**
: Use the <glossterm> element to specify the term that you describe in the glossary entry. Only one <glossterm> element is permitted for each <glossentry>.

**<glossdef> glossary definition**
: Use the <glossdef> element to enter a definition for your term. Only one <glossdef> element is permitted for each <glossentry>. If the same term has multiple definitions, create multiple <glossentry> elements.

**<glossBody> glossBody**
: Use the <glossBody> element as a container for additional information about the glossary entry. The <glossBody> element contains elements to describe part of speech, status, usage, alternative terms, and more.

**<glossPartOfSpeech> glossary part of speech**
: Use the <glossPartOfSpeech> element to describe how the term is used in a sentence. Use the *@value* attribute to define the part of speech; for example,

noun, proper noun, verb, adjective, or adverb are each possible parts of speech. If undefined, the default value for <glossPartOfSpeech> is "noun".

**<glossSurfaceForm> glossary surface form**

Use the <glossSurfaceForm> element to specify the full term and its acronym, if one exists, when it first appears in the text. For example, terms that will later be referred to by their acronym should on first occurrence include the full term and the acronym, i.e., Federal Communication Commission (FCC). The <glossSurfaceForm> provides a means for the translator to provide the correct form of the term, especially when no acronym is available or the acronym appears before rather than after the term.

**<glossAlt> glossary alternative**

Use the <glossAlt> as a container for variant terms. The <glossAlt> element can contain only one alternate term (acronym, abbreviation, synonym) as well as elements such as status and usage to describe the alternate term. To include multiple alternate terms, use multiple <glossAlt> elements.

**<glossAcronym> glossary acronym**

Use the <glossAcronym> element to provide the accepted acronym for the term, which is often formed from the initials of the several words making up the glossary term. The <glossAcronym> may be left blank if a term does not have an acronym in a target language. Also consider leaving a blank <glossAcronym> in your source language if the translator will need to add an acronym in a target language.

**<glossAbbreviation> glossary abbreviation**

Use the <glossAbbreviation> element to provide an abbreviated form of the term. For example, you might specify that after an initial introduction of the term "zoological gardens," the abbreviated form "zoo" may be used.

**<glossSynonym> glossary synonym**

Use the <glossSynonym> element to list a word that has the same definition as the glossary term.

**<glossStatus> glossary status**

Use the <glossStatus> element to provide information about the permitted use of a term. Use the *@value* attribute to define the accepted use; for example, preferred, restricted, prohibited, or obsolete are each possible statements about the status of a term in your terminology database.

**<glossUsage> glossary usage**

Use the <glossUsage> element to provide additional information about how and where the term should be used. For example, you might indicate that a term is colloquial or slang or is permitted only in certain contexts.

The following example illustrates the use of these glossary elements in a DITA file.

```
<?xml version="1.0" encoding="UTF-8"?>
<!DOCTYPE glossgroup PUBLIC "-//OASIS//DTD DITA Glossary Group//EN"
   "glossgroup.dtd">
<glossgroup id="glossary">
  <title>Glossary</title>
  <glossentry id="estimate">
    <glossterm>estimate</glossterm>
    <glossdef>to calculate the approximate cost of an activity</
glossdef>
    <glossBody>
      <glossPartOfSpeech value="verb"/>
      <glossStatus value="preferred"/>
      <glossAlt>
        <glossSynonym>project</glossSynonym>
        <glossUsage>Do not use because of the easy confusion with the
           noun.</glossUsage>
     </glossAlt>
    </glossBody>
  </glossentry>
  <glossentry id="PUBEstimator">
    <glossterm>PUB$Estimator</glossterm>
    <glossdef>a program used to estimate and track time spent
developing
       publications</glossdef>
    <glossBody>
      <glossPartOfSpeech value="properNoun"/>
      <glossStatus value="preferred"/>
      <glossAlt>
        <glossAbbreviation>PUB$</glossAbbreviation>
        <glossUsage>Use when describing the actions that the program
           takes in response to steps; i.e. PUB$ calculates a new
           hours/page.</glossUsage>
     </glossAlt>
    </glossBody>
  </glossentry>
  <glossentry id="ROI">
    <glossterm>return on investment</glossterm>
    <glossdef>a performance measure used to calculate the efficiency of
       an investment. Calculated by dividing the benefit of the
investment
       by the cost of the investment.</glossdef>
    <glossBody>
      <glossSurfaceForm>return on investment (ROI)</glossSurfaceForm>
      <glossAlt>
        <glossAcronym>ROI</glossAcronym>
     </glossAlt>
    </glossBody>
  </glossentry>
</glossgroup>
```

**Glossary review questions**

What are the two glossary topic types provided by DITA?

What element do you use when you want to provide a form of the term that includes its acronym?

To provide multiple meanings for a single glossary term, include multiple <glossdef> tags within the <glossentry> container.

- True
- False

What is wrong with the following code?

```
<glossentry id="automobile">
   <glossterm>automobile</glossterm>
   <glossdef>a passenger vehicle propelled by an
      internal-combustion engine, suitable for use
      on a street</glossdef>
   <glossBody>
      <glossPartOfSpeech value="noun"/>
      <glossAlt>
         <glossAbbreviation>auto</glossAbbreviation>
         <glossSynonym>car</glossSynonym>
         <glossUsage>Do not shorten automobile. Use
            the word car instead.</glossUsage>
      </glossAlt>
   </glossBody>
</glossentry>
```

**a.** The <glossentry> element must be contained within a <glossgroup> container.

**b.** The <glossAlt> container cannot contain a <glossUsage> element.

**c.** The <glossAlt> container cannot contain more than one variant.

**d.** Noun should be declared as a *@type* attribute, not a *@value* attribute, within the <glossPartOfSpeech> element.

The <glossBody> element enables you to provide what additional information about a term. Select all that apply.

- **a.** Antonym
- **b.** Synonym
- **c.** Part of speech
- **d.** Abbreviation
- **e.** How and where to use it

# SECTION H

# Understanding Bookmap Basics

Bookmaps extend the hierarchical structure provided by DITA maps. Like a DITA map, the bookmap provides a mechanism for ordering topics and creating hierarchy. In addition, the bookmap provides semantic elements to define your publication's structure and publication-specific metadata. Bookmaps address the requirement of grouping and organizing DITA topics using a traditional, book-based approach.

We group the main features of bookmaps into three categories: 1) frontmatter and backmatter; 2) parts, chapters, and appendices; and 3) book metadata. Using these three categories you can create a publication with a traditional book structure.

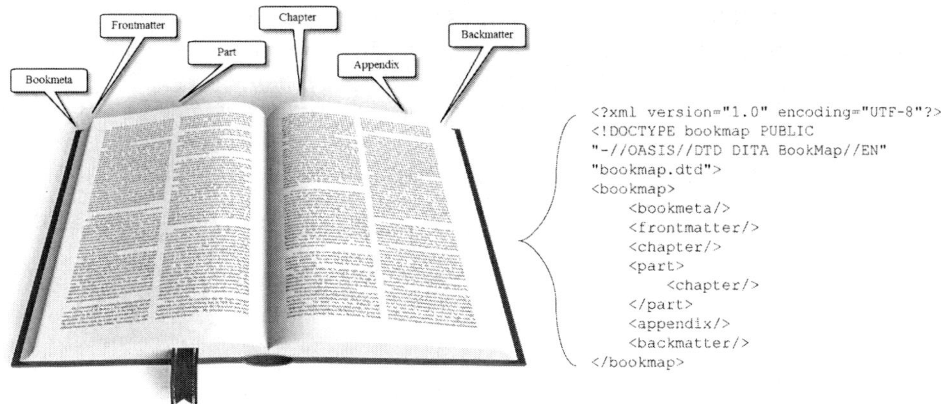
Frontmatter
Chapter
Backmatter
Part
Appendix
Bookmeta
<?xml version="1.0" encoding="UTF-8"?>
<!DOCTYPE bookmap PUBLIC
"-//OASIS//DTD DITA BookMap//EN"
"bookmap.dtd">
<bookmap>
<bookmeta/>
<frontmatter/>
<chapter/>
<part>
<chapter/>
</part>
<appendix/>
<backmatter/>
</bookmap>

**Figure 15: Bookmap parts and supporting code**

### Frontmatter and backmatter support

Bookmaps provide a mechanism to include traditional frontmatter and backmatter in your publication. For you example, you can choose to add tables of contents and figures to your frontmatter, as well as acknowledgments, trademarks, legal notices, colophons, and a preface. In your backmatter, you might include a glossary and an index.

### Parts, chapters, and appendices

Parts, chapters, and appendices are used to build the body of your publication. Bookmaps allow many configurations of these elements. All three elements can either point directly to topics or other maps using the *@href* attribute or can act as container elements, holding nested <topicref> elements. The <part> element also serves as a container for <chapter> elements.

You will find it especially useful to construct your bookmaps by referencing chapter- or part-level maps. These submaps contain the topics and allow different sections of a book to be managed independently. A team of writers can work together to create independent maps for chapters or parts and combine them to create one or more bookmaps.

Standard chapter maps may be reused in multiple bookmaps. For example, one organization uses a standard map of the required safety information as the second chapter in all of their installation and operations manuals.

### Book metadata

Book metadata provides a very rich set of metadata for the bookmap. The elements range from information about names and addresses and book identification numbers to book restrictions and change history. Book metadata provides a way to collect information about the publication. It is also used to define the content required for a book's front and back covers and other areas where standard information occurs.

The content of book metadata can be used to populate standard elements in your output. For example, you can use the content of the <mainbooktitle> and <bookrights> elements to build the front cover of your publication.

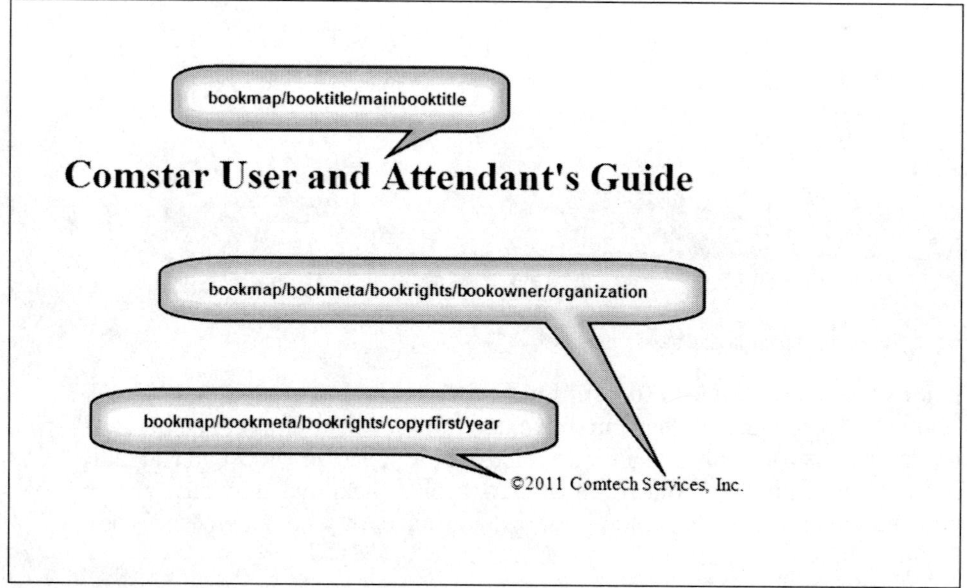

You can also use the same information in a header or footer. Note in this example, the page header repeats the book title. By using book metadata to define these elements, your content is correctly and consistently tagged with DITA elements.

14 Comstar User and Attendant's Guide

**Reentering a conference call**

1. Lift the handset or press Speaker.
   The Speaker button is the last button on the left.
2. Press the appropriate line or station button of the parties you wish to consult with.
3. Press Conference.
   This will connect you with the parties on the conference call.

# LESSON 17

## Bookmap Structure

Just like the DITA map, the bookmap functions as a collection of pointers to the content of a publication. By nesting references to content, you create hierarchy. You can nest references to maps or topics in a bookmap, but you cannot nest a reference to another bookmap.

In this lesson you learn to create a bookmap. This lesson contains four exercises:

- Creating a bookmap
- Creating submaps
- Adding bookmap content
- Adding book metadata

**Creating a bookmap**

This exercise introduces the standard XML markup included in a bookmap. In this exercise, you learn to

- create a bookmap
- add a book title
- add frontmatter and backmatter to the bookmap
- include a table of contents, glossary, and index in your bookmap

**1.** Create a new bookmap.

You can start a new bookmap in a text editor or in an XML editor. In most XML editors, you can choose **file > new > DITA bookmap** . As it does when you create any topic, your XML editor usually includes the DTD declaration, XML declaration, and <bookmap> start and end tags automatically. If you choose to use a text editor, enter the markup shown here.

```
<?xml version="1.0" encoding="utf-8"?>
<!DOCTYPE bookmap PUBLIC "-//OASIS//DTD DITA BookMap//EN"
   "bookmap.dtd">
<bookmap xml:lang="en-us">
</bookmap>
```

**2.** Add an *@id* attribute to your <bookmap> element.

A unique ID allows you to easily identify your map. As with all *@id* attributes, the ID value must be unique. It can contain numbers, letters, and underscores, but it must start with a letter or a number.

```
<?xml version="1.0" encoding="utf-8"?>
<!DOCTYPE bookmap PUBLIC "-//OASIS//DTD DITA BookMap//EN"
   "bookmap.dtd">
<bookmap id="ComstarUserAndAttendantsGuide" xml:lang="en-us">
</bookmap>
```

3. Add a <booktitle> element container to your bookmap.

```
<bookmap id="ComstarUserAndAttendantsGuide" xml:lang="en-us">
   <booktitle>
   <booktitle>
</bookmap>
```

4. Add a <mainbooktitle> element to your <booktitle> container element, and enter a title.

   You can also choose to enter any number of alternate book titles (<booktitlealt>) within the <booktitle> element.

```
<bookmap id="ComstarUserAndAttendantsGuide" xml:lang="en-us">
   <booktitle>
      <mainbooktitle>Comstar User and Attendant's
         Guide</mainbooktitle>
   </booktitle>
</bookmap>
```

5. Add <frontmatter> start and end tags after the <booktitle> end tag.

   The <frontmatter> element is a container for information that appears at the beginning of the publication before the body content.

```
<bookmap id="ComstarUserAndAttendantsGuide" xml:lang="en-us">
   <booktitle>
      <mainbooktitle>Comstar User and Attendant's
         Guide</mainbooktitle>
   </booktitle>
   <frontmatter>
   </frontmatter>
</bookmap>
```

6. Add an empty <preface> element between the <frontmatter> tags, and set its href attribute to "ComstarPreface.dita".

```
<bookmap id="ComstarUserAndAttendantsGuide" xml:lang="en-us">
   ⋮
   <frontmatter>
      <preface href="ComstarPreface.dita"/>
   </frontmatter>
</bookmap>
```

7. Add <booklists> start and end tags after the <preface> tag.

The <booklists> element is a container for any list in the publication. In the frontmatter, it might contain tables of contents, figures, and tables; in backmatter, it typically contains the glossary and index.

```
<bookmap id="ComstarUserAndAttendantsGuide" xml:lang="en-us">
   ⋮
   <frontmatter>
      <preface href="ComstarPreface.dita"/>
      <booklists>
      </booklists>
   </frontmatter>
</bookmap>
```

**8.** Add an empty <toc> element between the <booklists> tags.

On publication, the processor recognizes the presence of the <toc> element and generates a table of contents.

```
<bookmap id="ComstarUserAndAttendantsGuide" xml:lang="en-us">
   ⋮
   <frontmatter>
      <preface href="ComstarPreface.dita"/>
      <booklists>
         <toc/>
      </booklists>
   </frontmatter>
</bookmap>
```

**9.** Nest <booklists> start and end tags within <backmatter> start and end tags after the <frontmatter> end tag.

```
<bookmap id="ComstarUserAndAttendantsGuide" xml:lang="en-us">
   ⋮
   <frontmatter>
      ⋮
   </frontmatter>
   <backmatter>
      <booklists>
      </booklists>
   </backmatter>
</bookmap>
```

**10.** Nest <glossarylist> start and end tags within the backmatter <booklists> tags, and add <topicref> elements for each of your glossary term files.

Alternatively, you can include an *@href* attribute in the <glossarylist> pointing to a single <glossgroup> file, submap of glossary terms, or another manually generated glossary file. The referenced file or map will then be added to your book. Your processor may also be able to generate a glossary list from the terms used in the book. If so, do not include an *@href* attribute or reference another file.

**Note:** The glossary files will be placed into your book in the order you put them in the map. Be sure to include the files so that your terms are alphabetical.

```
<bookmap id="ComstarUserAndAttendantsGuide" xml:lang="en-us">
   ⋮
   <backmatter>
      <booklists>
         <glossarylist>
            <topicref href="g_confcall.dita"/>
            <topicref href="g_fcc.dita"/>
         </glossarylist>
      </booklists>
   </backmatter>
</bookmap>
```

**11.** Add an empty <indexlist> tag after the <glossarylist> end tag.

As with the <glossarylist> element, the <indexlist> element can include an *@href* attribute pointing to manually generated index files. If no *@href* attribute is included, the processor should generate the list.

```
<bookmap id="ComstarUserAndAttendantsGuide" xml:lang="en-us">
   ⋮
   <backmatter>
      <booklists>
         <glossarylist>
            <topicref href="g_confcall.dita"/>
            <topicref href="g_fcc.dita"/>
         </glossarylist>
         <indexlist/>
      </booklists>
   </backmatter>
</bookmap>
```

**12.** Save this file as ComstarUserAndAttendantsGuide.ditamap.

### ComstarUserAndAttendantsGuide.ditamap

Your entire bookmap should now look like this example.

```
<?xml version="1.0" encoding="utf-8"?>
<!DOCTYPE bookmap PUBLIC "-//OASIS//DTD DITA BookMap//EN"
   "bookmap.dtd">
<bookmap id="ComstarUserAndAttendantsGuide" xml:lang="en-us">
   <booktitle>
      <mainbooktitle>Comstar User and Attendant's
         Guide</mainbooktitle>
   </booktitle>
   <frontmatter>
      <preface href="ComstarPreface.dita"/>
      <booklists>
         <toc/>
      </booklists>
   </frontmatter>
   <backmatter>
```

```
      <booklists>
         <glossarylist>
            <topicref href="g_confcall.dita"/>
            <topicref href="g_fcc.dita"/>
         </glossarylist>
         <indexlist/>
      </booklists>
   </backmatter>
</bookmap>
```

**Creating submaps**

Because several sections in the *Comstar User Guide* can be used in other deliverables, it is helpful to group these sections into submaps. Submaps are created with the <map> element and can be referenced in maps and bookmaps with the *@href* attribute. Submaps are ideal for collaborative content creation. Each author can create one or several submaps that are referenced by a lead writer who builds the final publication map or bookmap.

In this exercise, you will create four DITA maps that will be used in the following exercise. The four maps that you will create are

- Hold Call
- Transfer Call
- Forward Call
- Conference Call

1. Start a new DITA map.

   Make sure to include the XML and DTD declarations and the root element <map>.

   ```
   <?xml version="1.0" encoding="utf-8"?>
   <!DOCTYPE map PUBLIC "-//OASIS//DTD DITA Map//EN"
      "map.dtd">
   <map xml:lang="en-us">
   </map>
   ```

2. Add an *@id* attribute and value to your <map> element.

   ```
   <?xml version="1.0" encoding="utf-8"?>
   <!DOCTYPE map PUBLIC "-//OASIS//DTD DITA Map//EN"
      "map.dtd">
   <map id="HoldCall" xml:lang="en-us">
   </map>
   ```

3. Add a <title> element and value to your map.

   ```
   <?xml version="1.0" encoding="utf-8"?>
   <!DOCTYPE map PUBLIC "-//OASIS//DTD DITA Map//EN"
      "map.dtd">
   <map id="HoldCall" xml:lang="en-us">
      <title>Holding a Call</title>
   </map>
   ```

4. After the map title, add <topicref> start and end tags and assign an *@href* attribute of "AboutHold.dita".

```
<?xml version="1.0" encoding="utf-8"?>
<!DOCTYPE map PUBLIC "-//OASIS//DTD DITA Map//EN"
   "map.dtd">
<map id="HoldCall" xml:lang="en-us">
   <title>Holding a Call</title>
   <topicref href="AboutHold.dita">
   </topicref>
</map>
```

5. Nest an empty <topicref> tag within the AboutHold.dita <topicref> start and end tags and assign an *@href* attribute of "HoldingACall.dita".

```
<?xml version="1.0" encoding="utf-8"?>
<!DOCTYPE map PUBLIC "-//OASIS//DTD DITA Map//EN"
   "map.dtd">
<map id="HoldCall" xml:lang="en-us">
   <title>Holding a Call</title>
   <topicref href="AboutHold.dita">
      <topicref href="HoldingACall.dita"/>
   </topicref>
</map>
```

6. Save this file as HoldCall.ditamap.
7. Repeat these steps to create three additional submaps, Transfer Call, Forward Call, and Conference Call, as shown in the examples.

```
<?xml version="1.0" encoding="utf-8"?>
<!DOCTYPE map PUBLIC "-//OASIS//DTD DITA Map//EN"
   "map.dtd">
<map id="TransferCall" xml:lang="en-us">
   <title>Transferring a Call</title>
   <topicref href="AboutTransfer.dita">
      <topicref href="TransferringACall.dita"/>
   </topicref>
</map>
```

```
<?xml version="1.0" encoding="utf-8"?>
<!DOCTYPE map PUBLIC "-//OASIS//DTD DITA Map//EN"
   "map.dtd">
<map id="ForwardCall" xml:lang="en-us">
   <title>Forwarding a Call</title>
   <topicref href="AboutForward.dita">
      <topicref href="ForwardingACall.dita"/>
   </topicref>
</map>
```

```
<?xml version="1.0" encoding="utf-8"?>
<!DOCTYPE map PUBLIC "-//OASIS//DTD DITA Map//EN"
   "map.dtd">
<map id="ConferenceCall" xml:lang="en-us">
   <title>Conference Calls</title>
   <topicref href="AboutConferenceCalls.dita">
      <topicref href="PlacingACall.dita"/>
      <topicref href="LeavingAConferenceCallTemporarily.dita"/>
```

```
        <topicref href="ReenteringAConferenceCall.dita"/>
        <topicref href="ConsultingPrivatelyOnTheConferenceCall.dita"/>
        <topicref href="ReenteringACallWithAllPeople.dita"/>
    </topicref>
</map>
```

**Adding bookmap content**

This exercise explains how to add content to your bookmap using the submaps you created in the previous exercise. In this exercise, you learn to

- add chapters
- group chapters in parts
- add an appendix

1. Open the bookmap you started in the first exercise of this lesson.

```
<?xml version="1.0" encoding="utf-8"?>
<!DOCTYPE bookmap PUBLIC "-//OASIS//DTD DITA BookMap//EN"
   "bookmap.dtd">
<bookmap id="ComstarUserAndAttendantsGuide" xml:lang="en-us">
   <booktitle>
      <mainbooktitle>Comstar User and Attendant's
         Guide</mainbooktitle>
   </booktitle>
   <frontmatter>
      <preface href="ComstarPreface.dita"/>
      <booklists>
         <toc/>
      </booklists>
   </frontmatter>
   <backmatter>
      <booklists>
         <glossarylist>
            <topicref href="g_confcall.dita"/>
            <topicref href="g_fcc.dita"/>
         </glossarylist>
         <indexlist/>
      </booklists>
   </backmatter>
</bookmap>
```

2. Insert an empty <chapter> element between the <frontmatter> end tag and <backmatter> start tag, and assign an href of "QuickGuide.dita".

   The <chapter> element contains references to topics that appear in the publication's first chapter. There is no limit to the number of <chapter> elements your bookmap may contain.

   The *@href* attribute on the <chapter> element is optional. When you include an *@href* within the <chapter> element, the title of the referenced topic or map becomes the chapter title. When you do not include an *@href* attribute, you can include a <topicmeta> container within the <chapter> container and set the name of the chapter using a <navtitle> element. In this case, the title defined in the QuickGuide.dita file, Quick Guide to Basic Telephone Use, is the title of the first chapter.

```
<bookmap id="ComstarUserAndAttendantsGuide" xml:lang="en-us">
   ⋮
   </frontmatter>
   <chapter href="QuickGuide.dita"/>
   <backmatter>
   ⋮
</bookmap>
```

3. Add <part> start and end tags after the QuickGuide.dita chapter.

   A <part> element groups multiple topics or chapters together. Once you have included a <part> in a bookmap, you cannot include a <chapter> element without embedding it within a part.

```
<bookmap id="ComstarUserAndAttendantsGuide" xml:lang="en-us">
   ⋮
   <chapter href="QuickGuide.dita"/>
   <part>
   </part>
   ⋮
</bookmap>
```

4. Provide a title for the part by nesting a <navtitle> element within <topicmeta> tags.

```
<bookmap id="ComstarUserAndAttendantsGuide" xml:lang="en-us">
   ⋮
   <chapter href="QuickGuide.dita"/>
   <part>
      <topicmeta>
         <navtitle>Basic Functions</navtitle>
      </topicmeta>
   </part>
   ⋮
</bookmap>
```

5. Add three empty <chapter> elements after the <metadata> end tag, and assign their *@href* attributes to the three submaps you created in the previous exercise.

   In this case, the *@href* attribute points to the location of a DITA map rather than to an individual topic. By creating your book chapters using a series of chapter-level maps, you can more easily manage the content. If you have several writers working on independent chapter-level map content, you can combine these maps into any number of different bookmaps, facilitating content reuse. If you define a reference to content other than DITA topics within the <chapter> *@href* attribute, you should also include the *@format* attribute to identify the kind of resource being referenced.

```
<bookmap id="ComstarUserAndAttendantsGuide" xml:lang="en-us">
   ⋮
   <chapter href="QuickGuide.dita"/>
   <part>
      <topicmeta>
         <navtitle>Basic Functions</navtitle>
      </topicmeta>
      <chapter href="HoldCall.ditamap" format="ditamap"/>
      <chapter href="TransferCall.ditamap" format="ditamap"/>
      <chapter href="ForwardCall.ditamap" format="ditamap"/>
   </part>
   ⋮
</bookmap>
```

6. Add a second part titled "Advanced Functions", and include the ConferenceCalls.ditamap file in that part.

```
<bookmap id="ComstarUserAndAttendantsGuide" xml:lang="en-us">
   ⋮
   <chapter href="QuickGuide.dita"/>
   <part>
      <topicmeta>
         <navtitle>Basic Functions</navtitle>
      </topicmeta>
      <chapter href="HoldCall.ditamap" format="ditamap"/>
      <chapter href="TransferCall.ditamap" format="ditamap"/>
      <chapter href="ForwardCall.ditamap" format="ditamap"/>
   </part>
   <part>
      <topicmeta>
         <navtitle>Advanced Functions</navtitle>
      </topicmeta>
      <chapter href="ConferenceCall.ditamap" format="ditamap"/>
   </part>
   ⋮
</bookmap>
```

7. Add <appendices> start and end tags after the second part.

   The <appendices> element is an optional wrapper for <appendix> elements within a book.

```
<bookmap id="ComstarUserAndAttendantsGuide" xml:lang="en-us">
   ⋮
   <part>
      <topicmeta>
         <navtitle>Advanced Functions</navtitle>
      </topicmeta>
      <chapter href="ConferenceCall.ditamap" format="ditamap"/>
   </part>
   <appendices>
   </appendices>
   ⋮
</bookmap>
```

8. Add a title for the <appendices> section.

```
<bookmap id="ComstarUserAndAttendantsGuide" xml:lang="en-us">
   ⋮
   <appendices>
      <topicmeta>
         <navtitle>Appendices</navtitle>
      </topicmeta>
   </appendices>
   ⋮
</bookmap>
```

9. Add two empty <appendix> tags within the <appendices> wrapper. Point the first to the "../Components/Accessories.ditamap" file and the second to the "../../ComstarPricing.pdf" file.

```
<bookmap id="ComstarUserAndAttendantsGuide" xml:lang="en-us">
   ⋮
   <appendices>
      <topicmeta>
         <navtitle>Appendices</navtitle>
      </topicmeta>
      <appendix href="../Components/Accessories.ditamap"
         format="ditamap"/>
      <appendix href="../../ComstarPricing.pdf" format="pdf"/>
   </appendices>
   ⋮
</bookmap>
```

10. Save your work in the ComstarUserAndAttendantsGuide.ditamap file.

### ComstarUserAndAttendantsGuide.ditamap

The example shows the complete ComstarUserAndAttendantsGuide.ditamap, which includes a preface, table of contents, five chapters, two appendices, a glossary, and an index. After an introductory chapter, the remaining chapters are divided into two parts, and the appendixes are grouped into an appendices section.

```
<?xml version="1.0" encoding="utf-8"?>
<!DOCTYPE bookmap PUBLIC "-//OASIS//DTD DITA BookMap//EN"
   "bookmap.dtd">
<bookmap id="ComstarUserAndAttendantsGuide" xml:lang="en-us">
   <booktitle>
      <mainbooktitle>Comstar User and Attendant's
         Guide</mainbooktitle>
   </booktitle>
   <frontmatter>
      <preface href="ComstarPreface.dita"/>
      <booklists>
         <toc/>
      </booklists>
   </frontmatter>
   <chapter href="QuickGuide.dita"/>
   <part>
      <topicmeta>
         <navtitle>Basic Functions</navtitle>
```

```
      </topicmeta>
      <chapter href="HoldCall.ditamap" format="ditamap"/>
      <chapter href="TransferCall.ditamap" format="ditamap"/>
      <chapter href="ForwardCall.ditamap" format="ditamap"/>
   </part>
   <part>
      <topicmeta>
         <navtitle>Advanced Functions</navtitle>
      </topicmeta>
      <chapter href="ConferenceCall.ditamap" format="ditamap"/>
   </part>
   <appendices>
      <topicmeta>
         <navtitle>Appendices</navtitle>
      </topicmeta>
      <appendix href="../Components/Accessories.ditamap"
         format="ditamap"/>
      <appendix href="../../ComstarPricing.pdf" format="pdf"/>
   </appendices>
   <backmatter>
      <booklists>
         <glossarylist>
            <topicref href="g_confcall.dita"/>
            <topicref href="g_fcc.dita"/>
         </glossarylist>
         <indexlist/>
      </booklists>
   </backmatter>
</bookmap>
```

**Adding metadata to your bookmap**

Book metadata is used to hold information about your publication as a whole, such as the copyright year and holder. You can leverage the contents of book metadata for search. And, using your stylesheet, you can include the content of <bookmeta> elements in your final publication. For example, you may want to include the copyright year on the front cover of a PDF. By including the copyright year in <bookmeta>, you have this option.

In this exercise, you learn to

- add the book's International Standard Book Number (ISBN) to your bookmap
- add copyright information to your bookmap

1. Open the bookmap you created in the previous exercise.
2. Insert <bookmeta> start and end tags after the <booktitle> end tag.

   The <bookmeta> element is the container for the publication's metadata.

```
<bookmap id="ComstarUserAndAttendantsGuide" xml:lang="en-us">
   <booktitle>
      <mainbooktitle>Comstar User and Attendant's
         Guide</mainbooktitle>
   </booktitle>
   <bookmeta>
   </bookmeta>
   ⋮
</bookmap>
```

3. Nest <isbn> tags within <bookid> start and end tags, and define the book's ISBN.

   The <bookid> container includes the publisher's information for the book, such as part number, edition and volume, and ISBN.

```
<bookmap id="ComstarUserAndAttendantsGuide" xml:lang="en-us">
   ⋮
   <bookmeta>
      <bookid>
         <isbn>012-3456789012</isbn>
      </bookid>
   </bookmeta>
   ⋮
</bookmap>
```

4. Insert <bookrights> start and end tags after the <bookid> end tag.

   The <bookrights> element is a container for the publication's copyright information.

```
<bookmap id="ComstarUserAndAttendantsGuide" xml:lang="en-us">
   ⋮
   <bookmeta>
      <bookid>
         <isbn>012-3456789012</isbn>
      </bookid>
      <bookrights>
      </bookrights>
   </bookmeta>
   ⋮
</bookmap>
```

5. In the <bookrights> element, nest a <year> element within a <copyrfirst> container element, and enter the copyright year.

   The <copyrfirst> element contains the first year of publication. If you need to display more than one publication year, use the <copyrlast> element in addition to <copyrfirst>.

```
<bookmap id="ComstarUserAndAttendantsGuide" xml:lang="en-us">
   ⋮
   <bookmeta>
      <bookid>
         <isbn>012-3456789012</isbn>
      </bookid>
```

```
      <bookrights>
         <copyrfirst>
            <year>2011</year>
         </copyrfirst>
      </bookrights>
   </bookmeta>
   ⋮
</bookmap>
```

6. After the <copyrfirst> end tag, nest an <organization> element within a <bookowner> container element, and enter the copyright holder's name.

```
<bookmap id="ComstarUserAndAttendantsGuide" xml:lang="en-us">
   ⋮
   <bookmeta>
      <bookid>
         <isbn>012-3456789012</isbn>
      </bookid>
      <bookrights>
         <copyrfirst>
            <year>2011</year>
         </copyrfirst>
         <bookowner>
            <organization>Comtech Services, Inc.</organization>
         </bookowner>
      </bookrights>
   </bookmeta>
   ⋮
</bookmap>
```

7. Save your work in the ComstarUserAndAttendantsGuide.ditamap file.

### ComstarUserAndAttendantsGuide.ditamap

This example shows the complete ComstarUserAndAttendantsGuide.ditamap after entering <bookmeta> information.

```
<?xml version="1.0" encoding="utf-8"?>
<!DOCTYPE bookmap PUBLIC "-//OASIS//DTD DITA BookMap//EN"
   "bookmap.dtd">
<bookmap id="ComstarUserAndAttendantsGuide" xml:lang="en-us">
   <booktitle>
      <mainbooktitle>Comstar User and Attendant's
         Guide</mainbooktitle>
   </booktitle>
   <bookmeta>
      <bookid>
         <isbn>012-3456789012</isbn>
      </bookid>
      <bookrights>
         <copyrfirst>
            <year>2011</year>
         </copyrfirst>
         <bookowner>
            <organization>Comtech Services, Inc.</organization>
         </bookowner>
      </bookrights>
```

```
    </bookmeta>
    <frontmatter>
       <preface href="ComstarPreface.dita"/>
       <booklists>
          <toc/>
       </booklists>
    </frontmatter>
    <chapter href="QuickGuide.dita"/>
    <part>
       <topicmeta>
          <navtitle>Basic Functions</navtitle>
       </topicmeta>
       <chapter href="HoldCall.ditamap" format="ditamap"/>
       <chapter href="TransferCall.ditamap" format="ditamap"/>
       <chapter href="ForwardCall.ditamap" format="ditamap"/>
    </part>
    <part>
       <topicmeta>
          <navtitle>Advanced Functions</navtitle>
       </topicmeta>
       <chapter href="ConferenceCall.ditamap" format="ditamap"/>
    </part>
    <appendices>
       <topicmeta>
          <navtitle>Appendices</navtitle>
       </topicmeta>
       <appendix href="../Components/Accessories.ditamap"
          format="ditamap"/>
       <appendix href="../../ComstarPricing.pdf" format="pdf"/>
    </appendices>
    <backmatter>
       <booklists>
          <glossarylist>
             <topicref href="g_confcall.dita"/>
             <topicref href="g_fcc.dita"/>
          </glossarylist>
          <indexlist/>
       </booklists>
    </backmatter>
 </bookmap>
```

### Bookmap elements

You can use the elements described below in a bookmap. For more information on bookmap elements, see the *OASIS Darwin Information Typing Architecture (DITA) Version 1.2 (OASIS Standard, 1 December 2010).*

**<booktitle> book title**

Use the <booktitle> element as a container for the main title of the book and any alternate titles.

**<mainbooktitle> main book title**

Use the <mainbooktitle> element to define the primary title for the book.

**<booktitlealt> alternate book title**

Use the <booktitlealt> element to define any alternate titles for the book, including short titles and subtitles.

**<frontmatter> front matter**

Use the <frontmatter> element to wrap content that appears at the beginning of the publication before the body content. The <frontmatter> element usually contains one or more of the following elements: <booklists>, <notices>, <dedication>, <colophon>, or <preface>. All of these elements are optional. You may also choose simply to point to content that precedes the body of the publication by nesting <topicref> or <topicgroup> elements as children of the <frontmatter> element. Because the *@href* attribute is not available on the <frontmatter> element, content cannot be directly referenced, only nested.

**<booklists> book lists**

Use the <booklists> element to reference different lists in the publication. When contained by a <frontmatter> element, <booklists> usually holds a table of contents element, <toc>. When contained by a <backmatter> element, it usually holds an index element, <indexlist>. It can also contain lists of abbreviations, bibliographies, figures, tables, trademarks, books, and glossary entries.

**<toc> table of contents**

Use the <toc> element to indicate that you want to generate a table of contents at that location. If you have created a table of contents manually, use the *@href* attribute to point to that topic.

**<glossarylist> glossary list**

Use the <glossarylist> element to indicate that you want to generate a glossary at that location. If you have created a glossary file manually, use the *@href* attribute to point to that topic.

**<indexlist> index list**

Use the <indexlist> element to indicate that you want to generate an index at that location. The processor will scan your topics for <indexterm> tags and compile an alphabetical index of terms. If you have created an index manually, use the *@href* attribute to point to that topic.

**<notices> notices**

Use the <notices> element to reference a topic containing legal notices, if required.

**<dedication> dedication**

Use the <dedication> element to reference a topic containing the book's dedication page, if any.

**<colophon> colophon**

Use the <colophon> element to reference a topic that contains the details about the production of the book, for example, the software used to create the content, the fonts used, and so on.

**<preface> preface**

Use the <preface> element to reference a topic containing introductory information about the book, such as the purpose, intended audience, and structure of the book.

**<part> part**

Use the <part> element to group chapters or topics together in the bookmap. The <part> element can contain a <chapter> element, but a <chapter> element cannot contain a <part> element. A <part> element may reference content directly by its *@href* attribute or may contain various configurations of nested content.

**<chapter> chapter**

Use the <chapter> element to group topics together in the bookmap. A <chapter> element may reference content directly by its *@href* attribute or may contain different configurations of nested content. You can add <chapter> elements to a bookmap until you add a <part> element after which you can only add more <part> elements and nest <chapter> elements within them.

**<appendices> appendices**

Use the <appendices> element to group multiple <appendix> elements into one section in a bookmap. An <appendices> element may reference content directly with an *@href* attribute or may contain different configurations of nested content.

**<appendix> appendix**

Use the <appendix> element for supplemental information. You can point to content by the appendix's *@href* attribute, or you can nest different configurations of <topicref> or <topicgroup> elements.

**<backmatter> back matter**

Use the <backmatter> element to wrap content that appears at the end of the publication, after the body content. The <backmatter> element usually contains one or more of the following elements: <booklists> and <notices>. You can also nest <topicref> or <topicgroup> elements. Because the *@href* attribute is not available on the <backmatter> element, content cannot be directly referenced, only nested.

```
<?xml version="1.0" encoding="utf-8"?>
<!DOCTYPE bookmap PUBLIC "-//OASIS//DTD DITA BookMap//EN"
   "bookmap.dtd">
<bookmap id="PUBEstimatorUserGuide">
   <booktitle>
      <mainbooktitle>PUB$Estimator User Guide</mainbooktitle>
      <booktitlealt>PUB$UG</booktitlealt>
   </booktitle>
   <frontmatter>
      <notices href="LegalNotices.dita"/>
      <dedication href="Dedication.dita"/>
      <preface href="AboutThisBook.dita"/>
      <booklists>
         <toc/>
      </booklists>
   </frontmatter>
   <part>
      <topicmeta>
         <navtitle>Estimating Your Project</navtitle>
      </topicmeta>
      <chapter href="DependencyCalculator.ditamap" format="ditamap"/>
      <chapter href="CreatingASchedule.ditamap" format="ditamap"/>
   </part>
   <part>
      <topicmeta>
         <navtitle>Tracking Your Project</navtitle>
      </topicmeta>
      <chapter href="EnteringHours.dita">
         <topicref href="GeneratingWeeklyTimesheet.dita"/>
         <topicref href="GeneratingMonthlyTimesheet.dita"/>
      </chapter>
      <chapter href="GeneratingProjectStatusReports.dita"/>
   </part>
   <appendices>
      <topicmeta>
         <navtitle>Appendices</navtitle>
      </topicmeta>
      <appendix href="SampleProjectScenario.dita"/>
      <appendix href="SpreadsheetTemplates.pdf" type="pdf"/>
   </appendices>
   <backmatter>
      <booklists>
         <glossarylist href="PUBGlossary.dita"/>
         <indexlist/>
      </booklists>
      <colophon href="Colophon.dita"/>
   </backmatter>
</bookmap>
```

**<bookmeta> book metadata**

Use the <bookmeta> element to include information about the publication, such as copyright and publisher information. The information you enter in <bookmeta> can be used for search or for placing information within the final publication.

**<bookid> book ID**

Use the <bookid> element as a container for publisher information about the book. The <bookid> element contains the <isbn> element, as well as other elements such as part, volume, and edition numbers.

**<isbn> isbn**

Use the <isbn> element to identify the book's International Standard Book Number.

**<bookrights> book rights**

Use the <bookrights> element as a container for information about the legal rights associated with the book, including copyright dates and owners. The <bookrights> element contains the <copyrfirst> and <bookowner> elements.

**<copyrfirst> first copyright**

Use the <copyrfirst> element to provide the first copyright year within a multiyear copyright statement. The <copyrfirst> element contains a <year> element.

**<copyrlast> last copyright**

Use the <copyrlast> element to provide the latest copyright year within a multiyear copyright statement. The <copyrlast> element contains a <year> element.

**<bookowner> book owner**

Use the <bookowner> element as a container for the owner of the copyright. The <bookowner> element will contain either an <organization> element or a <person> element, depending on the entity that owns the copyright.

```
<?xml version="1.0" encoding="utf-8"?>
<!DOCTYPE bookmap PUBLIC "-//OASIS//DTD DITA BookMap//EN"
   "bookmap.dtd">
<bookmap id="PUBEstimatorUserGuide">
   <bookmeta>
      <bookid>
         <isbn>123-4567890123</isbn>
      </bookid>
      <bookrights>
         <copyrfirst>
            <year>2011</year>
         </copyrfirst>
         <bookowner>
            <person>JoAnn Hackos</person>
         </bookowner>
      </bookrights>
   </bookmeta>
</bookmap>
```

**Bookmap review questions**

What is the difference between a DITA map and a bookmap?

- **a.** Bookmaps address the requirements of grouping and organizing DITA topics in a traditional, book-based approach.
- **b.** Bookmaps enable you to produce tables of contents, which you cannot produce using a DITA map.
- **c.** DITA maps reference topics and other maps, while bookmaps reference chapters and appendices.
- **d.** You can nest DITA maps within bookmaps, but you cannot nest bookmaps within DITA maps.

You cannot nest a bookmap within another bookmap.

- True
- False

What is the element that contains elements such as <toc>, <indexlist>, and <glossarylist>?

What happens if you include an *@href* attribute within a <toc> element?

- **a.** You receive an error. The <toc> element does not have an *@href* attribute.
- **b.** The processor updates the file named by the *@href* attribute with the current page numbers.
- **c.** The processor generates a table of contents and saves it to the file named in the *@href* attribute.
- **d.** The processor embeds the file named by the *@href* attribute as the table of contents.

You cannot directly reference content within the <frontmatter> and <backmatter> elements.

- True
- False

What is wrong with the following code?

```
<bookmap id="UserGuide">
   <chapter href="Installation.dita"/>
   <part>
      <topicmeta>
         <navtitle>Basic Tasks</navtitle>
      </topicmeta>
      <chapter href="Task1.dita"/>
      <chapter href="Task2.pdf" format="pdf"/>
      <chapter href="Task3.ditamap" format="ditamap"/>
   </part>
   <chapter>
      <topicref href="AdvancedTasks.ditamap" format="ditamap"/>
   </chapter>
   <appendix href="Menus.dita"/>
</bookmap>
```

- **a.** You cannot have an unnested <chapter> element after a <part> element has been used within the bookmap.
- **b.** The <appendix> element must be nested within an <appendices> element.
- **c.** You cannot reference pdf files within <chapter> element tags.
- **d.** The *@href* attribute is required on all <chapter> elements.

Chapters, parts, and appendices can either point directly to topics or other maps using the *@href* attribute, or can act as container elements, holding nested <topicref> or <mapref> elements.

- True
- False

Which of the following are contained within the <bookmeta> tag? Select all that apply.

- **a.** <booklists>
- **b.** <bookrights>
- **c.** <bookid>
- **d.** <booktitle>

Match the container element to the element it contains.

| <frontmatter> | <toc> |
|---|---|
| <bookid> | <isbn> |
| <bookrights> | <year> |
| <copyrfirst> | <organization> |
| <booklist> | <preface> |
| <bookowner> | <bookowner> |

# PART IV

# Content Reuse

DITA offers many opportunities for information developers to use content in multiple contexts, reducing duplication of effort, improving productivity, and increasing the consistency and quality of the information. DITA topics, carefully typed according to the content they contain, provide the foundation for content reuse. You can reference the same topics in multiple DITA maps to build content assemblies that meet the needs of any user communities. You can use the same topic more than once in a DITA map, reducing maintenance costs and improving accuracy and consistency. But topic reuse is not the only mechanism that DITA provides to optimize your information-development resources.

Using the DITA model, you can select individual content units, defined by XML elements, for multiple use. Information developers can identify warnings, cautions, legal statements, repetitive sets of steps, and other content snippets that are common to many deliverables. By storing this content separately and referencing it using the DITA *@conref* (content reference) or*@ keyref* (key reference) mechanisms, you can easily and consistently maintain common content.

By developing the topics and content units once rather than multiple times, you can

- improve accuracy and consistency. When you use the same topic in different contexts, you reduce redundancy and eliminate inaccuracies. When authors follow DITA-supported authoring guidelines to develop topics, you reduce the time required for editing and rewriting. DITA topic standards, whether you use the core information types for technical communication or create your own specializations, help to enforce business rules for content development and ensure consistency. When topics are consistently written, they are more amenable to be used in multiple contexts.
- increase efficiency. When one information developer authors a topic so that it can be used effectively in multiple contexts, you increase the productivity of all your information developers. When information developers create format-free XML source content, you reduce the time required for final production in multiple media. You also increase productivity of reviewers and approvers. You reduce the

confusion that results when reviewers repeatedly comment on the same content in different contexts, often recommending contradictory changes.

- streamline processes. By authoring topics that are free of proprietary format code, you reduce the time required for final production in multiple media. Deliverables in PDF, HTML, help systems, and other formats can be produced quickly and easily. Styling is consistent because style sheets are added at the end of the production cycle rather than during authoring.
- simplify updating. Topic-based authoring and content reuse helps information developers provide updated and improved content to customers as soon as it is approved.
- decrease translation costs. Once a topic or a content unit is translated, it need not be translated again when it appears in multiple deliverables. With some content management systems, you can send for translation only those topics that have not already been translated. Organizations have experienced significant reductions in their translation costs from content reuse.
- shorten publication cycles. Because you can use topics that are already approved in new publications, you decrease the review and approval times by limiting reviews only to new topics or changes in existing topics. Because you update only in one place, you decrease the amount of time required to update content when late changes occur in the product-development life cycle.

# SECTION I

# Understanding Content Reuse in DITA

In DITA, you will discover many ways to define and output content to multiple deliverables and to vary content to accommodate multiple products, platforms, and audiences.

In this section, you will find several methods for reusing content. It is important that you use this information and your own experimentation to define your overall content reuse strategy.

**Reference the same DITA topic in more than one DITA map**
: You might use a task in multiple deliverables that are created for different versions of a product, different products, or different audiences. Using topics in multiple maps is one of the core reuse functions in DITA.

**Use DITA maps in other DITA maps**
: You can build groups of topics that usually work together into smaller submaps that you can use in larger maps.

**Output content to different deliverables using the same DITA map**
: You can use a single map to produce a PDF version for printing, an XHTML version for the web, and a version for a help system. All you need to do is apply different stylesheets to your original XML content. You can also use attributes on the topics in a map so that you can apply conditional processing. The conditional processing attributes allow you to produce different output from the same map.

**Reference the same content in more than one DITA topic**
: You may have a instructions for performing a basic task that is used in multiple tasks. You can include the basic instructions in multiple topics using the *@conref*, *@keyref*, or *@conkeyref* mechanisms.

**Filter content using conditional processing**
: DITA conditional processing enables you to filter content that you want to include or exclude from a particular deliverable. With conditional processing,

you create a master topic that contains content variations for different users, products, platforms, or other conditions that you define.

**Flagging content using conditional processing attributes**

Not only can you filter content using conditional processing, DITA allows you to flag content using colors or symbols like change bars. With flagging attributes, you can indicate to reviewers or users exactly which content has been updated.

Through content reuse mechanisms, you can minimize the number of topics you create, maintain, and manage, and you can deliver more consistent and accurate content to your user community.

### Using DITA topics in multiple DITA maps

The topic is the fundamental reusable structure in DITA. DITA topics should be carefully designed so that they can be read and used independently of other topics. The lessons in the Topic section of this guide demonstrate how to structure your content so that it follows the standard DITA information typing architecture. The Information Model that you create for your organization as you plan your DITA implementation should establish the structural rules that you want your authors to follow to create consistent topics.

At the beginning of your projects, plan the topics you need to author, and build the maps that organize those topics for the final deliverables. By doing so, you will maximize your reuse potential. Many DITA architects advocate setting up your DITA maps, outlining the topics needed in each map, and identifying topics that will appear in multiple maps before assigning topic authoring to your team.

If you have a repository of DITA maps and topics, begin a new project by identifying the existing maps that are most like the maps you will need for the new project, especially if the new project updates an existing project.

### Using DITA maps in multiple DITA maps

One of the most efficient ways to build final maps for book, web, or help delivery is to create a series of submaps. A submap might represent a product component or function, such as installation or operations, a chapter in a book, or a section of an XHTML output. You can then use these submaps by reference in larger maps to organize a book, a help system, or a website. You may also find it useful to create small maps to organize topics for authoring or review.

When you have a series of subject-specific submaps, you can use them in multiple maps. The use of submaps increases the potential for content reuse across the deliverables for multiple products and helps to maintain consistency at a higher level of granularity than for the topics alone.

### Using a single DITA map for multiple deliverables

By using conditional processing at the topic level in your map, you can generate more than one deliverable from a single map. For example, one organization created a user guide for a telephone system. They also wanted to generate a quick reference guide that was a subset of the content in the user guide. They developed a quick reference stylesheet that extracted a subset of the content (title and numbered steps) from the user guide, and they assigned an attribute to the topic references to exclude many of the topics from the quick reference guide.

You might want to use the same map for both PDF and XHTML output, but at the same time include some topics in the PDF that you do not want to appear in the XHTML version. You can add the *@printonly* attribute to the topic references in the map that you want to exclude from the XHTML version.

However, you may also choose to use multiple maps for different deliverables to simplify the processing and manage the complexity that conditional processing can add to your production process.

**Using multiple stylesheets to publish a single DITA map**

To create your deliverables, you reference your topics in a DITA map. When you process the map for publication, you specify the stylesheets to use to format the content. In the DITA Open Toolkit, you can choose to apply

- a Cascading Style Sheet (CSS) to create XHTML output for web delivery
- an Extensible Stylesheet Language - Formatting Object (XSL-FO) stylesheet to create PDF output for printing
- stylesheets that support Eclipse or various help systems, such as HTML Help and Java Help

Using the same map, you can automatically produce multiple formats. You do not have to build separate maps for different formats. You can also use conditional processing on topic references in a map to exclude certain topics from a final deliverable, providing you with even more flexibility.

**Using the same content in multiple DITA topics**

Many publications have content that is repeated in multiple topics. For example, you may have safety hazard statements such as warnings, dangers, and cautions that are frequently reused. You may have warranty or copyright notices or other frontmatter and backmatter that are used in multiple documents. You may have other standard words, phrases, paragraphs, or steps that are used in more than one topic.

Content is reused at the element level. You can establish a file, called a collection file, that contains a set of reusable elements that can be easily accessed by your authors and referenced automatically into your topics. Using the *@conref*, *@keyref*, and *@conkeyref* mechanisms in DITA, you can write these content units once and use them everywhere. Remember that you can then update them once and have them updated everywhere they are used. The lessons in this Part teach you how to create *@conrefs*, *@keyrefs*, and *@conkeyrefs* in your authoring environment.

**Filtering content using conditional processing**

In DITA, almost every element has a common set of attributes you use for conditional processing. These attributes are

- *@audience*—the intended audience for the content
- *@platform*—the platform on which the product is deployed
- *@product*—the product that is the subject of the content
- *@otherprops*—any other attribute that you want to define

You can use the *@audience* attribute to specify parts of a topic that apply to different audiences. For example, you may have written a concept that is appropriate for an advanced user, but you want to include only the first paragraph in a version for the beginner. By adding an *@audience* attribute with the value "beginner" to the first paragraph, you can include this paragraph and exclude the "expert" paragraphs to develop a beginner's manual.

You can enter more than one value for the *@audience* attribute. For example, you may decide that the second paragraph of your concept is appropriate for an expert and an administrator. The values you enter to label this paragraph would be "expert administrator". During processing you can produce both an expert and an administrator version of the topic.

**Flagging content using conditional processing attributes**

You can also add colors, change bars, or other symbols to highlight different types of information in your content. For example, if you have information that applies to only one audience, you might indicate it with a symbol. One company chose to use a Canadian flag image to identify information specific to Canadian laws.

In addition to the conditional processing attributes listed in the previous section, you might also choose to flag content based on the *@rev* attribute, which indicates when and by whom content was modified. You might use this attribute, for example, when making updates to your content to indicate to reviewers or readers that content has changed from one version to another.

**Deciding on the best reuse mechanisms**

With the variety of reuse mechanisms available in DITA, you need to establish a strategy that uses the best mechanism to help you reduce costs, eliminate rework, and improve the quality of your content deliverables. A comprehensive reuse strategy should be designed to take advantage of each mechanism, depending on the requirements of your content.

If you are already using *@conref* or conditional publishing in your DITA topics, you need to weigh the advantage of the advanced reuse mechanisms and decide if it is appropriate to replace an existing practice with a better one.

| Reuse mechanism | Best practice for use |
|---|---|
| Conref (content reference) | Use to reference standard content sets, such as hazard statements, in master topics, especially when the standard content is unlikely to vary from one application to another. The placement of content references is under the control of the author. Avoid translation problems by replacing only non-translated images or referencing words or information in full sentences. |
| Conditional publishing | Use to select among variable content when the variations are few and under the control of the author. |
| Conref range | Use to reference a set of elements, such as a set of steps or a set of list items that are under the control of the author. |
| Conref push | Use to replace or add content to a topic when the control of the inserted content is in the hands of another author. No action is required of the original author except for the presence of element IDs. |
| Keyref | Use to swap graphics, words, or phrases that vary among multiple versions of the content. Avoid translation problems by swapping only non-translated images or words or information in full sentences. |
| Conkeyref | Use to swap more complete content units, such as hazard statements, paragraphs, procedural steps, and other intact content that is managed using collection files. By referencing only a single file with the appropriate content, excessive conditional processing is avoided. |

**Table 6: Selecting reuse mechanisms**

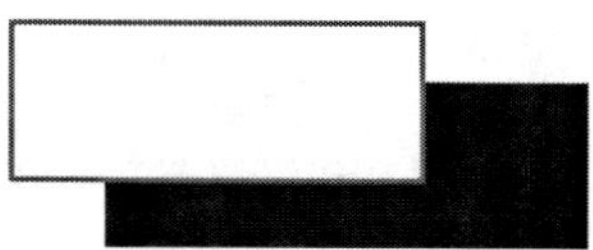

# LESSON 18

## The *@conref* Attribute

The conref mechanism enables you to easily reuse standard content in a DITA topic. When you use this mechanism, you point to a content unit in another topic, preferably located in a collection file that houses standard reusable content. Upon processing, the referenced content appears in place in your topic, as if you copied it. However, when you update the source content, it changes everywhere that you referenced it.

To use the conref mechanism, you must ensure that the content unit you reference will work in the new context. For example, you cannot conref a <properties> table element into a <concept> topic. You can only use a <properties> table in a <reference> topic.

The *@conref* attribute uses a unique *@id* attribute to identify the content unit you want to use. For example, if you want to use a <note> from one topic into another, you must add an *@id* attribute to the original note. Use a *@conref* attribute as you would an *@href* attribute. You point to the topic and the *@id* of the content unit that you want to reuse. The value of the *@conref* attribute must include an absolute or relative path to the topic and the id of the source content within the topic. For example, if you are working in a file system and you want to reference a step from a collection file, the typical format for the *@conref* attribute is systempathandfilename.dita#topicid/elementid.

**Note:** If you are using a content management system, you most likely need only point to the unique *@id* of the content unit you want to *@conref*. You do not need file paths and file names in the *@conref* attribute value.

**Referencing a range of elements**

You use a simple conref to add one element to a topic. However, to add a contiguous set of elements to a topic, use conref range. By using *@conref* range, you can reference more than one step, more than one list item, or other sets of contiguous content, thus avoiding the need to construct a series of small content references for individual steps, list items, or other information sets. As a result, the referencing process is simplified, and the cost of maintaining the referenced target elements is reduced.

By referencing a range of elements, you are able to reuse a standard set of steps as part of multiple procedures or add a set of standard items to a bulleted list. The first *conref* attribute marks the first step or the first list item. The *conrefend* attribute marks the last step or the last list item in the referenced collection file. When you resolve the content reference on publication, the additional steps or additional list items are placed in the topic.

For example, if you want to insert steps 2 through 4 into a topic, you must indicate that you want a range of elements by setting the *@conref* attribute on step 2 and the *@conrefend* on step 4. Both the starting and ending elements must be the same although the elements in between may be different.

For example, you must begin the reference to a set of steps with a <step> element and end it with another <step> element if all the referenced content represents the steps in a procedure. However, the elements between the <step> elements can be any sort of content, including substeps, informational paragraphs, graphics, notes, and so on.

A further restriction on *@conref* range requires that both elements at the beginning and end of the *@conref* have the same parent. In this example, both <step> elements have the same parent, <steps>.

**Pushing content into a topic**

As an author, you can decide to add content to your topic by setting up a *@conref* attribute. For example, you may decide to add a hazard statement from a collection file of hazard statements to your task topic. You create the content reference in the <prereq> element to bring in the external content.

However, you may want to add content to a topic that is managed by another author or to a topic that you want to update with new content without having to add the content to the original topic. In that case, you will use *@conaction* to push content into an existing topic. You will be using *@conref* in reverse.

Using the *@conaction* attribute, you may

- replace the content in an existing topic. For example, you may be writing about a new product that has a slightly different version of step 2 in a procedure. Use "pushreplace" to replace the existing step 2 with the different step 2.
- add content before an element in an existing topic. For example, if you are working with a product that requires an additional initial step in a procedure, use "pushbefore" to add a new step 1, moving the previous step 1 to step 2.
- add content after an element in an existing topic. For example, if you need to add a step after an existing step in a procedure, use "pushafter."

By pushing content into a topic, you avoid adding multiple conditional processing attributes to the topic. Multiple conditional processing attributes often make topics difficult to use.

*@conref* push allows other authors to insert content into a topic without requiring that the original author do anything in advance except establish an *@id* attribute on the elements. For example, an author managing content for a new

product may insert an additional step in a procedure or replace a step with a variations.

*@conref* push allows the author to insert content that replaces existing content or to add new content before or after existing content, as long as the structure of the target topic permits the content. The element that is pushed into a topic must be the same as the target element.

One of the uses of *@conref* push is to handle revisions to a topic during multiple release cycles. If Author A and Author B are both handling revisions to a topic before release, Author A can push the Release 1 revisions into the topic without affecting the work of Author B in updating the topic for Release 2. Nonetheless, collaboration among the authors of various releases is essential to avoid confusion and ensure that all versions are eventually merged into a master topic that moves forward.

In another case, Author A may want to add advanced content to a basic topic written by Author B. Using *@conref* push, Author A inserts the content without requiring that Author B take any action except to ensure that the elements in the topic have *@id*s. Author A's generated content is now appropriate for an expert audience, while Author B's content remains ready for a beginner audience.

You cannot, however, combine *@conref* push with *@conref* range.

**Adding content to a topic by reference**

This lesson explains how to add content to a DITA topic using the *@conref* attribute. In this lesson, you learn to

- create a collection file to hold a chunk of information that you want to insert in other topics
- add a *@conref* to the topic that will receive the referenced content

**1.** Create a collection file titled "Reusable Notes" using the DITA general topic information type and save it as ReusableNotes.dita.

A collection file is used to hold content that you want to reuse by reference in other topics. For example, a collection file might hold all your notes. Another collection file might hold all warnings or all dangers. Collection files enable you to edit similar content in one location and maintain simple and direct links between small pieces of reusable content and the topics in which they are used. Avoid creating content references (*@conref*) from content in one topic to content in another topic. Such cross-topic referencing can result in very complex linking and create multiple errors if a topic is removed from use.

Ensure that you create *@id* attributes for the topic and note that you will reference. In this case assign the topic an *@id* of "reusablenotes" and the note an *@id* of "hangupphone".

```
<?xml version="1.0" encoding="UTF-8"?>
<!DOCTYPE topic PUBLIC "-//OASIS//DTD DITA Topic//EN"
   "topic.dtd">
<topic id="reusablenotes" xml:lang="en-us">
   <title>Reusable Notes</title>
   <body>
      <p>
         <note id="hangupphone" type="tip">You must
            hang up your phone before you can make
            another call.</note>
      </p>
   </body>
</topic>
```

2. Open the TransferringaCall.dita file you created in Task Information Type on page 33 and last modified in Adding prolog metadata on page 101.

```
<?xml version="1.0" encoding="utf-8"?>
<!DOCTYPE task PUBLIC "-//OASIS//DTD DITA Task//EN"
   "task.dtd">
<task id="TransferringACall" xml:lang="en-us">
   <title><keyword>Transferring</keyword>
      a call</title>
   <shortdesc>When you transfer a call to another person
      in your office, you have two ways of handling the
      transfer.</shortdesc>
   <prolog>
      <author>John Smith</author>
      <copyright>
         <copyryear year="2009"/>
         <copyrholder>Comtech Services, Inc.</copyrholder>
      </copyright>
      <permissions view="all"/>
      <metadata>
         <keywords>
            <keyword>phone</keyword>
            <keyword>transfer</keyword>
            <keyword>transferring a call</keyword>
            <indexterm>transferring a call</indexterm>
            <indexterm>unannounced transfers
               <index-see-also>transferring a call</index-see-also>
            </indexterm>
            <indexterm>announced transfers
               <index-see-also>transferring a call</index-see-also>
            </indexterm>
            <indexterm>transfers
               <indexterm>unannounced</indexterm>
               <indexterm>announced</indexterm>
            </indexterm>
         </keywords>
      </metadata>
   </prolog>
   <taskbody>
      <context>When you transfer the call without speaking to
         the person, it is an unannounced transfer. When you
         speak to the person receiving the transferred call,
         it is an announced transfer.</context>
      <steps>
         <step>
            <cmd>Press the <uicontrol>transfer
```

```
                </uicontrol> button.</cmd>
         </step>
         <step>
            <cmd>Dial the number. </cmd>
            <info>Dial the number manually, use your
               pre-defined speed dial keys or go to your
               <xref href="AccessingCompanyDirectory.dita"
               type="task">company directory</xref>.
            </info>
         </step>
         <step>
            <cmd>Transfer the call.</cmd>
            <choicetable>
               <chhead>
                  <choptionhd>Type of Announcement</choptionhd>
                  <chdeschd>Steps to complete</chdeschd>
               </chhead>
               <chrow>
                  <choption>Announce a call transfer</choption>
                  <chdesc>
                     <ol>
                        <li>Speak to the person.</li>
                        <li>Hang up the phone.</li>
                     </ol>
                  </chdesc>
               </chrow>
               <chrow>
                  <choption>Transfer a call
                     unannounced</choption>
                  <chdesc>
                     <ul>
                        <li>Hang up the phone.</li>
                     </ul>
                  </chdesc>
               </chrow>
            </choicetable>
            <info>
               <note type="tip">If you announce a call and the
                  person refuses the transfer, do not hang
                  up the phone. Press the transfer button
                  again to retrieve the call on your phone
                  station.</note>
            </info>
         </step>
      </steps>
      <result>The call is transferred.</result>
   </taskbody>
   <related-links>
      <link href="AboutTransfer.dita" format="html"
         scope="local"/>
      <link href="../GeneralTopic/Glossary.dita"
         format="html" scope="peer"/>
      <link href="http://www.comtech-serv.com/Comstar"
         format="html" scope="external">
         <linktext>Comstar Phones</linktext>
         <desc>Order your Comstar phone today.</desc>
      </link>
   </related-links>
</task>
```

3. Add a <postreq> container after the <result> element end tag, and nest <note> start and end tags within it.

```
<task id="TransferringACall" xml:lang="en-us">
   ⋮
   <taskbody>
   ⋮
      <result>The call is transferred.</result>
      <postreq>
         <note></note>
      </postreq>
   </taskbody>
   ⋮
</task>
```

4. Add a *@conref* attribute to the note element, and assign a value.

   The value for the *@conref* attribute should point to the file and *@id* in the ReusableNotes.dita topic. When adding a *@conref* attribute, the value must have the following syntax, systempathandfilename.dita#topicid/elementid. In this example, assume that the ReusableNotes.dita topic is in the same folder as TransferringACall.dita. Notice that you don't include any content between the start and end tags for the note. If you did include content in this container, the content in the *@conref* would overwrite any content you include in the referencing topic.

```
<task id="TransferringACall" xml:lang="en-us">
   ⋮
   <taskbody>
   ⋮
      <result>The call is transferred.</result>
      <postreq>
         <note conref="ReusableNotes.dita#reusablenotes/
            hangupphone"></note>
      </postreq>
   </taskbody>
   ⋮
</task>
```

5. Save the TransferringACall.dita topic.

Your topic should now look like the example below. When processing the TransferringACall.dita topic, the content from the ReusableNotes.dita topic is inserted into the <note> element container.

```
<?xml version="1.0" encoding="utf-8"?>
<!DOCTYPE task PUBLIC "-//OASIS//DTD DITA Task//EN"
   "task.dtd">
<task id="TransferringACall" xml:lang="en-us">
   <title><keyword>Transferring</keyword>
      a call</title>
   <shortdesc>When you transfer a call to another person
      in your office, you have two ways of handling the
      transfer.</shortdesc>
   <prolog>
```

```
   <author>John Smith</author>
   <copyright>
      <copyryear year="2009"/>
      <copyrholder>Comtech Services, Inc.</copyrholder>
   </copyright>
   <permissions view="all"/>
   <metadata>
      <keywords>
         <keyword>phone</keyword>
         <keyword>transfer</keyword>
         <keyword>transferring a call</keyword>
         <indexterm>transferring a call</indexterm>
         <indexterm>unannounced transfers
            <index-see-also>transferring a call</index-see-also>
         </indexterm>
         <indexterm>announced transfers
            <index-see-also>transferring a call</index-see-also>
         </indexterm>
         <indexterm>transfers
            <indexterm>unannounced</indexterm>
            <indexterm>announced</indexterm>
         </indexterm>
      </keywords>
   </metadata>
</prolog>
<taskbody>
   <context>When you transfer the call without speaking to
      the person, it is an unannounced transfer. When you
      speak to the person receiving the transferred call,
      it is an announced transfer.</context>
   <steps>
      <step>
         <cmd>Press the <uicontrol>transfer
            </uicontrol> button.</cmd>
      </step>
      <step>
         <cmd>Dial the number. </cmd>
         <info>Dial the number manually, use your
            pre-defined speed dial keys or go to your
            <xref href="AccessingCompanyDirectory.dita"
            type="task">company directory</xref>.
         </info>
      </step>
      <step>
         <cmd>Transfer the call.</cmd>
         <choicetable>
            <chhead>
               <choptionhd>Type of Announcement</choptionhd>
               <chdeschd>Steps to complete</chdeschd>
            </chhead>
            <chrow>
               <choption>Announce a call transfer</choption>
               <chdesc>
                  <ol>
                     <li>Speak to the person.</li>
                     <li>Hang up the phone.</li>
                  </ol>
               </chdesc>
            </chrow>
            <chrow>
               <choption>Transfer a call
```

```
                  unannounced</choption>
               <chdesc>
                  <ul>
                     <li>Hang up the phone.</li>
                  </ul>
               </chdesc>
            </chrow>
         </choicetable>
         <info>
            <note type="tip">If you announce a call and the
               person refuses the transfer, do not hang
               up the phone. Press the transfer button
               again to retrieve the call on your phone
               station.</note>
         </info>
      </step>
   </steps>
   <result>The call is transferred.</result>
   <postreq>
      <note conref="ReusableNotes.dita#reusablenotes/
         hangupphone"></note>
   </postreq>
</taskbody>
<related-links>
   <link href="AboutTransfer.dita" format="html"
      scope="local"/>
   <link href="../GeneralTopic/Glossary.dita"
      format="html" scope="peer"/>
   <link href="http://www.comtech-serv.com/Comstar"
      format="html" scope="external">
      <linktext>Comstar Phones</linktext>
      <desc>Order your Comstar phone today.</desc>
   </link>
</related-links>
</task>
```

The following example shows what a PDF rendering of the topic might look like.

### Transferring a call

When you transfer a call to another person in your office, you have two ways of handling the transfer.

When you transfer the call without speaking to the person, it is an unannounced transfer. When you speak to the person receiving the transferred call, it is an announced transfer.

1. Press the transfer button.
2. Dial the number.
   Dial the number manually, use your pre-defined speed dial keys, or go to your company directory.
3. Transfer the call.

| Type of Announcement | Steps to complete |
|---|---|
| Announce a call transfer | **1.** Speak to the person.<br>**2.** Hang up the phone. |
| Transfer a call unannounced | Hang up the phone. |

**Tip:** If you announce a call and the person refuses the transfer, do not hang up the phone. Press the transfer button again to retrieve the call on your phone station.

The call is transferred.

**Tip:** You must hang up your phone before you can make another call.

**Adding multiple elements to a topic by reference**

This lesson explains how to add more than one element from a collection file to a DITA topic. In this lesson, you learn to

- create a collection file to hold multiple elements of information that you wish to insert in other topics
- add *@conref* and *@conrefend* to the topic that will receive the referenced content, where *@conref* marks the beginning of the group of elements and *@conrefend* marks the end of the group of elements you want to add

1. Create a collection file titled "Reusable Steps".

   This collection file contains the standard set of steps that you want to insert into other task topics.

```
<?xml version="1.0" encoding="UTF-8"?>
<!DOCTYPE task PUBLIC "-//OASIS//DTD DITA Task//EN"
   "task.dtd">
<task xml:lang="en-us">
```

```
   <title>Reusable Steps</title>
   <shortdesc>Task topic containing steps that can be reused in
      multiple tasks.</shortdesc>
   <taskbody>
      <steps>
         <step>
            <cmd>Lift the handset or press Speaker.</cmd>
            <info>the Speaker button is the last button on the
               left.</info>
         </step>
         <step>
            <cmd>Press the appropriate line or station button of
               the parties you wish to consult with.</cmd>
         </step>
      </steps>
   </taskbody>
</task>
```

2. Add *@id*s to the <task> element and each of the steps in the collection file. If possible, use *@id*s that describe the content. In this case, give the <task> element an *@id* of "reusablesteps", step 1 an *@id* of "lifthandset", and step 2 an *@id* of "pressbutton".

```
<?xml version="1.0" encoding="UTF-8"?>
<!DOCTYPE task PUBLIC "-//OASIS//DTD DITA Task//EN"
   "task.dtd">
<task id="reusablesteps" xml:lang="en-us">
   <title>Reusable Steps</title>
   <shortdesc>Task topic containing steps that can be reused in
      multiple tasks.</shortdesc>
   <taskbody>
      <steps>
         <step id="lifthandset">
            <cmd>Lift the handset or press Speaker.</cmd>
            <info>the Speaker button is the last button on the
               left.</info>
         </step>
         <step id="pressbutton">
            <cmd>Press the appropriate line or station button of
               the parties you wish to consult with.</cmd>
         </step>
      </steps>
   </taskbody>
</task>
```

3. Save the collection file as ReusableSteps.dita.
4. Create a task topic with the title, "Reentering a conference call", and an *@id*="reenteringconference".

```
<?xml version="1.0" encoding="utf-8"?>
<!DOCTYPE task PUBLIC "-//OASIS//DTD DITA Task//EN"
   "task.dtd">
<task id="reenteringconference" xml:lang="en-us" >
   <title>Reentering a conference call</title>
   <taskbody>
      <steps>
         <step>
            <cmd>Press Conference.</cmd>
```

```
            <stepresult>This will connect you with the parties
               on the conference call.</stepresult>
         </step>
      </steps>
   </taskbody>
</task>
```

5. Add an initial step containing the *@conref* attribute with the value, "ReusableSteps.dita#reusablesteps/lifthandset".

   The value of the *@conref* attribute consists of the name of the collection file, a # sign, the *@id* of the collection file, and the *@id* of the step you want to include in the task. This content reference will insert the first step from the collection file into the topic, Reentering a conference call, when you publish the DITA map.

```
<?xml version="1.0" encoding="utf-8"?>
<!DOCTYPE task PUBLIC "-//OASIS//DTD DITA Task//EN"
   "task.dtd">
<task id="reenteringconference" xml:lang="en-us" >
   <title>Reentering a conference call</title>
   <taskbody>
      <steps>
         <step conref="ReusableSteps.dita#reusablesteps/
            lifthandset"><cmd/>
         </step>
         <step>
            <cmd>Press Conference.</cmd>
            <stepresult>This will connect you with the parties
               on the conference call.</stepresult>
         </step>
      </steps>
   </taskbody>
</task>
```

6. Add a *@conrefend* attribute to the same <step> tag with the value, "ReusableSteps.dita#reusablesteps/pressbutton".

   This content reference will insert the last step from the collection file and any content between the first and last steps into the topic upon publication.

```
<?xml version="1.0" encoding="utf-8"?>
<!DOCTYPE task PUBLIC "-//OASIS//DTD DITA Task//EN"
   "task.dtd">
<task id="reenteringconference" xml:lang="en-us" >
   <title>Reentering a conference call</title>
   <taskbody>
      <steps>
         <step conref="ReusableSteps.dita#reusablesteps/
            lifthandset" conrefend="ReusableSteps.dita#
            reusablesteps/pressbutton"> <cmd/>
         </step>
         <step>
            <cmd>Press Conference.</cmd>
            <stepresult>This will connect you with the parties
               on the conference call.</stepresult>
            </step>
```

```
      </steps>
   </taskbody>
</task>
```

7. Save the file as "ReenteringAConferenceCall.dita".
8. Create a second task topic with the title "Placing a call" and an *@id*="placingcall".

```
<?xml version="1.0" encoding="utf-8"?>
<!DOCTYPE task PUBLIC "-//OASIS//DTD DITA Task//EN"
   "task.dtd">
<task id="placingcall" xml:lang="en-us" >
   <title>Placing a call</title>
   <taskbody>
      <steps>
      </steps>
   </taskbody>
</task>
```

9. Add two steps to the task, with the first referencing the "lifthandset" step in the collection topic and the second as shown in the example.

   This example shows that you can reuse elements of a collection file in more than one topic. The first topic you created references both steps in the collection file, while the second topic references only the first step.

```
<?xml version="1.0" encoding="utf-8"?>
<!DOCTYPE task PUBLIC "-//OASIS//DTD DITA Task//EN"
   "task.dtd">
<task id="placingcall" xml:lang="en-us" >
   <title>Placing a call</title>
   <taskbody>
      <steps>
         <step conref="ReusableSteps.dita#
            reusablesteps/lifthandset"><cmd/>
         </step>
         <step>
            <cmd>Dial the number.</cmd>
         </step>
      </steps>
   </taskbody>
</task>
```

10. Save the topic as "PlacingACall.dita".

Your published topics should now look like the examples below.

**Reentering a conference call**

1. Lift the handset or press Speaker.
   The Speaker button is the last button on the left.
2. Press the appropriate line or station button of the parties you wish to consult with.
3. Press Conference.
   This will connect you with the parties on the conference call.

**Placing a call**

1. Lift the handset or press Speaker.
   The Speaker button is the last button on the left.
2. Dial the number.

**Pushing content to an existing topic**

This lesson explains how to insert content into a DITA topic by using the *@conaction* attribute without revising the existing topic. In this lesson, you learn to

- establish a location in an existing topic that accommodates additional content
- dynamically replace content in an existing topic with new content
- dynamically add an element before or after an existing element

In this exercise, consider that you need to customize an existing task for a specific customer. Because you do not want to permanently change the generic task, you will push the special content into the topic instead. The content requires you to replace one step entirely and add a new step at the end.

1. Create a DITA task topic that will be the target for the content you want to push.

```
<?xml version="1.0" encoding="utf-8"?>
<!DOCTYPE task PUBLIC "-//OASIS//DTD DITA Task//EN"
   "task.dtd">
<task id="ForwardingACall" xml:lang="en-us" >
   <title>Forwarding a call</title>
   <taskbody>
      <steps>
         <step>
```

```
            <cmd>Press Program.</cmd>
         </step>
         <step>
            <cmd>Press Forward.</cmd>
         </step>
         <step>
            <cmd>Press an idle line button.</cmd>
         </step>
         <step>
            <cmd>Dial the outside number.</cmd>
         </step>
         <step>
            <cmd>Press Program.</cmd>
         </step>
      </steps>
   </taskbody>
</task>
```

2. Add unique *@id*s to the fourth and fifth steps of the procedure.

   By adding an *@id*, you specify a position at which content can be pushed into this topic. When establishing your content reuse strategies, you may want to require that *@id*s are always defined on certain element types. This strategy ensures that you can push content to a topic without having to go back and define *@id*s at the time you need to do the push. Remember that the topic itself must also have an *@id*. The *@id* of this topic is "ForwardingACall".

```
<task id="ForwardingACall" xml:lang="en-us" >
   <title>Forwarding a call</title>
   <taskbody>
      <steps>
         ⋮
         <step id="dialoutside">
            <cmd>Dial the outside number.</cmd>
         </step>
         <step id="finalprogram">
            <cmd>Press Program.</cmd>
         </step>
      </steps>
   </taskbody>
</task>
```

3. Save your work as ForwardingACall.dita.
4. Create a new task topic to contain the source content that you want to push into the ForwardingACall.dita file.

   A source topic that contains content to push into an existing target topic may be created by members of an information-development team who need to update a topic without making a permanent change to the topic. By pushing special content into the topic from an external source topic, you avoid cluttering the target topic with too much conditional text, especially conditional text that is used only once.

```
<?xml version="1.0" encoding="UTF-8"?>
<!DOCTYPE task PUBLIC "-//OASIS//DTD DITA Task//EN"
   "task.dtd">
<task id="PushContentForMajorClient" xml:lang="en-us" >
   <title>Push content for major client</title>
   <taskbody>
   </taskbody>
</task>
```

5. Add three step elements in the task body of this topic.

```
<task id="PushContentForMajorClient" xml:lang="en-us" >
   <title>Push content for major client</title>
   <taskbody>
      <steps>
         <step>
            <cmd/>
         </step>
         <step>
            <cmd/>
         </step>
         <step>
            <cmd/>
         </step>
      </steps>
   </taskbody>
</task>
```

6. In the first step, add a step that will replace the fourth step in the original ForwardingACall.dita topic.

```
<task id="PushContentForMajorClient" xml:lang="en-us" >
   <title>Push content for major client</title>
   <taskbody>
      <steps>
         <step>
            <cmd>Dial "9" followed by the outside number including
               area code.</cmd>
         </step>
         ⋮
      </steps>
   </taskbody>
</task>
```

7. Add a *@conref* attribute pointing to the *@id* of the fourth step in the original ForwardingACall.dita topic and a *@conaction* attribute of "pushreplace". The "pushreplace" value for the *@conaction* attribute indicates you want to replace the current content of the fourth step with this new content.

```
<task id="PushContentForMajorClient" xml:lang="en-us" >
   <title>Push content for major client</title>
   <taskbody>
      <steps>
         <step conref="ForwardingACall.dita#ForwardingACall/
```

```
            dialoutside" conaction="pushreplace">
            <cmd>Dial "9" followed by the outside number including
               area code.</cmd>
         </step>
         ⋮
      </steps>
   </taskbody>
</task>
```

**8.** In the second step of this topic, add a *@conref* attribute pointing to the id you established on the fifth step in the original ForwardingACall topic and a *@conaction* attribute equal to "mark".

When adding content before or after existing content, use the "mark" value of the *@conaction* attribute to indicate the element where the push operation will occur. When the conaction="mark" statement occurs before the content to be pushed, as in this example, the content will be pushed after the marked element. To push content before an element, reverse the order of this step and the next one so that the content to be pushed comes before the conaction="mark" statement.

Note that the <cmd> element of this step is empty; it is there only because the content model for the <step> element requires that it be present.

```
<task id="PushContentForMajorClient" xml:lang="en-us" >
   <title>Push content for major client</title>
   <taskbody>
      <steps>
         <step conref="ForwardingACall.dita#ForwardingACall/
            dialoutside" conaction="pushreplace">
            <cmd>Dial "9" followed by the outside number including
               area code.</cmd>
         </step>
         <step conref="ForwardingACall.dita#ForwardingACall/
            finalprogram" conaction="mark">
            <cmd/>
         </step>
         ⋮
      </steps>
   </taskbody>
</task>
```

**9.** In the third step, include the new content you want to add, and define the corresponding *@conref* and *@conaction* attributes.

This <step> element specifies the content you want pushed in the ForwardingACall.dita topic after the final step. The <cmd> element contains the content of the new step, and the *@conref* and *@conaction* attributes indicate that this content should be pushed *@after* the element with the corresponding conaction="mark" setting.

```
<task id="PushContentForMajorClient" xml:lang="en-us" >
   <title>Push content for major client</title>
   <taskbody>
      <steps>
         <step conref="ForwardingACall.dita#ForwardingACall/
            dialoutside" conaction="pushreplace">
            <cmd>Dial "9" followed by the outside number including
               area code.</cmd>
         </step>
         <step conref="ForwardingACall.dita#ForwardingACall/
            finalprogram" conaction="mark">
            <cmd/>
         </step>
         <step conref="ForwardingACall.dita#ForwardingACall/
            finalprogram" conaction="pushafter">
            <cmd>Validate that you have forwarded the line correctly
               by calling the original number and ensuring you are
               forwarded to the new number.</cmd>
         </step>
      </steps>
   </taskbody>
</task>
```

10. Save your work as PushContentForMajorClient.dita.
11. Add the new source topic to your ditamap for the *Comstar User Guide*, and set the attribute *@processing-role*="resource-only".

    By setting the processing role to "resource-only", you ensure that this source topic for your *@conref* push action does not appear as its own topic in the map.

```
<map id="ComstarUserGuide" xml:lang="en-us" >
   ⋮
   <topicref href="AboutForward.dita" format="dita"
      scope="local" type="concept" linking="sourceonly">
      <topicref href="ForwardingACall.dita" format="dita"
         scope="local" type="task" linking="normal"/>
      <topicref href="PushContentForMajorClient.dita"
         processing-role="resource-only"/>
   </topicref>
   ⋮
</map>
```

Your published topic should now look like the following example.

**Forwarding a call**

1. Press Program.
2. Press Forward.
3. Press an idle line button.
4. Dial "9" followed by the outside number including area code.
5. Press Program.
6. Validate that you have forwarded the line correctly by calling the original number and ensuring you are forwarded to the new number.

**_@conref_ attribute review questions**

The *@conref* attribute enables you to insert content into a topic without requiring that the original author do anything in advanced except establish an *@id* on the elements.

- True
- False

Why should you create a collection file to hold content that you want to reuse by reference in other topics?

a. Cross-topic referencing can result in very complex linking and create errors if a topic is removed from use.
b. *@conref*s are only valid when referencing a DITA general topic type.
c. A collection file does not need to contain valid XML so you can include out-of-context content more easily.
d. You cannot reference a range of information unless it is in a collection topic.

What is the proper syntax for a *@conref* attribute?

a. systempathandfilename.dita/topicid/elementid
b. systempathandfilename.dita/topicid#elementid
c. systempathandfilename.dita#elementid/topicid
d. systempathandfilename.dita#topicid/elementid

What must be true for this code to work? Select all that apply.

```
<task xml:lang="en-us" id="MakingACall">
   <title>Making a call</title>
   <taskbody>
      <steps>
         <step>
            <cmd>Lift the handset.</cmd>
         </step>
         <step>
            <cmd>Press an idle line button.</cmd>
         </step>
         <step conref="ClientSpecific.dita#
             Clientspecific/CustomerA">
            <cmd>Dial the outside number.</cmd>
         </step>
      </steps>
   </taskbody>
</task>
```

a. A topic with the @*id* of "ClientSpecific" must exist.
b. An element with the @*id* of "CustomerA" must exist within the ClientSpecific topic.
c. The element with the @*id* of "CustomerA" must be a step element.
d. The topic with the @*id* of "ClientSpecific" must be a task topic.

What must be true when using a @*conref* range? Select all that apply.

a. The elements at the beginning and end of the range must have the same parent.
b. All elements must be the same type.
c. The referenced content must be valid in the new context.
d. You must use an absolute path to the topic and id of the source content.

Which code is correct for inserting a range of content into a file?

**a.** <step conrefstart="SharedContent.dita#steps/step1" conrefend="SharedContent.dita#steps/step4"/>
**b.** <step conrefrange="SharedContent.dita#steps/step1" "SharedContent.dita#steps/step4/">
**c.** <step conref="SharedContent.dita#steps/step1" conrefend="SharedContent.dita#steps/step4"/>
**d.** <conrefrange><step conref="SharedContent.dita#steps/step1"/><step conref="SharedContent.dita#steps/step4"/></conrefrange>

When you are pushing information before the reference point in a file, which *@conaction* must be specified first in the source file, "mark" or "pushbefore"?

You cannot combine a *@conref* push with a *@conref* range.

- True
- False

What attribute should you set on the topic reference for your source file in a *@conref* push to prevent it from appearing as a topic in the output?

When might you use a *@conaction* attribute?

**a.** When you want to reuse a contiguous set of elements in another topic.
**b.** When you want to insert content into a topic without requiring the original author to do anything except establish *@id*s on the elements.
**c.** When you want to insert an element that would not be valid if it were embedded directly into the other file.
**d.** When you want to label content so that you can exclude it from certain outputs.

# LESSON 19

## Conditional Processing Attributes

The DITA conditional processing attributes allow you to label your content according the situations to which it applies. When you later process the content, you can use these labels to exclude content that does not apply to the current situation or to flag content to call attention to a change. This enables you to manage content for multiple purposes in a single source. For example, you may want a master concept topic to include variations for different versions of a software system. You might find it much more efficient to write one master topic that includes the software variations rather than maintain multiple similar topics that have to be individually maintained. You can use conditional processing attributes to label the variable content by the software version, perhaps using the *@product* attribute. Then, upon processing, you can exclude all the software versions that don't apply to your selected deliverable.

Conditional processing is best used to accommodate minor modifications for different situations. Consider it for situations in which you would originally have created two very similar files that have small differences in content. If you have significant variations, consider using *@keyref*s instead. See The Keyref Mechanism on page 272 for more information.

DITA supports the following conditional processing attributes:

- *@audience*
- *@product*
- *@platform*
- *@otherprops*

Each of these attributes can be given a standard set of values that authors can select. For example, the *@audience* attribute can have the following values, as determined by your information architect:

- novice
- experienced
- programmer
- administrator
- technician

An author who wants to specify that a specific paragraph applies only to an experienced user can select that paragraph and assign an *@audience* attribute and add or select the value "experienced".

```
<p audience="experienced">This paragraph has important information
   that is only appropriate for an experienced user.</p>
```

The *@otherprops* attribute is useful for adding additional conditional processing attributes that are not included in the three standard attributes: audience, product, and platform. For example, suppose the topic you are writing applies to more than one of your brands. You might need to indicate that some of the information applies only one specific band. You might use otherprops="brandXYZ" to label that paragraph. If you wanted to indicate a paragraph applied to more than one brand, you could add additional brands to the *@otherprops* attribute separated by spaces; for example, otherprops="brandXYZ brandABC".

You can also add more than one additional category of information to *@otherprops*. For example, suppose you also wanted to label content by country as well as brand. You would include both types of information in the same attribute tag. In the example, the brand is XYZ and the country is USA.

```
otherprops="XYZ USA"
```

**Note:** If you want to create other semantic categories, DITA also provides the *@props* attribute that can be specialized with to create new semantic conditional processing attributes. For information on creating such specializations, refer to the *OASIS Darwin Information Typing Architecture (DITA) Version 1.2 (OASIS Standard, 1 December 2010)*.

In addition to using these attributes to specify which information to include or exclude from specific output, any conditional processing attribute can also be highlighted with a flag. For example, you may want to use flagging to highlight content in your topics that is new and needs to be reviewed. You can use color changes in electronic output, or symbols in print or PDF output to call attention to this information. In addition to the filtering attributes listed earlier, DITA adds the *@rev* attribute specifically for flagging new or modified information. It indicates when you last modified or added the content. You might choose, for example, to add change bars or other highlighting to call attention to the changes during the review process.

You can use the conditional processing filtering and flagging attributes either on individual elements within a topic to affect only specific content or on the topic reference in a DITA map to affect the entire topic.

Once you have your content labeled for conditional processing, you activate the conditions using the .ditaval file. In this file, you specify the content that you want to exclude from the output or flag in a special way. For example, if you are generating content for brandABC, you would exclude content labelled for brandXYZ only. You can find information on using the .ditaval file in Creating the .ditaval file on page 355.

**Adding conditional processing attributes**

This lesson explains how to set up your topics to be filtered correctly during conditional processing. You will use one file to create both end user and administrator content, and to flag new content that you want reviewers to pay specific attention to. In this lesson, you learn to

- add *@audience* attributes to the elements you want to filter during processing
- add *@rev* attributes to elements to call attention to new information that must be reviewed carefully

**1.** Open the Transferring a call topic that you created in Task Information Type on page 33 and updated most recently in Adding content to a topic by reference on page 242.

```
<?xml version="1.0" encoding="utf-8"?>
<!DOCTYPE task PUBLIC "-//OASIS//DTD DITA Task//EN"
   "task.dtd">
<task id="TransferringACall" xml:lang="en-us">
   <title><keyword>Transferring</keyword>
      a call</title>
   <shortdesc>When you transfer a call to another person
      in your office, you have two ways of handling the
      transfer.</shortdesc>
   <prolog>
      <author>John Smith</author>
      <copyright>
         <copyryear year="2011"/>
         <copyrholder>Comtech Services, Inc.</copyrholder>
      </copyright>
      <permissions view="all"/>
      <metadata>
         <keywords>
            <keyword>phone</keyword>
            <keyword>transfer</keyword>
            <keyword>transferring a call</keyword>
            <indexterm>transferring a call</indexterm>
            <indexterm>unannounced transfers
               <index-see-also>transferring a call</index-see-also>
            </indexterm>
            <indexterm>announced transfers
               <index-see-also>transferring a call</index-see-also>
            </indexterm>
            <indexterm>transfers
               <indexterm>unannounced</indexterm>
               <indexterm>announced</indexterm>
            </indexterm>
```

```
      </keywords>
   </metadata>
</prolog>
<taskbody>
   <context>When you transfer the call without speaking to
      the person, it is an unannounced transfer. When you
      speak to the person receiving the transferred call,
      it is an announced transfer.</context>
   <steps>
      <step>
         <cmd>Press the <uicontrol>transfer
            </uicontrol> button.</cmd>
      </step>
      <step>
         <cmd>Dial the number. </cmd>
         <info>Dial the number manually, use your
            pre-defined speed dial keys or go to your
            <xref href="AccessingCompanyDirectory.dita"
            type="task">company directory</xref>.
         </info>
      </step>
      <step>
         <cmd>Transfer the call.</cmd>
         <choicetable>
            <chhead>
               <choptionhd>Type of Announcement</choptionhd>
               <chdeschd>Steps to complete</chdeschd>
            </chhead>
            <chrow>
               <choption>Announce a call transfer</choption>
               <chdesc>
                  <ol>
                     <li>Speak to the person.</li>
                     <li>Hang up the phone.</li>
                  </ol>
               </chdesc>
            </chrow>
            <chrow>
               <choption>Transfer a call
                  unannounced</choption>
               <chdesc>
                  <ul>
                     <li>Hang up the phone.</li>
                  </ul>
               </chdesc>
            </chrow>
         </choicetable>
         <info>
            <note type="tip">If you announce a call and the
               person refuses the transfer, do not hang
               up the phone. Press the transfer button
               again to retrieve the call on your phone
               station.</note>
         </info>
      </step>
   </steps>
   <result>The call is transferred.</result>
   <postreq>
      <note conref="ReusableNotes.dita#reusablenotes/
         hangupphone"></note>
   </postreq>
```

```
    </taskbody>
    <related-links>
        <link href="AboutTransfer.dita" format="html"
            scope="local"/>
        <link href="../GeneralTopic/Glossary.dita"
            format="html" scope="peer"/>
        <link href="http://www.comtech-serv.com/Comstar"
            format="html" scope="external">
            <linktext>Comstar Phones</linktext>
            <desc>Order your Comstar phone today.</desc>
        </link>
    </related-links>
</task>
```

2. Add two steps and a post requirement that will apply for administrators only, as shown in the example.

```
<task id="TransferringACall" xml:lang="en-us">
    ⋮
    <taskbody>
        <context>When you transfer the call without speaking to
            the person, it is an unannounced transfer. When you
            speak to the person receiving the transferred call,
            it is an announced transfer.</context>
        <steps>
            <step>
                <cmd>Activate the phone to use the transfer
                    feature.</cmd>
                <info>To activate your phone, go to the
                    options screen and turn the transfer feature
                    from off to on. Information about the options
                    screen is in the Options section of this
                    manual.</info>
            </step>
            <step>
                <cmd>Test the transfer feature to ensure
                    your phone is working correctly.</cmd>
                <info>Use the steps below to test your
                    phone</info>
            </step>
            <step>
                <cmd>Press the <uicontrol>transfer
                    </uicontrol> button.</cmd>
            </step>
            ⋮
        </steps>
        <result>The call is transferred.</result>
        <postreq>
            <note conref="ReusableNotes.dita#reusablenotes/
                hangupphone"></note>
            <p>If you encounter any problems testing
                your phone, contact the manufacturer.</p>
        </postreq>
    </taskbody>
    ⋮
</task>
```

If you use an XML editor, your screen image may render the first two steps. However, in the user guide, step 3 becomes step 1 when you produce your deliverable. After you process the information, the stylesheet numbers the steps correctly for the guide you produce.

3. Add *@audience* attributes with the value "administrator" to the information specific to the administrator.

```
<task id="TransferringACall" xml:lang="en-us">
   ⋮
   <taskbody>
      <context>When you transfer the call without speaking to
         the person, it is an unannounced transfer. When you
         speak to the person receiving the transferred call,
         it is an announced transfer.</context>
      <steps>
         <step audience="administrator">
            <cmd>Activate the phone to use the transfer
               feature.</cmd>
            <info>To activate your phone, go to the
               options screen and turn the transfer feature
               from off to on. Information about the options
               screen is in the Options section of this
               manual.</info>
         </step>
         <step audience="administrator">
            <cmd>Test the transfer feature to ensure
               your phone is working correctly.</cmd>
            <info>Use the steps below to test your
               phone</info>
         </step>
         <step>
            <cmd>Press the <uicontrol>transfer
               </uicontrol> button.</cmd>
         </step>
         ⋮
      </steps>
      <result>The call is transferred.</result>
      <postreq>
         <note conref="ReusableNotes.dita#reusablenotes/
            hangupphone"></note>
         <p audience="administrator">If you encounter any problems
            testing your phone, contact the manufacturer.</p>
      </postreq>
   </taskbody>
   ⋮
</task>
```

4. Add a *@rev* attribute to the first administrator step.

   The *@rev* attribute enables you to flag specific content during processing with a special symbol or color. Although you could also flag the content based on the audience="administrator" attribute, all administrator content would be flagged. Putting this attribute on just the one step enables you to call attention only to the specific information that you want to ensure is correct.

```
<task id="TransferringACall" xml:lang="en-us">
   ⋮
   <steps>
      <step audience="administrator" rev="1.1">
         <cmd>Activate the phone to use the transfer
            feature.</cmd>
         <info>To activate your phone, go to the
            options screen and turn the transfer feature
            from off to on. Information about the options
            screen is in the Options section of this
            manual.</info>
         </step>
         ⋮
   </steps>
   ⋮
</task>
```

**5.** Add *@audience* attributes with the value "enduser" to specify the original content of the user guide.

In the example, some content is specifically for the end user. For these elements, add "enduser" for the *@audience* attribute value. For all other elements, you can either omit the *@audience* attribute, or you can indicate that these elements apply to both audiences by separating the values with spaces. Both options are shown in the example.

```
<task id="TransferringACall" xml:lang="en-us">
   <title><keyword>Transferring</keyword>
      a call</title>
   <shortdesc>When you transfer a call to another person
      in your office, you have two ways of handling the
      transfer.</shortdesc>
   <prolog>
      <author>John Smith</author>
      <copyright>
         <copyryear year="2011"/>
         <copyrholder>Comtech Services, Inc.</copyrholder>
      </copyright>
      <permissions view="all"/>
      <metadata>
         <keywords>
            <keyword>phone</keyword>
            <keyword>transfer</keyword>
            <keyword>transferring a call</keyword>
            <indexterm>transferring a call</indexterm>
            <indexterm>unannounced transfers
               <index-see-also>transferring a call</index-see-also>
            </indexterm>
            <indexterm>announced transfers
               <index-see-also>transferring a call</index-see-also>
            </indexterm>
            <indexterm>transfers
               <indexterm>unannounced</indexterm>
               <indexterm>announced</indexterm>
            </indexterm>
         </keywords>
      </metadata>
```

```
</prolog>
<taskbody>
   <context audience="enduser">When you transfer the call
      without speaking to the person, it is an unannounced
      transfer. When you speak to the person receiving the
      transferred call, it is an announced transfer.</context>
   <steps>
      <step audience="administrator" rev="1.1">
         <cmd>Activate the phone to use the transfer
            feature.</cmd>
         <info>To activate your phone, go to the
            options screen and turn the transfer feature
            from off to on. Information about the options
            screen is in the Options section of this
            manual.</info>
      </step>
      <step audience="administrator">
         <cmd>Test the transfer feature to ensure
            your phone is working correctly.</cmd>
         <info>Use the steps below to test your
            phone.</info>
      </step>
      <step>
         <cmd>Press the <uicontrol>transfer
            </uicontrol> button.</cmd>
      </step>
      <step>
         <cmd>Dial the number. </cmd>
         <info>Dial the number manually, use your
            pre-defined speed dial keys or go to your
            <xref href="AccessingCompanyDirectory.dita"
            type="task">company directory</xref>.
         </info>
      </step>
      <step audience="administrator enduser">
         <cmd>Transfer the call.</cmd>
         <choicetable>
            <chhead>
               <choptionhd>Type of Announcement</choptionhd>
               <chdeschd>Steps to complete</chdeschd>
            </chhead>
            <chrow>
               <choption>Announce a call transfer<chdesc>
                  <ol>
                     <li>Speak to the person.</li>
                     <li>Hang up the phone.</li>
                  </ol>
               </chdesc>
            </chrow>
            <chrow>
               <choption>Transfer a call
                  unannounced</choption>
               <chdesc>
                  <ul>
                     <li>Hang up the phone.</li>
                  </ul>
               </chdesc>
            </chrow>
         </choicetable>
         <info>
            <note audience="enduser" type="tip">If you announce
```

```
                a call and the person refuses the transfer, do not
                hang up the phone. Press the transfer button
                again to retrieve the call on your phone
                station.</note>
            </info>
         </step>
      </steps>
      <result>The call is transferred.</result>
      <postreq>
         <note conref="ReusableNotes.dita#reusablenotes/
            hangupphone"></note>
         <p audience="administrator">If you encounter any problems
            testing your phone, contact the manufacturer.</p>
      </postreq>
   </taskbody>
   <related-links>
      <link href="AboutTransfer.dita" format="html"
         scope="local"/>
      <link href="../GeneralTopic/Glossary.dita"
         format="html" scope="peer"/>
      <link href="http://www.comtech-serv.com/Comstar"
         format="html" scope="external">
         <linktext>Comstar Phones</linktext>
         <desc>Order your Comstar phone today.</desc>
      </link>
   </related-links>
</task>
```

**6.** Save your work in the TransferringACall.dita file.

The following example illustrates the resulting output when you generate the topic for the administrator audience.

**Transferring a call**

1. Activate the phone to use the transfer feature.
   To activate your phone, go to the options screen and turn the transfer feature from off to on. Information about the options screen is in the Options section of this manual.
2. Test the transfer feature to ensure your phone is working correctly.
   Use the steps below to test your phone.
3. Press the transfer button.
4. Dial the number.
   Dial the number manually, use your pre-defined speed dial keys, or go to your company directory.
5. Transfer the call.

| Type of Announcement | Steps to complete |
|---|---|
| Announce a call transfer | **1.** Speak to the person.<br>**2.** Hang up the phone. |
| Transfer a call unannounced | Hang up the phone. |

The call is transferred.

**Tip:** You must hang up your phone before you can make another call.

If you encounter any problems testing your phone, contact the manufacturer.

The following example illustrates the resulting output when you generate the topic for the end user audience. For information about how these files are generated using the .ditaval file, see Creating the .ditaval file on page 355.

### Transferring a call

When you transfer a call to another person in your office, you have two ways of handling the transfer.

When you transfer the call without speaking to the person, it is an unannounced transfer. When you speak to the person receiving the transferred call, it is an announced transfer.

1. Press the transfer button.
2. Dial the number.
   Dial the number manually, use your pre-defined speed dial keys, or go to your company directory.
3. Transfer the call.

| Type of Announcement | Steps to complete |
|---|---|
| Announce a call transfer | **1.** Speak to the person.<br>**2.** Hang up the phone. |
| Transfer a call unannounced | Hang up the phone. |

**Tip:** If you announce a call and the person refuses the transfer, do not hang up the phone. Press the transfer button again to retrieve the call on your phone station.

The call is transferred.

**Tip:** You must hang up your phone before you can make another call.

**Conditional processing review questions**

Under what circumstances is it most appropriate to use conditional processing?

- **a.** When the conditions apply to elements within a topic, rather than the whole topic
- **b.** When you want to add or replace content without impacting the original topic
- **c.** When you have a complex array of variations dependent on audience, product, and platform
- **d.** When variations are minimal and under your control

Which of the following attributes can be used to filter the content that is included in a specific output? Select all that apply.

a. *@audience*
b. *@product*
c. *@rev*
d. *@status*

If an entire topic applies only to a single audience, you can use the *@audience* attribute on its topic reference in a DITA map rather than tag all the elements within the topic.

- True
- False

Suppose you are creating content for an application that runs on both the Macintosh and Windows operating systems. How might you tag information that is unique to only one of those systems?

To visually flag content you can use any of the standard conditional processing attributes as well as the *@rev* attribute.

- True
- False

Without defining a specialization, how might you indicate that a note applies to both a specific age range and gender?

a. <note otherprops="40to50, Female">
b. <note age="40to50" gender="Female">
c. <note otherprops="40to50 Female">
d. <note otherprops="40to50" otherprops="Female">

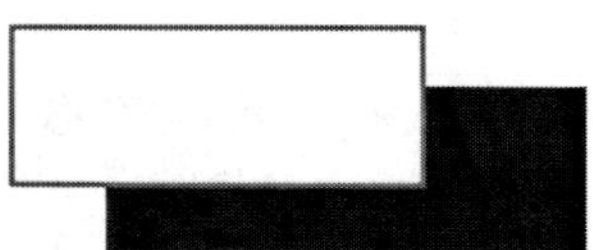

# LESSON 20

## The Keyref Mechanism

In the previous lessons, you learned how to manage reusable chunks of content by creating collection files and using the conref mechanism to draw the correct content into the final publication. The conref mechanism allows you to manage reusable content, such as safety hazards, in one location and use them everywhere. As a result, those chunks of reusable content are up to date everywhere they are inserted. You also learned how to apply conditional publishing attributes to variations of content in a master DITA topic. You may, for example, have several product lines that require small differences in the steps in a procedure or content that is applicable only to a subset of your users. By including the variations in a master topic, you avoid having to update the non-variable content in multiple topics.

Although both of these approaches can be useful, they both have limitations. Conditional publishing can cause difficulty in maintaining master topics. As long as there are only a small number of variations, it is reasonable to maintain. When the number of variations increase, however, the master topics begin to suffer from conditional bloat, making maintenance increasingly difficult and the topic almost completely unreadable for authors and reviewers. The conref approach does not allow for dynamic changes; all content must be predefined prior to processing. If a referenced topic is moved, for example, all *@conref* attributes must be updated to point to the new location.

The DITA keyref mechanism addresses the limitations of the other reuse options. This mechanism offers a solution for interchanging DITA content without having to rely on content references, hard-coded variables, or predefined conditional processing scenarios. It helps authors to avoid adding so many variations to master topics that they become unusable, and it makes it easy to swap content sets when you are ready to publish your topics.

Using the keyref mechanism, you move your variable content out of the topic and into the map, allowing you to replace variable content in the topic by simply updating the map. This is done by putting placeholders into your topics and then defining the content for those placeholders in one of two ways:

- Directly in the map or bookmap that you are using to generate your output
- In a file referenced by the map or bookmap that you are using to generate your output

Although the keyref mechanism is similar to the conref mechanism, the keyref mechanism enables a more simplified approach to conditional processing or profiling of content. Rather than relying on the DITA-OT to conditionally process content based on attribute values, you can change the content simply by changing the content of the key. The key placeholder stays the same, but the definition of that key is changed in the map or bookmap.

The keyref mechanism extends content reuse and content single sourcing within the DITA framework by allowing single or multiple components of any document to be populated at publication. Using this strategy, you avoid repetitive conditional processing. Possible implementations of keyref could include the following:

- A major phone manufacturer has many phone models that use the same OS but have different interface buttons.
- A product's name may change multiple times during a product-development cycle.
- An instructor wants to separate student and teacher web resources while using the same map to publish the course material.
- A manufacturer needs to produce two catalogs with the same content for two separate deliverables with different indexes depending on the target audience.

Like conref, keyref can present problems for translation. It is best to use keyref for content that is not translated, such as icons, wordless graphics, or product names. If longer phrases are substituted, we recommend that you swap full sentences so that the replaced phrases can be translated correctly.

**Keyref components**

The keyref mechanism is comprised of two components:

- The referencing key is found in the topic where the content will be included. When the content is defined in the map or bookmap, the referencing key is the *@keyref* attribute. When the content is in a file referenced by the map or bookmap, the referencing key is the *@conkeyref* attribute. These attributes point to the unique identifier of the defining key.
- The defining key is a single text string, image, topic, or map that will be placed at the location of the referencing key. Each key has a unique identifier, defined by the *@keys* attribute, which is then referenced by the referencing key. Use the <keydef> element to set the content to replace the placeholder.

Suppose for example, that you will not know the final name that marketing will give a product until the last minute. Using the *@keyref* attribute, you reference that information within your topic to be populated with content at a later date. In this example, the *@keyref* creates a placeholder for the "prodname" keyword in the sentence.

```
The new version of <keyword keyref="prodname"/> will be released on January
1.
```

In your map, you use the <keydef> element to set the name of the product, in this case "Quickstar". The *@keys* attribute corresponds to the *@keyref* attribute used as the placeholder in the topic. The product name, Quickstar, will be inserted into the appropriate placeholder at publication.

```
<keydef keys="prodname">
   <topicmeta>
      <keywords>
         <keyword>Quickstar</keyword>
      </keywords>
   </topicmeta>
</keydef>
```

If you are replacing more than a single word or phrase, however, you might prefer to reference a file outside of the map. Conkeyref is a variation on keyref in which the multiple versions are not stored in the map, but are referenced to collection files that hold the content in the repository. For example, suppose you have a line of products that a different set of icons representing the same functions. Using the *@conkeyref* attribute, you set a single key reference in the topic. Like the *@conref* attribute, the *@conkeyref* attribute takes content from the referenced topic. However, the *@conkeyref* refers to the topic indirectly using a *@keyref* attribute, rather than directly using the topic's file name. In this example, the *@conkeyref* creates a placeholder for the content with the id of "home" in the file defined by the "images" keyword. The *@href* attribute could be left blank in this case, but it is useful to provide a value like the # sign to avoid processing issues later.

```
<image conkeyref="images/home" href="#"/>
```

In your map, use the <keydef> element with the *@keys* attribute of "images" to point to a DITA topic, "key_file.dita".

```
<keydef keys="images" href="key_file.dita" type="concept" format="dita">
```

You can define multiple keys within a map or bookmap. However, once you define a key, that value will be used. If you define the same key a different way later in the map or bookmap, the later value will be ignored.

**Direct vs. indirect addressing**

The keyref mechanism is based on an indirect addressing strategy. With indirect addressing, an element in a topic (key) is given a temporary *@id* that another topic (placeholder) uses to take the content from the key element. By indirectly addressing content, you create a placeholder within a topic where the content will be resolved based on the value of the key. The defined key value can change as necessary, but you never need to change the placeholder.

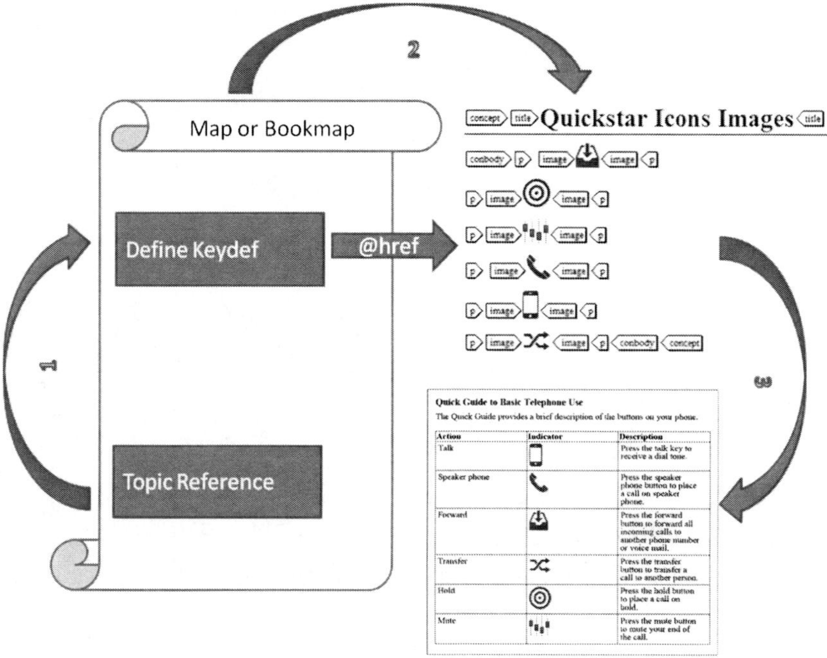


1. The target topic references a key within the map.
2. The <keydef> in the map references a file in the repository.
3. On publication, the target topic is populated with the content of the referenced file.

**Figure 16: Indirect Addressing**

By contrast, a *@conref* pulls content directly into a topic through direct addressing. The target topic (placeholder) points to the referenced topic (content) through an *@href* attribute which defines the file location and content in the file. The reference to the file and the location of the content does not change. If you need to switch the content being referenced, you must change the *@conref* attribute. When the document is processed the content that is conref'ed by the target topic is pulled in by the predefined *@href* path in the target topic. If the referenced content does not exist, then the conref fails. This process differs from indirect addressing because the *@conref* has a defined value prior to processing. In indirect addressing, the value is defined during processing.

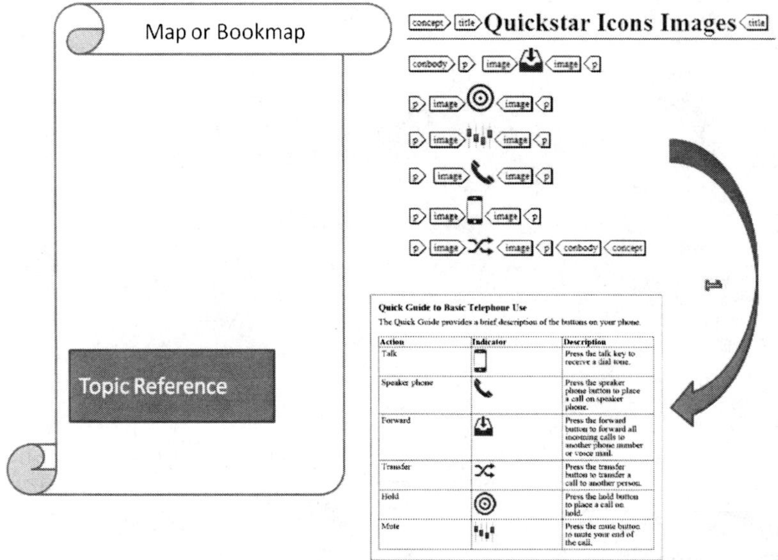


1. The target topic references a file in the repository.
2. On publication, the target topic is populated with the content of the referenced file.

**Figure 17: Direct Addressing**

**Reusing a group of images**

This exercise explains how to substitute one set of images for another in a DITA topic by using the *@conkeyref* attribute. In this exercise, assume you want to generate content for two different phone systems from the same set of content files. A primary difference between the systems are the icons used on the buttons. You want to be able to easily change the image file used when the book is generated.

In this exercise, you learn to

- create a set of images or icons that can be dynamically substituted in a topic using a single file reference
- using keys, interchange the icons without using a *@conref* for each icon or image

1. Start a new DITA concept topic and assign an *@id* attribute and value to the concept element.

   For this topic, we recommend using the unique *@id* ="keysImages". This *@id* represents your set of default icons. You can also create ids that reflect a product, model, or any other variable for conditional processing.

   ```
   <?xml version="1.0" encoding="UTF-8"?>
   <!DOCTYPE concept PUBLIC "-//OASIS//DTD DITA Concept//EN"
      "concept.dtd">
   <concept id="keysImages" xml:lang="en-us">
   </concept>
   ```

2. Give the topic a title of "Quickstar Default Icons".

   The title describes the content of the file. In this case, the file contains the images for the Quickstar product.

   ```
   <?xml version="1.0" encoding="UTF-8"?>
   <!DOCTYPE concept PUBLIC "-//OASIS//DTD DITA Concept//EN"
      "concept.dtd">
   <concept id="keysImages" xml:lang="en-us">
      <title>Quickstar Default Icons</title>
   </concept>
   ```

3. Insert <conbody> start and end tags and add six <image> tags to reference the six product icons.

   Because your icons are contained in image files, you must add *@href* attributes that point to the appropriate jpg files.

   ```
   <concept id="keysImages" xml:lang="en-us">
      <title>Quickstar Default Icons</title>
      <conbody>
         <image href="QuickStar_icons/forward.jpg"/>
         <image href="QuickStar_icons/hold.jpg"/>
         <image href="QuickStar_icons/mute.jpg"/>
         <image href="QuickStar_icons/speakerphone.jpg"/>
         <image href="QuickStar_icons/talk.jpg"/>
         <image href="QuickStar_icons/transfer.jpg"/>
      </conbody>
   </concept>
   ```

4. Add *@id* attributes and values for each image reference.

   Select names that represent the images themselves as the values for each id. For example, the first image is the FORWARD key on the phone. Give this image the *@id* value of “forward”. Remember that the *@id* value must have quotation marks surrounding it and contain no spaces or other illegal characters.

```
<concept id="keysImages" xml:lang="en-us">
   <title>Quickstar Default Icons</title>
   <conbody>
      <image href="QuickStar_icons/forward.jpg" id="forward"/>
      <image href="QuickStar_icons/hold.jpg" id="hold"/>
      <image href="QuickStar_icons/mute.jpg" id="mute"/>
      <image href="QuickStar_icons/speakerphone.jpg"
         id="speakerphone"/>
      <image href="QuickStar_icons/talk.jpg" id="talk"/>
      <image href="QuickStar_icons/transfer.jpg" id="transfer"/>
   </conbody>
</concept>
```

5. Save the key file as keys_buttons_Quickstar_icons.dita.
6. Open the ComstarUserAndAttendantsGuide.ditamap that you created in Adding metadata to your bookmap on page 222.

```
<?xml version="1.0" encoding="utf-8"?>
<!DOCTYPE bookmap PUBLIC "-//OASIS//DTD DITA BookMap//EN"
   "bookmap.dtd">
<bookmap id="ComstarUserAndAttendantsGuide" xml:lang="en-us">
   <booktitle>
      <mainbooktitle>Comstar User and Attendant's
         Guide</mainbooktitle>
   </booktitle>
   <bookmeta>
      <bookid>
         <isbn>012-3456789012</isbn>
      </bookid>
      <bookrights>
         <copyrfirst>
            <year>2011</year>
         </copyrfirst>
         <bookowner>
            <organization>Comtech Services, Inc.</organization>
         </bookowner>
      </bookrights>
   </bookmeta>
   <frontmatter>
      <preface href="ComstarPreface.dita"/>
      <booklists>
         <toc/>
      </booklists>
   </frontmatter>
   <chapter href="QuickGuide.dita"/>
   <part>
      <topicmeta>
         <navtitle>Basic Functions</navtitle>
      </topicmeta>
      <chapter href="HoldCall.ditamap" format="ditamap"/>
      <chapter href="TransferCall.ditamap" format="ditamap"/>
      <chapter href="ForwardCall.ditamap" format="ditamap"/>
   </part>
   <part>
      <topicmeta>
         <navtitle>Advanced Functions</navtitle>
      </topicmeta>
      <chapter href="ConferenceCall.ditamap" format="ditamap"/>
   </part>
```

```
      <appendices>
         <topicmeta>
            <navtitle>Appendices</navtitle>
         </topicmeta>
         <appendix href="../Components/Accessories.ditamap"
            format="ditamap"/>
         <appendix href="../../ComstarPricing.pdf" format="pdf"/>
      </appendices>
      <backmatter>
         <booklists>
            <glossarylist>
               <topicref href="g_confcall.dita"/>
               <topicref href="g_fcc.dita"/>
            </glossarylist>
            <indexlist/>
         </booklists>
      </backmatter>
   </bookmap>
```

7. Change the Quick Guide <chapter> element to a container and nest an empty <keydef> element that references the key file, keys_buttons_Quickstar_icons.dita.

   Although it is not necessary to place the <keydef> element near the topic that will use the key definitions, you may find it practical in order to keep track of related files in your map. You might also find it useful to define the *@type* and *@format* of the file as shown in the example.

```
<bookmap id="ComstarUserAndAttendantsGuide" xml:lang="en-us">
   ⋮
   <chapter href="QuickGuide.dita">
   <keydef href="keys_buttons_Quickstar_icons.dita"
      type="concept" format="dita"/>
   </chapter>
   ⋮
</bookmap>
```

8. Assign the value "buttons" to the *@keys* attribute in the <keydef> element.

   The *@href* attribute points to the file that contains the images that you want to use when you publish this map. The *@keys* attribute, "buttons", points to the file that contains the images that you will insert when you publish this map.

```
<bookmap id="ComstarUserAndAttendantsGuide" xml:lang="en-us">
   ⋮
   <chapter href="QuickGuide.dita">
   <keydef keys="buttons" href="keys_buttons_Quickstar_icons.dita"
      type="concept" format="dita"/>
   </chapter>
   ⋮
</bookmap>
```

9. Save your work in the ComstarUserAndAttendantsGuide.ditamap file.

10. Open the QuickGuide.dita topic that you created in Creating a reference topic on page 53.
Note that this file contains references to six images that are pictures of the icons on the phone. However, these images must be changed because you are now producing content for more than one version of the phone.

```
<?xml version="1.0" encoding="utf-8"?>
<!DOCTYPE reference PUBLIC "-//OASIS//DTD DITA
   Reference//EN" "reference.dtd">
<reference id="QuickGuide" xml:lang="en-us">
   <title>Quick Guide to Basic Telephone Use</title>
   <shortdesc>The Quick Guide provides a brief
      description of the buttons on your phone.
   </shortdesc>
   <prolog>
      <author>John Smith</author>
   </prolog>
   <refbody>
      <properties>
         <prophead>
            <proptypehd>Action</proptypehd>
            <propvaluehd>Indicator</propvaluehd>
            <propdeschd>Description</propdeschd>
         </prophead>
         <property>
            <proptype>Talk</proptype>
            <propvalue>
               <image href="talk.jpg"/>
            </propvalue>
            <propdesc>Press the talk key to receive a
               dial tone.</propdesc>
         </property>
         <property>
            <proptype>Speaker phone</proptype>
            <propvalue>
               <image href="speakerphone.jpg"/>
            </propvalue>
            <propdesc>Press the speaker phone button to
               place a call on speaker phone.</propdesc>
         </property>
         <property>
            <proptype>Forward</proptype>
            <propvalue>
               <image href="forward.jpg"/>
            </propvalue>
            <propdesc>Press the forward button to
               forward all incoming calls to another phone
               number or voice mail.</propdesc>
         </property>
         <property>
            <proptype>Transfer</proptype>
            <propvalue>
               <image href="transfer.jpg"/>
            </propvalue>
            <propdesc>Press the transfer button to
               transfer a call to another person.
            </propdesc>
         </property>
         <property>
```

```
            <proptype>Hold</proptype>
            <propvalue>
               <image href="hold.jpg"/>
            </propvalue>
            <propdesc>Press the hold button to place a
               call on hold.</propdesc>
         </property>
         <property>
            <proptype>Mute</proptype>
            <propvalue>
               <image href="mute.jpg"/>
            </propvalue>
            <propdesc>Press the mute button to mute
               your end of the call.
            </propdesc>
         </property>
      </properties>
   </refbody>
   <related-links>
      <link href="TransferringACall.dita"/>
   </related-links>
</reference>
```

**11.** In each <image> element in the QuickGuide.dita file, change the value of the *@href* attribute to "#".

You can leave this value blank but it is safer to provide a placeholder like the # sign to avoid processing issues later.

```
<reference id="QuickGuide" xml:lang="en-us">
   ⋮
   <refbody>
      <properties>
         <prophead>
            <proptypehd>Action</proptypehd>
            <propvaluehd>Indicator</propvaluehd>
            <propdeschd>Description</propdeschd>
         </prophead>
         <property>
            <proptype>Talk</proptype>
            <propvalue>
               <image href="#"/>
            </propvalue>
            <propdesc>Press the talk key to receive a
               dial tone.</propdesc>
         </property>
         <property>
            <proptype>Speaker phone</proptype>
            <propvalue>
               <image href="#"/>
            </propvalue>
            <propdesc>Press the speaker phone button to
               place a call on speaker phone.</propdesc>
         </property>
         <property>
            <proptype>Forward</proptype>
            <propvalue>
               <image href="#"/>
            </propvalue>
            <propdesc>Press the forward button to
```

```
            forward all incoming calls to another phone
            number or voice mail.</propdesc>
      </property>
      <property>
         <proptype>Transfer</proptype>
         <propvalue>
            <image href="#"/>
         </propvalue>
         <propdesc>Press the transfer button to
            transfer a call to another person.
         </propdesc>
      </property>
      <property>
         <proptype>Hold</proptype>
         <propvalue>
            <image href="#"/>
         </propvalue>
         <propdesc>Press the hold button to place a
            call on hold.</propdesc>
      </property>
      <property>
         <proptype>Mute</proptype>
         <propvalue>
            <image href="#"/>
         </propvalue>
         <propdesc>Press the mute button to mute
            your end of the call.
         </propdesc>
      </property>
   </properties>
</refbody>
   ⋮
</reference>
```

12. Add a *@conkeyref* attribute to each of the <image> elements to point to the "buttons" key that you defined earlier and the appropriate id that you defined in your key file.

```
<reference id="QuickGuide" xml:lang="en-us">
   ⋮
   <refbody>
      <properties>
         <prophead>
            <proptypehd>Action</proptypehd>
            <propvaluehd>Indicator</propvaluehd>
            <propdeschd>Description</propdeschd>
         </prophead>
         <property>
            <proptype>Talk</proptype>
            <propvalue>
               <image conkeyref="buttons/talk" href="#"/>
            </propvalue>
            <propdesc>Press the talk key to receive a
               dial tone.</propdesc>
         </property>
         <property>
            <proptype>Speaker phone</proptype>
            <propvalue>
               <image conkeyref="buttons/speakerphone" href="#"/>
            </propvalue>
```

```
            <propdesc>Press the speaker phone button to
               place a call on speaker phone.</propdesc>
         </property>
         <property>
            <proptype>Forward</proptype>
            <propvalue>
               <image conkeyref="buttons/forward" href="#"/>
            </propvalue>
            <propdesc>Press the forward button to
               forward all incoming calls to another phone
               number or voice mail.</propdesc>
         </property>
         <property>
            <proptype>Transfer</proptype>
            <propvalue>
               <image conkeyref="buttons/transfer" href="#"/>
            </propvalue>
            <propdesc>Press the transfer button to
               transfer a call to another person.
            </propdesc>
         </property>
         <property>
            <proptype>Hold</proptype>
            <propvalue>
               <image conkeyref="buttons/hold" href="#"/>
            </propvalue>
            <propdesc>Press the hold button to place a
               call on hold.</propdesc>
         </property>
         <property>
            <proptype>Mute</proptype>
            <propvalue>
               <image conkeyref="buttons/mute" href="#"/>
            </propvalue>
            <propdesc>Press the mute button to mute
               your end of the call.
            </propdesc>
         </property>
      </properties>
   </refbody>
   ⋮
</reference>
```

**13.** Save the QuickGuide.dita topic with the new content.

When you process your DITA map using the keys_buttons_Quickstar_icons.dita key file, the images of the buttons are be inserted into the properties table as shown in the example.

**Quick Guide to Basic Telephone Use**

The Quick Guide provides a brief description of the buttons on your phone.

| Action | Indicator | Description |
|---|---|---|
| Talk | | Press the talk key to receive a dial tone. |
| Speaker phone | | Press the speaker phone button to place a call on speaker phone. |
| Forward | | Press the forward button to forward all incoming calls to another phone number or voice mail. |
| Transfer | | Press the transfer button to transfer a call to another person. |
| Hold | | Press the hold button to place a call on hold. |
| Mute | | Press the mute button to mute your end of the call. |

To now change the images used in this topic for the second phone model, you need to create a second key file and change your ditamap to point to the new file.

1. Create a second key file as shown in the example and save it as "keys_buttons_Quickstar_words.dita".

```
<?xml version="1.0" encoding="UTF-8"?>
<!DOCTYPE concept PUBLIC "-//OASIS//DTD DITA Concept//EN"
  "concept.dtd">
<concept id="keysWords" xml:lang="en-us">
   <title>Quickstar Default Words</title>
   <conbody>
      <image href="QuickStar_words/forward.jpg"/>
      <image href="QuickStar_words/hold.jpg"/>
      <image href="QuickStar_words/mute.jpg"/>
      <image href="QuickStar_words/speakerphone.jpg"/>
      <image href="QuickStar_words/talk.jpg"/>
      <image href="QuickStar_words/transfer.jpg"/>
   </conbody>
</concept>
```

2. In the Comstaruserguide.ditamap file, redefine the *@keys* attribute in the <keydef> to point to your new key file and save your changes.

```
<bookmap id="ComstarUserAndAttendantsGuide" xml:lang="en-us">
   ⋮
   <chapter href="QuickGuide.dita"/>
   <keydef keys="buttons" href="keys_buttons_Quickstar_words.dita"
      type="concept" format="dita"/>
   ⋮
</bookmap>
```

When you process the bookmap using the keys_buttons_Quickstar_words.dita key file, the buttons will now become words as shown in the example.

**Quick Guide to Basic Telephone Use**

The Quick Guide provides a brief description of the buttons on your phone.

| Action | Indicator | Description |
|---|---|---|
| Talk | TALK | Press the talk key to receive a dial tone. |
| Speaker phone | SPEAKERPHONE | Press the speaker phone button to place a call on speaker phone. |
| Forward | FORWARD | Press the forward button to forward all incoming calls to another phone number or voice mail. |
| Transfer | TRANSFER | Press the transfer button to transfer a call to another person. |
| Hold | HOLD | Press the hold button to place a call on hold. |
| Mute | MUTE | Press the mute button to mute your end of the call. |

### Replacing variable words or phrases in a topic

This exercise explains how to set up placeholders in your topics so that you can populate them with new content when you publish your DITA map. In this exercise, you learn to

- create a variable in a topic that can be dynamically updated from a key definition in the DITA map
- insert a new product name dynamically into a target topic without using a *@conref* attribute

**Note:** Replacing single words or phrases in a topic may result in content that cannot be translated correctly or may result in errors in the source language. For example, in this lesson you change the noun phrase "Basic Telephone Use" to "ComstarPlus Use" in the title of the Quick Guide. Because product names are often not translated, the substitution should be reasonable for all translated versions. However, if the variable string replaces a singular noun with a plural noun, the verb may no longer be appropriate. For example, replacing "The policy explains ... " with "The human-resources policies explains ..." results in a grammar error. In addition, unlike most other languages, English is not heavily inflected, which means that words used as nouns, adjectives, verbs, and so on are often spelled the same way. In inflected languages, most words change depending on the part of speech or even the gender. Replacing words without considering the translation implications is inadvisable.

**1.** Open the QuickGuide.dita topic that you modified in the last exercise.

```
<?xml version="1.0" encoding="utf-8"?>
<!DOCTYPE reference PUBLIC "-//OASIS//DTD DITA
   Reference//EN" "reference.dtd">
<reference id="QuickGuide" xml:lang="en-us">
   <title>Quick Guide to Basic Telephone Use</title>
   <shortdesc>The Quick Guide provides a brief
      description of the buttons on your phone.
   </shortdesc>
   <prolog>
      <author>John Smith</author>
   </prolog>
   <refbody>
      <properties>
         <prophead>
            <proptypehd>Action</proptypehd>
            <propvaluehd>Indicator</propvaluehd>
            <propdeschd>Description</propdeschd>
         </prophead>
         <property>
            <proptype>Talk</proptype>
            <propvalue>
               <image conkeyref="buttons/talk" href="#"/>
            </propvalue>
            <propdesc>Press the talk key to receive a
               dial tone.</propdesc>
         </property>
         <property>
```

```
            <proptype>Speaker phone</proptype>
            <propvalue>
               <image conkeyref="buttons/speakerphone" href="#"/>
            </propvalue>
            <propdesc>Press the speaker phone button to
               place a call on speaker phone.</propdesc>
         </property>
         <property>
            <proptype>Forward</proptype>
            <propvalue>
               <image conkeyref="buttons/forward" href="#"/>
            </propvalue>
            <propdesc>Press the forward button to
               forward all incoming calls to another phone
               number or voice mail.</propdesc>
         </property>
         <property>
            <proptype>Transfer</proptype>
            <propvalue>
               <image conkeyref="buttons/transfer" href="#"/>
            </propvalue>
            <propdesc>Press the transfer button to
               transfer a call to another person.
            </propdesc>
         </property>
         <property>
            <proptype>Hold</proptype>
            <propvalue>
               <image conkeyref="buttons/hold" href="#"/>
            </propvalue>
            <propdesc>Press the hold button to place a
               call on hold.</propdesc>
         </property>
         <property>
            <proptype>Mute</proptype>
            <propvalue>
               <image conkeyref="buttons/mute" href="#"/>
            </propvalue>
            <propdesc>Press the mute button to mute
               your end of the call.
            </propdesc>
         </property>
      </properties>
   </refbody>
   <related-links>
      <link href="TransferringACall.dita"/>
   </related-links>
</reference>
```

2. Replace "Basic Telephone" in the title with an empty <keyword> element as a placeholder for the product name at the time of publication.

   In many companies, the product name changes frequently and often at the last moment before a publication is completed. Using a key to replace the product name at any time saves hours of topic maintenance.

```
<reference id="QuickGuide" xml:lang="en-us" >
   <title>Quick Guide to <keyword/> Use</title>
   ⋮
</reference>
```

3. Add the *@keyref* attribute with the value "prodname" to assign an identifier to the keyword element that will be used by the keyref mechanism to push the product name into the topic.

   It is best to use a keyref value that is easy to remember and correctly identifies the content being replaced.

```
<reference id="QuickGuide" xml:lang="en-us" >
   <title>Quick Guide to <keyword keyref="prodname"/> Use</title>
   ⋮
</reference>
```

4. Save the topic with the new content.
5. Open the bookmap, ComstarUserAndAttendantsGuide.ditamap, that you modified in the previous exercise.

```
<?xml version="1.0" encoding="utf-8"?>
<!DOCTYPE bookmap PUBLIC "-//OASIS//DTD DITA BookMap//EN"
   "bookmap.dtd">
<bookmap id="ComstarUserAndAttendantsGuide" xml:lang="en-us">
   <booktitle>
      <mainbooktitle>Comstar User and Attendant's Guide</mainbooktitle>
   </booktitle>
   <bookmeta>
      <bookid>
         <isbn>012-3456789012</isbn>
      </bookid>
      <bookrights>
         <copyrfirst>
            <year>2011</year>
         </copyrfirst>
         <bookowner>
            <organization>Comtech Services, Inc.</organization>
         </bookowner>
      </bookrights>
   </bookmeta>
   <frontmatter>
      <preface href="ComstarPreface.dita"/>
      <booklists>
         <toc/>
      </booklists>
   </frontmatter>
   <chapter href="QuickGuide.dita">
   <keydef keys="buttons" href="keys_buttons_Quickstar_words.dita"
      type="concept" format="dita"/>
   </chapter>
   <part>
      <topicmeta>
         <navtitle>Basic Functions</navtitle>
      </topicmeta>
      <chapter href="HoldCall.ditamap" format="ditamap"/>
      <chapter href="TransferCall.ditamap" format="ditamap"/>
```

```
      <chapter href="ForwardCall.ditamap" format="ditamap"/>
   </part>
   <part>
      <topicmeta>
         <navtitle>Advanced Functions</navtitle>
      </topicmeta>
      <chapter href="ConferenceCall.ditamap" format="ditamap"/>
   </part>
   <appendices>
      <topicmeta>
         <navtitle>Appendices</navtitle>
      </topicmeta>
      <appendix href="../Components/Accessories.ditamap"
         format="ditamap"/>
      <appendix href="../../ComstarPricing.pdf" format="pdf"/>
   </appendices>
   <backmatter>
      <booklists>
         <glossarylist>
            <topicref href="g_confcall.dita"/>
            <topicref href="g_fcc.dita"/>
         </glossarylist>
         <indexlist/>
      </booklists>
   </backmatter>
</bookmap>
```

6. Add <keydef> element start and end tags immediately after the <chapter> root element, and give the *@keys* attribute the value "prodname", the same name that you gave the *@keyref* attribute of the <keyword> element in the target topic.

```
<bookmap id="ComstarUserAndAttendantsGuide" xml:lang="en-us" >
   ⋮
   <chapter href="QuickGuide.dita">
   <keydef keys="prodname">
   </keydef>
   <keydef keys="buttons" href="keys_buttons_Quickstar_words.dita"
      type="concept" format="dita"/>
   </chapter>
   ⋮
</bookmap>
```

7. Nest <topicmeta> start and end tags within the <keydef> container.

   When defining a variable for a small piece of content, you combine <keydef> with the <keyword> element. As you learned earlier in this book, <keyword> elements are contained within the <topicmeta> structure. Thus, to define a <keyword> in a <keydef>, you include that structure within the <keydef> container.

```
<bookmap id="ComstarUserAndAttendantsGuide" xml:lang="en-us" >
   ⋮
   <chapter href="QuickGuide.dita">
   <keydef keys="prodname">
      <topicmeta>
      </topicmeta>
   </keydef>
   <keydef keys="buttons" href="keys_buttons_Quickstar_words.dita"
      type="concept" format="dita"/>
   </chapter>
   ⋮
</bookmap>
```

**8.** Nest the <keywords> and <keyword> start and end tags in the <topicmeta> element, and define the product name as the keyword.

In this lesson, use ComstarPlus as the <keyword>.

```
<bookmap id="ComstarUserAndAttendantsGuide" xml:lang="en-us" >
   ⋮
   <chapter href="QuickGuide.dita">
   <keydef keys="prodname">
      <topicmeta>
         <keywords>
            <keyword>ComstarPlus</keyword>
         </keywords>
      </topicmeta>
   </keydef>
   <keydef keys="buttons" href="keys_buttons_Quickstar_words.dita"
      type="concept" format="dita"/>
   </chapter>
   ⋮
</bookmap>
```

**9.** Save your work in the ComstarUserAndAttendantsGuide.ditamap file.

When you publish the ComstarUserGuide.ditamap file after making the changes in this lesson, the new product name appears in the Quick Guide heading, as shown in the example.

**Quick Guide to ComstarPlus Use**

The Quick Guide provides a brief description of the buttons on your phone.

| Action | Indicator | Description |
|---|---|---|
| Talk | TALK | Press the talk key to receive a dial tone. |
| Speaker phone | SPEAKERPHONE | Press the speaker phone button to place a call on speaker phone. |
| Forward | FORWARD | Press the forward button to forward all incoming calls to another phone number or voice mail. |
| Transfer | TRANSFER | Press the transfer button to transfer a call to another person. |
| Hold | HOLD | Press the hold button to place a call on hold. |
| Mute | MUTE | Press the mute button to mute your end of the call. |

**Generating related links dynamically**

When you learned to create <related-links> within a topic, you also learned that using such a mechanism could limit the reusability of the topic. When such links change or move, you may have a significant maintenance effort to update each topic with the new information. In addition, using <related-links> in a topic requires that the topic being linked to is present in the map or bookmap during publication. If the linked topic is missing, you will get a processing error. However, using a *@keyref* to define the <related-link> addresses these issues. You can more easily maintain the link and, since the linked topic is added at publication, it does not need to be present in the map or bookmap.

This exercise explains how to create related links for your topics that can be updated whenever you publish a DITA map. In this exercise, you learn to use keys to create related links dynamically so that they are easy to update.

1. Open the QuickGuide.dita topic you modified in the previous exercise.

```
<?xml version="1.0" encoding="utf-8"?>
<!DOCTYPE reference PUBLIC "-//OASIS//DTD DITA
   Reference//EN" "reference.dtd">
<reference id="QuickGuide" xml:lang="en-us">
   <title>Quick Guide to <keyword keyref="prodname"/> Use</title>
   <shortdesc>The Quick Guide provides a brief
      description of the buttons on your phone.
   </shortdesc>
   <prolog>
      <author>John Smith</author>
   </prolog>
   <refbody>
      <properties>
         <prophead>
            <proptypehd>Action</proptypehd>
            <propvaluehd>Indicator</propvaluehd>
            <propdeschd>Description</propdeschd>
         </prophead>
         <property>
            <proptype>Talk</proptype>
            <propvalue>
               <image conkeyref="buttons/talk" href="#"/>
            </propvalue>
            <propdesc>Press the talk key to receive a
               dial tone.</propdesc>
         </property>
         <property>
            <proptype>Speaker phone</proptype>
            <propvalue>
               <image conkeyref="buttons/speakerphone" href="#"/>
            </propvalue>
            <propdesc>Press the speaker phone button to
               place a call on speaker phone.</propdesc>
         </property>
         <property>
            <proptype>Forward</proptype>
            <propvalue>
               <image conkeyref="buttons/forward" href="#"/>
            </propvalue>
            <propdesc>Press the forward button to
               forward all incoming calls to another phone
               number or voice mail.</propdesc>
         </property>
         <property>
            <proptype>Transfer</proptype>
            <propvalue>
               <image conkeyref="buttons/transfer" href="#"/>
            </propvalue>
            <propdesc>Press the transfer button to
               transfer a call to another person.
            </propdesc>
         </property>
         <property>
            <proptype>Hold</proptype>
            <propvalue>
               <image conkeyref="buttons/hold" href="#"/>
            </propvalue>
            <propdesc>Press the hold button to place a
               call on hold.</propdesc>
```

```
            </property>
            <property>
               <proptype>Mute</proptype>
               <propvalue>
                  <image conkeyref="buttons/mute" href="#"/>
               </propvalue>
               <propdesc>Press the mute button to mute
                  your end of the call.
               </propdesc>
            </property>
         </properties>
      </refbody>
      <related-links>
         <link href="TransferringACall.dita"/>
      </related-links>
   </reference>
```

2. Remove the *@href* attribute value in the <link> element within the <related-links> container.

```
<reference id="QuickGuide" xml:lang="en-us" >
   ⋮
   <refbody>
   ⋮
   </refbody>
   <related-links>
      <link/>
   </related-links>
</reference>
```

3. Add a *@keyref* attribute and attribute value to the <link> element.

   The value you enter should represent the title of the topic that will be linked. In this case, use "TransferringACall". This name, which is not the filename of the topic file, is a placeholder for the link that you will define using a *@keydef* in your bookmap.

```
<reference id="QuickGuide" xml:lang="en-us" >
   ⋮
   <refbody>
   ⋮
   </refbody>
   <related-links>
      <link keyref="TransferringACall"/>
   </related-links>
</reference>
```

4. Save your work in the QuickGuide.dita topic.
5. Open the ComstarUserAndAttendantsGuide.ditamap that you modified in the previous exercise.

```
<?xml version="1.0" encoding="utf-8"?>
<!DOCTYPE bookmap PUBLIC "-//OASIS//DTD DITA BookMap//EN"
   "bookmap.dtd">
<bookmap id="ComstarUserAndAttendantsGuide" xml:lang="en-us" >
   <booktitle>
```

```
    <mainbooktitle>Comstar User and Attendant's Guide</mainbooktitle>
  </booktitle>
  <bookmeta>
    <bookid>
      <isbn>012-3456789012</isbn>
    </bookid>
    <bookrights>
      <copyrfirst>
        <year>2011</year>
      </copyrfirst>
      <bookowner>
        <organization>Comtech Services, Inc.</organization>
      </bookowner>
    </bookrights>
  </bookmeta>
  <frontmatter>
    <preface href="ComstarPreface.dita"/>
    <booklists>
      <toc/>
    </booklists>
  </frontmatter>
  <chapter href="QuickGuide.dita">
  <keydef keys="prodname">
    <topicmeta>
      <keywords>
        <keyword>ComstarPlus</keyword>
      </keywords>
    </topicmeta>
  </keydef>
  <keydef keys="buttons" href="keys_buttons_Quickstar_words.dita"
    type="concept" format="dita"/>
  </chapter>
  <part>
    <topicmeta>
      <navtitle>Basic Functions</navtitle>
    </topicmeta>
    <chapter href="HoldCall.ditamap" format="ditamap"/>
    <chapter href="TransferCall.ditamap" format="ditamap"/>
    <chapter href="ForwardCall.ditamap" format="ditamap"/>
  </part>
  <part>
    <topicmeta>
      <navtitle>Advanced Functions</navtitle>
    </topicmeta>
    <chapter href="ConferenceCall.ditamap" format="ditamap"/>
  </part>
  <appendices>
    <topicmeta>
      <navtitle>Appendices</navtitle>
    </topicmeta>
    <appendix href="../Components/Accessories.ditamap"
      format="ditamap"/>
    <appendix href="../../ComstarPricing.pdf" format="pdf"/>
  </appendices>
  <backmatter>
    <booklists>
      <glossarylist>
        <topicref href="g_confcall.dita"/>
        <topicref href="g_fcc.dita"/>
      </glossarylist>
      <indexlist/>
```

```
        </booklists>
    </backmatter>
</bookmap>
```

6. Add an empty <keydef> element immediately after the Quick Guide <chapter> root element that points to your TransferringACall.dita file.

   The *@href* attribute points to the topic that will become the related link in the TransferringACall.dita topic when processed. The value should be the path of the topic relative to the bookmap location.

```
<bookmap id="ComstarUserAndAttendantsGuide" xml:lang="en-us" >
   ⋮
   <chapter href="QuickGuide.dita">
   <keydef href="TransferringACall.dita"/>
   <keydef keys="prodname">
      <topicmeta>
         <keywords>
            <keyword>ComstarPlus</keyword>
         </keywords>
      </topicmeta>
   </keydef>
   <keydef keys="buttons" href="keys_buttons_Quickstar_words.dita"
      type="concept" format="dita"/>
   </chapter>
   ⋮
</bookmap>
```

7. Add attribute definitions to establish the topic type and format, how this file will be processed, and the name of the key.

   The *@keys* attribute is the same as the <keyref> you specified in your topic for the related link, in this case "TransferringACall". Use the *@type*, *@format*, and *@processing-role* attributes to indicate that the information type is task, the file is a DITA file, and the topic referenced by the <keydef> element will be included during processing.

```
<bookmap id="ComstarUserAndAttendantsGuide" xml:lang="en-us" >
   ⋮
   <chapter href="QuickGuide.dita">
   <keydef keys="TransferringACall" href="TransferringACall.dita"
      type="task" format="dita" processing-role="normal"/>
   <keydef keys="prodname">
      <topicmeta>
         <keywords>
            <keyword>ComstarPlus</keyword>
         </keywords>
      </topicmeta>
   </keydef>
   <keydef keys="buttons" href="keys_buttons_Quickstar_words.dita"
      type="concept" format="dita"/>
   </chapter>
   ⋮
</bookmap>
```

8. Save your work in the ComstarUserAndAttendantsGuide.ditamap file.

When you process the ComstarUserGuide.ditamap file for XHTML output, you will see a related link to "Transferring a Call" added to the Quick Guide topic as shown in the example.

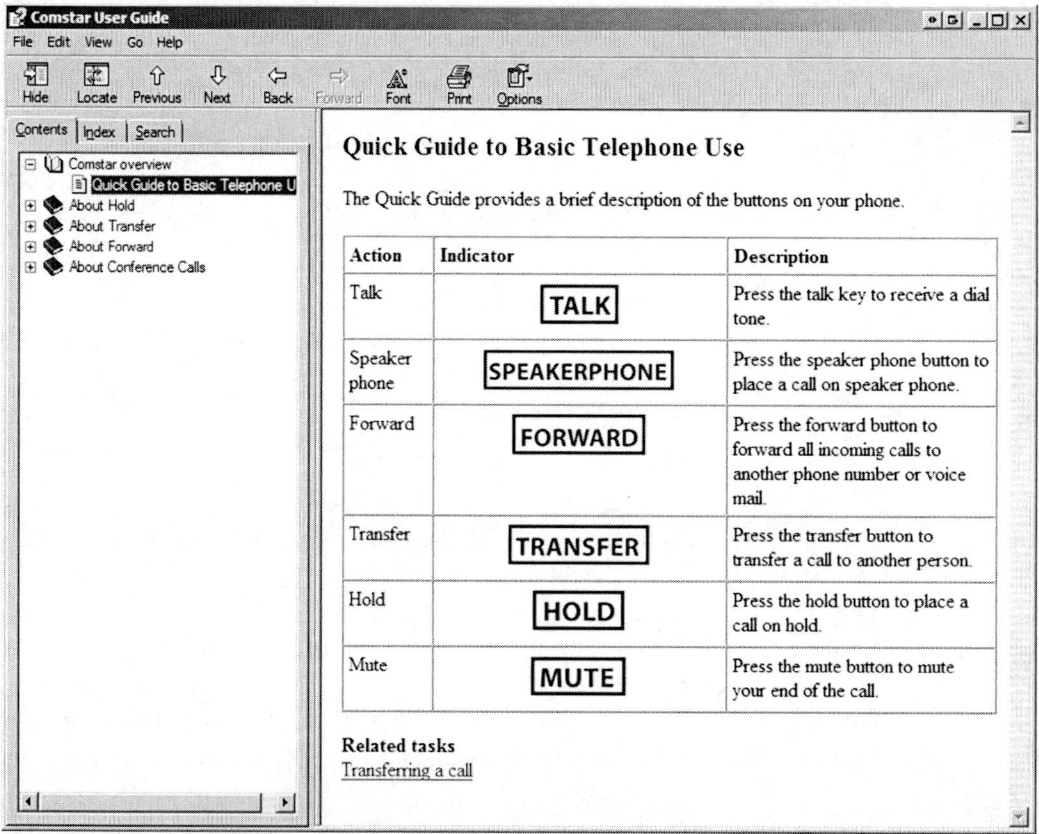


## Referencing glossary terms

You can use the keyref mechanism to insert glossary terms into your text or associate those terms with their definitions. You can also specify that the processor use the abbreviated form of a glossary term on all but the first occurrence of the word in the text. In this exercise you learn to

- insert a glossary term into your text
- create a hover definition for online deliverables
- insert the abbreviated form of a term on all but the first occurrence

1. Open the ComstarUserAndAttendantsGuide.ditamap that you modified in the previous exercise.

```
<?xml version="1.0" encoding="utf-8"?>
<!DOCTYPE bookmap PUBLIC "-//OASIS//DTD DITA BookMap//EN"
   "bookmap.dtd">
<bookmap id="ComstarUserAndAttendantsGuide" xml:lang="en-us" >
   <booktitle>
      <mainbooktitle>Comstar User and Attendant's Guide</mainbooktitle>
   </booktitle>
   <bookmeta>
      <bookid>
         <isbn>012-3456789012</isbn>
      </bookid>
      <bookrights>
         <copyrfirst>
            <year>2011</year>
         </copyrfirst>
         <bookowner>
            <organization>Comtech Services, Inc.</organization>
         </bookowner>
      </bookrights>
   </bookmeta>
   <frontmatter>
      <preface href="ComstarPreface.dita"/>
      <booklists>
         <toc/>
      </booklists>
   </frontmatter>
   <chapter href="QuickGuide.dita">
   <keydef keys="TransferringACall" href="TransferringACall.dita"
      type="task" format="dita" processing-role="normal"/>
   <keydef keys="prodname">
      <topicmeta>
         <keywords>
            <keyword>ComstarPlus</keyword>
         </keywords>
      </topicmeta>
   </keydef>
   <keydef keys="buttons" href="keys_buttons_Quickstar_words.dita"
      type="concept" format="dita"/>
   </chapter>
   <part>
      <topicmeta>
         <navtitle>Basic Functions</navtitle>
      </topicmeta>
      <chapter href="HoldCall.ditamap" format="ditamap"/>
      <chapter href="TransferCall.ditamap" format="ditamap"/>
      <chapter href="ForwardCall.ditamap" format="ditamap"/>
   </part>
   <part>
      <topicmeta>
         <navtitle>Advanced Functions</navtitle>
      </topicmeta>
      <chapter href="ConferenceCall.ditamap" format="ditamap"/>
   </part>
   <appendices>
      <topicmeta>
         <navtitle>Appendices</navtitle>
      </topicmeta>
```

```
      <appendix href="../Components/Accessories.ditamap"
         format="ditamap"/>
      <appendix href="../../ComstarPricing.pdf" format="pdf"/>
   </appendices>
   <backmatter>
      <booklists>
         <glossarylist>
            <topicref href="g_confcall.dita"/>
            <topicref href="g_fcc.dita"/>
         </glossarylist>
         <indexlist/>
      </booklists>
   </backmatter>
</bookmap>
```

2. Add a *@keys* attribute to each of the <topicref> elements that point to your glossary terms.

```
<bookmap id="ComstarUserAndAttendantsGuide" xml:lang="en-us" >
   ⋮
   <backmatter>
      <booklists>
         <glossarylist>
            <topicref keys="confcall" href="g_confcall.dita"/>
            <topicref keys="fcc" href="g_fcc.dita"/>
         </glossarylist>
         <indexlist/>
      </booklists>
   </backmatter>
</bookmap>
```

3. Save your work in the ComstarUserAndAttendantsGuide.ditamap file.
4. Open the AboutConferenceCalls.dita topic you created in Creating a concept topic on page 22.

```
<?xml version="1.0" encoding="utf-8"?>
<!DOCTYPE concept PUBLIC "-//OASIS//DTD DITA Concept//EN"
   "concept.dtd">
<concept id="AboutConferenceCalls" xml:lang="en-us">
   <title>About conference calls</title>
   <shortdesc>Use a conference call to speak with more
      than two people in two different locations at the
      same time.</shortdesc>
   <prolog>
      <author>John Smith</author>
   </prolog>
   <conbody>
      <p>Use one of the following types of conference calls
         to speak with multiple people.</p>
      <dl>
         <dlentry>
            <dt>Three-way conference call</dt>
            <dd>Three-way conference calling connects
               two other people to a call.</dd>
         </dlentry>
         <dlentry>
            <dt>Multi-line conference call</dt>
            <dd>Multi-line conference calling connects
               you to more than two but fewer than eight
```

```
                other people on a call.</dd>
          </dlentry>
          <dlentry>
             <dt>Dial-in conference call</dt>
             <dd>Dial-in conference calling uses a single
                conference call number to connect multiple
                people.</dd>
          </dlentry>
       </dl>
    </conbody>
    <related-links>
       <link href="SettingUpConfCall.dita" scope="local">
          <linktext>Conference call set-up</linktext>
       </link>
    </related-links>
</concept>
```

5. In the <shortdesc> element, replace the words "conference call" with a <term> element containing a *@keyref* attribute that points to the conference call glossary item.

   When the file is processed, this element will be replaced by the <glossterm> of the <glossentry> with the *@id* you have referenced using the *@keyref* attribute.

```
<concept id="AboutConferenceCalls" xml:lang="en-us">
   <title>About conference calls</title>
   <shortdesc>Use a <term keyref="confcall"/> to speak with
      more than two people in two different locations at the
      same time.</shortdesc>
   ⋮
</concept>
```

6. In the first paragraph of the <conbody>, surround the words "conference call" with <term> start and end tags and place a *@keyref* attribute in the start tag that points to the conference call glossary item.

   When the file is processed for an online output, the words "conference call" will be linked to the <glossdef> of the <glossentry> with the *@id* you have referenced using the *@keyref* attribute. Depending on your transform, the definition might appear as hover text over the word, or users might click the word to see the definition.

```
<concept id="AboutConferenceCalls" xml:lang="en-us">
   ⋮
   <conbody>
      <p>Use one of the following types of
         <term keyref="confcall">conference calls</term>
         to speak with multiple people.</p>
      ⋮
   </conbody>
   ⋮
</concept>
```

7. Save your work in the AboutConferenceCalls.dita topic.

**8.** Create a concept topic with a section titled "Notes, Warnings, and Cautions" and two notes as shown in the example.

```
<?xml version="1.0" encoding="UTF-8"?>
<!DOCTYPE concept PUBLIC "-//OASIS//DTD DITA Concept//EN"
   "http://docs.oasis-open.org/dita/v1.1/OS/dtd/concept.dtd">
<concept id="ComstarPreface" xml:lang="en-us" >
   <title>Preface</title>
   <conbody>
      <section>
         <title>Notes, Warnings, and Cautions</title>
         <note type="note">This equipment generates, uses, and can
            radiate radio frequency energy and if not installed and
            used in accordance with the instruction manual, may cause
            interference to radio communications. It has been tested
            and found to comply with the limits for a Class A
            computing device pursuant to Subpart J of Part 15 of FCC
            rules, which are designed to provide reasonable protection
            against such interference when operated in a commercial
            environment. Operation of this equipment in a residential
            area may cause interference, in which case the user, at
            his own expense, will be required to take whatever
            measures may be required to correct the interference.
            </note>
         <note type="note">For a list of applicable FCC
            certifications, refer to the Appendix.</note>
      </section>
   </conbody>
</concept>
```

**9.** Replace each abbreviation "FCC" with an empty <abbreviated-form> element pointing to the FCC glossary entry.

Upon processing, the first instance of the FCC term will be replaced by the <glossSurfaceForm> and subsequent FCC terms will be replaced by the <glossAcronym>.

```
<?xml version="1.0" encoding="UTF-8"?>
<!DOCTYPE concept PUBLIC "-//OASIS//DTD DITA Concept//EN"
   "http://docs.oasis-open.org/dita/v1.1/OS/dtd/concept.dtd">
<concept id="ComstarPreface" xml:lang="en-us" >
   <title>Preface</title>
   <conbody>
      <section>
         <title>Notes, Warnings, and Cautions</title>
         <note type="note">This equipment generates, uses, and can
            radiate radio frequency energy and if not installed and
            used in accordance with the instruction manual, may cause
            interference to radio communications. It has been tested
            and found to comply with the limits for a Class A
            computing device pursuant to Subpart J of Part 15 of
            <abbreviated-form keyref="FCC"/> rules,
            which are designed to provide reasonable protection
            against such interference when operated in a commercial
            environment. Operation of this equipment in a residential
            area may cause interference, in which case the user, at
            his own expense, will be required to take whatever
            measures may be required to correct the interference.
            </note>
```

```
            <note type="note">For a list of applicable
               <abbreviated-form keyref="FCC"/>
               certifications, refer to the Appendix.</note>
         </section>
      </conbody>
   </concept>
```

**10.** Save this file as "ComstarPreface.dita".

The examples show how the ComstarPreface.dita file would be processed based on whether the Federal Communications Commission term has appeared previously in the book.

### Notes, Warnings, and Cautions

**:** This equipment generates, uses, and can radiate radio frequency energy and if not installed and used in accordance with the instruction manual, may cause interference to radio communications. It has been tested and found to comply with the limits for a Class A computing device pursuant to Subpart J of Part 15 of Federal Communications Commission (FCC) rules, which are designed to provide reasonable protection against such interference when operated in a commercial environment. Operation of this equipment in a residential area may cause interference, in which case the user, at his own expense, will be required to take whatever measures may be required to correct the interference.

**Note:** For a list of applicable FCC certifications, refer to the Appendix.

### Keyref review questions

Match the reuse mechanism to its most appropriate use.

| | |
|---|---|
| *@keyref* | Reference standard content sets that are unlikely to vary from one application to another. |
| *@conkeyref* | Select from variable content when variations are few. |
| *@conref* | Swap complete content units that vary among multiple versions of the content. |
| Conditional processing | Swap graphics, words, or phrases that vary among multiple versions of the content. |

Select the true statements. Select all that apply.

- **a.** Both *@keyref* and *@conref* use indirect addressing.
- **b.** Conref@ requires you to touch fewer files when you need to update a reference.
- **c.** Use *@keyref*, rather than *@conref*, for dynamic linking.
- **d.** *@keyref* is better suited for inserting small pieces of information, while *@conref* is better suited for large standalone components of content.

What attribute do you use as a referencing key when the key value is defined in the map or bookmap.

To change content in a map using *@keyref*, change the value of the key placeholder.

- True
- False

What happens if you define a key multiple ways in the same map?

- **a.** The first key definition applies in all cases.
- **b.** The last key definition applies in all cases.
- **c.** The current location in the map determines the key definition.
- **d.** You will receive an error when you try to process the book.

What's wrong with this code: <keydef id=prodname>PUB$Estimator</keydef>

- **a.** The *@id* attribute should be a *@keys* attribute.
- **b.** The value being defined must be nested in <topicmeta><keywords><keyword> elements.
- **c.** The <keydef> element requires an *@href* attribute.
- **d.** prodname should be in quotes.

What is the proper syntax to reference a specific element (id) in an external key file (key)?

What is the expected output for this code: <term conkeyref="ATM">automated teller machine</term>?

- **a.** The acronym ATM will be substituted for the full term after the first occurrence.
- **b.** The definition of the term will be linked to this occurrence of the term.
- **c.** The term defined by the key "ATM" will be inserted into the text in place of the words enclosed by the <term> element..
- **d.** The term will be linked to the file "ATM".

To define a glossary file as a key file without also including the file in the book, use the <glossdef> tag within your bookmap.

- True
- False

# PART V

# The DITA Information-Development Environment

DITA allows organizations and information architects to create a custom environment within the framework of the base DITA information architecture. As you have seen throughout this guide, the base DITA information architecture supports a wide range of information types, content units, inline elements, and referencing mechanisms. However, you can change and simplify the information-development environment to assist your authors in making good structural decisions about their content and about the XML structures they use. You can also ensure that the structural choices your authors make are consistent across the organization and across the enterprise.

Through modifications, you can

- remove information types, entire element domains, or individual elements and attributes from the framework
- restrict the use of specific elements and attributes
- specify the type, order, and number of elements required within an information type
- specify the specific attributes required for an element
- limit attribute values to a pre-defined list
- create new information types and element tags

Such modifications help ease the transition to DITA and XML authoring and help you enforce your organization's information architecture.

As with any type of custom work, however, an organization has to weigh the benefit of the modifications against the amount of effort required to develop, implement, and maintain the changes. Modifications should not begin until you have completed a thorough content analysis and designed a DITA information architecture that will support the types of information you produce in your organization. You must have a strong information model that

- identifies the information types you require
- describes the structure of each information type, including the required and optional elements allowed in each
- defines the metadata required to describe your content

With this information, you can then describe the ideal information-development environment that will assist your authors most in creating content that conforms to your model. Part V then assists you then in selecting the appropriate methodologies that will help you implement that environment. It introduces the methodologies available for modifying the base DITA framework, describing the capabilities and limitations of each method and presenting the pros and cons of using each one. Unlike the rest of this guide, however, Part V does not provide step-by-step instructions for using these methodologies and making these changes. Modifications require experienced DITA experts and the input and cooperation of your tool vendor. We strongly recommend that you engage the assistance of a experienced DITA consultant and your tool vendor when you are ready to modify your authoring environment.

# SECTION J

# Understanding the DITA Information-Development Environment

The DITA architecture supports a variety of mechanisms you may use to modify the environment in which your organization develops information.

The DITA specialization mechanism, introduced in DITA 1.0, accommodates the needs of organizations that require information types, elements, and attributes that are unique to a particular subject area. In DITA 1.2, mechanisms were added, including constraints and controlled vocabularies, to allow organizations to modify the DITA architecture in less comprehensive ways than specialization. In addition, the developers of most XML editors provide additional methods to allow you to modify the XML authoring environment without changing the underlying DITA architecture. In this section, you learn how each of DITA modification mechanisms works so that you can meet the needs of your authors and your content and still ensure that you are using DITA in a way that is compliant with the DITA standard.

The DITA 1.2 architecture accommodates the requirements of many different information-development communities, from hardware and software products and machine equipment to learning and training materials. Consequently, the DITA 1.2 architecture embraces a rich architecture that contains capabilities to support the needs of a wide variety information-development activities. However, the wealth of information types, elements, and attributes provided may be more than your content requires or your authors are prepared to handle.

An information-development organization may modify the DITA architecture to best meet the requirements of its content and its information developers. For example, authors writing about heavy-equipment maintenance may not need DITA's software programming elements. A marketing organization producing product catalogs may not require the specialized DITA learning and training information types and elements. An information architect may want to prohibit writers from using some of DITA's highlighting elements like <b> and <i> to enforce the separation of format from content. At the same time, that information architect may want to ensure that all authors correctly enter the product names used to filter content topics and content units upon publication.

Some organizations discover that the DITA 1.2 architecture does not include the special maps and information types needed to structure their content correctly. The semiconductor industry, for example, has created a DITA specialization for the register description that is a foundation information type of their subject area. A service organization that relies on field support engineers to contribute occasional content may prefer a simplified authoring environment that relies heavily on basic word-processing elements like headings, paragraphs, and lists to produce DITA-compliant content.

Whatever the requirements, DITA supports several mechanisms for modifying and simplifying the authoring environment or creating unique information types, elements, and attributes. By degree of difficulty, from the simplest modifications to the most complex, these mechanisms include

- creating document-type shells to reduce the full set of DITA structures to those essential for a subject area
- constraining DITA maps, content units, and elements to reduce the options from which authors must choose
- implementing controlled vocabularies for metadata attributes, especially those used for filtering and flagging content upon publication
- creating specialized maps, information types, elements, and attributes to support subject-area requirements

**Note:** The DITA standard, unlike some other XML authoring standards, does not promote customizations. Customizations result in new Document Type Definitions (DTDs) that are no longer standard and, consequently, are no longer inter-operable with content produced using different customizations. We strongly recommend against customizing DITA DTDs, Rather, recognize that correctly developed, DITA shell models, constraints, controlled vocabularies, and specializations remain compliant with the DITA standard and its forthcoming releases, unless an explicit decision is made by the standards committee that backward compatibility will no longer be maintained.

**Modification evaluation**

As with any type of modifications, an organization has to weigh the benefit of the modifications against the amount of effort required to develop, implement, and maintain them. Use the simplest modification option possible to meet your needs.

This table summarizes the modifications you might want to make in your environment and shows the approaches that can help you achieve them.

| If you want to... | Document-type shells | Constraint mechanism | Controlled attribute values | Specialization |
|---|---|---|---|---|
| Eliminate entire domains or information types | X | | | X |
| Eliminate elements or attributes not needed | | X | | X |
| Make elements required or optional | | X | | X |
| Restrict the occurrence of elements | | X | | X |
| Restrict or require attributes for certain elements | | X | | X |
| Define acceptable values for attributes | | | X | X |
| Change the required order of elements within a topic | | | | X |
| Create new elements | | | | X |
| Create new information types | | X | | X |

**Table 7: Comparison of DITA Modification Options**

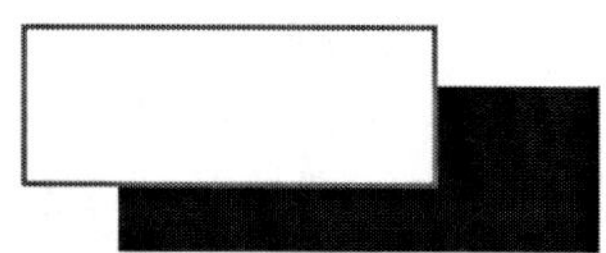

# LESSON 21

## DITA Information-Development Environment Modifications

No matter which option you choose to modify your environment, you need to be well versed in DITA and your authoring tools. We recommend that you consult DITA experts and your tool vendors when making these modifications. As a result, it is beyond the scope of this book to teach the mechanics for modifying your environment. Instead, this lesson is designed to introduce you to the things you need to consider when determining the customizations required. In this lesson, you consider when to implement

- document-type shells
- constraints
- controlled attribute values
- specializations

**Modifying the document-type shells**

The complete DITA architecture contains a set of information types to structure many types of content and many sets of elements to label words and phrases semantically. However, not every organization needs all the sets. In fact, authors may be confused by menus that display information types and domain elements that they should not use. Or, authors may use information types or elements incorrectly. Displaying all possible information types, elements, and attributes in your authoring environment usually leads to inconsistent and faulty markup that results in processing and styling errors. Different authors choose different, or even conflicting, ways to identify the same content.

You can limit the information types and elements sets available to your authors by creating document-type shells that contain only the information types and element sets that your authors need. By pointing your XML authoring tool to these document-type shells rather than the complete DITA architecture, authors will see only the choices that are allowed in your information architecture.

For example, if your marketing organization wants to use the concept information type with only the set of user-interface elements, you would construct a document-type shell for the concept information type and the user interface domain. Or, perhaps your technical documentation organization wants to use the concept, task, and reference information types and the programming and software element domains, but does not need the learning and training information types or the safety hazard element domain. In the document-type shell, you would include only the programming and software element domains.

Creating corporate- or department-specific document-type shells helps you simplify the DITA architecture and reduce complexity for authors. However, document-type shells function as a rough cut. You either include an information type, or you exclude it. You either include an entire domain of elements, or you exclude them all. For example, if you eliminate the highlighting domain, you eliminate bold and italic but you also eliminate subscript, superscript, and all the other elements in that domain. If you eliminate the task information type, you no longer have pre-requisite, steps, post-requisite, or any of the other structural elements of task available for your authors.

Consequently, you need to review carefully the list of possible information types and element domains that are available in the complete DITA document-type shell. The following table lists the information types and domains as defined in the DITA 1.2 specification. Note that all of these information types and domains are not discussed in this book; refer to the *OASIS Darwin Information Typing Architecture (DITA) Version 1.2 (OASIS Standard, 1 December 2010).*

| **Information Types** | **Domains** |
|---|---|
| Topic | Abbreviated form |
| Map | Hazard statement |
| Bookmap | Highlight |
| Concept | Indexing |
| Task | Learning |
| Reference | Learning meta |
| Learning assessment | Programming |
| Learning bookmap | Software |
| Learning content | User delayed resolution |
| Learning map | User interface |
| Learning overview | Utilities |
| Learning plan | |
| Learning summary | |
| Machine task | |

**Implementation considerations**

Implement document-type shells as soon as you know which information types and domains you want to use. Initially, you may want to use the complete DITA architecture during your pilot project and the development of your Information Model. However, before you roll out the model to your entire authoring community, you should create your organization-specific document-type shells.

Document-type shells that eliminate many unneeded information types and domain elements decrease the learning curve, increase markup consistency, and promote author productivity. Remember that you can always update your document-type shells by adding information types and element domains if you later determine they are needed.

At the time of this edition, a web-based tool is available to help you create document-type shells. See http://dita-generator.appspot.com/shell/ for a step-by-step procedure to create a document-type shell. You will also need an XML authoring environment that allows you to point to your shell. Any DITA-compliant XML editor should allow you to implement custom document-type shells.

By creating document-type shells for your authoring environment, you do not alter the base DITA document-type shell in any way. You simply leave parts out. As a result, you have compliant, non-specialized DITA. If someone were to modify a topic created using your document-type shells in an authoring environment that uses the complete DITA document-type shells, the topic would be valid DITA XML. However, you could no longer use that modified topic if that person were to add any elements that were not included in your shell because the new element added would not be valid in your version of DITA.

Be certain that by using different DITA document-type shells in your enterprise you do not make topic-reuse difficult.

**Constraining your authoring environment**

The DITA 1.2 constraints architecture allows you to manage your authors' use of particular structures and elements, as determined by your information architecture:

- You can remove optional elements such as the simple table <simpletable> because you want authors to select the OASIS table <table> instead.
- You can require optional elements on all topics, such as short description <shortdesc>, because you want your authors to add these elements to every topic.
- You may want to enforce a consistent style for writing notes, making them more concise. You can constrain the <note> element, restricting authors to only one <p> within a note, removing block elements such as <ol>, <ul>, and <table>, and eliminating phrase-level elements like <codeph>, <msgph>, and <term>.
- You can require that a context element always precede a prerequisites element in your version of a strict task model.
- You can allow superscript and subscript in the highlighting domain but omit bold, italic, and underline.

- You can require that a section always begin with a title and that authors may not enter text directly into the <section> element, a popular constraint among many information architects.
- You can constrain a bookmap to require that the table of contents always be in front matter and the index always be in back matter.

By applying constraints, you omit, make required, or specify the order of some part of the DITA information architecture. However, you cannot make a required attribute like the topic *@id* optional, and you cannot change the order of elements that already have a specified order.

Recall the comparison of the general and strict task models in Task Information Type on page 33. In DITA 1.2, the strict task model, which was the only task model in early versions of the specification, was replaced by the general task specialization. General task is looser than strict task. Unlike the strict task, it allows prerequisite, context, and section to occur in any order prior to steps. It also allows more than one instance of any of these content units. In fact, the DITA 1.2 strict task model is a constraint of the general task model. It omits the section and requires that prerequisite precede context. It also allows only one instance of either of these content units.

The general task model was developed to allow information architects to constrain the task model in ways required by the organizations. Note that the strict task model constrains the general task model, requiring authors to follow a prescribed structure for a task. Information architects wanting a different strict task structure can constrain the general task in a way of their own choosing. See Task Information Type on page 33 for more information about the strict and general task models.

By constraining DITA elements, you enforce the set of rules for using DITA elements and attributes properly, as defined by your information architecture. Constraints assist authors by limiting options that are valid but are not considered best practices in your authoring environment. They also simplify the code review process for your information architects.

Remember, however, that a less constrained topic or map may be incompatible with a more constrained topic or map. For example, the strict task model does not allow a section, while the general task does. A general task topic containing a section, although it correctly follows the general task model, will be invalid in an organization that requires the strict task model.

**Implementation considerations**

Implementing constraints requires a more well-defined information architecture than implementing document-type shells. You need to make explicit decisions with respect to each structure and element. Many of the elements in your group's information model may need a constraint, depending on how much enforcement of structure and element choice you want the authoring environment to handle. Implement constraints only after you've completed a thorough content analysis and designed a DITA information architecture to support all the types of information you produce.

If you constrain elements before completing a thorough analysis, you may fail to support certain content. Faced with too restrictive an environment, authors are likely squeeze content into inappropriate elements just to "make it fit."

Once your architecture is stable, you can apply constraints to your document-type shells and incorporate them into your XML authoring tools. You will need to work closely with your tools vendor, because different vendors have implemented the DITA 1.2 constraints mechanism differently.

**Developing controlled attribute values**

Attributes are used extensively in DITA to filter or flag content, typically either for conditional publishing or for search and retrieval. As a result, the values assigned to these attributes must be consistent across your entire organization. The DITA 1.2 architecture allows you to define sets of controlled attribute vocabularies and validate them at the DTD or schema level. To do so, you create a specialized map, called the SubjectScheme map, defining your attributes, their values, and even their relationships to each other. The allowed values are listed when an author adds an attribute, eliminating the potential for typographical errors or inconsistencies in terminology.

The SubjectScheme map allows organizations to

- define easily identifiable, consistent, valid names for attribute values. For example, a group using the *@platform* attribute may have authors who use different names for the same platform. One group regularly uses "phantom" while another group consistently refers to it as "PhantomOS". A controlled vocabulary would list only "phantom" among the options for the *@platform* attribute value.
- create labels to make the correct values easy to locate. Suppose the group using "PhantomOS" argues that this choice is more readable and useful to the authors. It is possible to create a label with the more readable option, "PhantomOS", in the value list, while the true value, "phantom" (with no spaces that would cause problems for XML), is correctly defined in the SubjectScheme map.
- develop subject-matter definitions to accompany the controlled vocabularies. Often more thorough definitions of attribute values are needed for authors to interpret and apply them correctly. For example, two authors may interpret the *@audience* values of "expert" and "administrator" to mean

the same thing. To avoid these issues, you can create a subject definition topic referenced by the SubjectScheme map to explain that "expert" users are end users, "administrator" users are certified technicians, and the two are mutually exclusive. You can then configure your authoring environment to display this subject definition using a mouse-over or some other user interface mechanism.

- define hierarchical relationships between attribute values. You might need to classify some attribute values more specifically than others. For example, you might need to differentiate a *@platform* of "Linux" between "RedHat" and "Ubuntu". Rather than list both RedHat and Ubuntu at the main level in the value list, making the list longer, you can nest attribute values to indicate their relationships and then structure the authoring interface to show that RedHat and Ubuntu are flavors of Linux. If authors choose "Linux" as the *@platform* attribute value, they must then specify the flavor.
- set one value as the default. If the author does not select a value from the values list, the value designated as the default applies.

**Note:** You cannot apply a SubjectScheme map to override values that are specified already in the DITA DTDs. For example, the *@importance* attribute has the values "high", "low", and others defined. You cannot remove those values. However, you can add to them.

By implementing a SubjectScheme map, you can fine tune your authoring environment by providing readable, consistent, sensible attribute value lists for authors, while at the same time ensuring that valid values are entered across the organization and potentially across the enterprise.

**Implementation considerations**

The key to implementing controlled attribute values is defining a metadata strategy, in particular metadata that will be used for conditional processing or any other sort of filtering, flagging, or searching. Controlled values cannot be implemented until you have defined basic metadata in your information architecture. The information model should lay out definitions for which attributes to use, for what purposes they are applied, and what the value selections are.

Applying the SubjectScheme maps prematurely risks the effort required to implement them. Once your architecture is stable, specify the controlled values you need and work with your tools vendor to implement the SubjectScheme map. Displaying controlled values in your authoring environment is dependent on the tools vendors. Vendors may have implemented the DITA 1.2 SubjectScheme map differently. In addition, many vendors have their own processes in place to configure the authoring environment for specific attribute values. However, keep in mind that these processes are likely unique to the individual tool and may not work with other tools. By using a SubjectScheme map, you ensure that your controlled values are available in any authoring environment.

**Specializing DITA**

When all other options for modifying the authoring environment have been exhausted, you may need to introduce special structures for DITA maps, new information types, or subject-area semantics to your DITA environment. Specialization, a fundamental feature of the DITA framework, allows you to create unique structures to support your content.

The DITA specialization mechanism allows you to specify new types of content, including specialized

- maps that mirror the larger organizational framework of your content. Note that the bookmap is a specialization of the basic DITA map.
- information types that meet specific subject-matter requirements. Note that the concept information type is a specialization of the basic DITA topic.
- elements that reflect the semantics of your subject matter. Note that <uicontrol> is a specialization of the <ph> element.

**Map specialization**

You use a structural specialization to add structures to the base DITA map. For example, the bookmap is a structural specialization of map. It includes parts like frontmatter, backmatter, parts, and chapters to define the structures needed by those producing print or PDF books.

**Information-type specialization**

To build a new structure for an information type, you construct a structural specialization. With a structural specialization, you create new content units that are used to support your subject matter. Information architects use structural specializations to create new authoring environments so that authors have the content units and elements they need. For example, the Learning Plan, part of the Learning and Training specialization, has sections that reflect the requirements of instructional designers as they plan a learning and training environment. The technical-communication information type, the general task, is a specialization of the DITA base topic, while the strict task is a constraint of the general task.

**Domain specialization**

With a domain specialization, you create semantic elements that more accurately describe your content and make it easier to style, search, and retrieve. There are many opportunities for domain specializations. For example, many industries, such as semiconductor, pharmaceuticals, transportation, telecommunications, and medical equipment, may develop specializations that relate specifically to the terminology and elements unique to their subject areas. Industry specializations allow you to standardize and information and to create consistent content for end users.

You might also develop domain specializations to describe information specific to a particular department, information type, or product. For example, companies might create a domain specialization for Application Programming Interfaces (APIs) because the content is significantly different from the previously defined user interface, programming, and software domains.

**Implementation considerations**

Using a specialization provides the opportunity to enforce your information architecture and to support information that is not adequately covered by the base DITA architecture or the specializations already included for technical communication, the machine industry, and learning and training. However, it is wise to begin your pilot project and early implementation of DITA using the out-of-the-box architecture. As you continue to understand your content needs, carefully consider whether you can meet your needs without specialization. If you believe you do need a specialization, work with consultants and your tool vendor to implement it correctly.

Although it is the most complex modification option, DITA specialization still greatly simplifies the process of creating new DTDs for unique information types. An average DTD might contain hundreds of lines of code, but a specialized DTD can be written with just a few lines of code because it inherits all the structure, semantics, and processing rules of the parent DITA DTD. Inheritance means that you can use the structures and semantics already defined in the base topic DITA DTD and the core DITA information types, effectively single sourcing your DTD set and simplifying its maintenance. In other words, specialization is the process of using existing structures from the base DITA structure to create new information types and elements that better fit your needs.

For example, you have learned that the core DITA information types, task, concept, and reference, each have the same basic structure (title, short description, prolog, body, and related links). The source of this basic structure is the topic.dtd. Each of the core information type DTDs is a specialization of the basic topic.dtd, as illustrated in Figure 18 on page 318.

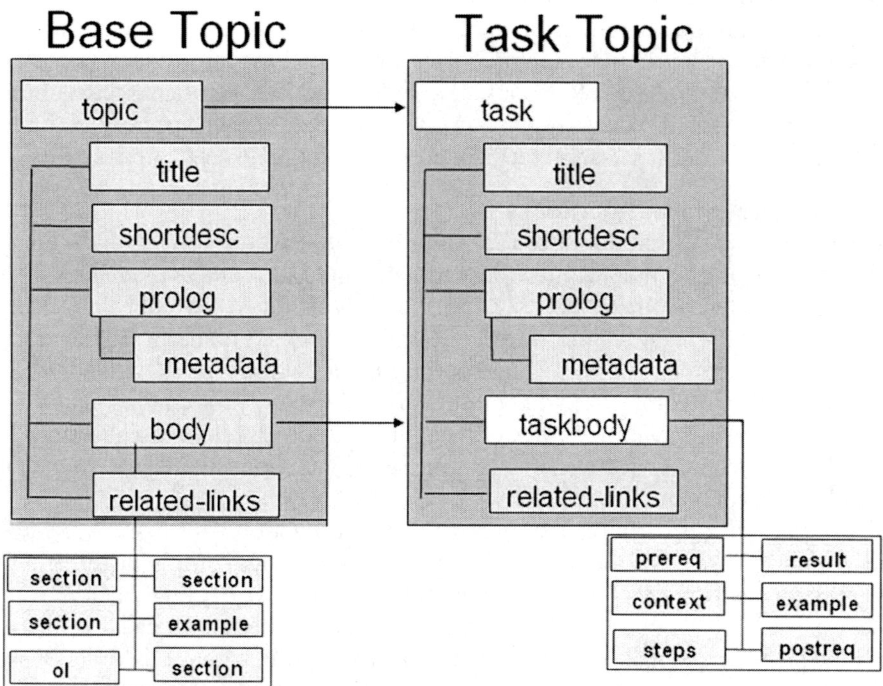


**Figure 18: Specialization of task topic**

In DITA 1.2, the Learning and Training topic specializations and glossary specialization have also been included in the base framework.

Similarly, specialized elements map to a base parent element and inherit the structure and styles of that parent. For example, the <steps> element that is the heart of the task information type is specialized from the ordered list <ol> in the base topic information type. Steps inherit the structure defined for the ordered list. Because the base structure is already established for the ordered list in a DITA stylesheet, you do not have to create a new style to account for <steps> in the task. Each <step> in the <steps> container element is formatted with the sequential numbers already defined for list items <li> inside the <ol> container element.

Because your specialized elements and information types inherit styles and structure rules from their parent elements, you can also generalize, or revert, your specialized information type or content unit back to the base structure and more generic content unit. For example, if you generalized the <steps> content unit, it will revert to an ordered list. Generalization, part of the inheritance principle, means that you can exchange DITA content with organizations that have different specializations. For example, you may work closely with an original equipment manufacturer (OEM) or a supplier that provides you with content. The OEM or supplier can deliver DITA content that includes its own specialized information types and content units. You can generalize the content to the base DITA topic information type and process it as part of your information set.

Specialization carries significant overhead with it. A specialization needs to be written, implemented, and maintained. It also restricts portability to a certain extent. The specialized structures are unique to a specific organization. Knowing that, a specialization should not be rushed into. Perform the following due diligence before specializing:

- Investigate other options, including document-type shells, constraints, controlled attribute values, and lightweight tools configurations.
- Develop a business case for the specialization, specifying the overhead it will take to develop, implement, and maintain the specialization in your authoring environment.

If you still believe that you need a specialization, work with your information architect to define your requirements. It may be possible to meet your needs without a specialization. If you decide to create a specialization, work with your information architect and a person knowledgeable about modifying the appropriate files and implementing the specialization correctly in your authoring environment.

**DITA modifications review questions**

You have determined that your organization will not use any of the user-interface domain elements. What form of modification is best suited to remove those elements from the authoring environment.

- **a.** Document-type shells
- **b.** Constraint mechanism
- **c.** Controlled attribute values
- **d.** Specialization

To require that authors always provide a title for a section in a DITA concept, use the constraints mechanism.

- True
- False

You have determined that your organization requires a new information type for tutorial topics. What form of customization is best suited to create this new information type?

**a.** Document-type shells
**b.** Constraint mechanism
**c.** Controlled attribute values
**d.** Specialization

The document-type shells enables you to leave out individual elements and information types.

- True
- False

Your applications run on multiple Windows, Apple, and Unix platforms, with minor differences that you plan to note through conditional processing. What form of modification can best help you ensure that your authors always specify the platforms consistently?

**a.** Document-type shells
**b.** Constraint mechanism
**c.** Controlled attribute values
**d.** Specialization

All elements in a values selection list must be at the same level, without sub-values.

- True
- False

You want to change the elements that are required in a concept topic. What is the best modification option to achieve this goal?

**a.** Document-type shells
**b.** Constraint mechanism
**c.** Controlled attribute values
**d.** Specialization

Carefully handled modifications, like document-type shells, the constraint mechanism, and controlled attribute values, change DITA's base semantics and processing rules.

- True
- False

You want to limit the situations in which specific elements can be used. What is the best modification option to achieve this goal?

**a.** Document-type shells
**b.** Constraint mechanism
**c.** Controlled attribute values
**d.** Specialization

The SubjectScheme map is used for which modification type?

**a.** Document-type shells
**b.** Constraint mechanism
**c.** Controlled attribute values
**d.** Specialization

# PART VI

# Processing

Processing your DITA topics and maps requires a suite of tools.

To create XHTML, HTML, or something that compiles HTML output, you need an XML parser and an XSLT processor. To create PDF or print output, you need to an XML parser and an XSL-FO processor. These tools are available in commercial products and open-source systems. Some bundle the tools pieces into a single processing unit with a user interface to guide you through the production options.

An XML parser reads the XML structure and provides the logic to move within the hierarchy of the XML elements and attributes. An XSLT processor analyzes an XML document and provides the functionality to alter the sequence, hierarchy, or markup of an XML document. For example, an XSLT processor could change the XML DITA tag <task> to an HTML tag <html> to generate web output. An XSL-FO processor interprets the XLS-FO file which could be generated by the XSLT processor and renders the PDF output.

Many people currently use the DITA Open Toolkit to process their DITA deliverables. Many vendors also use the Open Toolkit as the production tool in their products. The Open Toolkit includes an open source version of each of the required processors. The DITA-OT is packaged with the following technologies used during processing.

- Processing build script - ANT
- XML parser - Xerces
- XSLT processor - Saxon or Xalan
- XSL-FO processor - Apache FOP and support for Antenna House or Render X

The DITA Open Toolkit includes transforms and stylesheets contributed by volunteers to generate various output types. However, the Open Toolkit output styles may not match your organization's style requirements. In that case, you must learn to configure the styles to fit your needs or hire someone who specializes in such work.

The DITA Open Toolkit also includes the functionality you need to create build files. Build files process DITA maps and topics by providing instructions to the DITA-OT that specify the input files (bookmap/map/topic), the desired output type, the appropriate transform scripts and stylesheet, and the processing applications (Xerces, Saxon, Apache

FOP). By using a build file, you establish a repeatable set of rules to create a single deliverable or a set of deliverables. If you don't use build files, your processing tools will prompt you to enter the same information every time you want to create output.

# SECTION K

# Understanding the DITA Open Toolkit

The DITA Open Toolkit (DITA-OT) is an implementation of the OASIS DITA Technical Committee's specification for DITA DTDs and schemas. The Toolkit transforms DITA XML source content into deliverable formats such as PDF, HTML, and help systems. Although the DITA-OT is closely associated with the DITA specification, it is not a standard approved by the OASIS DITA Technical Committee and therefore should be considered as only one option for transforming DITA content.

The DITA-OT and all applications needed to run it are open source, free to download and use. However,authoring tools do not come with the DITA Open Toolkit. However, you can author in DITA using open-source or commercial tools.

**DITA Open Toolkit Components**

The current version of the DITA Open Toolkit includes the DTDs and schemas to support both DITA 1.1 and DITA 1.2 features. Versions prior to 1.5.1 do not support the DITA 1.2 features. In addition to the DTDs and schemas, the DITA-OT also includes the transforms and stylesheets necessary for PDF, XHTML, Java Help, HTML Help, Eclipse Help, and HTML-to-DITA transformations. You can also download additional DITA-OT transform from SourceForge.

The following applications are open source and needed by the DITA Open Toolkit to produce HTML, HTML Help, Java Help, and PDF output. With the exception of the Java Development Kit and the Microsoft HTML Help™ application, the necessary applications are all packaged with the DITA-OT versions 1.4.3 and higher and do not require separate installation steps.

**Java Development Kit (JDK)**

The Java Software Development kit is an Oracle product targeted for Java developers. You use it to write, compile, debug, and run Java applets and applications. The Java processor is needed to produce each output type. All of the tools are tied together through Java.

**Java Help**

JavaHelp allows users to create online help to support their Java platform applications, including both applet and standalone applications, javabeans components, applets in HTML pages, and server-based Java applications.. The JavaHelp system is a Java Platform, Standard Edition ("Java SE") optional package and can be run in both Windows and Linux environments.

**Microsoft HTML Help**

Microsoft HTML Help™ is an online help authoring tool used to develop and author online help for software applications or web sites. It is compiler used to generate the HTML Help files during the build process.

**Note:** The compiled HTML help transform requires that this authoring tool be installed and accessible by the DITA-OT.

**Apache FOP**

Apache Formatting Objects Processor (FOP) is a Java-based application that reads the XLS-FO standard and renders the resulting pages to a PDF file that can then be read by a PDF reader application like Adobe Acrobat® or Foxit®. Apache FOP is part the Apache XML Graphics Project and is licensed under the Apache License, version 2.0. Apache FOP is the rendering engine supplied with DITA-OT to generate PDF output through the intermediate XSL-FO standard.

**Note:** The rendering engine used to transform the XSL-FO standard into a PDF is an important piece of the DITA-OT transformation scenario. Although Apache FOP is a powerful rendering engine, it does have limitations when processing the XSL-FO standard, and it is not the only choice for rendering engine. Companies have designed proprietary rendering engines to interpret the XSL-FO standard for PDF output and have also built extensions to support advanced PDF requirements. In general, rendering engines used to interpret the XSL-FO standard will provide the logic required to build page sets, page flows, table of contents, headers, footers, and other page properties. In the context of DITA publishing, users have the option of extending the DITA-OT PDF transformation by using proprietary engines like Antenna House, Render X, Styler, XPP, or DB2. Each of these rendering engines provides additional capabilities that Apache FOP does not during formating. For a complete list of extensions and rendering engine capabilities, review the features set for each rendering engine.

**SAXON XSLT processor**

The SAXON XSLT processor is responsible for the intermediate step of transforming the source DITA XML content to the target source. The target source can include XHTML, JavaHelp, and XSL-FO. The DITA-OT publishing pipeline uses the XSLT processor to interpret the XSLT standard which provides the logic to go from one XML source to another. The DITA-OT is supplied with Saxon 9 which is an open source product available under the Mozilla Public License. Saxon 9.x provides implementations of XSLT 2.0, XQuery 1.0, and XPath 2.0 at the basic level of conformance defined by W3C. It is available for both Java and .NET.

**Apache Ant™**

Apache Ant™ is an XML-based, W3C-approved standard that defines a processing pipeline that evokes Java classes to initiate the DITA-OT build processes. Ant scripts define the build parameters to build output files such as HTML, PDF, and help systems. In addition to defining the different output types of the DITA-OT, Ant scripts also define specific processing parameters like input file, output folder, clean temp, process relation tables, and display draft comments. Many more Ant arguments can be found in the DITA 1.2 architectural specification.

### DITA Open Toolkit Folder Structure

The information in the table describes the folder structure and content of the DITA Open Toolkit directory (DITAOT) after installation.

| Folder | Contents |
|---|---|
| css | the styles for displaying XML source files in editors or browsers |
| demo | demonstrations and experiments for DITA capabilities |
| doc | documentation for DITA and the Open Toolkit |
| dtd | the document type definitions for the DITA vocabulary |
| lib | the Java implementation for advanced processing |
| out | the formatted output<br>**Note:** This folder is generated the first time a document is processed, not when the DITA Open Toolkit is installed. |
| plugins | reserved for additional plugins to extend or enhance the capabilities of the baseline DITA-OT |
| resource | the styles and other resources for XHTML and other output |
| samples | example DITA content for testing the processing |
| schema | the XML Schema definitions for the DITA vocabulary |
| tools | the files needed for ant as well as additional batch files used to process the DITA-OT |

| Folder | Contents |
| --- | --- |
| temp | the intermediate files created during processing<br>**Note:** This folder is generated the first time a document is processed, not when the DITA Open Toolkit is installed. |
| xsl | the XSLT files for XHTML and PDF processing |

**Table 8: DITA Open Toolkit folder structure**

# LESSON 22

## DITA Open Toolkit

In previous versions of the DITA-OT, users had to download and install individual components of the DITA-OT and set environmental variables to ensure that the DITA-OT would find the correct paths to each component. However, all versions of the DITA-OT starting with 1.4.3 include the required components, with the exception of the Java Development Kit and the Microsoft HTML Help™ application package, and automatically set the correct environmental variables at runtime.

This lesson contains three exercises:

- Installing the DITA-OT
- Installing the Java Development Kit (JDK)
- Installing Microsoft HTML Help

**Note:** This lesson assumes that you are installing the latest version of the DITA-OT on a Windows platform and does not provide instructions for installing individual components that are included in the OT or setting environmental variables. These instructions are valid for the release of the DITA-OT, JDK, and Microsoft HTML Help application current at the time of this book's publication. Installation may change with later releases, so check the installation instructions provided with the latest version of these components for any additional instructions relevant to the current release. If you are using a Linux system, see the DITA Open Toolkit installation instructions for that platform on http://sourceforge.net/.

**Installing the DITA Open Toolkit**

The DITA-OT is available from http://sourceforge.net/. In this exercise, you learn to download and install the DITA-OT and all included components. The JDK and Microsoft HTML Help are downloaded and installed separately.

1. Enter the URL: http://sourceforge.net/projects/DITA-ot/.
2. Click on the green download box.

   **Note:** If you are an Internet Explorer user and a yellow bar appears at the top of the screen with the message, "To help protect your security, Internet

Explorer blocked this site from downloading files to your computer. Click here for options," click on the bar and select "Download File".

3. Click **Save** to unzip the downloaded file and save it to your C:\ directory as DITAOT.

**Installing JDK (Java Development Kit)**

The Java Development Kit (JDK) is an Oracle product targeted for Java developers. In this exercise, you learn to download and install the JDK. The steps provide general instructions for downloading and installing the JDK. Refer to the installation instructions provided on the product download page for more specific information related to the current release.

1. Enter the URL: http://www.oracle.com.
2. Browse to the Java SE download page.
3. Click the download button for the JDK.
4. Accept the license agreement.
5. Select the appropriate version of the JDK for your platform.
6. Click **Run** and follow the steps in the install wizard to complete the installation.

**Installing Microsoft HTML Help™**

Microsoft HTML Help™ is available from the MSDN library. In this exercise, you learn to download and install the application.

**Note:** If you need instructions for installing Microsoft HTML Help on a Linux system, see the DITA Open Toolkit installation instructions on the http://sourceforge.net.

1. Enter the URL: http://msdn.microsoft.com/en-us/library/ms669985.
2. Select **Download Htmlhelp.exe**.
3. Click **Run** and navigate to an appropriate directory.
4. Follow the steps in the HTML Help install wizard to complete the installation.

**Testing DITA-OT Installation**

After installing the DITA-OT and JDK, you should test your installation before you begin processing your files. The DITA-OT provides a demo file (build_file.xml) to test your installation. In this exercise, you learn how to verify that all components have installed correctly.

1. Run the startcmd.bat file found in the root folder where you installed the DITA-OT.
2. Type `java -version`.

Your command prompt displays something similar to the example message below. If your command prompt does not display similar information, reinstall the JDK.

```
java version "1.6.0_25"
Java(TM) SE Runtime Environment, SE Runtime Environment
   (build 1.6.0_25-b06)
Java HotSpot(TM) 64-Bit Server VM (build 20.0-b11, mixed mode)
```

3. Type `ant -version`.
   Your command prompt displays something similar to the example below. If your command prompt does not display the information below, reinstall the DITA-OT.

   ```
   Apache Ant version 1.7.1 compiled on June 27 2008
   ```

   **Note:** If you see the message "Unable to locate tools.jar", the DITA-OT will still work. You can download this file, if desired, from the internet.
4. Type `ant all -f build_demo.xml` and press **Enter** to begin testing.

   If you see an Out of Memory Error, perform the following steps.

   a. In the command prompt under the DITA Open Toolkit directory (DITAOT), type `set ANT_OPTS=-Xmx256M`
   b. Test the DITA installation process again by typing `ant all -f build_demo.xml` in the command prompt.

   The processing finishes after a few minutes depending on the speed of your computer and how large your project is. When testing completes, the command prompt displays the confirmation message "`BUILD SUCCESSFUL`". If you do not see "`BUILD SUCCESSFUL`", look through the error messages on the command prompt to research the problem or reinstall the DITA Open Toolkit.

   **Note:** To read more about the DITA Open Toolkit options and functions, see C:\DITAOT\doc\DITA-readme.html on your local hard drive.

Another method you can use to create the samples and test your installation is to type `ant -f build_demo.xml` in your command prompt. When you type `ant -f`, you also have the option of putting in your own .ditamap file as a source and creating your own outputs. Your command prompt displays the following information requests:

- `Please enter the filename for the DITA map you want to build including the directory path (if any). The filename must have the .ditamap extension. Note that the relative paths that climb (../) are not supported yet. To build the sample,` press return without entering anything. The DITA map filename:

- Please enter the name of the output directory or press return to accept the default. The output directory (out):
- Please enter the type of output to generate. Options include eclipse, htmlhelp, javahelp, PDF, or web. Use lowercase letters. The output type: (eclipse, htmlhelp, javahelp, PDF, web, docbook)
- Continue? (Y,y,N,n)

You can also create Ant build scripts so that you don't have to answer the same questions at the command prompt each time you want to create your output. See Ant Build Files on page 335 for more information.

**DITA-OT review questions**

Which of the following components are included in the DITA-OT download? Select all that apply.

- **a.** Java Development Kit
- **b.** JavaHelp
- **c.** Microsoft HTML Help
- **d.** Apache FOP
- **e.** Saxon XSLT
- **f.** Apache Ant

Match each DITA-OT component to its function.

| | |
|---|---|
| JDK | Compiles online help to support Java platform applications |
| JavaHelp | Used to write, compile, debug, and run Java applets and applications |
| Microsoft HTML Help | Compiles HTML help for software applications or web sites |
| Apache FOP | Defines the build and processing parameters to build output files |
| Saxon XSLT | Reads the XLS-FO standard and renders the resulting pages to a PDF |
| Apache Ant | Responsible for the intermediate step of transforming the source DITA XML content to the target source |

From what web site can you download the DITA-OT?

What output types can you create using the DITA-OT out-of-the-box? Select all that apply.

- **a.** HTML
- **b.** Flash
- **c.** HTMLHelp
- **d.** JavaHelp
- **e.** PDF
- **f.** SharePoint
- **g.** InDesign

The DITA-OT version 1.4.3 and later automatically sets the correct environmental variables at runtime.

- True
- False

# SECTION L
## Understanding Build Files

When you use the DITA Open Toolkit to produce your deliverable, you can create an Ant build file to make processing easier. The purpose of the Ant build file is to

- set project and import properties to indicate where the tools are in your processing environment
- define targets for the output type (PDF, HTML Help (.chm), XHTML, Java Help, Eclipse, etc)
- invoke a property to identify your DITA map source file and your output directory.
- set additional processing variables
- extend publishing to include external processing resources

The Ant build file connects the source files (DITA map and stylesheets) and the production processes together. It can be complex or simple depending upon your needs. The basic build file defines where the map is located, which stylesheets you want to use to process your output (i.e., XHTML, PDF, HTML Help, Java Help, or Eclipse), and the directory where the output should be placed.

# LESSON 23

## Ant Build Files

After you download the DITA Open Toolkit, you can find several build file templates in the folder, samples/ant-sample. Figure 19 shows a sample of one build file template. Note that as versions of the DITA-OT are released, the template build files may change and therefore differ from the examples used in this lesson.

```
<?xml  version="1.0" encoding="UTF-8" ?>
<!-- revise @PLACEHOLDER@ names and values -->
<!--
  | basedir can be specified to other places base on your need.
  |
  | Note: input, output, and temp directories will base on the
  | basedir if they are relative paths.
-->
<project name="@PROJECT.NAME@_htmlhelp"
   default="@DELIVERABLE.NAME@2htmlhelp" basedir=".">
   <!-- dita.dir should point to the toolkit's root directory  -->
   <propertyname="dita.dir"
      value="${basedir}${file.separator}..${file.separator}.." />
   <!-- if file is a relative file name, the file name will be
      resolved relative to the importing file  -->
   <importfile="${dita.dir}${file.separator}integrator.xml" />
   <target name="@DELIVERABLE.NAME@2htmlhelp" depends="integrate">
      <ant antfile="${dita.dir}${file.separator}build.xml"
         target="init">
         <!-- please refer to the toolkit's document for supported
            parameters, and specify them base on your needs  -->
         <propertyname="args.input" value="@DITA.INPUT@" />
         <propertyname="output.dir" value="@OUTPUT.DIR@" />
         <propertyname="transtype" value="htmlhelp" />
      </ant>
   </target>
</project>
```

**Figure 19: Example of the htmlhelp template file in the ant-sample folder**

Because the Open Toolkit uses different processes and files to define each output type, you may want to create a new build file for each output. If you use the templates provided in the Open Toolkit samples/ant-sample folder, you will need to create one build file to produce HTML Help and another build file to produce PDF. If you want to create one build file to produce HTML and PDF output simultaneously, see Invoking multiple builds on page 338 in this lesson.

In the DITA Open Toolkit, Ant allows you to add custom functionality to create your output. For example, you can use properties to add customized cascading stylesheets or insert automatically generated headers and footers. Some other options you can include using customized Ant build files include invoking additions to the XSL stylesheets and overriding the DITA element processing with custom XSL stylesheets. You can learn more about Ant build options from the DITA-antscript.html file in the DITA Open Toolkit doc/readme folder.

This lesson contains four exercises that lead you through building, invoking, and modifying build files.

**Creating a build file**

This exercise explains how to create a build file for PDF output. All output build files are created in the same way; they just use different templates. The output template files are located in the DITAOT directory in the samples/ant-sample folder. In this exercise, you learn to

- start a build file for a specific project and deliverable
- point to a .ditamap file as your input
- add a folder location for your output files
- process the build file to create your output

**Note:** The exercises in this lesson assume that your Comstar User Guide files are located in DITAOT\samples\ComstarUserGuide\. If you have placed your files elsewhere, either move the folder to this location or change all file paths in the instructions to your specific path.

1. Open the template_pdf.xml file in a text editor such as notepad.

   The template_pdf.xml file is in the DITAOT/samples/ant_sample directory.

```
<?xml version="1.0" encoding="UTF-8" ?>
<!-- revise @PLACEHOLDER@ names and values -->
<!--
   | basedir can be specified to other places base on your need.
   |
   | Note: input, output, and temp directories will base on the
   | basedir if they are relative paths.
-->
<project name="@PROJECT.NAME@_pdf"
   default="@DELIVERABLE.NAME@2pdf" basedir=".">
   <!-- dita.dir should point to the toolkit's root directory  -->
   <property name="dita.dir"
      value="${basedir}${file.separator}..${file.separator}.." />
   <!-- if file is a relative file name, the file name will be
      resolved relative to the importing file  -->
   <import file="${dita.dir}${file.separator}integrator.xml" />
   <target name="@DELIVERABLE.NAME@2pdf" depends="integrate">
      <ant antfile="${dita.dir}${file.separator}build.xml"
         target="init">
      <!-- please refer to the toolkit's document for supported
         parameters, and specify them base on your needs  -->
```

```
            <property name="args.input" value="@DITA.INPUT@" />
            <property name="output.dir" value="@OUTPUT.DIR@" />
            <property name="transtype" value="pdf" />
         </ant>
      </target>
   </project>
```

2. Replace all @placeholders@, including the @ symbol, in the template.
   a. Change `@PROJECT.NAME@` to ComstarUserGuide, the name of your project.
   b. Change `@DELIVERABLE.NAME@` to ComstarUserGuide, the unique name for your deliverable.

      Because you can include multiple targets in a single build file, you need to create a specific deliverable name for each target. For more information about creating multiple deliverables with a single build file, see Invoking multiple builds on page 338.
   c. Change `@DITA.INPUT@` to ${dita.dir}${file.separator}samples${file.separator}ComstarUserGuide${file.separator}ComstarUserGuide.ditamap, the file path and file name of the DITA map you want to process.

      Use ${file.separator} in your path names so that the build file can be processed without errors on any platform.
   d. Change the `@OUTPUT.DIR@` to ${dita.dir}${file.separator}samples${file.separator}ComstarUserGuide${file.separator}pdf.

      The output directory is the file path to the folder where you want your output files to be stored after processing completes.
3. Save the build file as ComstarUserGuide_pdf.xml in the DITAOT/samples/ant_sample directory.

   The name of the build file must match the project name (@PROJECT.NAME@) you assigned in your build file.

```
<?xml version="1.0" encoding="UTF-8" ?>
<!-- revise @PLACEHOLDER@ names and values -->
<!--
   | basedir can be specified to other places base on your need.
   |
   | Note: input, output, and temp directories will base on the
   | basedir if they are relative paths.
-->
<project name="ComstarUserGuide_pdf"
   default="ComstarUserGuide2pdf" basedir=".">
   <!-- dita.dir should point to the toolkit's root directory  -->
   <property name="dita.dir"
      value="${basedir}${file.separator}..${file.separator}.." />
   <!-- if file is a relative file name, the file name will be
      resolved relative to the importing file  -->
```

```
    <import file="${dita.dir}${file.separator}integrator.xml" />
    <target name="ComstarUserGuide2pdf" depends="integrate">
       <ant antfile="${dita.dir}${file.separator}build.xml"
          target="init">
       <!-- please refer to the toolkit's document for supported
          parameters, and specify them base on your needs  -->
          <property name="args.input"
             value="${dita.dir}${file.separator}samples$
             {file.separator}ComstarUserGuide${file.separator}
             ComstarUserGuide.ditamap />
          <property name="output.dir"
             value="${dita.dir}${file.separator}samples$
             {file.separator}ComstarUserGuide${file.separator}
             pdf" />
          <property name="transtype" value="pdf" />
       </ant>
    </target>
</project>
```

4. Run the startcmd.bat file found in the root folder where you installed the DITA-OT.
5. At the command prompt, type `ant -f samples\ComstarUserGuide \ComstarUserGuide_pdf.xml` and press enter to begin processing.

   The file name located after samples\ComstarUserGuide\ is the name of the build file you created.

   The processing finishes after a few minutes depending on the speed of your computer and how large your project is. When the processing completes, the confirmation message "`BUILD SUCCESSFUL`" displays on your command prompt. If the build is not successful and displays "`BUILD FAILED`", look through the error messages on the command prompt to identify the problem. If you cannot resolve the build problem, contact a DITA Open Toolkit expert.

**Invoking multiple builds**

Use the multiple builds feature when creating different types of media output or processing different DITA maps at one time. You can include multiple targets for creating your output in one build file. Doing so decreases the time it takes to run multiple build files. In this exercise, you learn to

- modify a build file to output more than one deliverable type
- modify a build file to use two different map files

**Note:** This exercise assumes you have two revisions of the ComstarUserGuide. Before you begin, make a copy of your ComstarUserGuide.ditamap, and name it ComstarUserGuideRevTwo.ditamap. You do not need to make any changes to this file; however, if you would like to compare the different outputs generated by this single build file, consider making a few easily noticeable changes, such as removing a few of the topic references.

1. Open the ComstarUserGuide_pdf.xml file you created in the last lesson.

```
<?xml version="1.0" encoding="UTF-8" ?>
<!-- revise @PLACEHOLDER@ names and values -->
<!--
   | basedir can be specified to other places base on your need.
   |
   | Note: input, output, and temp directories will base on the
   | basedir if they are relative paths.
-->
<project name="ComstarUserGuide_pdf"
   default="ComstarUserGuide2pdf" basedir=".">
   <!-- dita.dir should point to the toolkit's root directory  -->
   <property name="dita.dir"
      value="${basedir}${file.separator}..${file.separator}.." />
   <!-- if file is a relative file name, the file name will be
      resolved relative to the importing file  -->
   <import file="${dita.dir}${file.separator}integrator.xml" />
   <target name="ComstarUserGuide2pdf" depends="integrate">
      <ant antfile="${dita.dir}${file.separator}build.xml"
         target="init">
      <!-- please refer to the toolkit's document for supported
         parameters, and specify them base on your needs  -->
         <property name="args.input"
            "${dita.dir}${file.separator}samples$
            {file.separator}ComstarUserGuide${file.separator}
            ComstarUserGuide.ditamap" />
         <property name="output.dir"
            value="${dita.dir}${file.separator}samples$
            {file.separator}ComstarUserGuide${file.separator}
            pdf" />
         <property name="transtype"  value="pdf" />
      </ant>
   </target>
</project>
```

2. Change the *@default* attribute on the <project> element to "all".

   The *@default* attribute indicates which targets the build file should process. Since you are now going to generate multiple outputs with one build file, you need to create a target that points to multiple targets. The processor will now look for a <target> element with the name of "all".

```
<project name="ComstarUserGuide_pdf"
   default="all" basedir=".">
   ⋮
</project>
```

3. Add a <target> element with a *@name* attribute of "all" and list each of the three target output files in the *@depends* attribute.

   When you run the build file in the toolkit, your processor uses the information in the "all" target and runs the targets listed in the *@depends* attribute value.

```
<project name="ComstarUserGuide_pdf"
   default="all" basedir=".">
   <!-- dita.dir should point to the toolkit's root directory  -->
   <property name="dita.dir"
      value="${basedir}${file.separator}..${file.separator}.." />
   <!-- if file is a relative file name, the file name will be
      resolved relative to the importing file  -->
   <import file="${dita.dir}${file.separator}integrator.xml" />
   <target name="all" depends="ComstarUserGuide2pdf,
      ComstarUserGuide2xhtml, ComstarUserGuideRevTwo2pdf"/>
   ⋮
</project>
```

4. Create a new target definition for an xhtml output after the current target definition.

   You can copy the target definition from the template_xhtml.xml file in the samples/ant-sample folder. Note that in this case, the args.input value remains the same because you are processing the same map to a different output type. However, you are changing the output.dir value to store the resulting output separately from the PDF.

```
<project name="ComstarUserGuide_pdf"
   default="all" basedir=".">
   ⋮
   <target  name="ComstarUserGuide2xhtml" depends="integrate">
      <ant antfile="${dita.dir}${file.separator}build.xml"
         target="init">
      <!-- please refer to the toolkit's document for supported
         parameters, and specify them base on your needs  -->
         <property name="args.input"
            value="${dita.dir}${file.separator}samples$
            {file.separator}ComstarUserGuide${file.separator}
            ComstarUserGuide.ditamap" />
         <property name="output.dir"
            value="${dita.dir}${file.separator}samples$
            {file.separator}ComstarUserGuide${file.separator}
            web" />
         <property name="transtype"  value="xhtml" />
      </ant>
   </target>
</project>
```

5. Create a new target definition to output another PDF file using a different revision of the Comstar User Guide.

   You can copy the target definition from the previous PDF target definition. Note that in this case, the args.input value changes to the new ditamap you want to process. However, you keep the output.dir value set to the PDF directory since you are creating another PDF file.

```
<project name="ComstarUserGuide_pdf"
   default="all" basedir=".">
   ⋮
   <target name="ComstarUserGuideRevTwo2pdf" depends="integrate">
```

```
        <ant antfile="${dita.dir}${file.separator}build.xml"
           target="init">
        <!-- please refer to the toolkit's document for supported
           parameters, and specify them base on your needs  -->
           <property name="args.input"
              value="${dita.dir}${file.separator}samples$
              {file.separator}ComstarUserGuide${file.separator}
              ComstarUserGuideRevTwo.ditamap" />
           <property name="output.dir"
              value="${dita.dir}${file.separator}samples$
              {file.separator}ComstarUserGuide${file.separator}
              pdf" />
           <property name="transtype" value="pdf" />
        </ant>
     </target>
  </project>
```

**6.** Save your work in the ComstarUserGuide_pdf.xml file.

The example shows the entire build file with the modifications to generate three different output files.

```
<?xml version="1.0" encoding="UTF-8" ?>
<!-- revise @PLACEHOLDER@ names and values -->
<!--
   | basedir can be specified to other places base on your need.
   |
   | Note: input, output, and temp directories will base on the
   | basedir if they are relative paths.
-->
<project name="ComstarUserGuide_pdf"
   default="all" basedir=".">
   <!-- dita.dir should point to the toolkit's root directory  -->
   <property name="dita.dir"
      value="${basedir}${file.separator}..${file.separator}.." />
   <!-- if file is a relative file name, the file name will be
      resolved relative to the importing file  -->
   <import file="${dita.dir}${file.separator}integrator.xml" />
   <target name="all" depends="ComstarUserGuide2xhtml,
      ComstarUserGuide_pdf2pdf, ComstarUserGuideRevTwo2pdf"/>
   <target name="ComstarUserGuide2pdf" depends="integrate">
      <ant antfile="${dita.dir}${file.separator}build.xml"
         target="init">
      <!-- please refer to the toolkit's document for supported
         parameters, and specify them base on your needs  -->
         <property name="args.input"
            "${dita.dir}${file.separator}samples$
            {file.separator}ComstarUserGuide${file.separator}
            ComstarUserGuide.ditamap" />
         <property name="output.dir"
            value="${dita.dir}${file.separator}samples$
            {file.separator}ComstarUserGuide${file.separator}
            pdf" />
         <property name="transtype"  value="pdf" />
      </ant>
   </target>
   <target name="ComstarUserGuide2xhtml" depends="integrate">
      <ant antfile="${dita.dir}${file.separator}build.xml"
         target="init">
      <!-- please refer to the toolkit's document for supported
         parameters, and specify them base on your needs  -->
```

```
         <property name="args.input"
            value="${dita.dir}${file.separator}samples$
            {file.separator}ComstarUserGuide${file.separator}
            ComstarUserGuide.ditamap" />
         <property name="output.dir"
            value="${dita.dir}${file.separator}samples$
            {file.separator}ComstarUserGuide${file.separator}
            web" />
         <property name="transtype"  value="xhtml" />
      </ant>
   </target>
   <target name="ComstarUserGuideRevTwo2pdf" depends="integrate">
      <ant antfile="${dita.dir}${file.separator}build.xml"
         target="init">
      <!-- please refer to the toolkit's document for supported
         parameters, and specify them base on your needs  -->
         <property name="args.input"
            value="${dita.dir}${file.separator}samples$
            {file.separator}ComstarUserGuide${file.separator}
            ComstarUserGuideRevTwo.ditamap" />
         <property name="output.dir"
            value="${dita.dir}${file.separator}samples$
            {file.separator}ComstarUserGuide${file.separator}
            pdf" />
         <property name="transtype" value="pdf" />
      </ant>
   </target>
</project>
```

When you run this build file, it creates two output folders:

- samples/ComstarUserGuide/pdf contains two pdf files, ComstarUserGuide.pdf and ComstartUserGuideRevTwo.pdf
- samples/ComstarUserGuide/web contains multiple html files, including index.html from which you can access the entire help system

**Adding a cascading stylesheet**

When you create your HTML-based output, you may want to override some styles defined in the stylesheets. If you created your own XSLT stylesheets, creating a cascading stylesheet (CSS) is not critical because you have already designed your XSLT stylesheets. However, if you choose to use the stylesheets provided out-of-the-box with the DITA-OT or if you want to customize a specific deliverable to have a different look and feel than defined in your XSLT stylesheets, you may need to add a custom CSS.

Figure 20 shows the default format provided by the DITA-OT for HTML output.

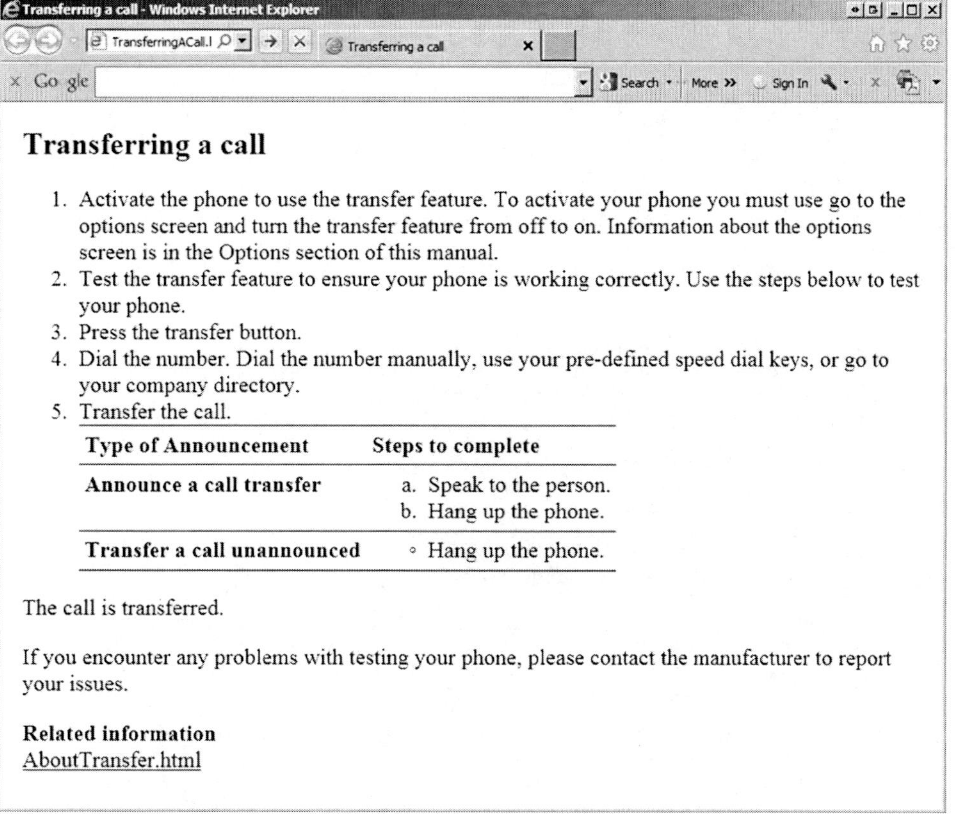


**Figure 20: Default HTML output from the DITA-OT**

Suppose, however, you want to change the background color to black, the text to white, links to yellow, and the heading font to a sans-serif. In this lesson, you learn to

- create a simple CSS to make these changes
- modify the build file to apply the CSS during processing

1. Create and save a CSS file called phones.css in a resources folder under your ComstarUserGuide directory.

```
body {
   background: black; color: white;
   }

a {
   color: yellow;
   }

h1.topictitle1 {
   font-family:  Verdana, Arial, Helvetica, sans-serif;
   }
```

2. Open the ComstarUserGuide_pdf.xml file you modified in the last exercise.

```
<?xml version="1.0" encoding="UTF-8" ?>
<!-- revise @PLACEHOLDER@ names and values -->
<!--
   | basedir can be specified to other places base on your need.
   |
   | Note: input, output, and temp directories will base on the
   | basedir if they are relative paths.
-->
<project name="ComstarUserGuide_pdf"
   default="all" basedir=".">
   <!-- dita.dir should point to the toolkit's root directory  -->
   <property name="dita.dir"
      value="${basedir}${file.separator}..${file.separator}.." />
   <!-- if file is a relative file name, the file name will be
      resolved relative to the importing file  -->
   <import file="${dita.dir}${file.separator}integrator.xml" />
   <target name="all" depends="ComstarUserGuide2xhtml,
      ComstarUserGuide_pdf2pdf, ComstarUserGuideRevTwo2pdf"/>
   <target name="ComstarUserGuide2pdf" depends="integrate">
      <ant antfile="${dita.dir}${file.separator}build.xml"
         target="init">
      <!-- please refer to the toolkit's document for supported
         parameters, and specify them base on your needs  -->
         <property name="args.input"
            "${dita.dir}${file.separator}samples$
            {file.separator}ComstarUserGuide${file.separator}
            ComstarUserGuide.ditamap" />
         <property name="output.dir"
            value="${dita.dir}${file.separator}samples$
            {file.separator}ComstarUserGuide${file.separator}
            pdf" />
         <property name="transtype"  value="pdf" />
      </ant>
   </target>
   <target  name="ComstarUserGuide2xhtml" depends="integrate">
      <ant antfile="${dita.dir}${file.separator}build.xml"
         target="init">
      <!-- please refer to the toolkit's document for supported
         parameters, and specify them base on your needs  -->
         <property name="args.input"
            value="${dita.dir}${file.separator}samples$
            {file.separator}ComstarUserGuide${file.separator}
            ComstarUserGuide.ditamap" />
```

```
         <property name="output.dir"
            value="${dita.dir}${file.separator}samples$
            {file.separator}ComstarUserGuide${file.separator}
            web" />
         <property name="transtype"  value="xhtml" />
      </ant>
   </target>
   <target name="ComstarUserGuideRevTwo2pdf" depends="integrate">
      <ant antfile="${dita.dir}${file.separator}build.xml"
         target="init">
      <!-- please refer to the toolkit's document for supported
         parameters, and specify them base on your needs  -->
         <property name="args.input"
            value="${dita.dir}${file.separator}samples$
            {file.separator}ComstarUserGuide${file.separator}
            ComstarUserGuideRevTwo.ditamap" />
         <property name="output.dir"
            value="${dita.dir}${file.separator}samples$
            {file.separator}ComstarUserGuide${file.separator}
            pdf" />
         <property name="transtype" value="pdf" />
      </ant>
   </target>
</project>
```

3. In the xhtml target, add three new property definitions for args.css, args.cssroot, and args.copycss.

   The args.css property specifies the name of the CSS file, while the args.cssroot property provides the path to that file. Setting args.copycss to "yes" indicates that the processor can copy the CSS to the appropriate directories for processing.

```
<project name="ComstarUserGuide_pdf"
   default="all" basedir=".">
   ⋮
   <target  name="ComstarUserGuide2xhtml" depends="integrate">
      <ant antfile="${dita.dir}${file.separator}build.xml"
         target="init">
         ⋮
         <property name="transtype"  value="xhtml" />
         <property name="args.css"
            value="phones.css" />
         <property name="args.cssroot"
            value="${dita.dir}${file.separator}samples$
            {file.separator}ComstarUserGuide${file.separator}
            resources" />
         <property name="args.copycss" value="yes"/>
      </ant>
   </target>
   ⋮
</project>
```

4. Save your work in the ComstarUserGuide_pdf.xml file.

When you now run the build file, your HTML output will look like the following example.

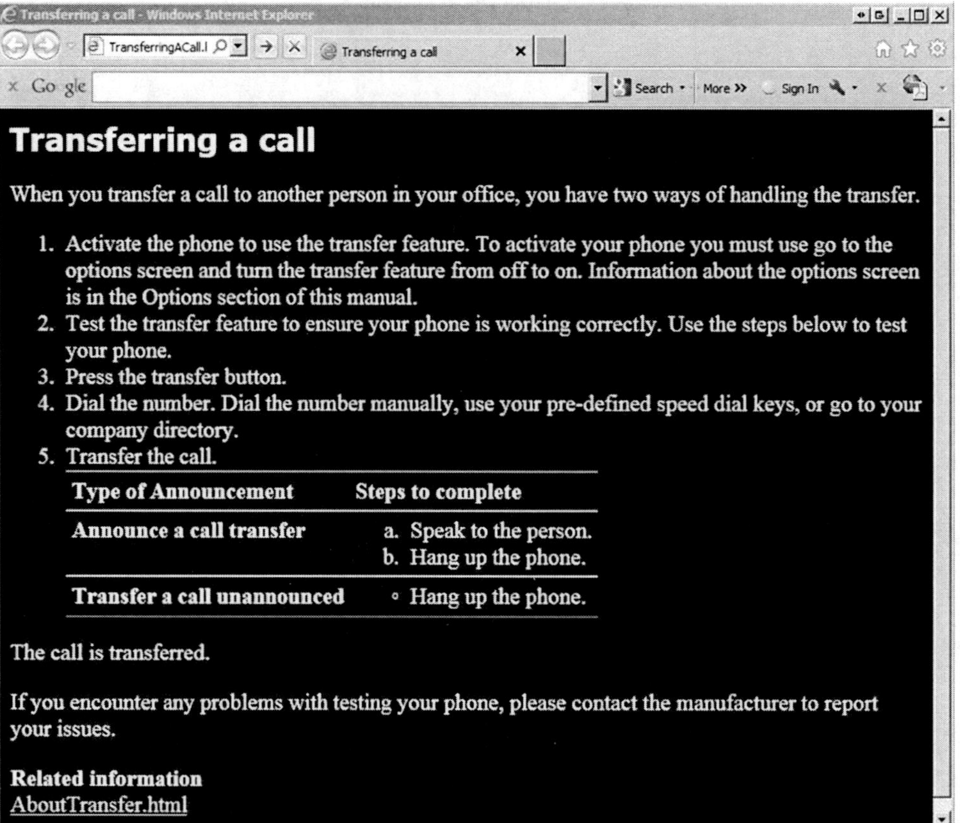

## Adding a header and footer

Adding custom headers and footers improves your content reuse abilities because you can produce custom header and footer information for different users' needs. For example, you might want to add a link to your home page at the top of your web pages, add custom HTML navigation to each of your builds, or place a copyright statement at the end of your web pages. Although you can include headers and footers in your stylesheet, you can also create a file containing the HTML markup and include this file automatically when you build your output. You might find this approach useful if you need different information for multiple audiences. Figure 21 shows the default format provided by the DITA-OT for HTML output.

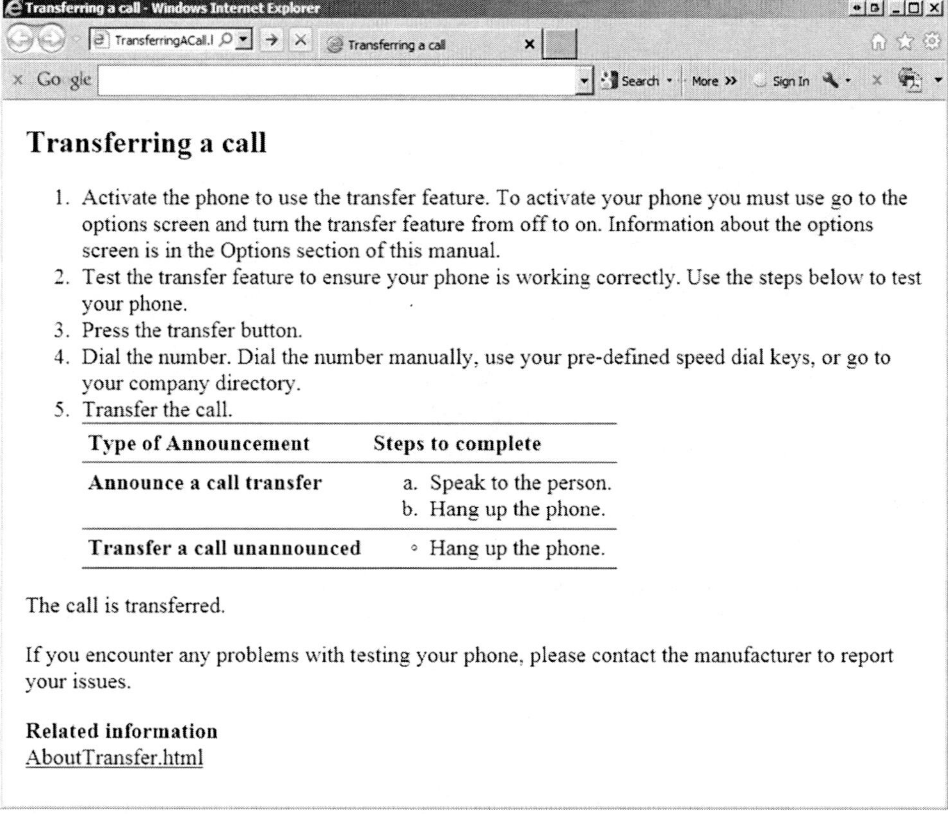


# Transferring a call

1. Activate the phone to use the transfer feature. To activate your phone you must use go to the options screen and turn the transfer feature from off to on. Information about the options screen is in the Options section of this manual.
2. Test the transfer feature to ensure your phone is working correctly. Use the steps below to test your phone.
3. Press the transfer button.
4. Dial the number. Dial the number manually, use your pre-defined speed dial keys, or go to your company directory.
5. Transfer the call.

| Type of Announcement | Steps to complete |
|---|---|
| **Announce a call transfer** | a. Speak to the person.<br>b. Hang up the phone. |
| **Transfer a call unannounced** | ◦ Hang up the phone. |

The call is transferred.

If you encounter any problems with testing your phone, please contact the manufacturer to report your issues.

**Related information**
AboutTransfer.html

**Figure 21: Default HTML output from the open toolkit**

Suppose, however, that you want to add a link to your home page at the top of each topic and a copyright statement in the footer. In this exercise, you learn to

- create HTML markup files for headers and footers
- modify the build file to include these markup files during processing

1. Create and save an HTML markup file named header.html in your ComstarUserGuide/resources folder.

```
<p><font style="color:red; font size: 20pt;">
    Visit <a href="http://www.comtech-serv.com">
    Comtech Services, Inc.</a></font></p>
```

2. Create and save an HTML markup file named footer.html in your ComstarUserGuide/resources folder.

```
<p><font style="color:white;">
    Copyright 2011 Comtech Services, Inc.</p>
```

3. Open the ComstarUserGuide_pdf.xml file you modified in the last exercise.

```
<?xml version="1.0" encoding="UTF-8" ?>
<!-- revise @PLACEHOLDER@ names and values -->
<!--
   | basedir can be specified to other places base on your need.
   |
   | Note: input, output, and temp directories will base on the
   | basedir if they are relative paths.
-->
<project name="ComstarUserGuide_pdf"
   default="all" basedir=".">
   <!-- dita.dir should point to the toolkit's root directory  -->
   <property name="dita.dir"
      value="${basedir}${file.separator}..${file.separator}.." />
   <!-- if file is a relative file name, the file name will be
      resolved relative to the importing file  -->
   <import file="${dita.dir}${file.separator}integrator.xml" />
   <target name="all" depends="ComstarUserGuide2xhtml,
      ComstarUserGuide_pdf2pdf, ComstarUserGuideRevTwo2pdf"/>
   <target name="ComstarUserGuide2pdf" depends="integrate">
      <ant antfile="${dita.dir}${file.separator}build.xml"
         target="init">
      <!-- please refer to the toolkit's document for supported
         parameters, and specify them base on your needs  -->
         <property name="args.input"
            "${dita.dir}${file.separator}samples$
            {file.separator}ComstarUserGuide${file.separator}
            ComstarUserGuide.ditamap" />
         <property name="output.dir"
            value="${dita.dir}${file.separator}samples$
            {file.separator}ComstarUserGuide${file.separator}
            pdf" />
         <property name="transtype"  value="pdf" />
      </ant>
   </target>
   <target  name="ComstarUserGuide2xhtml" depends="integrate">
      <ant antfile="${dita.dir}${file.separator}build.xml"
         target="init">
      <!-- please refer to the toolkit's document for supported
         parameters, and specify them base on your needs  -->
         <property name="args.input"
            value="${dita.dir}${file.separator}samples$
            {file.separator}ComstarUserGuide${file.separator}
            ComstarUserGuide.ditamap" />
         <property name="output.dir"
            value="${dita.dir}${file.separator}samples$
            {file.separator}ComstarUserGuide${file.separator}
            web" />
         <property name="transtype"  value="xhtml" />
         <property name="args.css"
            value="phones.css" />
         <property name="args.cssroot"
            value="${dita.dir}${file.separator}samples$
            {file.separator}ComstarUserGuide${file.separator}
            resources" />
         <property name="args.copycss" value="yes"/>
      </ant>
   </target>
   <target name="ComstarUserGuideRevTwo2pdf" depends="integrate">
      <ant antfile="${dita.dir}${file.separator}build.xml"
```

```
         target="init">
      <!-- please refer to the toolkit's document for supported
         parameters, and specify them base on your needs  -->
         <property name="args.input"
            value="${dita.dir}${file.separator}samples$
            {file.separator}ComstarUserGuide${file.separator}
            ComstarUserGuideRevTwo.ditamap" />
         <property name="output.dir"
            value="${dita.dir}${file.separator}samples$
            {file.separator}ComstarUserGuide${file.separator}
            pdf" />
         <property name="transtype" value="pdf" />
      </ant>
   </target>
</project>
```

4. In the xhtml target, add two new property definitions for args.hdr and args.ftr.

```
<project name="ComstarUserGuide_pdf"
   default="all" basedir=".">
   ⋮
   <target  name="ComstarUserGuide2xhtml" depends="integrate">
      <ant antfile="${dita.dir}${file.separator}build.xml"
         target="init">
      <!-- please refer to the toolkit's document for supported
         parameters, and specify them base on your needs  -->
         <property name="args.input"
            value="${dita.dir}${file.separator}samples$
            {file.separator}ComstarUserGuide${file.separator}
            ComstarUserGuide.ditamap" />
         <property name="output.dir"
            value="${dita.dir}${file.separator}samples$
            {file.separator}ComstarUserGuide${file.separator}
            web" />
         <property name="transtype" value="xhtml" />
         <property name="args.css"
            value="phones.css" />
         <property name="args.cssroot"
            value="${dita.dir}${file.separator}samples$
            {file.separator}ComstarUserGuide${file.separator}
            resources" />
         <property name="args.copycss" value="yes"/>
         <property name="args.hdr"
            value="${dita.dir}${file.separator}samples$
            {file.separator}ComstarUserGuide${file.separator}
            resources${file.separator}header.html" />
         <property name="args.ftr"
            value="${dita.dir}${file.separator}samples$
            {file.separator}ComstarUserGuide${file.separator}
            resources${file.separator}
            footer.html" />
       </ant>
   </target>
   ⋮
</project>
```

5. Save your work in the ComstarUserGuide_pdf.xml file.

When you now run the build file, your HTML output will look like the following example.

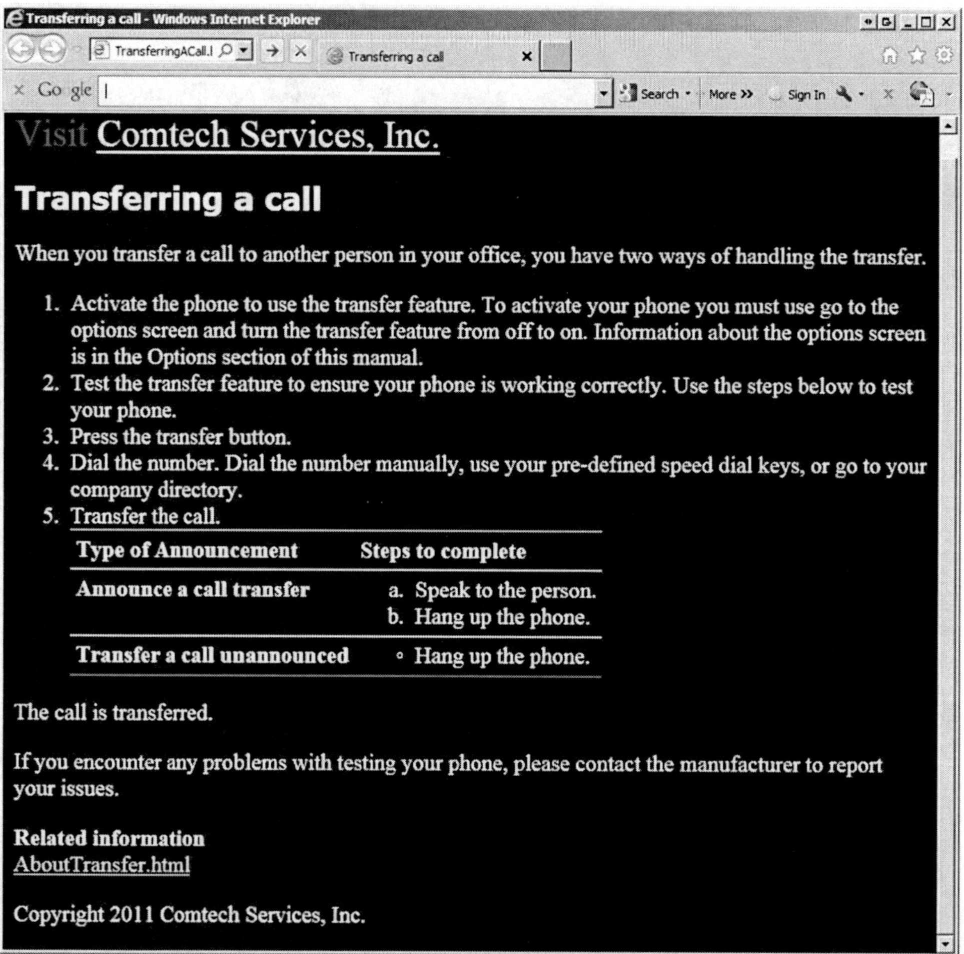

**Build file review questions**

What is the purpose of the Ant build file? Select all that apply.

- **a.** specify the location of key files
- **b.** define targets for the output type
- **c.** replace individual topic files within a map
- **d.** identify your source file
- **e.** point to your output directory
- **f.** indicate where the necessary processing tools are located

What command do you type to run a build file?

What are the four placeholders that you must change when starting with an Ant build file template? Select all that apply.

- **a.** @TARGET.NAME@
- **b.** @PROJECT.NAME@
- **c.** @SOURCE.NAME@
- **d.** @DELIVERABLE.NAME@
- **e.** @OUTPUT.DIR@
- **f.** @ARGS.CSS@
- **g.** @DITA.INPUT@

You must have one build file for each type of output you want to create.

- True
- False

Which property element is coded correctly?

- **a.** <property name="args.css" value="myprojects/project1/resources/project.css"/>
- **b.** <property name="args.css" value="myprojects${file.separator}project1${file.separator}resources${file.separator}project.css"/>
- **c.** <property name="args.css" value="project.css"/>
- **d.** <property name="args.css" value="myprojects{file.separator}project1{file.separator}resources{file.separator}project.css"/>

What property definition must you define to add a footer using the build file?

What attribute name goes in the blank? <target name="all" _______="ug2xtml, ug2pdf">

# SECTION M

# Understanding Conditional Processing

As you learned in Conditional Processing Attributes on page 260, for conditional processing to function correctly, you must label your content according to the situations to which it applies. During processing, you then use a .ditaval file to indicate the attributes and values that you want to process conditionally and the processing rules you want to apply.

**Filtering and flagging content**

In the <prop> element, you set parameters to include, exclude, or flag content. These parameters are defined by the following attributes:

- *@att* — the attribute that identifies the content you want to take action on, either *@audience*, *@product*, *@platform*, or *@otherprops*
- *@val* — the value of the specified attributes, such as internal/external (audience) or windows/linux (platform). If no value is specified, the action applies to all occurrences of the attribute.
- *@action* — the activity you want to perform, either include, exclude, or flag
- *@style* — the text style to use for the flagged content, either underline, double-underline, italics, bold, or overline. Applies only if *@action*=flag.
- *@color* — the text color you want to use for flagged content. The color can be either a name or an SRGB value. Applies only if *@action*=flag.
- *@backcolor* — the color you want to use to highlight flagged content. Applies only if *@action*=flag.

There are sixteen possible values for the *@color* or *@backcolor* attributes:

| | | | |
|---|---|---|---|
| black=#000000 | white=#FFFFFF | yellow=#FFFF00 | green=#008000 |
| silver=#C0C0C0 | navy=#000080 | maroon=#800000 | gray=#808080 |
| lime=#00FF00 | red=#FF0000 | blue=#0000FF | olive=#808000 |
| purple=#800080 | teal=#008080 | fuchsia=#FF00FF | aqua=#00FFFF |

Filtering is the most common option for conditional processing. To include or exclude content specific to a deliverable, use the "include" or "exclude" value for the *@action* attribute in your .ditaval <prop> element. You can filter at the map or at the topic level.

The other value you can use in the *@action* attribute on the <prop> element is "flag". Flagging with the <prop> element allows you to change the text style or color. Other flagging options are available through the <revprop> element.

**Flagging revised content**

The revision property <revprop> element in the .ditaval file allows you to flag a specific version of your document based on values you assigned previously to the *@rev* attribute. Using the <revprop> element lets you create a version for editors or reviewers so that they focus on content they have not yet reviewed. As with the <prop> element, the <revprop> element uses attributes to control its behavior. They include the following:

- *@val* — the version number of your output, such as 7.01. Unlike the <prop> attribute, you need not specify an attribute because the *@rev* attribute is assumed.
- *@action* — the activity you want to perform on your content, either flag or noflag.
- *@changebar* — the color, style, or character used for a changebar. The specified value must be compatible with the target output format.
- *@style* — the text style to use for the flagged content, either underline, double-underline, italics, bold, or overline.
- *@color* — the text color to use for the flagged content. The color can be any of those listed previously.
- *@backcolor* — the color used to highlight flagged content. The color can be any of those listed previously.

# LESSON 24

## The .ditaval File

Depending on the attributes that define the content you want to process conditionally, you use one of two elements in the .ditaval file:

- The <prop> element filters and flags content based on *@audience*, *@product*, *@platform*, and *@otherprops* attributes
- The <revprop> element flags content based on the *@rev* attribute

**Creating the .ditaval file**
To successfully produce output using conditional processing, you must create a .ditaval file to indicate which properties you want to filter or flag. In this lesson, you learn to

- filter content based on the *@audience* attribute
- flag content based on the *@rev* attribute
- modify your build file to point to the .ditaval file

The attribute values used in this lesson represent the values defined in Understanding Conditional Processing on page 353. In that lesson, you used the attribute *@audience* to distinguish between the information for the end user and the administrator. For this sample .ditaval file, assume you are creating the Administrator Guide. Include everything labeled "administrator" and exclude everything labeled "enduser".

1. Open a new file in your text editor.
2. Enter the xml declaration as the first line of your file.

```
<?xml version="1.0" encoding="utf-8"?>
```

3. Add <val> element start and end tags for the .ditaval file.

   <val> is the root element of a .ditaval file.

```
<?xml version="1.0" encoding="utf-8"?>
<val>
</val>
```

4. Add two empty <prop> elements between the <val> element start and end tags to specify your filtering criteria.

You use the <prop> element to add the metadata needed to conditionally process your topic. You can add as many <prop> elements as needed.

```
<val>
   <prop/>
   <prop/>
</val>
```

5. Add the following attributes and associated values to your <prop> elements.

```
<val>
   <prop att="audience" val="enduser" action="exclude"/>
   <prop att="audience" val="administrator"
      action="include"/>
</val>
```

6. Add a third <prop> element to specify flagging criteria.

   Use this <prop> element to flag steps that are unique to the administrators. Flagging enables administrators to quickly locate steps that they share with end users and steps that are uniquely their responsibility. Use the following attribute values:

   @*att*="audience"
   @*val*="administrator"
   @*action*="flag"
   @*backcolor*="gray"

```
<val>
   <prop att="audience" val="enduser" action="exclude"/>
   <prop att="audience" val="administrator"
      action="include"/>
   <prop att="audience" val="administrator" action="flag"
      backcolor="gray"/>
</val>
```

7. Add an empty <revprop> element after the last <prop> element.

```
<val>
   <prop att="audience" val="enduser" action="exclude"/>
   <prop att="audience" val="administrator"
      action="include"/>
   <prop att="audience" val="administrator" action="flag"
      backcolor="gray"/>
   <revprop/>
</val>
```

8. In the <revprop> element, specify that content for rev 1.1 be marked with change bars. The changebar value in the example is a "|" .

```
<val>
   <prop att="audience" val="enduser" action="exclude"/>
   <prop att="audience" val="administrator"
```

```
      action="include"/>
   <prop att="audience" val="administrator" action="flag"
      backcolor="gray"/>
   <revprop val="1.1" action="flag" changebar="|"/>
</val>
```

9. Save your file as phone.ditaval in the ComstarUserGuide/resources folder.

   The .ditaval file is usually a short file, but it becomes more complex as your conditions increase in complexity.

10. Open the build file you created in Adding a header and footer on page 346.

```
<?xml version="1.0" encoding="UTF-8" ?>
<!-- revise @PLACEHOLDER@ names and values -->
<!--
   | basedir can be specified to other places base on your need.
   |
   | Note: input, output, and temp directories will base on the
   | basedir if they are relative paths.
-->
<project name="ComstarUserGuide_pdf"
   default="all" basedir=".">
   <!-- dita.dir should point to the toolkit's root directory  -->
   <property name="dita.dir"
      value="${basedir}${file.separator}..${file.separator}.." />
   <!-- if file is a relative file name, the file name will be
      resolved relative to the importing file  -->
   <import file="${dita.dir}${file.separator}integrator.xml" />
   <target name="all" depends="ComstarUserGuide2xhtml,
      ComstarUserGuide_pdf2pdf, ComstarUserGuideRevTwo2pdf"/>
   <target name="ComstarUserGuide2pdf" depends="integrate">
      <ant antfile="${dita.dir}${file.separator}build.xml"
         target="init">
      <!-- please refer to the toolkit's document for supported
         parameters, and specify them base on your needs  -->
         <property name="args.input"
            "${dita.dir}${file.separator}samples$
            {file.separator}ComstarUserGuide${file.separator}
            ComstarUserGuide.ditamap" />
         <property name="output.dir"
            value="${dita.dir}${file.separator}samples$
            {file.separator}ComstarUserGuide${file.separator}
            pdf" />
         <property name="transtype"  value="pdf" />
      </ant>
   </target>
   <target  name="ComstarUserGuide2xhtml" depends="integrate">
      <ant antfile="${dita.dir}${file.separator}build.xml"
         target="init">
      <!-- please refer to the toolkit's document for supported
         parameters, and specify them base on your needs  -->
         <property name="args.input"
            value="${dita.dir}${file.separator}samples$
            {file.separator}ComstarUserGuide${file.separator}
            ComstarUserGuide.ditamap" />
         <property name="output.dir"
            value="${dita.dir}${file.separator}samples$
            {file.separator}ComstarUserGuide${file.separator}
            web" />
         <property name="transtype"  value="xhtml" />
```

```
         <property name="args.css"
            value="phones.css" />
         <property name="args.cssroot"
            value="${dita.dir}${file.separator}samples$
            {file.separator}ComstarUserGuide${file.separator}
            resources" />
         <property name="args.copycss" value="yes"/>
         <property name="args.hdr"
            value="${dita.dir}${file.separator}samples$
            {file.separator}ComstarUserGuide${file.separator}
            resources${file.separator}header.html" />
         <property name="args.ftr"
            value="${dita.dir}${file.separator}samples$
            {file.separator}ComstarUserGuide${file.separator}
            resources${file.separator}
            footer.html" />
      </ant>
   </target>
   <target name="ComstarUserGuideRevTwo2pdf" depends="integrate">
      <ant antfile="${dita.dir}${file.separator}build.xml"
         target="init">
      <!-- please refer to the toolkit's document for supported
         parameters, and specify them base on your needs  -->
         <property name="args.input"
            value="${dita.dir}${file.separator}samples$
            {file.separator}ComstarUserGuide${file.separator}
            ComstarUserGuideRevTwo.ditamap" />
         <property name="output.dir"
            value="${dita.dir}${file.separator}samples$
            {file.separator}ComstarUserGuide${file.separator}
            pdf" />
         <property name="transtype" value="pdf" />
      </ant>
   </target>
</project>
```

**11.** Add an empty <property> element for the dita.input.valfile parameter in each target that you want to conditionally process and set the value to the location of the .ditaval file.

For this exercise, assume you only want to conditionally process the ComstarUserGuide2pdf and ComstarUserGuide2xhtml targets.

```
<project name="ComstarUserGuide_pdf"
   default="all" basedir=".">
   <!-- dita.dir should point to the toolkit's root directory  -->
   <property name="dita.dir"
      value="${basedir}${file.separator}..${file.separator}.." />
   <!-- if file is a relative file name, the file name will be
      resolved relative to the importing file  -->
   <import file="${dita.dir}${file.separator}integrator.xml" />
   <target name="all" depends="ComstarUserGuide2xhtml,
     ComstarUserGuide_pdf2pdf, ComstarUserGuideRevTwo2pdf"/>
   <target name="ComstarUserGuide2pdf" depends="integrate">
      <ant antfile="${dita.dir}${file.separator}build.xml"
         target="init">
      <!-- please refer to the toolkit's document for supported
         parameters, and specify them base on your needs  -->
         <property name="args.input"
            "${dita.dir}${file.separator}samples$
```

```
            {file.separator}ComstarUserGuide${file.separator}
            ComstarUserGuide.ditamap" />
         <property name="output.dir"
            value="${dita.dir}${file.separator}samples$
            {file.separator}ComstarUserGuide${file.separator}
            pdf" />
         <property name="transtype"  value="pdf" />
         <property name="dita.input.valfile"
            value="${dita.dir}${file.separator}samples$
            {file.separator}ComstarUserGuide${file.separator}
            resources${file.separator}phone.ditaval"/>
      </ant>
   <target  name="ComstarUserGuide2xhtml" depends="integrate">
      <ant antfile="${dita.dir}${file.separator}build.xml"
         target="init">
      <!-- please refer to the toolkit's document for supported
         parameters, and specify them base on your needs  -->
         <property name="args.input"
            value="${dita.dir}${file.separator}samples$
            {file.separator}ComstarUserGuide${file.separator}
            ComstarUserGuide.ditamap" />
         <property name="output.dir"
            value="${dita.dir}${file.separator}samples$
            {file.separator}ComstarUserGuide${file.separator}
            web" />
         <property name="transtype"  value="xhtml" />
         <property name="args.css"
            value="phones.css" />
         <property name="args.cssroot"
            value="${dita.dir}${file.separator}samples$
            {file.separator}ComstarUserGuide${file.separator}
            resources" />
         <property name="args.copycss" value="yes"/>
         <property name="args.hdr"
            value="${dita.dir}${file.separator}samples$
            {file.separator}ComstarUserGuide${file.separator}
            resources${file.separator}header.html" />
         <property name="args.ftr"
            value="${dita.dir}${file.separator}samples$
            {file.separator}ComstarUserGuide${file.separator}
            resources${file.separator}
            footer.html" />
         <property name="dita.input.valfile"
            value="${dita.dir}${file.separator}samples$
            {file.separator}ComstarUserGuide${file.separator}
            resources${file.separator}phone.ditaval"/>
      </ant>
   </target>
   ⋮
</project>
```

**12.** Save your work in the ComstarUserGuide.pdf.xml build file.

The examples show a portion of the resulting pdf, which includes all content for the administrator audience, highlights unique administrator content in gray, and marks new content for version 1.1 with change bars.

### Transferring a call

1. **1.** Activate the phone to use the transfer feature.
   To activate your phone, go to the options screen and turn the transfer feature from off to on. Information about the options screen is in the Options section of this manual.
2. **2.** Test the transfer feature to ensure your phone is working correctly.
   Use the steps below to test your phone.
3. **3.** Press the transfer button.
4. **4.** Dial the number.
   Dial the number manually, use your pre-defined speed dial keys, or go to your company directory.
5. **5.** Transfer the call.

| Type of Announcement | Steps to complete |
|---|---|
| Announce a call transfer | **1.** Speak to the person.<br>**2.** Hang up the phone. |
| Transfer a call unannounced | Hang up the phone. |

The call is transferred.

If you encounter any problems testing your phone, contact the manufacturer.

**.ditaval review questions**

What is the purpose of a .ditaval file?

- **a.** To label the content you want to process conditionally
- **b.** To identify your source files, stylesheets, and other applications needed to create your deliverable
- **c.** To define keys and identify the location of key files
- **d.** To indicate the attributes and values that you want to process conditionally and the processing rules you want to apply

What is the root element of a .ditaval file?

What is the difference between <prop> and <revprop>? Select all that apply.

- **a.** The <revprop> is used only for flagging, while <prop> element is used only for filtering.
- **b.** The <revprop> element applies only to the rev attribute, while the <prop> element can apply to any other conditional processing attribute.
- **c.** The <revprop> element requires an *@att* attribute, while the <prop> element does not.
- **d.** The <revprop> element enables you to flag changes with changebars, while the <prop> element does not.

Which attribute would you use to change the background color of the flagged text?

The <revprop> element is used solely for flagging content. It cannot be used for filtering.

- True
- False

What property in your build file identifies the location of the .ditaval file?

# Appendix A

Throughout this book, you have created many topics and maps for the Comstar User Guide, a small user guide for a phone system. This appendix illustrates all files required to complete the entire book as built in the map and bookmap files in the lessons. For those files used in the lessons, the example code is the final result from all lessons in the book. The other files not created in the lessons are provided as further examples, but do not provide all the attributes and metadata that you learned to include in similar files. To generate the entire book file, you will need to create each of the files in this appendix. Use these files as opportunities for further practice using the DITA methodology and elements.

# Preface

**Notes, Warnings, and Cautions**

**Note:** This equipment generates, uses, and can radiate radio frequency energy and if not installed and used in accordance with the instruction manual, may cause interference to radio communications. It has been tested and found to comply with the limits for a Class A computing device pursuant to Subpart J of Part 15 of rules, which are designed to provide reasonable protection against such interference when operated in a commercial environment. Operation of this equipment in a residential area may cause interference, in which case the user, at his own expense, will be required to take whatever measures may be required to correct the interference.

**Note:** For a list of applicable certifications, refer to the Appendix.

# Preface code

The code below illustrates the example shown.

```
<?xml version="1.0" encoding="UTF-8"?>
<!DOCTYPE concept PUBLIC "-//OASIS//DTD DITA Concept//EN"
   "http://docs.oasis-open.org/dita/v1.1/OS/dtd/concept.dtd">
<concept id="ComstarPreface"  xml:lang="en-us">
 <title>Preface</title>
 <conbody>
  <section>
   <title>Warnings and Cautions</title>
   <note type="note">This equipment generates, uses, and can
      radiate radio frequency energy and if not installed and used
      in accordance with the instruction manual, may cause
      interference to radio communications. It has been tested and
      found to comply with the limits for a Class A computing device
      pursuant to Subpart J of Part 15 of
      <abbreviated-form keyref="fcc"/> rules, which are
      designed to provide reasonable protection against such
      interference when operated in a commercial environment.
      Operation of this equipment in a residential area may cause
      interference, in which case the user, at his own expense, will
      be required to take whatever measures may be required to
      correct the interference.</note>
  </section>
 </conbody>
</concept>
```

# Comstar overview

The Comstar User and Attendant's Guide is designed to help you use your telephone's features to your best advantage.

**Terms you'll need to know**
The following terms will help you understand some of the instructions in this guide.

**Attendant**
A receptionist or other person responsible for answering incoming calls.

**Dialpad**
The numbered keys on your telephone, including the # and *.

**Function buttons**
The buttons or keys on your telephone that allow you to press a single button to make conference calls, program your telephone, use the speakerphone, and others.

**Handset**
The telephone receiver that you use to listen and speak.

**Intercom calls**
The calls you make to other telephones inside your organization.

**Line buttons**
The buttons you use to select the outside line you want to use to make a call.

**Line lamps**
The small lights next to the line buttons on your telephone.

**Speakerphone**
A built-in feature of your telephone that lets you speak and hear a conversation without using the handset. The following telephones have a built-in speakerphone: 16-button, 30-button, and 42-button.

**Station**
An individual telephone set.

**Station buttons**
The buttons you use to select other extensions in the system.

**Switchhook**
On the single-line telephone, the button in the handset cradle.

**64-button DSS/BLF**
The 64-button accessory that contains 60 telephone line buttons and lamps and four function buttons. DSS/BLF stands for Direct Station select/Busy Lamp Field.

# Comstar overview code

The code below illustrates the example shown.

```
<?xml version="1.0" encoding="utf-8"?>
<!DOCTYPE concept PUBLIC "-//OASIS//DTD DITA Concept//EN"
   "http://docs.oasis-open.org/dita/v1.1/OS/dtd/concept.dtd">
<concept id="ComstarOverview" xml:lang="en-us">
   <title>Comstar overview</title>
   <shortdesc>The Comstar User and Attendant's Guide is
      designed to help you use your telephone's features to
      your best advantage.</shortdesc>
   <conbody>
      <section>
         <title>Terms you'll need to know</title>
         <p>The following terms will help you understand
            some of the instructions in this guide.</p>
         <dl>
            <dlentry>
               <dt>Attendant</dt>
               <dd>A receptionist or other person
                  responsible for answering incoming calls.
               </dd>
            </dlentry>
            <dlentry>
               <dt>Dialpad</dt>
               <dd>The numbered keys on your telephone,
                  including the # and *.</dd>
            </dlentry>
            <dlentry>
               <dt>Function buttons</dt>
               <dd>The buttons or keys on your telephone
                  that allow you to press a single button to
                  make conference calls, program your
                  telephone, use the speakerphone and
                  others.</dd>
            </dlentry>
            <dlentry>
               <dt>Handset</dt>
               <dd>The telephone receiver that you use to
                  listen and speak.</dd>
            </dlentry>
            <dlentry>
               <dt>Intercom calls</dt>
               <dd>The calls you make to other telephones
                  inside your organization.</dd>
            </dlentry>
            <dlentry>
               <dt>Line buttons</dt>
               <dd>The buttons you use to select the
                  outside line you want to use to make
                  a call.</dd>
            </dlentry>
            <dlentry>
               <dt>Line lamps</dt>
               <dd>The small lights next to the line
                  buttons on your telephone.</dd>
            </dlentry>
            <dlentry>
```

```
            <dt>Speakerphone</dt>
            <dd>A built-in feature of your telephone
               that lets you speak and hear a
               conversation without using the handset.
               The following telephones have a built-in
               speakerphone: 16-button, 30-button, and
               42-button.</dd>
         </dlentry>
         <dlentry>
            <dt>Station</dt>
            <dd>An individual telephone set.</dd>
         </dlentry>
         <dlentry>
            <dt>Station buttons</dt>
            <dd>The buttons you use to select other
               extensions in the system.</dd>
         </dlentry>
         <dlentry>
            <dt>Switchhook</dt>
            <dd>On the single-line telephone, the
               button in the handset cradle.</dd>
         </dlentry>
         <dlentry>
            <dt>64-button DSS/BLF</dt>
            <dd>The 64-button accessory that contains
               60 telephone line buttons and lamps and
               four function buttons. DSS/BLF stands for
               Direct Station select/Busy Lamp Field.
            </dd>
         </dlentry>
      </dl>
   </section>
</conbody>
</concept>
```

# Quick Guide to Basic Telephone Use

The Quick Guide provides a brief description of the buttons on your phone.

| Action | Indicator | Description |
|---|---|---|
| Talk | TALK | Press the talk key to receive a dial tone. |
| Speaker phone | SPEAKERPHONE | Press the speaker phone button to place a call on speaker phone. |
| Forward | FORWARD | Press the forward button to forward all incoming calls to another phone number or voice mail. |
| Transfer | TRANSFER | Press the transfer button to transfer a call to another person. |
| Hold | HOLD | Press the hold button to place a call on hold. |
| Mute | MUTE | Press the mute button to mute your end of the call. |

## Quick guide code

The following code illustrates the example shown.

```
<?xml version="1.0" encoding="utf-8"?>
<!DOCTYPE reference PUBLIC "-//OASIS//DTD DITA
   Reference//EN" "reference.dtd">
<reference id="QuickGuide" xml:lang="en-us">
   <title>Quick Guide to <keyword keyref="prodname"/> Use</title>
   <shortdesc>The Quick Guide provides a brief
      description of the buttons on your phone.
   </shortdesc>
   <prolog>
      <author>John Smith</author>
   </prolog>
   <refbody>
      <properties>
         <prophead>
            <proptypehd>Action</proptypehd>
```

```
            <propvaluehd>Indicator</propvaluehd>
            <propdeschd>Description</propdeschd>
         </prophead>
         <property>
            <proptype>Talk</proptype>
            <propvalue>
               <image conkeyref="buttons/talk" href="#"/>
            </propvalue>
            <propdesc>Press the talk key to receive a
               dial tone.</propdesc>
         </property>
         <property>
            <proptype>Speaker phone</proptype>
            <propvalue>
               <image conkeyref="buttons/speakerphone" href="#"/>
            </propvalue>
            <propdesc>Press the speaker phone button to
               place a call on speaker phone.</propdesc>
         </property>
         <property>
            <proptype>Forward</proptype>
            <propvalue>
               <image conkeyref="buttons/forward" href="#"/>
            </propvalue>
            <propdesc>Press the forward button to
               forward all incoming calls to another phone
               number or voice mail.</propdesc>
         </property>
         <property>
            <proptype>Transfer</proptype>
            <propvalue>
               <image conkeyref="buttons/transfer" href="#"/>
            </propvalue>
            <propdesc>Press the transfer button to
               transfer a call to another person.
            </propdesc>
         </property>
         <property>
            <proptype>Hold</proptype>
            <propvalue>
               <image conkeyref="buttons/hold" href="#"/>
            </propvalue>
            <propdesc>Press the hold button to place a
               call on hold.</propdesc>
         </property>
         <property>
            <proptype>Mute</proptype>
            <propvalue>
               <image conkeyref="buttons/mute" href="#"/>
            </propvalue>
            <propdesc>Press the mute button to mute
               your end of the call.
            </propdesc>
         </property>
      </properties>
   </refbody>
   <related-links>
      <link keyref="TransferringACall"/>
   </related-links>
</reference>
```

# About hold

The hold feature allows you to keep a phone call on the line while you step away from your desk. The person on the call will still be connected but will hear silence or music depending upon how your system was configured.

## About hold code

The code below illustrates the example shown.

```
<?xml version="1.0" encoding="utf-8"?>
<!DOCTYPE concept PUBLIC "-//OASIS//DTD DITA Concept//EN"
   "http://docs.oasis-open.org/dita/v1.1/OS/dtd/concept.dtd">
<concept id="AboutHold" xml:lang="en-us">
   <title>About hold</title>
   <conbody>
      <p>The hold feature allows you to keep a phone call
         on the line while you step away from your desk. The
         person on the call will still be connected but will
         hear silence or music depending upon how your
         system was configured.</p>
   </conbody>
</concept>
```

# Holding a call

1. Press Hold/Callback to place a call on hold.
2. Press the Hold/Callback to retrieve a call on hold.

## Holding a call code

The code below illustrates the example shown.

```
<?xml version="1.0" encoding="utf-8"?>
<!DOCTYPE task PUBLIC "-//OASIS//DTD DITA Task//EN"
   "http://docs.oasis-open.org/dita/v1.1/OS/dtd/task.dtd">
<task id="HoldingACall" xml:lang="en-us">
   <title>Holding a call</title>
   <taskbody>
      <steps>
         <step>
            <cmd>Press Hold/Callback to place a call on
               hold.</cmd>
         </step>
         <step>
            <cmd>Press the Hold/Callback to retrieve a
               call on hold.</cmd>
         </step>
      </steps>
   </taskbody>
</task>
```

# About transfer

When you transfer a call to another person in your office, you have two ways to handle the transfer. When you transfer a call without speaking to the person, it is an unannounced transfer. When you speak to the person receiving the transferred call, it is an announced transfer.

## About transfer code

The code below illustrates the example shown.

```
<?xml version="1.0" encoding="utf-8"?>
<!DOCTYPE concept PUBLIC "-//OASIS//DTD DITA Concept//EN"
   "http://docs.oasis-open.org/dita/v1.1/OS/dtd/concept.dtd">
<concept id="AboutTransfer" xml:lang="en-us">
   <title>About transfer</title>
   <conbody>
      <p>When you transfer a call to another person in
         your office, you have two ways to handling the
         transfer. When you transfer a call without
         speaking to the person, it is an unannounced
         transfer. When you speak to the person receiving
         the transferred call, it is an announced transfer.
      </p>
   </conbody>
</concept>
```

# Transferring a call

When you transfer a call to another person in your office, you have two ways of handling the transfer.

When you transfer the call without speaking to the person, it is an unannounced transfer. When you speak to the person receiving the transferred call, it is an announced transfer.

1. Press the transfer button.
2. Dial the number.

   Dial the number manually, use your pre-defined speed dial keys, or go to your company directory.
3. Transfer the call.

| Type of Announcement | Steps to complete |
|---|---|
| Announce a call transfer | 1. Speak to the person.<br>2. Hang up the phone. |
| Transfer a call unannounced | ■ Hang up the phone. |

**Tip:** If you announce a call and the person refuses the transfer, do not hang up the phone. Press the transfer button again to retrieve the call on your phone station.

The call is transferred.

## Transferring a call code

The code below illustrates the example shown.

```
<?xml version="1.0" encoding="utf-8"?>
<!DOCTYPE task PUBLIC "-//OASIS//DTD DITA Task//EN"
   "task.dtd">
<task id="TransferringACall" xml:lang="en-us">
   <title><keyword>Transferring</keyword>
      a call</title>
   <shortdesc>When you transfer a call to another person
      in your office, you have two ways of handling the
      transfer.</shortdesc>
   <prolog>
      <author>John Smith</author>
      <copyright>
         <copyryear year="2009"/>
         <copyrholder>Comtech Services, Inc.</copyrholder>
      </copyright>
```

```
    <permissions view="all"/>
    <metadata>
       <keywords>
          <keyword>phone</keyword>
          <keyword>transfer</keyword>
          <keyword>transferring a call</keyword>
          <indexterm>transferring a call</indexterm>
          <indexterm>unannounced transfers
             <index-see-also>transferring a call</index-see-also>
          </indexterm>
          <indexterm>announced transfers
             <index-see-also>transferring a call</index-see-also>
          </indexterm>
          <indexterm>transfers
             <indexterm>unannounced</indexterm>
             <indexterm>announced</indexterm>
          </indexterm>
       </keywords>
    </metadata>
 </prolog>
 <taskbody>
    <context audience="enduser">When you transfer the call
       without speaking to the person, it is an unannounced
       transfer. When you speak to the person receiving the
       transferred call, it is an announced transfer.</context>
    <steps>
       <step audience="administrator" rev="1.1">
          <cmd>Activate the phone to use the transfer
             feature.</cmd>
          <info>To activate your phone, go to the
             options screen and turn the transfer feature
             from off to on. Information about the options
             screen is in the Options section of this
             manual.</info>
       </step>
       <step audience="administrator">
          <cmd>Test the transfer feature to ensure
             your phone is working correctly.</cmd>
          <info>Use the steps below to test your
             phone</info>
       </step>
       <step>
          <cmd>Press the <uicontrol>transfer
             </uicontrol> button.</cmd>
        </step>
       <step>
          <cmd>Dial the number. </cmd>
          <info>Dial the number manually, use your
             pre-defined speed dial keys or go to your
             <xref href="AccessingCompanyDirectory.dita"
             type="task">company directory</xref>.
          </info>
       </step>
       <step audience="administrator enduser">
          <cmd>Transfer the call.</cmd>
          <choicetable>
             <chhead>
                <choptionhd>Type of Announcement</choptionhd>
                <chdeschd>Steps to complete</chdeschd>
             </chhead>
             <chrow>
```

```
                  <choption>Announce a call transfer</choption>
                  <chdesc>
                     <ol>
                        <li>Speak to the person.</li>
                        <li>Hang up the phone.</li>
                     </ol>
                  </chdesc>
               </chrow>
               <chrow>
                  <choption>Transfer a call
                     unannounced</choption>
                  <chdesc>
                     <ul>
                        <li>Hang up the phone.</li>
                     </ul>
                  </chdesc>
               </chrow>
            </choicetable>
            <info>
               <note audience="enduser" type="tip">If you announce
                  a call and the person refuses the transfer, do
                  not hang up the phone. Press the transfer button
                  again to retrieve the call on your phone
                  station.</note>
            </info>
         </step>
      </steps>
      <result>The call is transferred.</result>
      <postreq>
         <note conref="ReusableNotes.dita#reusablenotes/hangupphone">
         </note>
         <p audience="administrator">If you encounter any problems
            testing your phone, contact the manufacturer.</p>
      </postreq>
   </taskbody>
   <related-links>
      <link href="AboutTransfer.dita" format="html"
         scope="local"/>
      <link href="../GeneralTopic/Glossary.dita"
         format="html" scope="peer"/>
      <link href="http://www.comtech-serv.com/Comstar"
         format="html" scope="external">
         <linktext>Comstar Phones</linktext>
         <desc>Order your Comstar phone today.</desc>
      </link>
   </related-links>
</task>
```

# About forward

You can ask the system to forward all your calls to another extension or to an outside telephone number.

When you forward your calls, inside and outside calls are forwarded to another extension. While your phone is in "call forwarding," you will hear a single ring to remind you that you are using this feature.

You also have the ability to forward your calls in a chain with up to four forwards. With chaining, call A will forward to phone B, phone B to phone C, and so on. The fourth phone will always ring even if it is also on call forwarding.

And, if you have programmed a distinctive ring for your phone, the extension that receives your forwarded calls will ring your calls with the same distinctive sound.

## About forward code

The code below illustrates the example shown.

```
<?xml version="1.0" encoding="utf-8"?>
<!DOCTYPE concept PUBLIC "-//OASIS//DTD DITA Concept//EN"
   "http://docs.oasis-open.org/dita/v1.1/OS/dtd/concept.dtd">
<concept id="AboutForward" xml:lang="en-us">
   <title>About forward</title>
   <shortdesc>You can ask the system to forward all your
      calls to another extension or to an outside telephone
      number.</shortdesc>
   <conbody>
      <p>When you forward your calls, an inside and
         outside calls are forwarded to another extension.
         While your phone is in "call forwarding," you will
         hear a single ring to remind you that you are using
         this feature.</p>
      <p>You also have the ability to forward your calls
         in a chain with up to four forwards. With
         chaining, call A will forward to phone B, phone B
         to phone C, and so on. The fourth phone will always
         ring even if it is also on call forwarding.</p>
      <p>And, if you have programmed a distinctive ring
         for your phone, the extension that receives your
         forwarded calls will ring your calls with the same
         distinctive sound.</p>
   </conbody>
</concept>
```

# Forwarding a call

1. Press Program.
2. Press Forward.
3. Press an idle line button.
4. Dial the outside number.
5. Press Program.

## Forwarding a call code

The code below illustrates the example shown.

```
<?xml version="1.0" encoding="utf-8"?>
<!DOCTYPE task PUBLIC "-//OASIS//DTD DITA Task//EN"
   "task.dtd">
<task xml:lang="en-us" id="ForwardingACall">
   <title>Forwarding a call</title>
   <taskbody>
      <steps>
         <step>
            <cmd>Press Program.</cmd>
         </step>
         <step>
            <cmd>Press Forward.</cmd>
         </step>
         <step>
            <cmd>Press an idle line button.</cmd>
         </step>
         <step id="dialoutside">
            <cmd>Dial the outside number.</cmd>
         </step>
         <step id="finalprogram">
            <cmd>Press Program.</cmd>
         </step>
      </steps>
   </taskbody>
</task>
```

# About conference calls

Use a conference call to speak with more than two people in two different locations at the same time. Use one of the following types of conference calls to speak with multiple people.

**Three-way conference call**
: Three-way conference calling connects two other people to a call.

**Multi-line conference call**
: Multi-line conference calling connects you to more than two but fewer than eight other people on a call.

**Dial-in conference call**
: Dial-in conference calling uses a single conference call number to connect multiple people.

## About conference call code

The code below illustrates the example shown.

```
<?xml version="1.0" encoding="utf-8"?>
<!DOCTYPE concept PUBLIC "-//OASIS//DTD DITA Concept//EN"
   "concept.dtd">
<concept id="AboutConferenceCalls" xml:lang="en-us">
   <title>About conference calls</title>
   <shortdesc>Use a <term keyref="confcall"/> to speak with more
      than two people in two different locations at the
      same time.</shortdesc>
   <prolog>
      <author>John Smith</author>
   </prolog>
   <conbody>
      <p>Use one of the following types of
         <term conkeyref="confcall">conference calls</term>
         to speak with multiple people.</p>
      <dl>
         <dlentry>
            <dt>Three-way conference call</dt>
            <dd>Three-way conference calling connects
               two other people to a call.</dd>
         </dlentry>
         <dlentry>
            <dt>Multi-line conference call</dt>
            <dd>Multi-line conference calling connects
               you to more than two but fewer than eight
               other people on a call.</dd>
         </dlentry>
         <dlentry>
            <dt>Dial-in conference call</dt>
            <dd>Dial-in conference calling uses a single
```

```
               conference call number to connect multiple
               people.</dd>
         </dlentry>
      </dl>
   </conbody>
   <related-links>
      <link href="SettingUpConfCall.dita" scope="local">
         <linktext>Conference call set-up</linktext>
      </link>
   </related-links>
</concept>
```

# Placing a call

1. Lift the handset or press speaker.
2. Dial the number.

## Placing a call code

The code below illustrates the example shown.

```
<?xml version="1.0" encoding="utf-8"?>
<!DOCTYPE task PUBLIC "-//OASIS//DTD DITA Task//EN"
   "task.dtd">
<task xml:lang="en-us" id="placingcall">
   <title>Placing a call</title>
   <taskbody>
      <steps>
         <step conref="ReusableSteps.dita#reusablesteps/lifthandset">
            <cmd/>
         </step>
         <step>
            <cmd>Dial the number.</cmd>
         </step>
      </steps>
   </taskbody>
</task>
```

# Leaving a conference call temporarily

1. Press Hold/Callback.
2. Hang up the phone.

   The other parties can continue to talk together until you return.

## Leaving a conference call temporarily code

The code below illustrates the example shown.

```
<?xml version="1.0" encoding="utf-8"?>
<!DOCTYPE task PUBLIC "-//OASIS//DTD DITA Task//EN"
   "http://docs.oasis-open.org/dita/v1.1/OS/dtd/task.dtd">
<task xml:lang="en-us" id="LeavingAConferenceCallTemporarily">
   <title>Leaving a conference call temporarily</title>
   <taskbody>
      <steps>
         <step>
            <cmd>Press Hold/Callback.</cmd>
         </step>
         <step>
            <cmd>Hang up the phone.</cmd>
            <info>The other parties can continue to talk together
               until you return.</info>
         </step>
      </steps>
   </taskbody>
</task>
```

# Reentering a conference call

1. Lift the handset or press Speaker.
2. Press the appropriate line or station button of the parties you wish to consult with.
3. Press Conference.

   This will connect you with the parties on the conference call.

## Reentering a conference call code

The code below illustrates the example shown.

```
<?xml version="1.0" encoding="utf-8"?>
<!DOCTYPE task PUBLIC "-//OASIS//DTD DITA Task//EN"
   "http://docs.oasis-open.org/dita/v1.1/OS/dtd/task.dtd">
<task id="ReenteringAConferenceCall" xml:lang="en-us">
   <title>Reentering a conference call</title>
   <taskbody>
      <steps>
         <step>
            <cmd>Lift the handset or press Speaker.</cmd>
         </step>
         <step>
            <cmd>Press the appropriate line or station button of the
               parties you wish to consult with.</cmd>
         </step>
         <step>
            <cmd>Press Conference.</cmd>
            <info>This will connect you with the parties on the
               conference call.</info>
         </step>
      </steps>
   </taskbody>
</task>
```

# Consulting privately on the conference call

1. Press the appropriate line or station button of the person you wish to consult with.

   You will be privately connected with that person. The third party will be placed on Hold.
2. Press Conference to connect with one person.

   The system will choose the person. The other person will be placed on Hold.

## Consulting privately on the conference call code

The code below illustrates the example shown.

```
<?xml version="1.0" encoding="utf-8"?>
<!DOCTYPE task PUBLIC "-//OASIS//DTD DITA Task//EN"
   "http://docs.oasis-open.org/dita/v1.1/OS/dtd/task.dtd">
<task id="Consulting" xml:lang="en-us">
   <title>Consulting privately on the conference call</title>
   <taskbody>
      <steps>
         <step>
            <cmd>Press the appropriate line or station button of the
               person you wish to consult with.</cmd>
            <info>You will be privately connected with that person.
               The third party will be placed on Hold.</info>
         </step>
         <step>
            <cmd>Press Conference to connect with one person.</cmd>
            <info>The system will choose the person. The other person
               will be placed on Hold.</info>
         </step>
      </steps>
   </taskbody>
</task>
```

# Reentering a call with all people

1. Lift handset or press Speaker.
2. Press Conference or Hold/Callback.

## Reentering a call with all people code

The code below illustrates the example shown.

```
<?xml version="1.0" encoding="utf-8"?>
<!DOCTYPE task PUBLIC "-//OASIS//DTD DITA Task//EN"
   "http://docs.oasis-open.org/dita/v1.1/OS/dtd/task.dtd">
<task id="ReenteringACallWithAllPeople" xml:lang="en-us">
   <title>Reentering a call with all people</title>
   <taskbody>
      <steps>
         <step>
            <cmd>Lift handset or press Speaker.</cmd>
         </step>
         <step>
            <cmd>Press Conference or Hold/Callback.</cmd>
         </step>
      </steps>
   </taskbody>
</task>
```

# Glossary

**conference call**
: a telephone call in which a caller may speak with several people in different locations at the same time

**Federal Communications Commission**
: a government agency that regulates and oversees communications by radio, television, wire, satellite and cable

## Glossary code

The code below illustrates the code for the two terms shown.

```
<?xml version="1.0" encoding="utf-8"?>
<!DOCTYPE glossentry PUBLIC "-//OASIS//DTD DITA Glossary//EN"
   "http://docs.oasis-open.org/dita/v1.1/OS/dtd/glossary.dtd">
<glossentry "xml:lang="en-us" id="confcall">
   <glossterm>conference call</glossterm>
   <glossdef>a telephone call in which a caller may speak with
      several people in different locations at the same time
   </glossdef>
</glossentry>


<?xml version="1.0" encoding="utf-8"?>
<!DOCTYPE glossentry PUBLIC "-//OASIS//DTD DITA Glossary//EN"
   "http://docs.oasis-open.org/dita/v1.1/OS/dtd/glossary.dtd">
<glossentry id="fcc">
   <glossterm>Federal Communications Commission</glossterm>
   <glossdef>a government agency that regulates and oversees
      communications by radio, television, wire, satellite,
      and cable</glossdef>
   <glossBody>
      <glossPartOfSpeech value="properNoun"/>
      <glossSurfaceForm>Federal Communications Commission (FCC)
      </glossSurfaceForm>
      <glossAlt>
         <glossAcronym>FCC</glossAcronym>
      </glossAlt>
   </glossBody>
</glossentry>
```

# Reusable Content

The following examples show the files that were created in this book to provide reusable content to the various topics in the Comstar User Guide.

## Reusable notes code

The code below illustrates the file used to provide a common note to all files that need it.

```
<?xml version="1.0" encoding="UTF-8"?>
<!DOCTYPE topic PUBLIC "-//OASIS//DTD DITA Topic//EN"
   "topic.dtd">
<topic id="reusablenotes"  xml:lang="en-us">
   <title>Reusable Notes</title>
   <body>
      <p>
         <note id="hangupphone" type="tip">You must hang up your
            phone before you can make another call.</note>
      </p>
   </body>
</topic>
```

## Reusable steps code

The code below illustrates the file used to provide common steps to all tasks that need it.

```
<?xml version="1.0" encoding="UTF-8"?>
<!DOCTYPE task PUBLIC "-//OASIS//DTD DITA Task//EN"
   "task.dtd">
<task id="reusablesteps" xml:lang="en-us">
   <title>Reusable Steps</title>
   <shortdesc>Task topic containing steps that can be reused in
      multiple tasks.</shortdesc>
   <taskbody>
      <steps>
         <step id="lifthandset">
            <cmd>Lift the handset or press Speaker.</cmd>
            <info>the Speaker button is the last button on the
               left.</info>
         </step>
         <step id="pressbutton">
            <cmd>Press the appropriate line or station button of
               the parties you wish to consult with.</cmd>
         </step>
      </steps>
   </taskbody>
</task>
```

# Push content for a major client code

The code below illustrates a file containing content that can be pushed to other files as required.

```
<?xml version="1.0" encoding="UTF-8"?>
<!DOCTYPE task PUBLIC "-//OASIS//DTD DITA Task//EN"
   "task.dtd">
<task id="PushContentForMajorClient"  xml:lang="en-us">
   <title>Push content for major client</title>
   <taskbody>
      <steps>
         <step conref="ForwardingACall.dita#ForwardingACall/dialoutside"
            conaction="pushreplace">
            <cmd>Dial "9" followed by the outside number including area
               code.</cmd>
         </step>
         <step conref="ForwardingACall.dita#ForwardingACall/finalprogram"
            conaction="mark">
            <cmd/>
         </step>
         <step conref="ForwardingACall.dita#ForwardingACall/finalprogram"
            conaction="pushafter">
            <cmd>Validate that you have forwarded the line correctly by
               calling the original number and ensuring you are forwarded
               to the new number.</cmd>
         </step>
      </steps>
   </taskbody>
</task>
```

# Maps

The following examples show the maps, submaps, and bookmaps that were created in this book as ways to create the *Comstar User Guide.*

## Comstar map code

```
<?xml version="1.0" encoding="utf-8"?>
<!DOCTYPE map PUBLIC "-//OASIS//DTD DITA Map//EN"
   "map.dtd">
<map id="ComstarUserGuide" xml:lang="en-us">
   <title>Comstar User Guide</title>
   <topicmeta>
      <copyright>
         <copyryear year="2011"/>
         <copyrholder>Comstar Phones</copyrholder>
      </copyright>
   </topicmeta>
   <topicref href="ComstarOverview.dita" format="dita" scope="local"
      collection-type="family">
      <topicref href="QuickGuide.dita" locktitle="yes" format="dita"
         scope="local" type="reference" linking="targetonly">
         <topicmeta>
            <navtitle>Get Started Now</navtitle>
         </topicmeta>
      </topicref>
      <topicref href="AboutHold.dita" navtitle="Hold" format="dita"
         scope="local" type="concept" linking="sourceonly">
         <topicmeta>
            <audience type="user"/>
            <audience type="administrator"/>
         </topicmeta>
         <topicref href="HoldingACall.dita" format="dita"
            scope="local" type="task" linking="normal">
         </topicref>
      </topicref>
      <topicref href="AboutTransfer.dita" format="dita" scope="local"
         type="concept" linking="sourceonly">
         <topicref href="TransferringACall.dita" format="dita"
            scope="local" type="task" linking="normal"/>
      </topicref>
      <topicref href="AboutForward.dita" format="dita" scope="local"
         type="concept" linking="sourceonly">
         <topicref href="ForwardingACall.dita" format="dita"
            scope="local" type="task" linking="normal"/>
         <topicref href="PushContentForMajorClient.dita"
            processing-role="resource-only"/>
      </topicref>
      <topicref href="AboutConferenceCalls.dita" format="dita"
         scope="local" type="concept" collection-type="sequence">
         <topicref href="PlacingACall.dita" format="dita" scope="local"
            type="task"/>
         <topicref href="LeavingAConferenceCallTemporarily.dita"
```

```
            format="dita" scope="local" type="task"/>
         <topicref href="ReenteringAConferenceCall.dita" format="dita"
            scope="local" type="task"/>
         <topicref href="ConsultingPrivatelyOnTheConferenceCall.dita"
            format="dita" scope="local" type="task"/>
         <topicref href="ReenteringACallWithAllPeople.dita" format="dita"
            scope="local" type="task"/>
      </topicref>
   </topicref>
   <topicref href="http://www.comtech-serv.com/Comstar/" format="html"
      scope="external" locktitle="yes" print="no">
      <topicmeta>
         <navtitle>Comtech Services: Comstar Phone Information
         </navtitle>
         <shortdesc>Online ordering for your choice of any Comstar
            phones.</shortdesc>
      </topicmeta>
   </topicref>
   <topicref href="../../ComstarPricing.pdf" format="pdf"
      scope="external">
      <topicmeta>
         <shortdesc>Comstar phones provide a variety of different plans
            you can purchase to use with your phone.</shortdesc>
      </topicmeta>
   </topicref>
   <mapref href="../Components/Accessories.ditamap" format="ditamap"
      scope="peer" toc="no"/>
</map>
```

# Comstar map code with relationship table

```
<?xml version="1.0" encoding="utf-8"?>
<!DOCTYPE map PUBLIC "-//OASIS//DTD DITA Map//EN"
   "map.dtd">
<map id="ComstarUserGuide">
   <title>Comstar User Guide</title>
   <topicref href="ComstarOverview.dita"/>
   <topicref href="QuickGuide.dita"/>
   <topicref href="AboutHold.dita">
      <topicref href="HoldingACall.dita"/>
   </topicref>
   <topicref href="AboutTransfer.dita">
      <topicref href="TransferringACall.dita"/>
   </topicref>
   <topicref href="AboutForward.dita">
      <topicref href="ForwardingACall.dita"/>
   </topicref>
   <topicref href="AboutConferenceCalls.dita">
      <topicref href="PlacingACall.dita"/>
      <topicref href="LeavingAConferenceCallTemporarily.dita"/>
      <topicref href="ReenteringAConferenceCall.dita"/>
      <topicref href="ConsultingPrivatelyOnTheConferenceCall.dita"/>
      <topicref href="ReenteringACallWithAllPeople.dita"/>
   </topicref>
   <mapref href="../Components/Accessories.ditamap"/>
   <topicref href="g_confcall.dita"/>
   <reltable>
      <relheader>
```

```
         <relcolspec type="concept"/>
         <relcolspec type="task"/>
         <relcolspec type="reference"/>
      </relheader>
      <relrow>
         <relcell>
            <topicref href="AboutHold.dita"/>
         </relcell>
         <relcell>
            <topicref href="HoldingACall.dita"/>
         </relcell>
         <relcell></relcell>
      </relrow>
      <relrow>
         <relcell>
            <topicref href="AboutTransfer.dita"/>
         </relcell>
         <relcell>
            <topicref href="TransferringACall.dita"/>
         </relcell>
         <relcell></relcell>
      </relrow>
      <relrow>
         <relcell>
            <topicref href="AboutForward.dita"/>
         </relcell>
         <relcell>
            <topicref href="ForwardingACall.dita"/>
         </relcell>
         <relcell></relcell>
      </relrow>
      <relrow>
         <relcell>
            <topicref href="AboutConferenceCalls.dita"/>
         </relcell>
         <relcell>
            <topicgroup collection-type="sequence">
               <topicref href="PlacingACall.dita"/>
               <topicref href="LeavingAConferenceCallTemporarily.dita"/>
               <topicref href="ReenteringAConferenceCall.dita"/>
               <topicref
                  href="ConsultingPrivatelyOnTheConferenceCall.dita"/>
               <topicref href="ReenteringACallWithAllPeople.dita"/>
            </topicgroup>
         </relcell>
         <relcell></relcell>
      </relrow>
      <relrow>
         <relcell>
            <topicgroup collection-type="family">
               <topicref href="AboutHold.dita"/>
               <topicref href="AboutTransfer.dita"/>
               <topicref href="AboutForward.dita"/>
               <topicref href="AboutConferenceCalls.dita"/>
            </topicgroup>
         </relcell>
         <relcell></relcell>
         <relcell>
            <topicgroup linking="targetonly">
               <topicref href="QuickGuide.dita"/>
               <topicref href="../Components/Accessories.ditamap"/>
```

```
            <topicref href="g_confcall.dita"/>
         </topicgroup>
      </relcell>
   </relrow>
   <relrow>
      <relcell></relcell>
      <relcell>
         <topicref href="HoldingACall.dita"/>
         <topicref href="TransferringACall.dita"/>
         <topicref href="ForwardingACall.dita"/>
         <topicref href="PlacingACall.dita"/>
         <topicref href="LeavingAConferenceCallTemporarily.dita"/>
         <topicref href="ReenteringAConferenceCall.dita"/>
         <topicref href="ConsultingPrivatelyOnTheConferenceCall.dita"/>
         <topicref href="ReenteringACallWithAllPeople.dita"/>
      </relcell>
      <relcell>
         <topicref href="../Components/Accessories.ditamap"
            linking="targetonly"/>
         <topicref href="g_confcall.dita" linking="targetonly"/>
      </relcell>
   </relrow>
</reltable>
</map>
```

# Submaps code

The code below illustrates the submaps created for use in the bookmap file.

### HoldCall.ditamap

```
<?xml version="1.0" encoding="utf-8"?>
<!DOCTYPE map PUBLIC "-//OASIS//DTD DITA Map//EN"
   "map.dtd">
<map id="HoldCall" xml:lang="en-us">
   <title>Holding a Call</title>
   <topicref href="AboutHold.dita">
      <topicref href="HoldingACall.dita"/>
   </topicref>
</map>
```

### TransferCall.ditamap

```
<?xml version="1.0" encoding="utf-8"?>
<!DOCTYPE map PUBLIC "-//OASIS//DTD DITA Map//EN"
   "map.dtd">
<map id="TransferCall" xml:lang="en-us">
   <title>Transferring a Call</title>
   <topicref href="AboutTransfer.dita">
      <topicref href="TransferringACall.dita" />
   </topicref>
</map>
```

### ForwardCall.ditamap

```
<?xml version="1.0" encoding="utf-8"?>
<!DOCTYPE map PUBLIC "-//OASIS//DTD DITA Map//EN"
   "map.dtd">
<map id="ForwardCall" xml:lang="en-us">
   <title>Forwarding a Call</title>
   <topicref href="AboutForward.dita">
      <topicref href="ForwardingACall.dita" />
   </topicref>
</map>
```

### ConferenceCall.ditamap

```
<?xml version="1.0" encoding="utf-8"?>
<!DOCTYPE map PUBLIC "-//OASIS//DTD DITA Map//EN"
   "map.dtd">
<map id="ConferenceCall" xml:lang="en-us">
   <title>Conference Calls</title>
   <topicref href="AboutConferenceCalls.dita">
      <topicref href="PlacingACall.dita" />
      <topicref href="LeavingAConferenceCallTemporarily.dita" />
      <topicref href="ReenteringAConferenceCall.dita" />
      <topicref href="ConsultingPrivatelyOnTheConferenceCall.dita" />
      <topicref href="ReenteringACallWithAllPeople.dita" />
   </topicref>
</map>
```

## Bookmap code

```
<?xml version="1.0" encoding="utf-8"?>
<!DOCTYPE bookmap PUBLIC "-//OASIS//DTD DITA BookMap//EN"
   "bookmap.dtd">
<bookmap id="ComstarUserAndAttendantsGuide" xml:lang="en-us">
   <booktitle>
      <mainbooktitle>Comstar User and Attendant's Guide</mainbooktitle>
   </booktitle>
   <bookmeta>
      <bookid>
         <isbn>012-3456789012</isbn>
      </bookid>
      <bookrights>
         <copyrfirst>
            <year>2011</year>
         </copyrfirst>
         <bookowner>
            <organization>Comtech Services, Inc.</organization>
         </bookowner>
      </bookrights>
   </bookmeta>
   <frontmatter>
      <preface href="ComstarPreface.dita"/>
      <booklists>
         <toc/>
      </booklists>
   </frontmatter>
   <chapter href="QuickGuide.dita">
```

```
   <keydef keys="TransferringACall" href="TransferringACall.dita"
      type="task" format="dita" processing-role="normal"/>
   <keydef keys="prodname">
      <topicmeta>
         <keywords>
            <keyword>ComstarPlus</keyword>
         </keywords>
      </topicmeta>
   </keydef>
   <keydef keys="buttons" href="keys_buttons_Quickstar_words.dita"
      type="concept" format="dita"/>
   </chapter>
   <part>
      <topicmeta>
         <navtitle>Basic Functions</navtitle>
      </topicmeta>
      <chapter href="HoldCall.ditamap" format="ditamap"/>
      <chapter href="TransferCall.ditamap" format="ditamap"/>
      <chapter href="ForwardCall.ditamap" format="ditamap"/>
   </part>
   <part>
      <topicmeta>
         <navtitle>Advanced Functions</navtitle>
      </topicmeta>
      <chapter href="ConferenceCall.ditamap" format="ditamap"/>
   </part>
   <appendices>
      <topicmeta>
         <navtitle>Appendices</navtitle>
      </topicmeta>
      <appendix href="../Components/Accessories.ditamap"
         format="ditamap"/>
      <appendix href="../../ComstarPricing.pdf" format="pdf"/>
   </appendices>
   <backmatter>
      <booklists>
         <glossarylist>
            <topicref keys="confcall" href="g_confcall.dita"/>
            <topicref keys="fcc" href="g_fcc.dita"/>
         </glossarylist>
         <indexlist/>
      </booklists>
   </backmatter>
</bookmap>
```

# Appendix B

Appendix B provides a table of elements referenced in this book. Because the book does not account for all the elements in the *@OASIS Darwin Information Typing Architecture (DITA) Version 1.2 (OASIS Standard, 1 December 2010)* , this table includes the main elements needed to get started with DITA. The table illustrates the element name, the formal name, and where it is discussed in the book. If you need an element not mentioned in Appendix B, reference the *@OASIS Darwin Information Typing Architecture (DITA) Version 1.2 (OASIS Standard, 1 December 2010)* for the full list.

# DITA element glossary

| Element | Element name | Refer to |
|---|---|---|
| <abbreviated-form> | abbreviated form | Referencing glossary terms on page 296 |
| <abstract> | abstract | <abstract> abstract on page 29 |
| <apiname> | API name | <apiname> API name on page 85 |
| <appendices> | appendices | <appendices> appendices on page 227 |
| <appendix> | appendix | <appendix> appendix on page 227 |
| <audience> | audience | <audience> audience on page 108 |
| <author> | author | <author> author on page 108 |
| <b> | bold | <b> bold on page 88 |
| <backmatter> | back matter | <backmatter> back matter on page 227 |
| <body> | body | <body> body on page 30 |
| <brand> | brand | <brand> brand on page 109 |
| <bookid> | book ID | <bookid> book ID on page 229 |
| <booklists> | book lists | <booklists> book lists on page 226 |
| <bookmap> | bookmap | Understanding Bookmap Basics on page 209 |
| <bookmeta> | book metadata | <bookmeta> book metadata on page 228 |
| <bookowner> | book owner | <bookowner> book owner on page 229 |
| <bookrights> | book rights | <bookrights> book rights on page 229 |
| <booktitle> | book title | <booktitle> book title on page 225 |

| Element | Element name | Refer to |
|---|---|---|
| <booktitlealt> | alternative book title | <booktitlealt> alternate book title on page 226 |
| <chapter> | chapter | <chapter> chapter on page 227 |
| <chdesc> | choice description | <chdesc> choice description on page 48 |
| <chdeschd> | choice description head | <chdeschd> choice description head on page 47 |
| <chhead> | choice head | <chhead> choice head on page 47 |
| <choice> | choice | <choice> choice on page 47 |
| <choices> | choices | <choices> choices on page 47 |
| <choicetable> | choice table | <choicetable> choice table on page 47 |
| <choption> | choice option | <choption> choice option on page 48 |
| <choptionhd> | choice option head | <choptionhd> choice option head on page 47 |
| <chrow> | choice row | <chrow> choice row on page 48 |
| <cmd> | command | <cmd> command on page 45 |
| <cmdname> | command name | <cmdname> command name on page 86 |
| <codeblock> | code block | <codeblock> code block on page 84 |
| <colophon> | colophon | <colophon> colophon on page 227 |
| <colspec> | column specification | <colspec> column specification on page 71 |
| <conbody> | concept body | <body> body on page 30 |
| <concept> | concept | <task> <concept> <reference> root elements on page 29 |

| Element | Element name | Refer to |
|---|---|---|
| <context> | context | <context> context on page 44 |
| <copyrholder> | copyright holder | <copyrholder> copyright holder on page 108 |
| <copyright> | copyright | <copyright> copyright on page 108 |
| <copyrfirst> | copyright first year | <copyrfirst> first copyright on page 229 |
| <copyrlast> | copyright last year | <copyrlast> last copyright on page 229 |
| <copyryear> | copyright year | <copyryear> copyright year on page 108 |
| <created> | created date | <created> created date on page 108 |
| <critdates> | critical dates | <critdates> critical dates on page 108 |
| <dd> | definition description | <dd> definition description on page 70 |
| <ddhd> | definition head | <ddhd> definition description head on page 70 |
| <dedication> | dedication | <dedication> dedication on page 226 |
| <desc> | description | <desc> description on page 96 |
| <dl> | definition list | <dl> definition list on page 70 |
| <dlentry> | definition list entry | <dlentry> definition list entry on page 70 |
| <dlhead> | definition list head | <dlhead> definition list head on page 70 |
| <dt> | definition term | <dt> definition term on page 70 |
| <dthd> | term head | <dthd> definition term head on page 70 |
| <entry> | entry | <entry> entry on page 71 |

| Element | Element name | Refer to |
|---|---|---|
| <example> | example | <example> example on page 67 |
| <example> | example (task) | <example> example on page 49 |
| <fig> | figure | <fig> figure on page 68 |
| <filepath> | file path | <filepath> file path on page 86 |
| <frontmatter> | front matter | <frontmatter> front matter on page 226 |
| <glossAbbreviation> | glossary abbreviation | <glossAbbreviation> glossary abbreviation on page 205 |
| <glossAcronym> | glossary acronym | <glossAcronym> glossary acronym on page 205 |
| <glossAlt> | glossary alternate | <glossAlt> glossary alternative on page 205 |
| <glossarylist> | glossary | <glossarylist> glossary list on page 226 |
| <glossBody> | glossary body | <glossBody> glossBody on page 204 |
| <glossdef> | glossary definition | <glossdef> glossary definition on page 204 |
| <glossentry> | glossary entry | <glossentry> glossary entry on page 204 |
| <glossgroup> | glossary group | <glossgroup> glossary group on page 204 |
| <glossPartOfSpeech> | glossary part of speech | <glossPartOfSpeech> glossary part of speech on page 204 |
| <glossStatus> | glossary status | <glossStatus> glossary status on page 205 |
| <glossSurfaceForm> | glossary surface form | <glossSurfaceForm> glossary surface form on page 205 |
| <glossSynonym> | glossary synonym | <glossSynonym> glossary synonym on page 205 |

| Element | Element name | Refer to |
|---|---|---|
| <glossterm> | glossary term | <glossterm> glossary term on page 204 |
| <glossUsage> | glossary usage | <glossUsage> glossary usage on page 205 |
| <i> | italic | <i> italic on page 88 |
| <image> | image | <image> image on page 68 |
| <indexlist> | index | <indexlist> index list on page 226 |
| <indexterm> | index term | <indexterm> indexterm on page 110 |
| <index-see> | index see | <index-see> index see on page 110 |
| <index-see-also> | index term see also | <index-see-also> index see also on page 110 |
| <index-sort-as> | index term sort as | <index-sort-as> index sort as on page 110 |
| <info> | information | <info> information on page 45 |
| <isbn> | isbn | <isbn> isbn on page 229 |
| <keydef> | key definition | Keyref components on page 273 |
| <keyword> | keyword | <keyword> keyword on page 81 |
| <keywords> | keywords | <keywords> keywords on page 109 |
| <li> | list item | <li> list item on page 69 |
| <link> | link | <link> link on page 96 |
| <linkinfo> | link information | <linkinfo> link information on page 97 |
| <linklist> | link list | <linklist> link list on page 97 |
| <linkpool> | link pool | <linkpool> link pool on page 97 |
| <linktext> | link text | <linktext> link text on page 97 |

| Element | Element name | Refer to |
|---|---|---|
| <map> | map | DITA Map Structure on page 118 |
| <mapref> | map reference | <mapref> map reference on page 131 |
| <mainbooktitle> | main book title | <mainbooktitle> main book title on page 225 |
| <menucascade> | menu cascade | <menucascade> menu cascade on page 87 |
| <metadata> | metadata | <metadata> metadata on page 108 |
| <msgph> | message phrase | <msgph> message phrase on page 85 |
| <navtitle> | navigation title | <navtitle> navigation title on page 29 |
| <note> | note | <note> note on page 45 |
| <notices> | notices | <notices> notices on page 226 |
| <ol> | ordered list | <ol> ordered list on page 69 |
| <organization> | organization | <bookowner> book owner on page 229 |
| <p> | paragraph | <p> paragraph on page 67 |
| <parml> | parameter list | <parml> parameter list on page 84 |
| <part> | part | <part> part on page 227 |
| <pd> | parameter description | <pd> parameter description on page 84 |
| <permissions> | permissions | <permissions> permissions on page 109 |
| <person> | person | <bookowner> book owner on page 229 |
| <ph> | phrase | <ph> phrase on page 81 |
| <platform> | platform | <platform> platform on page 109 |
| <plentry> | parameters list entry | <plentry> parameter list entry on page 84 |

| Element | Element name | Refer to |
|---|---|---|
| <postreq> | post requirement | <postreq> post requirement on page 49 |
| <preface> | preface | <preface> preface on page 227 |
| <prereq> | prerequisite | <prereq> prerequisite on page 44 |
| <prodinfo> | product information | <prodinfo> product information on page 109 |
| <prodname> | product name | <prodname> product name on page 109 |
| <prolog> | prolog | <prolog> prolog on page 29 |
| <propdesc> | property description | <propdesc> property description on page 60 |
| <propdeschd> | property description head | <propdeschd> property description head on page 60 |
| <properties> | properties | <properties> properties on page 60 |
| <property> | property (DITA element) | <property> property on page 60 |
| <prophead> | property head | <prophead> property head on page 60 |
| <proptype> | property type | <proptype> property type on page 60 |
| <proptypehd> | property type head | <proptypehd> property type head on page 60 |
| <propvalue> | property value | <propvalue> property value on page 60 |
| <propvaluehd> | property value head | <propvaluehd> property value head on page 60 |
| <pt> | parameter term | <pt> parameter term on page 84 |
| <refbody> | reference body | <body> body on page 30 |
| <reference> | reference | <task> <concept> <reference> root elements on page 29 |

| Element | Element name | Refer to |
|---|---|---|
| <related-links> | related links | <related-links> related links on page 30 |
| <relcell> | relationship table cell | <relcell> relationship table cell on page 192 |
| <relcolspec> | relationship column specification | <relcolspec> relationship column specification on page 191 |
| <relheader> | relationship head | <relheader> relationship head on page 191 |
| <relrow> | relationship table row | <relrow> relationship table row on page 191 |
| <reltable> | relationship table | <reltable> relationship table on page 191 |
| <result> | result | <result> result on page 48 |
| <revised> | revised date | <revised> revised date on page 108 |
| <row> | row | <row> row on page 71 |
| <searchtitle> | search title | <searchtitle> search title on page 29 |
| <section> | section | <section> section on page 67 |
| <section> | section (task) | <section> section on page 44 |
| <shortdesc> | short description | <shortdesc> short description on page 29 |
| <simpletable> | simple table | <simpletable> simple table on page 73 |
| <sl> | simple list | <sl> simple list on page 68 |
| <sli> | simple list item | <sli> simple list item on page 68 |
| <stentry> | simple table cell (entry) | <stentry> simple table cell (entry) on page 73 |
| <step> | step | <step> step on page 45 |
| <stepresult> | step result | <stepresult> step result on page 46 |

| Element | Element name | Refer to |
| --- | --- | --- |
| <steps> | steps | <steps> steps and <steps-unordered> steps unordered on page 45 |
| <steps-informal> | steps informal | <steps-informal> steps informal on page 46 |
| <steps-unordered> | steps unordered | <steps> steps and <steps-unordered> steps unordered on page 45 |
| <stepxmp> | step example | <stepxmp> step example on page 45 |
| <stentry> | simple table row | <stentry> simple table cell (entry) on page 73 |
| <sthead> | simple table head | <sthead> simple table head on page 73 |
| <strow> | simple table row | <strow> simple table row on page 73 |
| <sub> | subscript | <sub> subscript on page 88 |
| <substep> | sub-step | <substep> sub-step on page 46 |
| <substeps> | sub-steps | <substeps> sub-steps on page 46 |
| <sup> | superscript | <sup> superscript on page 88 |
| <systemoutput> | system output | <systemoutput> system output on page 87 |
| <table> | table | <table> table on page 71 |
| <task> | task | <task> <concept> <reference> root elements on page 29 |
| <taskbody> | task body | <body> body on page 30 |
| <tbody> | table body | <tbody> table body on page 71 |
| <term> | term | <term> term on page 82 |
| <tgroup> | table group | <tgroup> table group on page 71 |

| Element | Element name | Refer to |
|---|---|---|
| <thead> | table head | <thead> table head on page 71 |
| <title> | title | <title> title on page 29 |
| <titlealts> | title alternatives | <titlealts> title alternatives on page 29 |
| <toc> | table of contents | <toc> table of contents on page 226 |
| <topicgroup> | topic group | <topicgroup> topic group on page 130 |
| <topichead> | topic heading | <topichead> topic heading on page 129 |
| <topicmeta> | topic metadata | <topicmeta> topic metadata on page 130 |
| <topicref> | topic reference | <topicref> topic reference on page 129 |
| <tt> | teletype | <tt> teletype on page 88 |
| <uicontrol> | user interface control | <uicontrol> user interface control on page 87 |
| <ul> | unordered list | <ul> unordered list on page 69 |
| <userinput> | user input | <userinput> user input on page 86 |
| <varname> | variable name | <varname> variable name on page 86 |
| <vrm> | version, release, and modification | <vrm> version, release, modification on page 109 |
| <vrmlist> | version, release, and modification list | <vrmlist> version, release, modification list on page 109 |
| <xref> | cross reference link | <xref> cross reference link on page 82 |

# Index

## D

## E

## F



## G

## H

## L



## M

## N



## O



## P

## R

## S

## T